QUEER BUDAPEST, 1873–1961

QUEER BUDAPEST
1873–1961

ANITA KURIMAY

THE UNIVERSITY OF CHICAGO PRESS

CHICAGO AND LONDON

The University of Chicago Press, Chicago 60637
The University of Chicago Press, Ltd., London
© 2020 by The University of Chicago
All rights reserved. No part of this book may be used or reproduced in any manner whatsoever without written permission, except in the case of brief quotations in critical articles and reviews. For more information, contact the University of Chicago Press, 1427 E. 60th St., Chicago, IL 60637.
Published 2020

29 28 27 26 25 24 23 22 21 20   1 2 3 4 5

ISBN-13: 978-0-226-70565-1 (cloth)
ISBN-13: 978-0-226-70579-8 (paper)
ISBN-13: 978-0-226-70582-8 (e-book)
DOI: https://doi.org/10.7208/chicago/9780226705828.001.0001

Library of Congress Cataloging-in-Publication Data

Names: Kurimay, Anita, author.
Title: Queer Budapest, 1873–1961 / Anita Kurimay.
Description: Chicago ; London : University of Chicago Press, 2020. | Includes bibliographical references and index.
Identifiers: LCCN 2019046572 | ISBN 9780226705651 (cloth) | ISBN 9780226705798 (paperback) | ISBN 9780226705828 (ebook)
Subjects: LCSH: Homosexuality—Hungary—Budapest—History—20th century. | Homosexuality—Hungary—Budapest—History—19th century. | Budapest (Hungary)—Social life and customs—20th century. | Budapest (Hungary)—Social life and customs—19th century.
Classification: LCC HQ76.3.H92 B834 2020 | DDC 306.76/609439/12—dc23
LC record available at https://lccn.loc.gov/2019046572

For members of the Hungarian LGBTQ community
and scholars of gender and sexuality in East-Central Europe

CONTENTS

	Introduction. Sexual Politics in the "Pearl of the Danube"	1
1.	Registering Sex in Sinful Budapest	19
2.	The "Knights of Sick Love": The Queers of Kornél Tábori and Vladimir Székely	53
3.	Rehabilitating "Sexual Abnormals" in the Hungarian Soviet Republic	91
4.	Peepholes and "Sprouts": A Lesbian Scandal	119
5.	Unlikely Allies: Queer Men and Horthy Conservatives	153
6.	The End of a Precarious Coexistence: The Prosecution of Homosexuals	194
	Epilogue. Queers and Democracy: The Misremembering of the Queer Past	231
	Acknowledgments	237
	Notes	241
	Bibliography	293
	Index	315

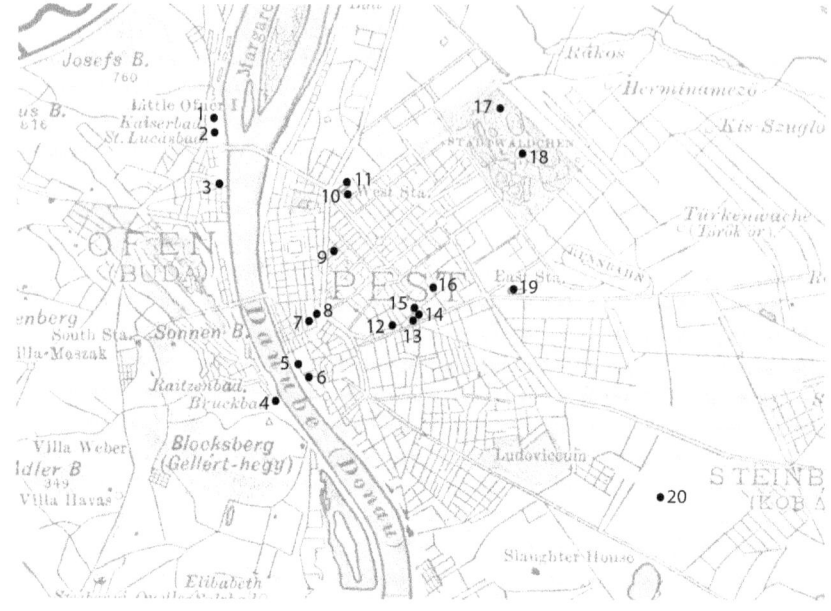

Queer meeting places in Budapest. Map locations:
1. Császár Bath
2. Lukács Bath
3. Király Bath
4. Rudas Bath
5. Duna Promenade/Dunakorzó
6. Petőfi Square
7. Elisabeth Square/ Erzsébet tér
8. Deák Square
9. Minta Café
10. Nyugati Train Station
11. Nyugati (Marx) Square
12. Hungária Bath
13. Emke Café
14. Beer sanatorium/Sörszanatorium
15. Hungária Restaurant and Café
16. Bar on Szövetség Street
17. Széchenyi Bath
18. City Park/Városliget
19. Keleti Train Station
20. People's Park/Népliget

INTRODUCTION

Sexual Politics in the "Pearl of the Danube"

In 1908, the celebrated Hungarian writer Soma Guthi published *Homosexual Love*, as part of his new crime novel series.[1] The novel, a tragic love story between two wealthy gentlemen, stands as one of the few Hungarian sources from the turn of the century that directly addresses same-sex love and sexuality. Through the eyes of its main character, Detective Tuzár, the book offers a rare window into early twentieth-century representations of homosexuality in Hungary. Guthi's frankness with his readers about homosexual people remains striking and seems remarkably progressive, even over a century later:

> The papers do not provide enough information [about homosexuality] for the curious lay reader. This is despite the fact that the nature of homosexuality can be described in two short words: sensual friendship. Brave definition, but I believe it is quite accurate. In friendship, the existence of sensuality is nothing else than a wonderful exception to the rule . . .
>
> The passion of the urnings [male homosexuals] is also human passion. . . . They also feel the anguish of jealousy, the pain of cheating and the bitterness of rejection or despised love. . . . And where there is great passion, there is sin, since sin luxuriates in the depth of passion.
>
> Whoever knows them, knows very well that they are different from their fellow men only in the nature of their sexual desire, and otherwise, they are, by and large, intelligent, kind-hearted, and honest people, who never sin against public morality because of their unnatural desire.[2]

Detective Tuzár, who is assigned to a homosexual murder case, was not only familiar with the latest sexological and social/activist theories on homosexuality (as he cites Krafft-Ebing and Karl Ulrichs, for instance), but as the excerpt hints at, believed that homosexuals were "normal" people who become criminals only due to the outdated criminal laws of European countries. In the two-hundred-page novel, the author conveys a view that it was not the "innate" nature of homosexuals but rather the laws that made them more likely to be suicidal and easy prey for criminals. Moreover, Guthi was also a lawyer who defended homosexual clients against bribery schemes and was thus intimately familiar with legal and police matters concerning homosexuals in Budapest. Featuring a murder case that brought homosexuals into direct contact with the police, *Homosexual Love* demonstrates an ambiguous legal discourse regarding same-sex sexuality, which, on the one hand, criminalized male homosexuals and, on the other, left a lot of room for the police to avoid prosecuting them.

Guthi, along with Hungarian officials and many of their contemporaries, was aware of the growing presence of men who had sex with, bought sex from, and sold sex to other men in Budapest. Indeed, it was obvious to anyone visiting Budapest at the turn of the century that the new capital embraced a public sexual culture. The liberal atmosphere that surrounded sex in Budapest at this time—whether due to publications about sex, illustrations and photography of naked bodies, the prevalence of prostitution, or the rapid expansion of commercial establishments like pubs and cafés—was recognized both at home and abroad.[3] As *The Morality of Budapest*, a satirical social critique dating from 1902, observed:

> The parameters of Budapest today are actually small enough that people cannot hide their actions from each other. In spite of this, the city's moral standards stand at such surprising[ly] low levels that they are almost impossible to characterize. With the most certainty, we can conclude that no city in the world so openly cultivates the profiteering of all forms of vice, at the expense of morality, than does Budapest. Vice is openly present in public spaces, with official assistance. Frankly, this city operates as a real sex expo, where sex is considered as the most comfortable, most natural form of work, and actually thought of as a perfectly normal industry; people give and take, without anyone being offended by it, or protesting against it. At every street corner, there stand five or six painted pieces of merchandise, who in broad daylight sell themselves just as freely as under the night's wet air, when they throw themselves on anyone who comes their way.[4]

The relatively small size of the city may have made anonymity more difficult, but the author suggests that the city's inhabitants valued neither secrecy nor moral purity. As satirical as the author's tone is, his description of the liberal sexual atmosphere reflected a widespread contemporary view of the Hungarian capital. And he was not alone in publishing such observations. Spurred by the growth of the urban mass media and the penny press in the 1880s, Budapest's journalists regularly discussed prostitution, liberal sexual morals, and the lax regulation of the sex industry.[5] Despite a growing number of conservative voices that characterized fin de siècle Budapest as the "Sinful City," sex sold newspapers, which in turn became key vehicles for disseminating discourse and knowledge about sexuality.[6]

Same-sex love and desire did not figure prominently in this explosion of virtually uncensored printed sexual discourse until the first decade of the twentieth century. At that time a few books and articles about erotic relations between men began to appear, such as *Homosexual Love*, but most took a decidedly less tolerant tone than Guthi did.[7] Acknowledging the pervasiveness and visibility of same-sex sexuality in Budapest, a 1908 book titled *Metropolitan Mores* characterized participants as "perversities," ominously warning readers that such "sick love" would corrupt the very essence of "natural" love:

> If we take a closer look at Budapest's love life, and also want to introduce it in its truest form, we have to divide the types of love that exist in the city into two main groups: the natural, healthy love and sick love. . . . The life of the capital provides thousands and thousands of examples of the different manifestations of sexual life all day long, from morning until night. After all, that is why our nice Budapest is a large city. A myriad of nightclubs and cafés further develop and shape the already awakened desires. In turn, all desires of humankind are experienced in the city, including the *wild offshoots of nature*. These wild offshoots are well-known and cunning perversities, which proliferate at the places of love, just like they do within so many families. After all, even here there can be some distinction made, considering that nowadays there are some perversities that have plunged themselves into the public consciousness, almost as if they were natural.[8]

Dividing Budapest's sexual culture into two camps—one "natural" and "healthy," the other composed of those "wild offshoots of nature" who engaged in same-sex love—the author of *Metropolitan Mores* feared that the latter group would move beyond the public sphere and into the privacy of family life, ultimately becoming as normalized and "natural" as the love between a man and a woman.

Significantly, many contemporaries took a similarly bifurcated view of Budapest's sexual culture, displaying a willingness to discuss "natural" expressions of sexuality—even playfully, as in the satirical *Morality of Budapest*—but taking the opposite stance on what they considered "sick" or "unnatural" love. In fact, despite the prevalence and visibility of same-sex sexuality, both authorities and social critics believed that *not* talking about "perversities," especially homosexuality, was essential to stop the spread of the "disease" in European societies. Regardless of disagreements about the root causes of same-sex desire, there was tacit agreement among them that talking about it, even if only to condemn it, would inevitably ignite same-sex desire in some people. As a result, in the period between 1873 and the 1960s (apart from a series of articles during the 1900s), there are few traces of men who had sex with men and what was eventually labeled "male homosexuality" in official documents, and only slightly greater discussion about them in the popular press. The notion that reading or talking about homosexuality could "infect" people remained pervasive throughout Hungary's most tumultuous decades. It prevailed even when the country experienced radically different political constellations: monarchy (1867–1918); liberal democracy in 1918; Communism in 1919; authoritarian conservatism (1920–44); brief fascist rule in 1944–45; and during the initial years of the Communist dictatorship (1948–89).[9] The collective silencing around issues of homosexuality cut across political and ideological divides. Outside of the medical and legal professions and internal police discussions, the subject of homosexuality was taboo.

What was common, if suppressed, knowledge for contemporaries about same-sex sexuality in Budapest throughout the first three decades of the twentieth century, however, has been similarly silent in the historical record. Unlike Berlin, Paris, London, and Vienna, the historical existence of a vibrant queer sexual culture of Budapest has not been acknowledged, either in public memory or in the broad historical scholarship.[10] In this way, the story of queer life in Hungary is similar to that of other East-Central European capitals. For instance, comparing the sexual morale of early twentieth-century Budapest to that of Paris and Vienna, even eminent cultural historian John Lukacs's asserted that "another rarity in Budapest (and in Hungary) was the evidence of homosexuality among males. In all of the records, including those of the police, and, even more significant, in the rich and gossipy journalism and literature of the period, we find very few examples of it."[11] According to Lukacs homosexuality was simply not part of Hungarian culture. This book categorically refutes Lukacs's assertion. In locating queer sexualities in Hungary's past, it reinserts sexuality into the cultural and political history of Hungary and also uncovers the reasons behind the historical silencing of queer subjects.

Queer Budapest is a history of nonnormative sexualities in Budapest as they were understood, experienced, and policed between the birth of the city as a unified metropolis in 1873 and the decriminalization of male homosexual acts in 1961 (which went into effect in 1962). This is an era characterized by shifting and often ideologically opposed political systems, from the Austro-Hungarian monarchy, through the Hungarian Soviet Republic of 1919, the conservative authoritarian interwar regime, the fascist Hungarian Arrow Cross, and finally through the Communist dictatorship of the 1950s and early 1960s. Yet, tracing the relationship between these different regimes and the regulation and policing of sexuality reveals surprising continuities in how authorities approached queer sexuality in practice. While most histories of modern Hungary emphasize ruptures and differences among its political systems, *Queer Budapest* shows that divergent political regimes built upon each other in their attitudes toward sexuality.

Moreover, I argue that men who had sex with men and women who were sexual with women were an integral part of establishing a modern Hungarian capital. From the late nineteenth century until the decriminalization of male homosexual acts in 1961, Hungarian state building was intimately tied to the management of nonnormative sexual and gender behavior. By the turn of the century, authorities in Budapest were acutely aware of a growing queer culture and in fact regarded it as evidence of Budapest's rise as a modern metropolis, although not necessarily welcome evidence. To legal, medical, and police officials, methods of handling homosexuality were important markers of the Hungarian state's place among rapidly modernizing European nation-states. To that end, in the late 1880s, the Metropolitan Police became one of the first police forces to create a "homosexual registry." The registry that collected names and the extensive socioeconomic background information of men who had sex with men ironically contributed to both official and public silence around homosexuality. By combining the latest law enforcement and criminological theories, the registry served as a means to demonstrate that Budapest was ready to take its place in the modern West—a testament to the city's ambitiously modern and scientifically progressive population management.[12] Even though the homosexual registry did not function effectively for two more decades, it remained constant during the turbulent political changes of the early twentieth century, was in use at least until the decriminalization of homosexuality in 1961, and continued to have a function until the end of Communism in 1989. In this way, regulating same-sex sexuality was central to the project of Hungarian modernity.

In addition, by selectively incorporating what they saw as the most effective ways of managing queer sexualities from London, Berlin, Vienna, and Paris, authorities in Budapest actively confronted widespread Western perceptions of Eastern European and Hungarian backwardness. As a result, Budapest became intimately involved in European conversations about sex and its management, as a crossroad of exchange about ideas of sexuality. The specific ways authorities in Budapest responded to leading Western theories on sexuality, criminology, and penal reform attest to a genuinely interconnected European urban community where information was relatively transparent and widely circulated. Further, although scholarship has tended to privilege Western metropoles as central sites and disseminators of knowledge, that Hungarian authorities incorporated the ideas of Magnus Hirschfeld, Richard von Krafft-Ebing, and Sigmund Freud into their treatment of nonnormative sexualities, at times ahead of their British, French, and American counterparts, offers evidence that Budapest was not a cultural backwater. Instead, it was an important contributor to European conversations about sexuality that are usually associated with Berlin, London, and Paris. Thus, *Queer Budapest* reframes ideas about transnational information exchange, communications, culture, and everyday practices, demonstrating that the transmission of knowledge was never a one-way flow nor did it reflect any conventionally imagined East/West divide.[13]

Queer Budapest also considers queer sexualities from the ground up, showing that, although sex between men was criminalized by the Hungarian penal code of 1878, its unlawfulness did not prevent men from having sex and romantic relationships with other men. In fact, the collective silence around homosexual relationships paradoxically facilitated a sexual culture in Budapest that provided space for an active queer culture, at least among men.[14] Gender is an important factor here; even though authorities increasingly policed nonnormative sexuality for both men and women, for a number of reasons nonnormative male sexuality continued to be tolerated and at times even protected. During the conservative interwar years, for example, a crackdown on prostitution and the curtailing of women's rights led to repressive rhetoric, policies, and actions disproportionately directed toward women, sparing men with same-sex desires. Other factors, including the perceived effects of the Great War on Hungarian men and the belief that, unlike women, men were inherently sexual, also contributed to tolerance around some forms of male homosexual activity under an authoritarian conservative regime.[15] In addition, the concept of "respectability," couched in gender ideologies and class-based assumptions about sexual privacy, was a decisive factor in determining the fate of men who engaged in homosexual behavior.[16] Across regimes, such cultural understandings were often more important than political and legislative frameworks in shaping the treatment of men who had sex with men.[17]

As for women, issues of female same-sex sexuality are almost invisible in public records and conversations. Since female homosexuality was not criminalized, legal and police sources remained mostly silent about women who had sexual relationships with other women. During the first decade of the twentieth century, there was a brief period when sex and love between women was more openly discussed, particularly in popular literature. Love between women was also discussed in the context of prostitution. According to contemporary accounts, "it [was] a well-known fact that most prostitutes, whose numbers by the turn of century were considerable, 'kept their' hearts for their female lovers."[18] Generally, however, from the 1880s on, official accounts (government, police, or public health sources) intentionally avoided addressing the issue of female homosexuality.[19] Interestingly, it was Hungary's greatest political scandal—a celebrated divorce trial of the 1920s—that provided the most important break with the imposed silence of the authorities, as well as one of the richest sites for recovering female same-sex sexuality in Budapest. Concerning Cécile Tormay and Eduardina Pallavicini, two of the most visible conservative women of interwar Hungary, charges of female homosexuality surrounded the trial and created a national sex scandal that ultimately neither damaged the women's reputations nor halted their political aspirations. Surviving records of the trial and its press coverage make it possible to reconstruct interwar discourses on female homosexuality, still a rarity in queer histories, and particularly in East-Central European historiography. The Tormay case is a remarkable example of the coexistence of conservative politics and tolerance of certain forms of queer sexuality in interwar Hungary.

From the coexistence of the criminalization of male homosexual acts and a growing homosexual culture of fin de siècle Budapest to the lesbian scandal of the 1920s to the conservative interwar regime's tolerance of certain forms of queer sexualities, the history of Hungarian queer sexualities highlights how both the understanding and treatment of homosexuality remained stable between the last decade of the nineteenth century and the first three decades of the twentieth. Gender ideologies and respectability were paramount in sustaining the coexistence of queer sexualities and different political systems. The reconstruction of queer Budapest reveals the interconnectedness of Central European and more generally of European cities in terms of legal, police, sexological, and social/activist discourses on sexuality.

FROM GOLDEN AGE TO COMMUNIST CRACKDOWN

Since *Queer Budapest* covers almost a century of Hungarian history characterized by rapidly shifting political regimes, it is necessary to provide a brief contextual overview. A latecomer to urbanization and other aspects of modernity, Hungary and particularly Budapest experienced an era of rapid transformation following the Austro-Hungarian Compromise and the establishment of the dual monarchy in 1867. By granting sovereignty to Hungary to manage its own internal affairs, the *Kiegyezés* or *Ausgleich* (Compromise) of 1867 opened the way for progressive Hungarian forces. The establishment of a modern Hungarian capital that embodied the liberal vision of the Hungarian elite was one outcome. The administrative establishment of Budapest in 1873, with the merging of Buda, Óbuda, and Pest, provided a kick start to the creation of a modern metropolis. The Hungarian political elite had a clear vision for the new capital: to demonstrate Hungary's strength vis-à-vis its Austrian counterpart and the progress of the nation within the larger European context.

In 1892, Dr. Albert Shaw, an American journalist and editor of the *American Monthly and Review of Reviews*, published an article after returning from a European trip that surely pleased Budapest's modernity-minded elite. Entitled "Budapest: The Rise of a Metropolis," it was a description of the growth of a new, distinctly urban, European capital city:

> To the world at large, Budapest, the capital and metropolis of Hungary, is the least known of all the important cities of Europe. No other falls so far short of receiving the appreciation of its merits. Several reasons may be assigned for this comparative obscurity, among which are remoteness from the chief thoroughfares of travel and commerce, the isolation of Magyar language and literature, and the subordination of all things Hungarian to the Austrian name and fame. But the most important reason is the simplest of all: the Budapest of today is so new that the world has not had time to make its acquaintance. Its people justly claim for it the most rapid growth of all the European capitals, and is fond of likening its wonderful expansion to that of San Francisco, Chicago, and other American cities.[20]

Characteristic of American idealism, Shaw's writing reflects a kind of late nineteenth-century optimism that was, perhaps for the only time in history, also shared by Hungarians and especially the inhabitants of Budapest. In his delightful portrait of a city that in three decades grew from three sleepy towns into a buzzing metropolis, Shaw explained to his readers that the spectacular rise of Budapest was the result of several distinct developments: the establishment of a national and international transportation network with Budapest at its center; the creation of a sovereign financial and commercial system; and investments in industry that ultimately made the city the mill capital of the world.[21] Indeed, historians of Hungary agree that the political, economic, cultural, and social developments made in the late nineteenth and early twentieth century produced the Golden Age of Budapest.[22]

The interplay of these factors, similar to major American and Western European cities at the time, facilitated rapid population growth.[23] Within a fifty-year period, Budapest's population exploded. People poured in from the countryside by the thousands, with the hope of finding jobs in the many new factories and industries that guaranteed higher pay than seasonal and irregular agricultural work. By the outbreak of the Great War, the population of Budapest was almost a million, making it one of the largest European metropolises. Rapid population growth, however, was not accompanied by spatial expansion. The city remained relatively small and incorporated nearby villages rather than building new suburbs. The geographic attributes of Budapest also played a role in the concentration of the population. Buda, located on the west side of the Danube with its picturesque rolling hills, remained relatively sparsely populated aside from the districts surrounding the Royal Castle. In 1841 there were approximately thirty-eight thousand people living on the Buda side, while in 1890 about ninety thousand inhabited the area.[24] It was the Pest side that absorbed most of the newly arriving people: sixty-eight thousand in 1840 grew to half a million inhabitants in 1890.[25] Budapest accommodated this population growth in Pest by cramming more and more people into a small two-by-three-mile area. As a result, Budapest's spatial constellation produced some of the densest living conditions in Europe, ironically experienced by people who had migrated from some of the most sparsely populated parts of the continent.[26] Unlike Paris, London, Vienna, and other European capitals in the era, the physical organization of Budapest resulted in members of different classes residing in close proximity to one another. Similar to Berlin, there were a surprising number of middle- and working-class tenants living together in the same buildings.[27] This fluid use of space across class lines was also true for public areas and to some extent even neighborhoods.[28] And in their midst were various sites of homosocial bonding and homosexual pleasure, including cafés, the promenades at the Danube and the City Park, and an extensive thermal bath scene that catered to an increasingly visible, although still fugitive, queer world of men and, to a lesser extent, women.

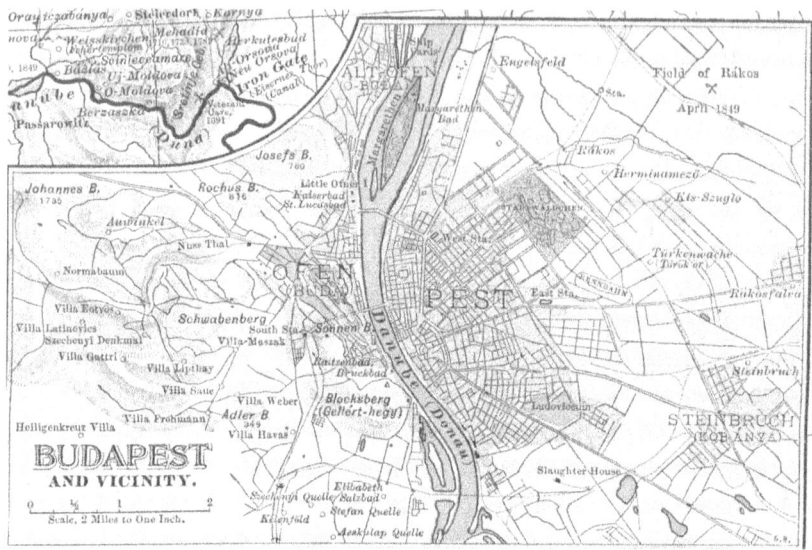

Figure 1. Budapest, 1899. Map 89 in Benjamin E. Smith, *The Century Atlas of the World* (New York: Century Co., 1899).

Although its territory expanded between the wars, the city's spatial composition did not change significantly until the end of World War II as a result of an urgent need to rebuild the bomb-decimated city. During the siege of Budapest, three-fourth of the city's approximately forty thousand buildings were damaged, with the castle district worst hit where 40 percent of the 6,500 homes became uninhabitable.[29] Following the Soviet model of socialist realism, the Communist government undertook the largest urban development of Budapest and fundamentally altered its visual landscape.[30]

According to standard narratives, the Golden Age of Budapest and also of Hungary came to an abrupt end at the outbreak of World War I and the fall of Habsburg monarchy in 1918.[31] Overnight, the country that in partnership with Austria constituted the second largest European empire became one of the smallest and most battered nations on the continent. Most historians consider the brief existence of the Democratic Republic (November 1918– March 1919) under Mihály Károlyi, and the subsequent Hungarian Soviet Republic (March 1919–August 1919), led by Béla Kun, as ill-fated and even disastrous political experiments.[32] These historians emphasize how both regimes were incompetent in dealing with the victorious powers or defending Hungary's territorial claims against those of neighboring countries. As a result, Hungary lost about two-thirds of its former territory and a population comprising millions of ethnic Hungarians. In addition, most histories stress the mass terror, ad hoc actions, and overall negative consequences of the Hungarian Communist revolutionary regime.[33] However, viewing the revolutionary period of 1918–19 through the lens of sexuality, and specifically nonnormative sexuality, introduces a different narrative and yields important insights into the nature of the Hungarian Soviet Republic. Rather than instituting terror and punitive discipline, Communist revolutionary ideology and policies viewed queer sexuality as both treatable and transient, and officials put forth a serious effort to judge crime through the eyes of a comprehensive sociomedical approach that incorporated psychoanalytical theories. Interestingly, Communists, believing that homosexuals could be treated and reintegrated into society as "normal" heterosexuals, did not recognize a category of persons defined as homosexual men and women. Homosexuality as an identity or as an innate and intrinsic part of the self and a Communist subjectivity were mutually exclusive.

Following the short-lived democratic and Communist governments of the immediate post–World War I period, an authoritarian and conservative political leadership came to power. Hungary now became a constitutional monarchy without a king. Admiral Miklós Horthy, the leader of the counterrevolutionary forces, became the regent and served as the head of state of Hungary from 1920 until 1944. Between 1920 and 1944, two conservative groups vied for political preeminence: the old conservative right that represented the traditional Hungarian aristocracy and a new radical right whose leaders came from the gentry and lower classes. While most old conservatives believed in some form of conservative parliamentary political system, the new radical right was openly hostile to representative government, militaristic, violently anti-Semitic, and antidemocratic.[34] In contrast to the era before 1914, historians have considered the interwar years in Hungary as a period of stagnation. Since many of Budapest's intellectual elite had left the country, it was viewed as a second-rate cultural center under a repressive conservative government with authoritarian tendencies.[35] The Horthy era did not simply bring a halt to Budapest's liberal capitalist and democratic development. In many ways it actively attempted to turn the tide back. Aggressive nationalism, antisemitism, antiliberalism, the renewed empowerment of the Catholic Church, and irredentism within the formerly liberal elite and intelligentsia delivered a killing blow to the capital's former ascendancy.[36]

With the drastic antiliberal changes ushered in by conservative forces during the interwar years, one might expect that the treatment of sexuality would also be affected. Indeed, the conservative Horthy regime instituted major changes on both the discursive and practical levels. The rhetoric that called for chastity before marriage and stressed the sanctity of the family was accompanied by a regulatory system that was more interventionist than it had been previously. This included discriminatory laws that instituted the first explicitly anti-Semitic law in twentieth-century Europe and also increased the power of law enforcement agencies.[37] The conservative state drove prostitution underground by eradicating the formerly relaxed regulation of female prostitution whereby the state made it easy for prostitutes and brothels to procure a license and increased the regulation of nonnormative sexualities. However, these conservative crackdowns focused predominately on women, and many men with same-sex desires emerged unscathed. Surprisingly, and for various reasons, Horthy's authoritarian regime chose to tolerate a growing homosexual subculture.

An end to the precarious coexistence of the Hungarian state and tolerance of homosexuality came with Hungary's entry into World War II. Once Hungary committed itself to Nazi Germany in the hope of regaining its pre–World War I territories and entered the war in 1941, homosexuality became irreconcilable with the idea of national community. Also, rising Nazi influence on the expanding Hungarian state resulted in the more systematic targeting of homosexuals and homosexuality. By the outbreak of the war, institutions such as the police and state bureaucracy had expanded and were highly functional. Once the tide began to turn following the battle of Stalingrad and Hungarian forces suffered terrible losses, Horthy and the Hungarian leadership actively sought peace with the Allies. The strategic location of Hungary in East-Central Europe made this possibility especially threatening for Nazi Germany. As a preventive measure, Hitler ordered German troops to occupy Hungary in March 1944. Following Hungary's attempt to get out of the war by signing an armistice with the Soviet Union on October 15, 1944, the Germans forced Horthy to name Ferenc Szálasi, the leader of the Arrow Cross Party, as the new prime minister. Under the proposed Family Law of the fascist Arrow Cross's Government of National Unity (October 1944–March 1945), both male and female homosexual acts were criminalized, and male homosexuals were to be castrated. But thanks to the Soviet invasion, these policies were never implemented.

It was not until after World War II and the establishment of the Communist dictatorship in 1948 that a Hungarian state systematically prosecuted homosexual men and men who had sex with men for the first time. Until the decriminalization of "unnatural fornication" in 1961, homosexual men were seen as the enemies of the Hungarian state and were relentlessly prosecuted. Homosexual men and women were seen as a threat to socialism, yet the Hungarian State Security Service used them for such nefarious means: as blackmail to frame people for crimes and as a way of turning some into useful informants for the growing State Security apparatus. In addition, homosexuals were still being registered in the homosexual registry. Thus, despite the end of Stalinist repressive rule and the decriminalization of homosexuality in 1961, queer sexuality in Budapest continued to be policed, repressed, and vilified.

Although scholars have emphasized the upheaval of rapid political changes during this period in Hungary's history, *Queer Budapest* demonstrates striking continuities in approaches to regulating—and tolerating—same-sex sexualities, even as ideologically distinct governments took power. Prior to World War II, liberal and conservative political regimes alike tolerated certain queer sexualities, although not in quite the same way or for the same reasons. It was World War II and the subsequent Communist one-party system that destroyed the curious coexistence of queer sexualities and the Hungarian state. In this way, *Queer Budapest* offers a unique portrait of twentieth-century Hungarian history.

FINDING ARCHIVES OF QUEER SEXUALITIES IN EAST-CENTRAL EUROPE

While the twentieth century, as historian Dagmar Herzog recently remarked, is often considered "the century of sex," until fairly recently it has been explored only in the context of the Western world, often defined as the US and Western Europe.[38] The historiography of European sexuality in English has conspicuously lacked works on same-sex sexuality in East-Central Europe.[39] In fact, when this project began, there were no published histories nor archives or collections dedicated to the subject of sexuality and, especially, queer sexuality. Thus, my work could not build on an established Hungarian source base.[40] There are two main reasons for this. First, both within and without the walls of East-Central European academic institutions, homophobia and sexism are present. The perceived association of one's intellectual subject with one's sexual identity makes writing on queer history a challenging endeavor. A second reason for the dearth of work on same-sex sexuality in East-Central Europe is the scarcity of sources. In addition to the devastation of World War II that destroyed many historical archives, four decades of Communist rule contributed to the erasure (both literally and figuratively) of historical sources on nonnormative sexuality. In fact, most court cases involving nonnormative sexualities at the Budapest Criminal Court system prior to 1918 were destroyed and many of the records of the interwar period were also damaged in the winter of 1944 during the Battle of Budapest. Their destruction posed a significant obstacle to writing a comprehensive history. Historical records on sexuality, especially nonnormative sexuality, along with those on other sensitive issues have been closely guarded even after 1989. The dearth of primary sources particularly on female same-sex sexuality explains why it is treated considerably less fully than its male counterpart. I have tried to evoke the historical female experience of same-sex desire despite the limitation of available sources.[41] In light of these obstacles, the excavation of a lost or forgotten pre–World War II queer community whose very existence has been denied by East-Central European governments is an important step in reintegrating East-Central European queer histories into a pan-European discourse.[42] *Queer Budapest* joins a handful of English language books on homosexual and queer history on East-Central Europe and is the first on Hungary's capital city.[43] It draws on and in turn contributes to multiple scholarly enterprises, including the history of sexuality and gender studies, along with cultural, urban, political, and social histories of East-Central Europe.

Queer Budapest recovers narratives about same-sex sexuality from sources as diverse as contemporary detective novels, police journals, popular newspapers, and the writings of sexologists. The fragmented and greatly varied nature of the source materials compels quite different kinds of narratives, some focused on a few influential figures in Hungarian history and others on obscure women and men. For instance, the sensational lesbian scandal surrounding Hungary's best-known conservative woman of the interwar era, Cécile Tormay, produced an archival richness of trial records that allows for an intimate perspective from many points of view. These sources, including rural voices on queer female sexuality provided by servants who gave sworn testimony at the trial, take the reader into the realms of private life, love, and politics and provide a window into the sexual lives of individuals, as well as the dissemination of popular knowledge about sexuality.[44]

At other times, *Queer Budapest* adopts a panoramic view that analyzes broad trends in the treatment and relationship between different political systems and nonnormative sexualities. Here were serious impediments to the archival research as even "normative" sexuality was and is still not particularly well represented or cataloged in any of the Hungarian archives. But since sex between men was criminalized prior to 1962, the documents of the Budapest Criminal Court, housed in the Budapest City Archives (BFL), served as a starting point and constitute the basis for my chapters on the interwar period.[45] The Hungarian National Archives (OSZK) were the other main repository of primary sources. Housing all existing Hungarian publications on issues of sexuality, a wealth of Hungarian and foreign newspapers, and the official Hungarian police journal, the National Archives was indispensable for my project. In addition, the Parliamentary Archives provided primary sources for the discussion of legal discourse, and the Hungarian Medical Archives was helpful for supplying information on medical discourse.[46] The Historical Archives of the Hungarian State Security (ÁBTL) provided crucial information to the post–1948 period. Finally, the digital primary source database Arcanum was instrumental for locating a wide range of sources (popular and medical, as well as official government and party sources) from the late nineteenth century through the Communist dictatorship.

While reading into the silences that surround homosexuality and nonnormative sexuality, I could rely on a growing historical scholarship that has demonstrated innovative approaches to locating both male and female same-sex erotic desire, feelings, and experience in the past.[47] Along with contextualizing the political, cultural, and social context of Hungary and particularly that of Budapest, I focused on the wider debates around women's rights, prostitution, venereal disease, and syphilis that all possess a considerable historiography.[48] In addition, there are some secondary sources on Hungarian feminists and their attitudes toward sexuality.[49] Even if these sources rarely address same-sex sexuality directly, subtle hints about nonnormative sexuality therein and reading between the lines of official sources in term of their views on issues of prostitution, sexually transmitted diseases, and questions concerning "respectable" masculinity and femininity were important for my study. To understand how people understood nonnormative sexualities, I needed to uncover how they understood normative gender roles for men and women.[50] Thus, identifying the premises of Hungarian masculinity and femininity and how they changed over time became central to my analysis.[51] In light of the dearth of secondary literature on gender and in particular on ideas of masculinity in Hungary prior to 1945, I read contemporary sources, both popular and official, with the intent of deciphering normative understandings of gender and sexuality. Furthermore, I relied on the extensive secondary literature on the history of gender and masculinity in other contexts, mostly Western with a few notable exceptions on East-Central Europe.[52]

Finally, I placed Budapest within a greater European context in terms of the legal, medical, political, and cultural discourses on issues of sexuality and events that undoubtedly influenced what happened there. Whether it was the Oscar Wilde trial, the Eulenburg affair, other scandals involving homosexuality, new cultural trends, urban and national policy, or laws that were enacted in Paris, London, or Berlin, such matters affected what was taking place in Budapest both in terms of discourses and the treatment and experience of queer sexualities. The rapid information exchange that we tend to associate with the digital age was in many ways present even at the end of the nineteenth century. News traveled fast via telegraph and other means, and both authorities and the public were informed about the latest sexual scandals and new theories about sexuality. Moreover, the authorities—city officials, police, members of the legal and medical establishment—were tuned in to transnational information channels and learned about the latest developments regarding the treatment and policing of nonnormative sexualities, even if these discussions did not feature in the mainstream media.

The combination of these research methods allowed me to read and interpret sources that directly addressed queer sexualities with a critical eye. The fusing of political, cultural, and urban histories of East-Central Europe with gender and sexuality as a dual central analytical lens has also enabled me to recreate narratives around queer sexuality and reconstruct multiple discourses and experiences around it. Furthermore, by not wedding to a singular theoretical framework, my approach incorporates representations of sexuality, while at the same time paying attention to the multiple ways discourses were received and adapted. Thus, even though none of the subjects of my study (men, women, and the authorities) existed outside of the discursive system, the actual effects of those various discursive powers (language and representation) were by no means uniform. Having exposed these discursive frameworks, I then turned to studying their effects.

Who and what are the subjects of the book? The debates around the terminology describing same-sex sexual activities by now have their own considerable historiography.[53] I made a conscious choice to not commit myself to using one expression such as "same-sex sex," "queer sex," or "nonnormative sex," because I wanted to use them interchangeably.[54] I did so partly because of the archival limitations of recovering and historicizing nonheterosexual identities.[55] More importantly, my use of these terms interchangeably is grounded in a conviction of the fluidity and instability of sexual identity and the very complexity of sexuality itself. Throughout this work, "same-sex sex," "queer sex," or "nonnormative sex" refers to men or women who engaged or were assumed to be engaged in sexual activities with their own sex. I use the terms "homosexual" and "homosexuality" much more carefully, and only apply them when contemporaries (popular or official sources) used the terminology.[56] I use these terms with the full awareness that many if not most people who engaged in nonnormative sexual behavior would not have embraced a nonnormative or homosexual identity. Indeed, especially in the case of women, a homosexual identity would not have been imaginable prior to the interwar era. Furthermore, as much as this is a study of same-sex sexuality, I also use same-sex sexuality as an analytical tool, not just an object of the study. Thinking of Budapest and Hungary's turbulent history through the lens of sexuality challenges standard narratives of the political history of Budapest. According to political histories, 1918 marks a distinct, conservative turn in Budapest's history; however, a lens of same-sex sexuality instead reveals deep continuities between Budapest's liberal and subsequent conservative political eras.

THE EVOLUTION OF *QUEER BUDAPEST*

The book opens in fin de siècle Budapest as the Hungarian capital is looking to establish itself as a modern European metropolis. The first chapter contextualizes Budapest within the late nineteenth-century European regulatory system of sex. The second chapter turns to early twentieth-century popular representations of homosexuality. The writings of Hungary's leading investigating journalists, Vladimir Székely and Kornél Tábori, simultaneously attend to the actual existence of an extensive culture of men who had sex with men in the Hungarian capital and also to a surprisingly fluid information exchange within European capitals about queer sexualities. Chapter 3 looks at how, during its brief existence in 1919, the Hungarian Soviet Republic approached nonnormative sexuality in an entirely new fashion. Ironically, despite conceptualizing nonheteronormative sexuality as a result of psychological trauma, the Communists ultimately granted no space for homosexual identity. The sensational divorce and libel trials of Hungary's two most influential women during the 1920s is the subject of chapter 4. The fifth chapter tracks how legal approaches to male homosexuality changed once more in an unpredictable fashion. In spite of Hungary's conservative and increasingly authoritarian political climate between 1920 and 1941, the discourses, regulation, and policing of same-sex sexuality show remarkable continuities from the pre–World War I era. Without denying the hardships and repressions that same-sex acts could produce for individuals, the chapter chronicles the coexistence of a thriving same-sex culture and the conservative Horthy regime. The final chapter traces the end to the precarious coexistence of the Hungarian state and tolerance of homosexuality to Hungary's entry into World War II and the establishment of the Communist dictatorship in 1948. The recently accessible court documents suggest that until the decriminalization of "unnatural fornication" in 1961, homosexual men were seen as the enemies of the Hungarian state and were relentlessly prosecuted.

By unearthing the nuanced ways in which political conservatism and the toleration of nonnormative sexualities coexisted within increasingly authoritarian regimes, the book offers historical insights into current debates about the relationship between authoritarian states and sexuality.[57] As anyone who has been paying attention to European and East-Central European politics will attest, Hungary (and Poland) are the most acute examples of the fragility of democracy in post–1989 Europe. Hungary, with its increasingly right-wing governing party, Fidesz, and its leader, Prime Minister Viktor Orbán, has become infamous in the Western media. News coverage about the crackdown on the Hungarian media, restriction of judicial freedom, and a virulent antirefugee stance, along with the Hungarian government's portrayal of the European Union as a colonial power, are only a few of the features of what critics have come to label as "Orban's illiberal democracy."[58] In this context, the state-supported homophobia and backlash against recent legal victories of the LGBTQ community may not be surprising. Unlike in most Western European countries where conservatives and far-right parties alike have come to embrace their respective LGBTQ communities as supposed signs of their cultural superiority vis-à-vis their homegrown and recently arrived Muslim communities, in East-Central Europe this has not been the case.[59] Gone are the days when would-be members of the European Union held up the more humane treatment of homosexuals as proof of the "cultural maturity" of East-Central European countries on their way to becoming mature Western democracies and, thus, worthy of EU membership. In the Hungarian context, where the appeal of the far-right party, Jobbik, has never been greater and the governing Fidesz has fully embraced right-wing populist rhetoric and authoritarian methods, queers have become the physical embodiments of the perils of Western cultural influence, neoliberal capitalism, and liberal democracy. Such representation is founded on the belief that the visibility of homosexuals and queer people more generally are a product of the post-1989 democratic era. In turn, the belief that queers are Western imports provides a convenient ideological foundation for the ongoing effort to resist granting Hungary's LGBTQ community equal rights and recognition. But what happens if we actually put these assumptions to the test?

Queer Budapest exposes the faultiness of these assumptions and dismantles the claim that queerness and LGBTQ people arrived only on the wings of Western democracy. Instead, by recovering and analyzing Hungary's queer past, this book contends that today's discourse is a product of the official silencing of LGBTQ history that characterized regimes prior to 1989 and, in particular, of the Communist regime's exploitation of sexuality and homosexuality for its own purposes. And while, following 1989, there were important legal victories for the queer community, more recent events fit squarely within the last major turn of the history of Hungarian homosexualities in which the long history of coexistence between illiberal governments and queer sexuality has shattered.

CHAPTER ONE

Registering Sex in Sinful Budapest

Urban love is also love. It lacks naivety and poetry . . . but urban love also has its own poems, which poets will not be able to ignore much longer. Sooner or later they will have to versify it. In fact it is the true modern love. The country love is out of date. The love in the metropolis is more genuine, more tangible, more naturalistic in its expressions, makes its way to its goal in a more direct and straightforward way, which is at the end of the day the same thing in the field, as it is in the City Park: many times marriage with Amor, but more frequently Amor—without a marriage certificate. It is the love making of poorer classes that provide the character and glowing warm colors of Budapest's love. Not only because there are more poor people in love than of wealth, but also because the love of poor people is more candid, boisterous, less shy, does not hide from the eyes of the world, more unassuming, would be satisfied with a bench, a tiny shrubby space, where one can whisper and kiss.
—Kornél Tábori, "Budapest in Love," 1905[1]

By the dawn of the twentieth century, Budapest was on its way to becoming a cosmopolitan metropolis notable for its emerging working class and culturally assertive and economically powerful urban middle class committed to advancing the city's liberal politics.[2] This was Budapest's Golden Age. But the "Pearl of the Danube," as late nineteenth-century Budapest was referred to by contemporaries who marveled at the city's architectural beauty, was also becoming internally infamous for its boisterous sexual culture and plentitude of gifted "butterflies of the night [Hungarian corollary for the American euphemism "ladies of the night"]."[3] Journalist Kornél Tábori's assertion in his essay "Budapest in Love," "the country love is out of date" reflected contemporary views that the norms and laws that had been regulating romantic and sexual behavior in Budapest for centuries were being challenged and were rapidly changing. In the Hungarian capital, as in most places prior to the 1900s, religion had reigned over marriage, divorce, and fertility in Hungary. The Catholic Church, which had the greatest influence among religious denominations, argued for chastity before marriage and that sex was about procreation between a married man and woman whose bond of marriage could only be broken by death. The family and power of men within it was embedded not only in canon law but also in existing legal codes of Hungary. The church was not alone in its traditional and restrictive view of sexual matters. The historic aristocracy and the bourgeois classes were also notoriously proper in upholding traditional piety in regard to gender and sexual norms, which nevertheless, as this chapter will demonstrate, showed willful ignorance toward the sexual transgressions of men. And while the Catholic Church would not change its ideas about sex well into the twentieth century and higher classes were also slow to change, as Tábori noted, the rest of society and especially urban society began to embrace a more liberal attitude toward sexuality. Moreover, as an unintended consequence of the secularization of marriage and divorce, which was intended to aid the integration of ethnic and religious diversity within Hungary and the Austro-Hungarian monarchy more generally, divorce rates in Budapest skyrocketed, and Hungarian divorce rates became one of the highest in Europe.[4] The secularization of marriage and divorce was only one of the signs of changing times. Urbanization and higher mobility of single men and women contributed to changing marriage and family patterns, what conservative critics saw as signs of the dangerous destabilization of the institution of the patriarchal family. Thanks to the rapid economic and population growth of Budapest, in tandem with liberal politics, the stronghold of the Catholic Church and of the patriarchal family on sexual morality weakened significantly. At the same time, a lack of affordable living spaces in Budapest led to crammed living conditions and little to no privacy for the growing urban working classes. This was especially true for young people and contributed to public spaces becoming more sexually charged. As a result, at the dawn of the twentieth century, as the words of Tábori conveyed, there seemed to be something novel about love and sexuality. Love, which in the case of Tábori was also a euphemism for engaging in sexual activity, appeared omnipresent in Budapest. In a moment of increasing leisure time even for the working classes, there was, as historian John Lukacs notes in regard to Budapest, "the sense of erotic promises, earthy and tangible, as well as transcendent. It penetrated the hearts of the people, and not only the young."[5] More visible, more scandalous, and increasingly impossible to ignore, sex in Budapest was there to stay.

The cultural and economic modernity that facilitated a new sexual urban climate also enabled the emergence of a homosexual subculture.[6] Queer men and women who preferred their own sex were part of the emerging sexual landscape of Budapest. Less visible but growing in numbers, it was also the first time that authorities began to acknowledge their presence and set out to deal with them. This chapter reconstructs the history of a remarkable document: the homosexual registry of the Budapest Metropolitan Police. Although contemporary publications from the late nineteenth century onward took up the issue of same-sex sexuality, most of them either omitted or provided only subtle references to the homosexual registry. In one of the few surviving sources that explicitly talks about the registry, neurologist Zoltán Nemes Nagy in 1933 makes the following claim:

> In the entire world, Budapest is the first metropolis where homosexuals are (semi) officially registered. The police keep a registry for known notorious homosexuals, mostly the blackmailers. This is especially important for policing purposes, since male homosexuals are followed like a shadow and threatened by blackmailers.[7]

The candid analysis of Nemes Nagy provides the basis of this chapter, which explores why the homosexual registry was first created, how it was maintained and used, and the ways in which contemporaries acknowledged its existence. Since the actual registry, as well as most historical traces of it, is gone, I use a multilayered approach. The chapter is based on the sources that directly or indirectly address, talk about, mention, or provide information about the historical origins, purpose, and implementation of the homosexual registry. In using these documents, I decode, deduce, and read into silences. I also rely on historical works that discuss contemporaneous policing of sexualities in other European cities. As part of reconstructing the registry, the chapter examines the approaches of the Metropolitan Police of Budapest to sexual crimes and more specifically to nonnormative sexuality. I argue that the establishment and increasingly more proficient implementation of the homosexual registry was a manifestation of the Hungarian state's expanding ability to control people's lives. Placing the policing of same-sex desire and the police's homosexual registry center stage corroborates and deepens the history of a spectacularly rapid modernization and the growing power of the state. It also offers new insights into the ways in which Hungarian officials during an increasingly liberal political environment understood Budapest's place in modern Europe. More specifically, this chapter argues that (homo)sexuality prior to World War I offered the authorities in Budapest both the concrete challenge of urban modernity as a well as the means to deal with it. The homosexual registry was part of a conscious and collaborative effort on the part of governing authorities to "catch up" and make Budapest into a modern capital. Yet, the activities perceived as catching up by authorities in terms of thinking about and policing sexuality were taking place in Budapest at the same time as they were in other major European cities. Furthermore, the registry while originally conceived as a bureaucratic tool to regulate same-sex sexuality, paradoxically proved neither wholly repressive nor regulatory.

HOMOSEXUALITY AND THE MODERN PENAL CODE

Following the Compromise of 1867 and the establishment of the Austro-Hungarian monarchy, Hungary could have its own legal system, including a new penal code. In contrast to what was perceived by the liberal Hungarian elite as Austria's antiquated penal code (enacted in 1803 and amended in 1852), the new Hungarian Penal code, or *Büntető törvénykönv*, was to assist Hungary's modernization and catching up to established European powers.[8] Being a latecomer to modernization in terms of political and economic as well as social processes yielded certain advantages. Most importantly, Hungarian officials and their immediate staff had been educated and traveled to the most advanced countries and had had firsthand experience of how the most developed countries functioned. Thus, they felt confident identifying the specific areas, whether in regulation, infrastructure, or execution, in which Hungary needed reforms. In drafting the new penal code in the early 1870s, Károly Csemegi, undersecretary of the Ministry of Interior, carefully analyzed leading European countries' penal codes in order to pick which system might offer a framework that would be most appropriate to Hungary.[9] After considering most Western European penal codes, Csemegi chose to follow the outlines of the German penal code of 1871. Ratified in 1878, the Hungarian penal code remained largely in place until 1961.[10] Although in comparison the Hungarian penal code was relatively more "enlightened" in its view of crimes than many others, the new justice system followed in the footsteps of established nation-states. It aimed to keep order and reduce crime by focusing on punishment, as opposed to treating crimes in a more comprehensive manner and focusing on prevention.

With the criminalization of consensual sex between adult men in 1878, the Hungarian regulation chose not to follow states, such as France, Holland, or Italy, that did not criminalize same-sex sexual relations as long as they were consensual and took place outside of the public sphere.[11] Nevertheless, the law was more lenient than the majority of European criminal codes.[12] In terms of the regulation of same-sex sexuality, the Hungarian penal code rejected Austria's approach, which criminalized both female and male homosexuality; instead like most countries that criminalized homosexuality, Hungary only criminalized sex between men.[13] They did so for a variety of reasons. Hungarian lawmakers wanted to create a more liberal penal code than what they considered the draconian Austrian code of 1852 to be. Not criminalizing sex between women would have been seen as one of the markers of Hungary's more progressive approach to criminal justice. More importantly, as in the case of most criminal codes, the authors of Hungarian penal code considered sex between women not worthy of criminalization for a variety of—often circular—reasons. In the eyes of lawmakers (all of whom were male), female homosexuality was less threatening to public morals since women tended to be more private about their sexual affairs and also more conforming in their gender representation. In their logic, since women's homosexuality was expressed only privately and most female homosexuals did their best to conceal their sexuality in public, female homosexual acts (as opposed to male homosexuality and female prostitution) posed little danger to public morality. At the same time, others argued that the same private nature of female homosexuality also made its prosecution impossible.[14] Ultimately, female homosexuality was not criminalized because sexual acts between women "constitute[d] far from being of the moral and punitive significance as unnatural fornication between men."[15]

Closely following Prussian law Paragraph 175, Paragraph 241 of the Hungarian penal code criminalized sexual acts between men and bestiality as *terrnèszet elleni fajtalanság*. The term *terrnèszet elleni fajtalanság* is the Hungarian equivalent of *widernatürliche unzucht*, or "unnatural fornication" in English. Charges of Paragraph 241 were treated as misdemeanors that could be punished by up to one year of *fogház* (the most lenient form of Hungary's three-tier prison system).[16] What exactly constituted an act of "unnatural fornication" was never concretely defined and remained open to different interpretations until its ultimate decriminalization in 1961. Depending on the interpreter, the parameters could be broader, such as "all sexual acts intended to arouse unnatural sexual desire," or more limited, in which case only penetrative intercourse would fulfill the legal definition of unnatural fornication. Generally speaking, similar to the German jurisdiction, acts that resembled "natural" (heterosexual intercourse–like) sexual acts and anal and oral sex were seen as "unnatural fornication."[17] Subject to the judge, mutual masturbation could also fulfill Paragraph 241. Paragraph 242 made nonconsensual, which included sex with minors under the age of twelve, "unnatural fornication" a felony, which was punishable by up to five years in prison, and potentially life imprisonment if the act caused the death of the victim. In addition to nonconsensual sex between adults, same-sex pedophilia also fell into this category. While in the case of a misdemeanor there was no ancillary punishment, a guilty conviction for Paragraph 242 could also mean the temporary loss of office and titles.[18] And importantly, both Paragraphs 241 and 242 were chargeable offenses; that is, if information was brought to the police's knowledge, the police had the right and responsibility to prosecute same-sex acts between men.[19] That is, once police acquired knowledge about sex between men in the form of accusations by members of the public or reports from the police themselves, the police were obligated to investigate the matter. The almost impossible task of catching people in the act that a guilty conviction of consensual homosexuality required was instrumental in the establishment of the homosexual registry.

THE METROPOLITAN POLICE OF BUDAPEST AND THE ESTABLISHMENT OF THE HOMOSEXUAL REGISTRY

Following a gradual political liberalization that continued after the Austro-Hungarian Compromise of 1867, Budapest gained control over its internal affairs. Between the Revolution of 1848–49 and the Compromise of 1867, the Habsburg bureaucracy in Vienna ruled with draconian vigor and made most of the major decisions about Hungary's internal affairs.[20] As testament to the new relationship between Austria and Hungary as a joint partnership between equals, the Hungarian capital was to have its own Hungarian police force. The arm of law enforcement in the Hungarian capital, the Budapest Metropolitan Police, was established in 1871. After the unification of Pest, Buda, and Óbuda in 1873, the state under the aegis of the Ministry of Justice assumed control over the Metropolitan Police, a nascent step in expanding the influence of the national Hungarian government.[21]

The internal structure of the police was finally established in the mid-1880s.[22] This was the era of the infamous Captain Elek Thaisz (1829–92), who served as the first chief captain of the Budapest Metropolitan Police.[23] Captain Thaisz, who was notorious for his love of "members of the oldest profession" (he was married to a madam and had lucrative business deals with the criminal underworld), actually facilitated prostitution's development and fostered a liberal attitude toward sexuality in general.[24] By 1881 the Metropolitan Police were responsible for about seventy-five square miles, the second largest area of enforcement in Europe after London. For such a vast area, there was only one policeman for every six hundred inhabitants and for approximately every seventy-seven thousand acres; thus, the number of policemen per inhabitant in Budapest was significantly lower than in other European capitals.²⁵ The Metropolitan Police underwent a series of reforms during the last years of the nineteenth and the beginning of the twentieth century. The establishment of the criminal registry was one of the notable results. The real change and a new era for the police came following the resignation of Thaisz in the wake of the preparations for the millennium celebration of the *Honfoglalás* (the settlement of Hungarians into the Carpathian Basin) in 1896. In an effort to clean up corruption and improve Budapest's public safety, crucial developments in terms of policing and implementation of regulations took place during the captaincy (the Hungarian name for the head of police) of Béla Rudnay (1896–1906).²⁶

In a conscious effort to modernize the police force, among other things the leadership under Rudnay set out to establish a system to track criminals in the city. Since Budapest had only recently claimed its city status and was a relative latecomer to modernization, the Metropolitan Police had the opportunity to set up a new system based on the hard-learned experiences of other cities. In an effort to implement the latest scientific methods to regulate and most effectively police Budapest, officers visited police headquarters in other major cities such as Berlin and London and educated themselves about existing criminal registries.²⁷ At the end, instead of the anthropometric Bertillon system (named after its creator Alphonse Bertillon, a French police officer) that measured the physical sizes of heads and faces and was used in most European countries and the United States, it was the Galton-Henry classification method of fingerprinting that the Metropolitan Police of Budapest adopted as the basis of its criminal registry.²⁸ In so doing, Hungary became the second country after England to introduce fingerprinting as the basis of identifying and keeping the records of criminals.²⁹ By 1903 there were 75,445 people in the criminal registry, which also included pictures of 10,807 people. In 1908 the criminal registry was made national, and the Office of National Criminal Registry by 1925 had almost three hundred thousand fingerprints stored.³⁰

It was the same desire to modernize and be on par with leading European police forces that led to the establishment of the homosexual registry. Being part of modern Europe required a more transparent and effective police and urban management system. Following the lead of Metropolitan Police in some of the largest Western European cities, the Hungarian authorities set up a file system for each crime in order to track individuals.³¹ The creation of a registry for homosexuals was part of this effort. Like many of their counterparts in other European capitals, there was a special unit within the Budapest

Metropolitan Police that cataloged information of men arrested for same-sex sexual activities in order to help identify and keep track of men who had sex with men.[32] The exact date for the creation of the homosexual registry is uncertain, but it appears to have reached its final form in 1908. In 1908, following the Vice Squad Department's move to a separate building, the registry was restructured along the lines of the so-called American style card-filing system, which presumably functioned in that form throughout the existence of the registry.[33] Although none of the sources acknowledge it explicitly, the data on homosexuals was most likely permanently housed alongside the registry of prostitutes, which served as a blueprint for the homosexual registry.[34] The special unit within the Metropolitan Police tasked with the monitoring of homosexuals in Budapest was closely aligned and cooperated with the vice police. Having been set up in the Austro-Hungarian monarchy, the chapters ahead will explain how the registry operated throughout every subsequent political regime until 1989.

THE CHARACTERISTICS OF THE HOMOSEXUAL REGISTRY

Some of the most informative details about the homosexual registry come from medical professionals from the 1930s. There are surviving references and hints about the existence of the registry in police, legal, and popular sources from the 1890s onward. But it is from two physicians that we learn the most about the exact makeup as well as the content of the homosexual registry. In *Catastrophies of Love Life*, Dr. Zoltán Nemes Nagy, a sexual pathologist and a medical doctor, provides a candid introduction to the background of the registry:

> There are about 5000 (in 1933) homosexual men in the Metropolitan police's registry. But by no means does the registry contain all the homosexuals, only those individuals who have had run-ins with the police. . . . The registry has been introduced in Budapest for about 15 years. But it contains mostly those who are passive or working for money and material interest.[35]

We know nothing as to why and how sexologist Nemes Nagy gained access to the otherwise covert registry, which was almost never openly acknowledged or talked about throughout the registry's eight-decade-long existence. Nemes Nagy in his private practice had homosexual patients from whom he could have gotten some of the information, but it seems that he also had contacts at the Vice Department of the Metropolitan Police. His statement about the duration of the registry is slightly off, since it is more likely that at the time of his writing the registry had been in operation for about twenty-five years. Nevertheless, his description of the registry and the personal accounts of his patients that he includes from the registry offer invaluable insights. To begin, we learn that homosexuals entered the registry *mostly* when they encountered the law as lawbreakers and potentially as victims of blackmail. While this will change during the post–World War II Communist era, during the first three decades of the twentieth century, men entered the registry for the most part not based on rumors or informants or sightings at certain venues, but rather through direct run-ins with the police. What this meant was that men had to be caught in the act or in some practice resembling the act of sex or suspected having performed the act in order to gain a place in the registry. Once men were in the homosexual registry, Nemes Nagy informs us, "their entire life: every bit of information about them was documented."[36] The registry contained the following information:

Homosexual Registry

Name:	Native tongue:
Birthplace and birth date:	Eye color:
Religion:	Mouth:
Marital status:	Nose:
Occupation:	Ears:
Address:	
Face:	
Location, where picked up:	Hands:
Nationality:	Hair:
Languages spoken:	Mustache:
Female name:	Beard:
Inclination:	Special peculiarities:
Social affiliations:	Criminal record:[37]

Most of the information that the homosexual registry contained was a standard feature of all criminal registries, regardless of the crime committed. Some of the specific descriptors were taken from the prostitution registry, which looked remarkably similar in Budapest and Vienna.[38] The police, even if they did not employ the physical measurements of the anthropometric Bertillon system, took detailed descriptions of physical attributes of those arrested. They also recorded people's social history.

The types of categories and overall information gathered on the registry point to the influence of criminal sociology and criminal anthropology as they emerged during the last part of nineteenth and early twentieth century.[39] But the registry reflects the approach of the so-called *közvetítő iskola* (go-between school), otherwise referred to as the neoclassical school, which from the late nineteenth century characterized the Hungarian legal system.[40] Due to late modernization, "in Hungary neither criminal sociology nor criminal anthropology attracted major fans."[41] Rather it was the German jurist and criminologist Franz Eduard Ritter von Liszt (1851–1919) whose progressive school became the most influential and whose approach Hungarian legal scholars and the legal system adopted.[42] As seen in the homosexual registry, this approach combined both exogenous (environmental) and endogenous (biological) factors in explaining the causes of crime. Questions about the individual's social, economic, and educational background reflect the exogenous focus, which was central to criminal sociology, while questions about people's physical attributes point to the anthropometric or biological focus. Whereas the "sociological school" located the seeds of criminal activities in the external environment, the criminal anthropology school located them in innate physical features that were the result of biology. Physical attributes, such as hair color and nose and ear shape, were especially thought to be important for future identification of the registered person as well as potentially as an explanation of his homosexuality.[43] In the rapidly growing city, where people frequently changed their address and location, keeping track of *notórius homosexuálisok*, or notorious homosexuals, was by no means an easy task.[44] Documenting social and economic background, as well as education level and occupation, was important for identifying and also explaining someone amidst the flow of incoming and unregistered inhabitants of Budapest.[45] The category of social affiliation was meant to map people's social world in terms of who they knew and what organizations, clubs, and societies (if any) they belong to or frequented. That knowledge, along with rest of the details that the registry supplied, could be useful in identifying individuals in cases dealing with male homosexual prostitution and the blackmailing of what I call respectable homosexuals—men who engaged in same-sex acts in private and who aside from their sexual object choice lived a reputable life. And as we will shortly see, the details about individuals were available for statistical analysis.[46]

THE EFFECTS OF FORENSIC MEDICINE

In the process of gathering information, data was collected that was specific to the homosexual registry. In addition to the generic information collected on all criminals, the registry included two additional categories: the person's inclination and female name. These features provide important clues about the operation of the registry as well as clues on police assumptions about the disposition of the homosexual population. To begin with, the question of "inclination" reflects the extent to which sexuality and in particularly nonnormative sexuality had become medicalized by the early twentieth century as Hungarian forensic science and psychiatry, as elsewhere in Europe, were enthusiastically claiming authority over sexuality.[47] Similar to the legal discourse, Hungarian medical discourse on sexuality was deeply influenced by the German-speaking world. At the onset of discussing nonnormative and in particular homosexualities, it was customary for Hungarian physicians to provide a summary of how most prominent physicians across Europe conceptualized homosexuality before detailing their own views and discussing specific Hungarian cases. As the following excerpt from one of the most prominent Hungarian forensic medicine textbooks of the time, written by Ernő Moravcsik (1858–1924), internationally renowned forensic psychiatrist, illustrates, Hungarian medical vocabulary, as well as conceptualization of homosexuality, was heavily influenced by the German-speaking world.

> The manifestation of sexual instinct between people of the same sex we call homosexuality, which stands in contrast to the heterosexuality of the opposite sexes. Krafft-Ebing calls this abnormal instinct a perversion, whereas actions of perversions he refers to as perversity. Westphal refers to such cases as "konträre Sexualempfindung" [sic] that is, a contrary feeling to a person's physical and developmental conditions. The French mainly use the expression of inversion to indicate the transformation through which a man ends up feeling like a woman. The most common designation of abnormal sexual instincts in men is *uranism* recommended by Ulrichs. Perverse feelings in women are known as *tribadia* (amor lesbicus).[48]

One does not have to be a linguist to detect that most of these terms that describe homosexuality came from the German language. Considering the predominance of German medicine along with the powerful and historically robust Hungarian relationship with the Habsburgs and the Hungarian elite's admiration of German culture, this comes as no surprise. German was the language of the imperial court of the Austro-Hungarian monarchy; even though Hungarian became the official language within the Hungarian kingdom after 1867, most people continued to be at least bilingual. In addition, since Hungary, and especially Budapest, prior to 1918, was an ethnically and linguistically diverse society, people who spoke different languages would often fall back on German as an intermediary language of communication.[49] This explains why many of the Hungarian expressions and references about homosexuality came from German and were often adopted without translation into Hungarian. Consequently, the word *urning* and expressions such as *warme bruder* and *schwester* or *warme schwester* were used by both the authorities as well as homosexuals themselves. *Urning*, the term introduced by Karl Heinrich Ulrichs, was meant to refer to people who preferred their own sex. According to Ulrichs's ideas, *urnings* possessed a male body with a female soul. The terms *urning*, which predated the word "homosexual," and *schwester*, which means sister in German, were the most commonly used terms to describe people who preferred their own sex until the beginning of the twentieth century.[50] That men who desired their own sex referred to each other as sisters literally embodied Ulrichs's theories about homosexual men being psychological hermaphrodites—that is, biologically male with a feminine character.[51] Over time, the word *warme*, which was literally translated into Hungarian as *meleg* to signify homosexual and gay, became the most used and politically correct reference to homosexuality. *Tribadia*, which referred to sexual love between women, however, was used by authorities but not by women themselves. Even as the term, as we will see in chapter 4, continued to be used by authorities into the interwar era, it was never embraced by lesbians. Perhaps no other word can better illustrate the symbiosis of Hungarian and German languages in the Hungarian language of sexuality than the word *homosexualis*, or homosexual. "Homosexuality" was coined by Karl-Maria Kertbeny, or Károly Mária Kertbeny, who, in his own words, "was born in Vienna, yet I am not a Viennese, bur rightfully Hungarian."[52] Yet, Kertbeny's mother tongue remained German, and it was also in German that he first used the term "homosexuality."[53] The word eventually entered into the Hungarian legal, medical, and popular discourse through German publications, first and foremost through Richard von Krafft-Ebing's (1840–1902) *Psychopathia Sexualis*, whose case studies featured a number of Hungarian patients with feelings for their own sex.[54] Some of them, like Sándor/Sarolta Vay who was born female but lived as part of the Austro-Hungarian male gentry, served as foundational case studies on homosexuality for the international sexological community.[55]

Even as references were made to French, and later to British and American medical theorists, Hungarian forensic scientists came to embrace Krafft-Ebing's ideas that homosexuality was a perversion and therefore a medical rather than criminal matter.[56] They also believed that homosexuality could be innate, "constitutional," or acquired, "pseudo": while some people were born with it, many more developed homosexuality.[57] However, unlike Krafft-

Ebing, who by the end of his life (he died in 1902) understood homosexuality as a variant of sexual inclination without necessarily any pathological origins or effects, Moravcsik and most of his Hungarian counterparts continued to believe that the majority of homosexual cases were the consequence of mental or nervous disorders.[58] The majority of men who engaged in sexual activities with other men were therefore not to be considered congenital homosexuals, but rather pathologically induced formerly heterosexual men.[59] And even as some Hungarian physicians, from the second decade of the twentieth century onward, perceived homosexuality as a sexual inclination without necessarily having any identifiable pathological causes, many continued to see homosexuality as a medically pathological condition well into the post–World War II era. As the specific questions on the homosexual registry demonstrate, in dealing with men who were caught having sex with other men or who confessed to have same-sex sexual desires, determining one's true sexual inclination became the first step not only for medical professionals but also for law enforcement.

The question of "inclination" in particular suggests that the Metropolitan Police were serious about determining whether or not the person was a real or authentic homosexual. The official police journal *Rendőri Lapok* (Police Pages) helps to provide additional details to contextualize the police's view and approach.[60] The journal as the official organ of the police was tasked with disseminating information—conceptual as well as technical—about matters of policing, in this case about queer sexualities, to police stations nationwide. In doing so, the journal played an important role in establishing norms of how policemen across Hungary approached and dealt with men who had sex with men and more generally with nonnormative forms of sexualities. In the first decade of the twentieth century, during the time when the homosexual registry was being set up, the journal featured a number of article series such as "The Pathological Aberrations of Sexual Life," "Sexual Offenses in the Criminal Code," and others explicitly on homosexuality.[61] In a similar fashion to forensic medical books, the articles in these series present a tour de force of the latest international views of sexologists and criminal anthropologists on sexual abnormalities such as masturbation, sadism, and masochism, as well the various forms of same-sex love, followed by workable definitions of various abnormalities and some actual experiences of the Metropolitan Police in dealing with them. During the same period, the journal also published articles about how police vice departments in some of the largest European cities such as Berlin and Paris dealt with homosexuality.[62] The articles illustrate the remarkable transnational influence sexological theories had in shaping public perceptions of sexuality. They also reveal the importance of information exchange among law enforcement agencies across large European cities that facilitated the Metropolitan Police's rather complex view of homosexuality and a surprisingly nuanced approach to men who had sex with men.

The police believed there were two major types of homosexuals. In one group homosexuality was innate; in the second group, it was acquired. This is clearly expressed in an article titled "Third Gender":

> Homosexuality and its seed is something that people bear within themselves since birth—and regardless of the circumstances it will take hold of those who have it and it is almost impossible to suppress it. It requires the utmost energy and self-control in order to hide one's perversity. But he will be always aware of it. Aside from the congenital perverts, there are quite a number of people in whose case it is not nature's fault that is to blame. Their perversity comes about as a result of their education, environment, their general life style, and sometimes as the consequence of an ill-considered moment or act.[63]

Thus, authentic homosexuals were born desiring their own sex and could not help their inclination. Unlike forensic doctors and sexologists, the police seemed much less interested in finding pathological origins for congenital homosexuals. Instead, which must have come from actual experience in dealing with homosexual men, the police took the homosexuality of those men for granted. The same sort of sexual drive that was believed to drive men to nonmonogamy and prostitution was in the instance of authentic male homosexuals seen as a drive "impossible to suppress." In the eyes of the police, congenital homosexuals required, if not sympathy, at least legitimacy. This was in contrast to people who were thought to acquire their homosexuality by developing it artificially through being exposed to it. According to the police, these men actually had a choice about their sexuality but did not resist. Consequently, the term "inclination" on the homosexual registry was meant to indicate this important distinction circulating in police circles at the time the registry's categories were created. The exact procedure that the police used to determine innate versus acquired homosexuality is not explicitly documented in records. It is likely that such determinations were the result of a combination of self-admission, the assessment of police medical experts, and the pressure of interrogation. There is no question that in between those men who from their earliest memories were attracted to their own sex and those who got involved with men in all-male institutions out of sheer curiosity, there was a wide range of men who fell in the gray zone. The registry's inclusion of "female name" in theory could supplement the differentiation by providing the adopted names by which authentic homosexuals were known within the queer community. However, it is more likely that female name was recorded in order to match the identity of individuals with their queer persona. This could help in identifying and tracking queer men.

Nemes Nagy's observation that the registry contained only those homosexuals who are "passive and working for money" provides further clues. For one, the police differentiated between men on the registry based on gender representation and sexual performativity. In doing so their approach supports a growing body of literature that highlights a transnational phenomenon during the first decades of the twentieth century of a differential (by and large preferential) treatment of manly homosexual men compared to that of male homosexuals who acted feminine and whose gender representation transgressed traditional gender norms.[64] There were so-called active men who had sex with other men whom the police did not necessarily consider "authentic" homosexuals. Those thought to be "authentic" in the eyes of the police were usually "passive" and "could not help their sexual inclination." The sexual role men played was bound to understandings of "authenticity"—only men who were sodomized (i.e., accepted anal penetration) could be authentic homosexuals. This conceptualization by the police conflated gendered assumptions about the essentially "active" nature of normal men—and the passive or feminine nature of queer men—with sexual selfhood. From the standpoint of the police, authentic homosexuals were born with the sexual desire of being sexually acted on by other men as passive "women." Second, as Nemes Nagy points out, the police made note of men who were selling their sexual services to other men. These men were considered not only "inauthentic" but also particularly dangerous. The following excerpt from the article "The Male Prostitute" that *Rendőri Lapok* published in 1908 illustrates the disdain that the police held for male prostitutes:

> The male prostitute is very far from a nomination for the "Legion of Honor"! Who sells his body has given up his soul, respect, and moral decency. The female prostitute has a lot of excuses. Just to mention one, there are quite a few among both registered and clandestine prostitutes whose unstoppable licentious blood and exotic desire for men place them among the condemned. This would be almost impossible among male prostitutes. They are all businessmen, who destroy the last drop of human decency by throwing themselves even to perverted bestialities,

for money. It is understandable therefore that their moral insanity soon becomes criminality. This is the case for almost all of them. There are thieves, swindlers, cynical murderers among them, but the majority of them are blackmailers. They have nothing to lose, unlike their *"respectable"* partners, whose entire existence crumbles in a minute if their secret is revealed.[65]

In contrast to female prostitutes, whose work the police could excuse for material and even biological reasons, male prostitutes were given no excuse for their behavior. By selling their male bodies to men, they committed "moral insanity." Moreover, most of them were believed to be criminals whose prostituting of their bodies was only one among many criminal activities. The blackmailing of authentic homosexuals, many of whom came from the middle and upper echelons of society, was equally concerning for the police. The registering and keeping of these men on the radar of the police at all times became a priority of a special "homosexual squad" within the police. What this meant was that the homosexual registry, which theoretically included all men who had sex with another man, made a distinction between men who engaged in consensual sex and male prostitutes. Before setting up a separate registry for male prostitutes sometime in the late 1920s, the police marked men who sold sex for money in the homosexual registry with "monetary interest."[66]

QUANTIFYING DATA FROM THE HOMOSEXUAL REGISTRY

Another medical doctor provides both quantitative and qualitative information about the registered individuals. Dr. Jenő Szántó, in a 1933 article on homosexuality in Budapest, presents some colorful data on the socioeconomic background of men who were in the registry of the Metropolitan Police.[67] Szántó, like Nemes Nagy, had contact with the police and was allowed to study the specific content of the registry, which he openly discussed more than once in a widely circulated medical journal.[68] He presents statistics on 3,425 registered men in terms of their occupation, marital status, religion, and criminal history (table 1).

Szántó's data, which comes from the early 1930s, resembles what we know of the distribution of homosexuals across professions from the pre–World War I period. While, overall, working-class and lower-class people are the majority, people of means (professionals, merchants, civil servants) make up a considerable segment of the registry. The fact that "merchant and salesmen" is the second largest category, followed by "business owners" and

TABLE 1. Occupational statistics of registered homosexuals

Occupation of 3,425 registered men*	#	%
Factory worker, day laborer, house servant	431	12.58
Merchant, salesman	422	12.38
Private officeholder, factory owner, landowner, property owner	309	9.09
Civil servant, civil worker	243	7.09
Tailors (both for men and women)	233	6.80
Ironworkers, chauffeurs	222	6.47
Waiters, bartenders, barkeepers	168	4.99
Carpenters, masons, glazers	163	4.76
Gardener, digger	158	4.61
Baker, cook, confectioner	137	4.00
Shoemaker	137	3.70
Manservant	107	3.12
Jeweler, artificer, optician, photographer	103	3.00
Pupil, university student	90	2.61
Hairdresser, barber	77	2.24
Upholsterer, decorator, painter	74	2.15
Artist, actor, music teacher	50	1.48
Butcher, slaughterer	46	1.33
Engineer, architect, chemist	40	1.16
Teacher, instructor	33	0.96
Nurse, masseur	32	0.93
Artiste, dancer	31	0.90
Musician	28	0.81
Textile worker, weaver	24	0.70
Bookbinder, printer	24	0.70
Medical doctor	19	0.55
Soldier (incomplete data)	15	0.43
Writer, journalist	10	0.29
Lawyer	9	0.26

* Szántó, "A homosexualitásról, különös tekintettel a budapesti viszonyokra," *Bőrgyógyászati, Urológiai és Venereologiai Szemle*, no. 2 (1933): 40.

"civil servants," is a clear indication that the Metropolitan Police registered men regardless of their social and economic status.

Szántó also provides information about the marital status of the men in the registry (table 2). The great majority (almost 80 percent) of registered men were single, which had likely also been the case in the last part of the nineteenth and early twentieth century since most people in the Budapest criminal registry during that time were single.[69]

Table 3 details the men's religious affiliation. All religions were proportionately represented in terms of the religious demographics of Budapest, except for Jews, who were underrepresented. In this respect, the situation of Budapest seems to resemble other cities, such as London, where Jewish men tended to be underrepresented in queer urban life.[70]

As for the data on age, over half of the men on the registry were between twenty and forty years old (table 4). This pattern seems to correspond with demographic trends in Budapest, with young single men flocking to the city for work.[71] These general characteristics are in line with the police's "typical registered male" on the Budapest criminal registry prior to World War I:

TABLE 2. Marital status of registered homosexuals

Family status of 3,425 registered men*	#	%
Single	2,691	78.58
Married	605	17.68
Widowed	64	1.87
Divorced	65	1.87

* Szántó, A homosexualitásról, különös tekintettel a budapesti viszonyokra," Bőrgyógyászati, Urológiai és Venereologiai Szemle, no. 2 (1933): 41.

TABLE 3. Religious affiliation of registered homosexuals

Religion of 3,425 homosexual men*	# of homosexuals	% of homosexuals	% of Budapest's population (in 1930)
Roman Catholic	2,236	65.28	59.9
Greek Catholic	53	1.54	1.0
Calvinist	494	14.42	11.4
Lutheran	153	4.52	4.8
Jewish	445	12.99	21.6
Other	44	1.28	1.3

* Szántó, "A homosexualitásról, különös tekintettel a budapesti viszonyokra," Bőrgyógyászati, Urológiai és Venereologiai Szemle, no. 2 (1933): 41.

TABLE 4. Age distribution of registered homosexuals

Age of 3,425 homosexual men*	#	%
Under 20 years of age	124	3.62
20–30 years of age	1,235	36.08
30–40 years of age	997	29.10
40–50 years of age	599	17.48
50–60	331	9.67
60 and above	139	4.05

* Szántó, "A homosexualitásról, különös tekintettel a budpesti viszonyokra," Bőrgyógyászati, Urológiai és Venereologiai Szemle, no. 2 (1933): 42.

between twenty and forty years old, born in the countryside, and unmarried.[72] Furthermore, the information that the homosexual registry conveys on homosexual men and men who had sex with men in Budapest is consistent with what historians have discovered about other urban communities: the majority of men who were caught for sex with men tended to be in their twenties and thirties, unmarried, and at the time of their arrest, gainfully employed.

The last set of data Szántó provides is the criminal history of the registered men (table 5). This information hints at a more complicated purpose and operation of the registry than the simple tracking of men who had sex with men would imply. We learn that about one in five (20 percent) of the registered men had had prior contact with the justice system. Nine percent of them had been convicted for homosexuality under Paragraph 241 or 242, and 10 percent had been convicted for other reasons. While the statistics from Szántó, as well as from police sources, do not specify, it seems that these men were most often convicted for petty crimes and theft.[73] In an essay on homosexuality that was written as part of a major publication on modern criminality, József Vogl, a police captain, stressed that while relatively few homosexuals were prosecuted for unnatural fornication, most homosexuals arrested, similar to other larger European cities, were charged with petty crimes such as theft.[74] Considering how difficult it would have been to catch people in the act, one could imagine that charging suspected homosexuals with petty crimes would have allowed police to bring these men into the police system and register them on the homosexual registry. At the same time, it is also possible that the police could arrest suspected homosexual men with petty charges in order to bring them into the station and then force them to confess to having sexual relations with men. Either way, it was not

TABLE 5. Criminal history of registered homosexuals

Criminal history of 3,425 homosexual men*	#	%
Convicted for blackmailing	40	1.16
Convicted for fornication	307	8.96
Convicted for other reasons	357	10.42

* Szántó, "A homoszexualitásról, különös tekintettel a budpesti viszonyokra," *Bőrgyógyászati, Urológiai és Venereologiai Szemle*, no. 2 (1933): 41.

only in the case of an unnatural fornication charge that men would enter the homosexual registry. The third category of crimes—blackmailing—is numerically small. However, for the purpose of the operation of the registry, it had a much greater significance than its numbers indicate.

THE HOMOSEXUAL REGISTRY IN PRACTICE

What principles informed how the "homosexual squad" and the police in general treated homosexuals, and how did they use the registry? The homosexual registry represented the application of modern rational technologies of power and the intensification of policing of nonnormative sexualities. In practice, local circumstances and understandings of sexuality were much more important in shaping its application and influence on the daily lives of queers in Budapest. In contrast to subsequent historical accounts, which praised the police for setting up a modern criminal registry, contemporary sources highlighted the continuing inability of the police to sufficiently implement it. Although rarely writing explicitly about the registry—homosexual or any other ones—the daily newspapers reported on and even ridiculed police corruption and "spectacular" (in)efficiencies on a regular basis throughout the first decade of the twentieth century.[75] The portrayal of the police in the most circulated and most popular comic journal of the day, *Borsszem Jankó* (Mighty small Johnny), indicates how denizens of Budapest thought about their law enforcement.[76] For two decades prior to World War I, this popular weekly journal featured a character, András Mihaszna (Useless Andrew), whose portrayal of the police achieved national fame.[77] Mihaszna was representative of contemporary urban satires of helpless police that were popular on both sides of the Atlantic.[78] As historian Géza Buzinkay states,

> His purpose not only to serve as a tool for presenting jokes about policemen; he embodied the awkward constable with his sense of omnipotence, a representative of official arrogance and conceit, the officer whose duty

it is to keep order in the chaotic metropolis but who is, of course, always clumsy, always in the wrong place at the wrong time.⁷⁹

The character of András Mihaszna, along with a dozen of his helpless counterparts who were featured in the contemporary press, highlights the struggles of the police to meet even minimal expectations. At the same time that the public was expressing its skepticism, the civic leadership also voiced concerns about the effectiveness of the police. Being understaffed and ill equipped to catch criminals would have been one thing. But the police were at times accused of actually intentionally failing at fulfilling their obligation. During a parliamentary debate in 1881, for example, one parliament member stated that "in comparison to the Metropolitan Police in London and in Vienna, where two-third of the police staff works during the night and one-third during the day, here (in Budapest) one-tenth of the police works at night. That is the source of our public safety or more precisely the lack thereof."⁸⁰ The relationship between the Metropolitan Police and the mayor and more generally the civic leadership of Budapest was far from harmonious throughout the life of the dual monarchy, and there was lingering criticism of the police for being lenient with criminals at best and indifferent and careless at worst until into twentieth century.⁸¹ These criticisms implied both qualitative and quantitative shortcomings. What this meant for the operation of the criminal registry system (and its subparts, like the registries of sexual vice crimes) is that it faced significant impediments.

In fact, the police themselves admitted that the implementation of the criminal registry was a slow process and that it was not fully operational even by the turn of the century. An 1899 article entitled "The National Registry System" in the *Rendőri Lapok* declared that "the Criminal registry (in Hungary) only exists in one place, in Budapest." It cited a lack of funding as the reason that no registry functioned elsewhere in Hungary and lamented that "the police struggled with operational problems and certainly lacked personnel, resources and organization to efficiently manage the registry even in Budapest."⁸² Another article from 1902, echoing the critical voices in parliament, went further in acknowledging that "amidst the continuing rise of population the police are not only unable to keep up with the rising crime rates (let alone register them), but that they are not even able to assure basic public safety."⁸³ When the official journal of the police explicitly acknowledged the incapacity to fulfill their most basic function of protection, it is not surprising that registering men who had sex with other men was not a high priority or even feasible. Furthermore, law enforcement authorities admitted that "this [the late nineteenth century] was the golden age of prostitution, when sex trafficking, procuring, pimping as well as *all other forms of crimes against morality*, were charged simply with a misdemeanor."[84] In addition, contemporary police articles also reasoned that while the police were supposed to protect the public from "perverse deeds," "and even as the public itself views sexual crimes as ignominious, in actuality they either do not even notice them, or more likely, the people themselves in fact engage in such deeds."[85] In 1903, the police declared that it was "worrisome that perversion between men is quite common in the capital."[86] They blamed the situation on a lack of adequate executive and regulatory power, asserting that fighting moral vices, including sex between men, brought little success. In response to the police's self-justification and complaints, the otherwise liberal city council expressed its own opinions about the ways in which the police handled prostitution and other issues of public morality: "The shocking state of things (around procuring and such) has nothing to do with the lack of existing regulations, rather with the fact that the regulations are not enforced with necessary might."[87] Contemporary reports and articles, including those in the official police journal, agreed that the actual accomplishment (or lack thereof) of the police in dealing with homosexuality and managing sexuality was far from ideal. In regard to same-sex sexuality more specifically, the articles explicitly acknowledge that while "the law in theory is relatively strict about male homosexuality in real life its application is not."[88] Surely, these aforementioned statements would suggest that the police's ineptness had a great deal to do with the lack of adequate attention to queers. But one could also easily argue that the Metropolitan Police of Budapest were no different than most urban police forces in Western capitals, a target of both popular jokes and internal criticisms. A look at the police's approach more closely shows how the police's lack of attention to queers was less about competency and more about a pragmatic choice.

SEX IN THE EYES OF THE POLICE

In the eyes of Hungarian authorities, concern for public and social order and facilitating a vibrant sexual culture were not mutually exclusive. As Budapest was expanding at lightning speed, authorities on both the state and city level were deeply concerned about maintaining order, especially social order and social hierarchies. Because the social composition of the city included a rapidly growing working-class population, the safeguarding of the respectable classes from "immoral" and "uncultured" elements was an important priority from the onset. In the densely populated central districts of the city, there was little physical separation between the rich and respectable and the urban poor, viewed by authorities as immoral elements in society. The police saw their role as safeguarding public spaces and ensuring the protection of the respectable classes.[89] Alongside keeping the unruly and rowdy denizens from disrupting public order, a top priority of police and city authorities alike was to prevent criminal behavior, as the number of thefts and property-related crimes had been on the rise.[90] City authorities made begging and vagrancy strictly illegal and subject to police prosecution.[91] As understaffed as the police were in the 1880s and 1890s, subsequent police chiefs paid particular attention and allocated considerable resources to policing the urban poor. The police also monitored socialist and workers' movements. The growing appeal of socialist ideas among workers kept the police on their toes, as they had to preempt major strikes or other disruptions in the life of the modern metropolis.[92] As it happened, being tough on these issues did not automatically translate into toughness on sex.[93]

Until the outbreak of World War I, the top priority for law enforcement consisted of battling with the two most pertinent criminal activities: property crimes (mostly in the form of theft) and physical assault.[94] Regulating sexuality in Budapest was, for the most part, a low priority. Despite the fact that after a change of leadership in 1885 the top-ranking officers at the Metropolitan Police of Budapest became less corrupt and at least no longer personally financially benefited from the city's booming sex industry through bribery or actual ownership, it was not until the interwar period that policing sexuality became a central concern.[95] This does not mean that general discussions about sex and sexuality did not occur. But until the end of the nineteenth century, and in terms of same-sex sexuality into the first decade of the twentieth, these discussions by and large tended to happen outside the arena of the police and governing authorities. As the next chapter will demonstrate, with the exception of the issue of the regulation of prostitution, it was on the pages of daily newspapers, medical journals, and social commentaries of various forms that people addressed the "problems" of the sex industry and the sexual culture of Budapest. The police and especially the Vice Squad Department was intimately familiar with and exposed to sex and increasingly frequent public displays of sexuality. But just as their counterparts in Vienna, Berlin, and elsewhere in Europe, they remained less concerned with prostitution and the rapidly growing sex industry than with controlling what they viewed as their undesirable effects.[96]

Concern to mitigate the negative consequences of public sexual immorality predated the establishment of the Metropolitan Police; the police forces of Pest, Buda, and Óbuda all had their own Vice Squad Departments.

These departments dealt with prostitution, fornication, trafficking, pornography, and what came to be labeled as "unnatural fornication," their term for sex between men. Following the unification of Budapest in 1873 and the establishment of Metropolitan Police, a Vice Squad Department was set up that was now to serve as the "moral police" of the integrated city. The founding document outlining the responsibilities of the department made it clear that the primary goal of the police was to prevent the scandals, spread of venereal disease, and trafficking of women. The leadership of the police was unequivocal about their role in society, and that did not include the suppression of prostitution. The following excerpt from a memorandum published in the *Bulletin of the Chief of the Police* describes the responsibilities of the vice police as the following:

> Immorality is just as much a product of society as morality is, and it is therefore a concern of the police only as long as it leads to damage, problems, or dangers for specific individuals. The responsibility of the Vice Squad is to prevent and lessen these effects.... The squad does not aspire to eradicate or suppress prostitution, rather it aims to prevent its consequences; scandals, spread of venereal disease and trafficking in girls.[97]

Writing in 1894, the chief captain articulates how it was neither the Vice Squad nor the police's role to change public morals. The police could not be expected to eradicate prostitution or any sexual activities considered "immoral" as long as these were thought to be an inevitable part of the social fabric of a modern metropolis. And even as the police's understanding of prostitution changed over time—from an essentialist view that "ever since human society was born it has been carrying a heavy burden, which it has not been able to get rid of and never will; prostitution," to a more sociologically based explanation that "young poor men in a cramped industrial city could simply not afford to marry and have respectable wives"—the police operated on the belief that the sex industry was there to stay.[98] Understanding sex—outside of marriage and the home—as a natural part of a modern urban city, the police's role became highly pragmatic. It was centered on safeguarding morality *in* public and limiting effects of the sex industry, namely, sexually transmitted diseases, theft, blackmailing, and the trafficking of young girls.

It was not until city officials and authorities came to see it as a burden and impediment to Budapest and Hungary's development that more comprehensive steps to control sex were initiated. Initially, sexuality and its control were a more pressing priority for the army. The rates of syphilis and venereal disease were growing at an alarming rate, essentially incapacitating the monarchy's soldiers.[99] Amidst a persistent outcry from the medical profession, army officials, and social critics, and as part of the growing international movement to fight the trafficking of women, city officials introduced legislative as well as regulatory changes that granted more power to the police to enforce new laws that were aimed to regulate public behavior.[100] Two important new laws were passed in 1908 and 1912. The 1908 law entrusted the police with greater powers to prosecute people who were unlawfully "pimping" women. In addition, following the international agreement reached in Paris in 1904 to fight the global trafficking of women, the Hungarian parliament passed laws criminalizing trafficking—Article XLIX of 1912. The same year, again modeling an international agreement that prohibited the distribution of pornographic publications (Paris 1910), the Hungarian parliament adopted similar laws.[101] Finally, a criminal vice court was established in 1911 under the aegis of the vice police, which became solely responsible for dealing with female prostitution and related charges.[102] As part of a transnational phenomenon, similar to the 1912 Criminal Law Amendment Act in England, Hungary saw the toughening of regulations as well as empowering of the law enforcement in dealing with sexual immoralities.[103] In theory, the Metropolitan Police, similar to police elsewhere in Europe, was in a significantly stronger position to regulate female prostitution and queer sexualities. The actual effects of these laws on the ground is difficult to assess. It seems that even if there was an intention by legislators and other authorities to modify law enforcement practices in policing sexual behaviors, the economic downturn of 1912–13 shifted the attention of the police to other matters. From 1912 onward, "due to economic hardship, Budapest experienced growing crime rates, the possibility of war was looming ... political tension was high, and there were frequent street protests." All of these circumstances consumed the police's resources.[104] The outbreak of World War I only reinforced the priorities of the police: keeping order and managing the city during wartime, monitoring the growing black market, and during the last year of the war, keeping an eye on social unrest.[105]

THE MAKINGS OF HUNGARIAN MASCULINITY AND FEMININITY

The ways that authorities perceived public morality and social order and dealt with sexuality were all highly gendered. What historians of Western Europe have illustrated about the moral double standards for men and women could not have been truer for Hungary during the late nineteenth and early twentieth centuries.[106] Bourgeois ideals of respectability, prescribed chastity, and modesty for women made them the natural guardians of public and private morality. While for women the parameters of *respectable* femininity were quite confined, the ideal of respectable male behavior was significantly more inclusive and its boundaries far more porous. At the same time that men were entrusted with representing Austria-Hungary's strength by being virile and honorable, the Hungarian male *dzsentri* (gentry), which made up a considerable part of society and had great cultural influence, was notorious for having a different understanding of respectability.[107] In the Hungarian context, the *dzsentri* class encompassed the former small landholder nobility who, having lost their estates, took up positions in the expanding state bureaucracy and in the military. However, while they, along with the assimilated Jewish and German urban middle class, effectively became part of the emerging middle class in Hungary, culturally the *dzsentri* continued to think of themselves as if, and act like, they were nobility. Perhaps no other Hungarian writer described the situation of the gentry in the late nineteenth and early twentieth century more accurately than the novelist Kálmán Mikszáth. Two of his novels, *A Noszty Fiú Esete Tóth Marival: Regény*, (1906–8) and *Gavallérok* (1897), provide a particularly poignant portrayal of the different cultural norms for men and women in the period. Considered the bastions of Hungarian patriotism and chivalry, the male *dzsentri* enjoyed a certain romanticized admiration. Their imagined lifestyle and cultural values were aspirational for both middle- and urban lower-class males. But it wasn't just their chivalry and love of the motherland that were found inspirational. There was another side to the masculinity of Hungarian *dzsentri* that in the eyes of contemporaries manifested itself in lavish spending, decadent parties, and a bohemian lifestyle.[108] This masculinity was also—as John Lukacs in *Budapest 1900* describes it—a virile and a chauvinistic one. In 1900 "masculinity and virility were still very dominant; the supremacy of [the] male was unquestioned and unquestionable, sometimes to the detriment of female sensitivities."[109] Within this milieu that took for granted the unquestionability of male superiority, there were a number of additional cultural assumptions about maleness that prevailed. Thanks to the historical association of male virility with sexual prowess, female prostitution and public (hetero)sexual culture had been considered a "necessary evil." For many Hungarian men who could afford it, visiting prostitutes was understood as a coming of age and an expected expression of masculinity.[110] In contrast, for women, losing their virginity before marriage was considered a capital sin, and merely the suspicion of having an inappropriate male friend could ruin a woman's respectability forever. Sexuality and female respectability were mutually exclusive. Such marked differences between the cultural norms for the sexes, which were by no means unique to Hungary, continued into the twentieth century even as social critics, politicians, and particularly religious institutions increasingly demanded moral purity for both sexes.[111]

The approach of the authorities (lawmakers and law enforcement) toward female prostitution embodied these moral double standards. Female prostitution was officially legalized in 1869, although there was no uniform national law regulating the practice until the post–World War I period. It was up to each municipality to regulate the sex trade. Lawmakers in Budapest and the rest of Hungary created laws that granted police the power to regulate prostitution. The local Vice Squad Departments registered female prostitutes, and the places that wanted to employ them (bordellos, cafés, and restaurants) were granted permits by the police. Female prostitutes were subjected to police harassment, forced regular medical exams, and social opprobrium and contempt. Their male clientele was typically not prosecuted and usually left alone. Captain Thaisz was instrumental in establishing the Metropolitan Police's approach. Thaisz and successive police chiefs in Budapest considered men purchasing sex a staple part of the male metropolitan experience. Yet they increasingly policed women who sold their own bodies. By the twentieth century, there was a discourse shift that in terms of the regulation of prostitution emphasized the necessity of protecting the health of citizens. As the following excerpt from an article, "Prostitution and the Vice Police," in *Rendőri Lapok* illustrates, the policing of women was no longer justified only in the name of protecting morality; it was now also done in the name of protecting national health.

> If we agree that there always was and always will be prostitution, then it cannot be left alone, because the State owes its citizens the protection of their health. That is because the danger of prostitution lies less in attacking our morality than in breeding venereal diseases. Thus, the most important thing in its regulation is not the policing and administrative registering, but rather its health aspects and medical care, which has been the case in most countries.[112]

With rising rates of sexually transmitted diseases and the criminality surrounding prostitution, the police focused its limited resources on policing women who were either already registered prostitutes or suspected of being clandestine ones. As Susan Zimmermann explains, this had consequences for all women in the city, especially the lower classes, who were often assumed to be prostitutes. Policing female sexuality imposed strict norms of female respectability on all women in public. In contrast, the police felt much less inclined to police male sexual behavior. An illustrative example of the police's double standard of policing male versus female behavior in public is that from the 1890s onward, there were undercover male detectives on the street making sure that women behaved in a respectable and ladylike manner, but there were no counterparts for monitoring respectable gentlemanlike behavior.[113]

The information collected within the homosexual registry and the ways in which it was used was enmeshed in contemporary assumptions about gender norms. The interpretation of the data, especially on the occupation and physical attributes of the registered men, reflected as well as helped to reinforce sexist typologies about who could become a homosexual, or a "homosexual criminal." Contemporary police statements such as "Statistical data supports the fact that men who have female occupations tend to fall ill of perversity" show the close association of effeminacy with homosexuality.[114] That consequently the police could declare that men in traditionally female occupations (such as tailors) were in danger of becoming homosexuals highlights how homosexuality was as much considered a transgression of gender norms as it was seen as a sexual transgression. It was not only men who transgressed traditional gender norms at work who were in danger, however. The police also had warnings for women who pushed the boundaries of gender norms. The same article that made the statement about homosexuals and their occupational preference also makes the following claims about women's place in society:

> And here we cannot but make a statement, which might seem a mockery. Could not the facts [from the registry] offer a lesson for those who support the fashionable social wave of feminism? It is unquestionable that the nature of one's profession has profound effects on one's mentality, character, and even on one's appearance. What would remain of a woman if she were to decide to take all areas from men even those, which require his strength and maleness? We would not declare that in this way, women would drift away from their own natural ways, but it is quite evident that within a feminist society, the essence of a woman sooner or later would fill up with mixed-gender subjects.[115]

In an age of heightened anxiety about the consequences of women entering into formerly male professions along with increasing visibility of Hungarian feminists who were calling attention to the police's double standards, it turned out that the information from the homosexual registry could be handy in more ways than one.¹¹⁶ It was not only useful for creating stereotypes about homosexuals but also to clarify and substantiate the police's negative attitude toward feminism.¹¹⁷

SAME-SEX SEXUALITY IN THE EYES OF THE POLICE

The moral double standard held by the police and municipal authorities had implications for queer male sexualities. Taking men's sexuality and sexual behavior for granted, the police were primarily concerned with safeguarding *public* safety and morality displayed *in* public. In light of the scant attention to same-sex sexuality (male or female) in police publications before the 1900s, we can infer that initially the police did not particularly concern themselves with sex between men (or between women).¹¹⁸ Men having sex with men, like female prostitution, was seen as an inevitable and unfortunate characteristic of rapid urbanization and modern life. By the time *Rendőri Lapok* made the question of homosexuality a regular feature of the official journal, the police had embraced the medicalized view that some people were born with congenital homosexuality. Nevertheless, their understanding of homosexuality remained far from monolithic, and there were different coexisting and often contradictory interpretations. Whether the law enforcement officers understood male homosexuality as an "aberration" of love and an "unhealthy" behavior or as an immoral perversion, the police did not see it as their responsibility to eradicate same-sex sexuality. Instead, they conceived their responsibility to be making sure that what they saw as the ill effects of same-sex sexuality and other sexual aberrations would be reduced and potentially eliminated. This explains why, in their approach to homosexuality, the police focused on theft, blackmailing, and, increasingly, men soliciting their bodies for money. Within this context, the purpose and usage of the homosexual registry became more complex. Authorities believed that the very act of registering men who had sex with men would help reduce the crimes they saw as associated with male homosexuality. Although the evidence comes from the post–World War I era, it is almost certain that even during its infancy, the existence of the registry was known to contemporaries and men knew if they were registered. Although being registered on the homosexual registry did not impose any legal burden on an individual (unlike the case of female prostitutes), it implied a considerable social and psychological burden.

Men considered innately or congenitally homosexual who had sex with men privately and away from the eyes of the public and police, and who did not recruit or turn men seen as normal into homosexuals, were of no concern. It is likely that until World War I such individuals did not even get registered. On the other hand, those "authentic" homosexuals, who conducted their affairs in public or semipublic places, which in view of the housing situation in Budapest was much more likely, did indeed get registered.[119] It seems that although the police registered them, officers only pressed charges in specific circumstances; the intent was not necessarily to punish homosexuality with a prison sentence. Such leniency would have been supported by the enactment of Article 1908:36 in the 1908 law, which introduced conditional suspension of charges in the case of minor offenses.[120] Piecing together the available evidence suggests that men who were caught for having sex with men in public might spend a few days in custody but would rarely ever see a trial. As we will see in future chapters, even as the number of people in the homosexual registry increased, the actual number of people prosecuted, let alone sentenced, for violating Paragraph 241 of the penal code that criminalized same-sex activities between men remained low between the 1870s and 1939.

Low arrest and prosecution rates did not mean, however, that from the 1880s and especially during the period between 1900 and 1914, the policing strategies of the "homosexual squad" were unchanged. Like other Vice Squad Departments across Europe, the vice section of the Budapest Metropolitan Police became gradually more institutionalized and their policing technique more sophisticated.[121] There were also more open disagreements about the treatment of homosexuals. *Rendőri Lapok* addressed the different considerations from the police's perspective in 1912:

> Perverted love is blind. Its fault is not its fault, similarly to those who are born without eyes. Why punish such misfortune? This is how the humanitarian approach thinks. Everything should be understood and forgiven. Attractive theory. Homosexuality is more complicated though. Hundreds and hundreds of cases in the experience of the police show how homosexuality tends to accompany immoral acts. Thus, homosexuality almost always also trips on several other paragraphs of the Criminal Code. The desire [of homosexuality] drives people into acts and deeds because of which not even ill people should be excused. Therefore, in theory we should not give up the criminalization of homosexuality because then we would give up the possibility of punishing all other crimes that homosexuality generated. In addition, homosexuality is not always congenital. According to a famous physiologist, each person has some perverse inclination. There is no absolutely normal human being. An unlucky event

and the company of immoral people are all that is necessary to make one's unnatural inclination natural. A few ill-fated perverted people can make a lot of people ill-fatedly perverted. This is where the greatest danger of homosexuality lies and that is why we have to be merciless against it.[122]

The reference to supporters of the "humanitarian approach" illustrates how even within the police there was support for reforms spearheaded by Magnus Hirschfeld and his *Wissenschaftlich-humanitäres Komitee* (WhK) (Scientific-Humanitarian Committee), which campaigned to the decriminalize homosexuality.[123] By the end of the first decade of the twentieth century, there were voices in Hungary calling for the decriminalization of homosexuality on humanitarian and medical grounds.[124] The lenient approach of the police in fact was part of the reason *Huszadik Század* (Twentieth Century), Hungary's most prominent and progressive social science journal, argued for decriminalization. In a 1910 article, "To the Issue of Homosexuality," Gyula Kramolin called for decriminalization on the grounds that the police actually didn't uphold the law. Having listed a number of humanitarian and medical reasons supporting decriminalization of consensual male homosexual acts, Kramolin went on to stay that

> otherwise, the outdatedness of the law is best demonstrated from the fact that the police treat the [homosexual] question with certain forbearance (which I personally learned from prominent police personnel): if it [prosecution] is not "necessary," they ignore it [homosexuality], and only in cases of explicit and concrete accusation, do they prosecute it, when they cannot avoid it. I ask: what is the purpose of a law that even the police consider unnecessary, and if it is unnecessary, why should it be upheld?[125]

What is remarkable though is not necessarily how members of the police were aware and supportive of efforts to decriminalize homosexuality but more so how flexibly they engaged with the existing law based on sexological interpretations of (homo)sexuality. It is precisely because the police embraced Magnus Hirschfeld's theory of *sexuelle Zwischenstufen* (sexual intermediary stages), according to which every man had some feminine and every woman some masculine traits, and consequently that homosexuality or the "third sex" could become "natural" in the "right" circumstances, that the police in Budapest continued to support the criminalization of homosexuality so they could prosecute certain homosexual behaviors.[126]

Even as the number in the homosexual registry rose and the most frequented homosexual rendezvous places came under closer supervision, the police appear to have pressed charges against "noncriminal" homosexuals (those homosexuals who, other than committing a crime by acting on their homosexuality, did not break another law) only in specific cases—being in a public space that was frequented by respected citizens, nonconsensual sex, procuring, and sex with a minor. An individual's social class, time spent in Budapest, and especially the motives of sexual acts were the most important factors determining one's treatment by the police. In instances when the apprehended person was not a permanent resident or was a recent newcomer to Budapest, the authorities would escort him back to his native village or town. Once there, the detained person would be set free on the condition that he would not to return to Budapest any time soon.[127] And although socioeconomic background did not always prevent one's entry into the homosexual registry, a middle- or upper-class identity would significantly lower one's chances as well as affect the treatment received. Although the category of "private office-holder, factory owner, landowner, property owner," presumably men with financial means, became the third most numerous category in the homosexual registry by the 1930s, prior to World War I those with a more affluent or professional background rarely stood trial. Exceptions to this generalization were homosexual acts that fell under Paragraph 242, which criminalized nonconsensual sex between men, including making advances to boys under twelve years of age. Another was a charge brought by one or more individuals rather than by the police.

The primary concern of the police and a substantial number of those on the homosexual registry were men who acted out of monetary interest rather than "unstoppable innate desire." It was those who engaged in homosexual activities with an ulterior or criminal motive that interested the police. Contemporary police reports highlight the connection between homosexuality and criminal behaviors such as theft, blackmail, and prostitution.[128] Tracking homosexuals by registering them allowed the police to catch criminals who looked to take advantage of "authentic" homosexuals. As the physician Nemes Nagy noted, the registry was also important for "policing purposes, since male homosexuals are followed like a shadow and threatened by blackmailers."[129] In addition to blackmailers, homosexuals were also targeted by professional thieves, whom the police could sometimes arrest by monitoring individuals listed on the registry. Consequently, even if the homosexual registry generally functioned as a tool to control, intimidate, and manage individuals, it could also serve as a form of protection from blackmailers and criminals for those seen by authorities as "authentic" homosexuals.

As fragmentary as the surviving sources are on specific details of the interactions between members of the police and men engaging in homosexual behavior, there is evidence that prior to 1914 performativity (as well as class and gender) was a crucial factor determining one's fate. Along with policing the morality of respectable women and making sure that unhealthy prostitutes would not endanger the virility of Hungarian men, the police increasingly dealt with men who had sexual encounters with men. How Hungarian authorities approached and handled men who had sex with men seems to be consistent with what historians of sexuality in other cities of the period have observed. As was true in other cities, in Budapest it was primarily so-called passive men, who behaved sexually like a "woman," who concerned the police.[130] In the majority of cases, it was these passive men whom the police deemed as "authentic" homosexuals. Consequently, it was these men who "could not help their behavior" that the police initially focused on. In turn, those "active" men who had sex with men but otherwise led a "respectable" *manly* life were of a little concern to the police. In this respect, Budapest seemed to fit a larger urban/metropolitan trend: men who otherwise conformed to the Hungarian masculine ideal could engage in same-sex sexual encounters without being judged or punished.[131] They might be warned or temporarily detained. But considering the accepted notion that men were *inherently* sexual, as long as a man engaging in sex with another man *looked like* a man and *performed* as a man in the eyes of the police they did not threaten the social or gender order.

CONCLUSION

By the turn of the century, Budapest was developing with meteoric speed into a modern metropolis. It was not only known for its mills and factories but also became notorious for its boisterous bordello culture. The city's relatively lax regulation of prostitution, along with its nightlife, gained international fame, and Budapest became a destination for men in search of a good time. The extensive salon, tavern, and cheap entertainment industry in Pest was enjoyed by young and old, the poor and the well-to-do. It also provided the police with plenty to do. And since queers were secretive, often met in private places, and did not disturb the peace, the chronically understaffed law enforcement bodies showed little concern for them during the years prior to World War I. Given the continuous flow of people to the city, the crowded living conditions, and the infamous nightlife and other vices, policing homosexuals remained a low priority on the agenda of both the police and the liberal political leadership. Overburdened by having to deal with petty crimes and keeping public order, in practice the authorities investigated same-sex activities only when they perceived them as particularly dangerous. Examples of such activity were cases involving older men seeking underage male prostitutes or insider's tips about exceptionally wild parties. In the eyes of the authorities, furthermore, social class, economic status, and gender performativity were often more important in determining police actions and treatment of suspects than one's sexual preference and acts.

At the same time, the mere existence of the homosexual registry underscores the fact that by the end of the nineteenth century, there was a growing concern among police and government officials about men having sex with men. Rapid urbanization also brought a dramatic increase in what social critics, religious figures, and, eventually, local authorities saw as immoral and unhealthy behaviors. As in most other European cities, the registry of male homosexuals existed in part to monitor and police Budapest's sexual and moral economy. In this sense, the registry was part of the modernization and centralization efforts of Budapest officialdom during rapidly changing times. Tracing the medical, legal, and police discourse on the homosexual registry demonstrates that it served multiple functions. By condensing personal and private information about individuals, the registry functioned from the moment of its creation as one of the tools for "scientifically" managing the sexual economy of the city. However, the registry of homosexuals and an extensive same-sex subculture were not mutually exclusive. While serving as a means to keep track of the ebb and flow of homosexuals into and within the urban environment, the registry also attempted to provide a concrete action plan by which authorities could make sense of and navigate the increasingly complex sexual landscape of the city. Albert Shaw's 1892 observation that Budapest was a well-planned city underscores how the establishment of the homosexual registry marked or reflected the coming of age of the Metropolitan Police and the Hungarian government generally. The swiftly modernizing city required a modern police force. The establishment and increasingly more proficient implementation of the homosexual registry was a manifestation of the Hungarian state's expanding ability to control people's lives.

CHAPTER TWO

The "Knights of Sick Love": The Queers of Kornél Tábori and Vladimir Székely

> In general homosexuals have a tendency to be interested in white-collar jobs. Working class homosexuals are for the most part intellectually superior to their heterosexual counterparts. Their unluckiness makes them be introspective early on. Being different prompts them to learn to think about the existence of human nature. Each homosexual is their own philosopher. Normal people, especially of lower socioeconomic backgrounds never ever come to a place where they would ponder their own metaphysical existence and their relationship to the rest of the world, which is quite natural for a homosexual. The fantastic, and the dreaming quality within the mental world of a homosexual is much more prominent than any brutal sense of reality.
>
> Normally, they like to socialize with other homosexuals. They arrange their own rendezvous within their circles. But there are many among them who prefer the perverse [homosexuals] from outside of their circle as well as normal young people. The happiness of the hunter, a man in love, and the map of his emotions are at times one and the same.
>
> —Vladimir Székely, 1908[1]

These contemplative words on the nature and habits of homosexuals by Vladimir Székely, a journalist and member of the police, were indicative of how the literal visibility of homosexuals in fin de siècle Budapest was constitutive of a new discursive visibility about homosexuality. Székely's detailed characterization of homosexuals reflects contemporary curiosity about queer sexualities as well as an aim to label, categorize, and ultimately understand them. The writer of these lines and investigative journalist Kornél Tábori would become the celebrated experts on the queers of Budapest during the first decade of the twentieth century. Their representation had a lasting effect on the perception of Hungarian homosexuals. This chapter examines the emerging public discourse about nonnormative sexuality during the first decade of the twentieth century. More specifically, it looks at why and how the first public discussions of homosexuality (and queer sexuality more generally) took place in Budapest. In doing so, it sets out to answer three questions: What factors were present in Budapest in 1908 that facilitated the arrival of the "Hungarian homosexual" in the popular press? How were those people who desired, or had sex with, their own sex introduced and represented, and what can that tell us about early twentieth-century Budapest? Finally, what effect did publications on homosexuality have on the conceptualization and treatment of homosexuality? The public appearance of homosexuals in print and on the streets of Budapest coincided with the Hungarian capital's coming of age. The two, I argue, were intimately connected. An analysis of the representations of nonnormative sexuality reveals how reports on queer sexuality exemplified the complex and often conflicting ways in which Hungarian authorities and denizens of Budapest came to terms with the city's rapid modernization. Talking about issues relating to sexuality was never just about sex, however. Sexuality also served, as historian Dagmar Herzog remarked, as a "transmission belt for wider cultural conflict."[2] Sex, therefore, was a platform that allowed public discussion on a series of interconnected issues in fin de siècle politics, culture, and society. In particular, the discourse around "knights of sick love" (queer men) reflected contemporaries' anxiety about the future of Budapest and of "Hungarian" genetic stock. In this regard, the appearance of queers in the popular press cultivated growing awareness of a sexual subculture of Budapest and corroborated and deepened fears about the future of the city.[3] But analysis of their portrayal of same-sex sexuality suggests that homosexuals were hailed also as harbingers of Budapest's new status as a modern European metropolis. They simultaneously were manifestations of urban decline and "living proof" of Hungary's place in the modern "progressive" Western world.

By 1900, the Liberal Party had been in power for a quarter of a century; its aims were clear: securing Hungary's place as Austria's equal counterpart. This would require an efficient state bureaucracy, a strong economy, and first and foremost a unified "Magyarized" state. Until 1905, growing state bureaucracy and continuing industrialization, secularization, and assimilation of minorities, particularly Jews, were all taking place rapidly. During this time Hungary entered its first era of mass politics. By 1900, in addition to the opposition of the 48-ers who had been pushing for greater independence from Austria, social democrats, socialist, liberal democrats, peasant parties, Christian socialists, and feminists entered the political and public sphere and were making their demands heard.⁴ Despite the cacophony of political voices that made forming and running a government more difficult between 1905 and 1914, the 1900s were the height of liberal politics, economic growth, and cultural creativity in Budapest.⁵ There was a sense of pervasive optimism (very uncharacteristic of Hungarians) about individual and collective prospects of life that cut across class, gender, and age. Thanks to the liberal laws that aimed to protect freedom of speech over the state's right to censor, this was also a time when a booming mass culture went relatively uncensored, especially in the capital. And it was in this milieu that queers and same-sex sexuality made their grand entry into public discourse. While there had been literary references to queer sexualities prior, the publications of Kornél Tábori and Vladimir Székely, Hungary's vanguard investigative journalists, overnight made male homosexuals (and to a much lesser extent lesbians) a topic of conversation on the streets of the capital and in towns across the country. Their books, which were a commercial and critical success, offer a rare window into the world of queers and the public's conception of them.

The chapter is based on the published and unpublished writings of Székely and Tábori, who during the first two decades of the twentieth century were the most famous and widely read authors on the seamy side of Budapest.⁶ In what follows, I examine the particular ways in which Tábori and Székely approached, depicted, and employed nonnormative sexuality in their works. In my analysis, I treat the journalists not simply as tools of social and discursive forces outside their own control, although those forces clearly influenced them. I also study the journalists' personal feelings and agendas and show how they had to face ethical dilemmas about their subjects.⁷ I pay particular attention to the language, expressions, and words that the journalists used to describe same-sex sexuality. I contend that the inconsistency of their terminology and, at times, contradictory accounts of the nature of homosexuality were representative of their own, and in many ways of broader societal, confusion about what to make of and how to deal with people who desired their own sex. Tábori and Székely's ambiguous representation of homosexuality, at once criticizing but also openly tolerant toward "respectable" homosexuals, incited an intense public discussion about queer sexuality. It also provided guidance to their readers about queer life, love, and the boundaries of respectability. Like the authorities discussed in chapter 1, Tábori and Székely distinguished between "respectable" authentic and immoral inauthentic queers. In doing so, they were representative of Hungarian reformers who were ready to embrace urban modernity with all its complexities. Being the first (and in many ways until the 1990s the sole) initiators of a more open public discussion around homosexuality, Tábori and Székely's representation of homosexuality, their terminology, and their differentiation between respectable and nonrespectable homosexuals had a lasting impact on the status and understandings of queer people in Hungary.

THE PENNY PRESS AND SCANDALOUS SEXUALITIES

Although the issue of same-sex sexuality, along with concerns about other forms of deviance, appeared in public discourse in the last decades of the nineteenth century, discussions of deviance were not the only avenue by which homosexuality entered public discussion. The 1900s saw sexuality enter its way to the public sphere, discourse, and consciousness in Central European cities with a defiant openness.[8] Previously considered a disgraceful topic for respected classes, sexuality became mainstreamed through the convergence of multiple agents of change: Traditional forms of art such as fine arts or literature placed sexuality in the center of their inquiry. New mediums like photography and film graphically depicted sensuality. Social and intellectual movements of the fin de siècle made it their entire mission to fight the evil effects of uncontrolled sexuality. Most often these movements vehemently opposed the liberalization of sexual ethics. Nevertheless, by introducing sexuality into the public discourse, they contributed to expanding popular knowledge about sex. Finally, the emergence of psychoanalysis and its belief that sexual drives were a fundamental part of humanity helped to dismantle the previously private and clandestine discourse on sexuality.[9] However, the avenue through which sexuality made its entry most seamlessly into the public and private worlds of contemporaries was the printed press.

As Hungarian authorities were undertaking the management of a rapidly growing city by providing new residents with basic necessities, denizens of Budapest also attempted to create recreational activities for the city's quickly expanding population. Soon after the unification of Budapest in 1873, the print media established a new form of entertainment, the penny press. By infusing sensationalism into traditional news, the penny press became one of the most accessible forms of entertainment for the urban masses. Prior to the 1880s, political and politically oriented papers dominated the market; following the Ministry of Interior's decision to lift the ban on selling daily newspapers on the street in 1896, however, the "yellow press" inundated the city. While in 1870 there were about eighty different papers and journals, by 1900 there were 384.[10] There were no exclusively erotic or pornographic publications printed in Budapest. That did not mean that people could not get their hands on German and French erotic publications that circulated in the city (most spoke German and many of the middle and upper classes spoke French). And pornographic images required no language skills. More importantly, sex and sexuality were increasingly featured not just in sociological, academic legal, and medical professional journals, but in the contemporary press as well. Whether it was prostitution, the sex industry, sexually transmitted diseases, trials of sexual crimes, or news about strange sexual behaviors, newspapers candidly discussed sex and sexuality beginning in the 1890s. Talking about sex, it turned out, sold papers and increased profits. Soon even conservative papers featured stories involving strange sexualities, illicit desires, and sexual crimes. They also began to provide space for advertisements for sexual and romantic partners. Albeit often written in veiled language, advertisements for sex became a standard feature of the press in the first decade of the twentieth century.[11]

THE MOTIVES OF TÁBORI AND SZÉKELY

That newspapers increasingly incorporated coverage of news related to sex only made the exceptionality of the publications of Hungary's pioneer investigating journalists Vladimir Székely and Kornél Tábori on the sexual culture of Budapest more apparent. Among the reports of sex-related news and especially of Budapest's queer culture, the works of Székely and Tábori stood out with their detailed and informative depictions. In particular, their work provided the most thorough descriptions of homosexuals, or "the knights of sick love" as Székely and Tábori referred to them. We can trace the seeds of Székely and Tábori's unique reporting to three causes: 1) their educational and professional background, which granted them access to an extensive knowledge base about sexuality; 2) Tábori's experience with the sexual cultures of both the West and East (he traveled and reported from Germany, the Netherlands, Switzerland, and Belgium, as well as from Russian and Serbia) and Székely's intimate familiarity with Vienna and Berlin, which helped them to place Budapest in the greater European context; and 3) their talent for writing captivating stories that absorbed their readers. Their subsequent publications that fused investigative journalism on topics related to sex and sexuality with a sensationalist style of writing had a universal appeal, transcending social, cultural, and even age differences.[12]

As the head of public relations for Budapest's Metropolitan Police, police counselor Vladimir Székely was as connected and well informed about Budapest's sexual subculture as possible for someone on the "right side" of the law. Székely had joined the police during the mid-1890s as part of their new public relations office and by 1902 became head of the Metropolitan Police's Public Relation Department. A position he would hold until 1918.[13] His duties included overseeing the daily newscast to the press, the flow of information about police activity, and the publication of the annual *Bulletin of the Police*. He was a regular contributor and editor of *Rendőri Lapok* (Police Pages), the official police journal and also the editor of the "Criminal Chronicle" section of *Huszadik Század*. During the interwar period, Székely continued to work for the police and was the editor and author of number of police publications.[14] In his approach to writing and editing, Székely focused on factual evidence and its contextualization for his readers. Whether he was writing on homosexuals, petty thieves, or criminal financial schemes, he did not just report the facts and fulfill his police duties but also provided thoughtful analysis of the context and often humanized the criminals. In doing so his work was situated at the intersection of policing, social investigation, and journalism. Though his works were well known by contemporaries and historians often mention him in passing, there is very little information about Székely's personal life. Nevertheless, in terms of his professional and public life, it is telling that his professionalism and work on behalf of the police were not only approved, but also praised by liberals and conservatives alike. His professionalism and focus on practical issues rather than on politics explains how throughout his lifetime Székely could work for the progressive *Huszadik Század*, yet could also continue to play a significant role in the police during the interwar conservative regime.

Unlike Székely, who worked for the civil authorities, Kornél Tábori was paid to entertain as well as to inform. While he was attending law school, Tábori became a journalist. He held his first job in Budapest in 1901 at *Pesti Napló*, a popular political paper where he later would later become an editor.[15] He was a prolific writer and became a regular contributor to many popular daily and weekly papers.[16] Over the course of his life, he also worked as an editor and a series editor to more than one book series. Tábori was always interested in criminal behavior and soon set out to be a police reporter, eventually editing the police column for *Pesti Napló*. His fascination with criminals did not stop with reporting, and it was Tábori who, having translated them, introduced Sir Arthur Conan Doyle's Sherlock Holmes detective novels to Hungarian readership.[17] In 1904–5 Tábori covered the Russo-Japanese War and published books about the horrors he witnessed. During his journalistic career, he also traveled to numerous Western European capitals including Amsterdam, Bern, and Brussels and reported on urban developments and the special characteristics of each city.[18] In World

Figure 2. Vladimir Székely. Image courtesy of Fővárosi Szabó Ervin Könyvtár Budapest Gyűjtemény/Metropolitan Ervin, Szabó Library, Budapest.

War I, he was a war correspondent and later gave lectures in various Western European countries to help arrange aid for the poor as the war dragged on. For his support of the Hungarian Soviet Republic in 1919, he was pushed aside and could not continue his journalistic career. Nevertheless, he continued to work, editing a number of book series, translating literature, and even directing a film. During his career Tábori wrote and coauthored over forty books, the great majority of them on social issues. He truly was the father of Hungarian investigative journalism and photography.[19] Perhaps thanks to his Jewishness, which could have made him sensitive to being an outsider, Tábori possessed a level of compassion for his subjects and empathy for those who in the eyes of society were despicable that surpassed the empathy of most of his contemporaries. In sharp contrast to his friend and coauthor Vladimir Székely, Tábori was increasingly exposed to the discriminatory policies of the interwar authoritarian Horthy regime. In addition to being blacklisted, from the late 1930s, Tábori became subjected to Hungary's anti-Semitic laws, and none of his conspicuous achievements could save him from deportation to Auschwitz, where he was killed in July 1944.

Vladimir Székely and Kornél Tábori became friends and regular collabo-

Figure 3. Photograph of Kornél Tábori. Personal photograph of Péter Búza.

rators, writing about societal problems that they, along with many of their contemporaries, considered to be barriers to the progress of Budapest. Their interest in revealing social problems through investigative reporting was part of a new focus on urban poverty, crime, and their scientific measurement. Around the turn of the century, Budapest saw the emergence of new associations, agencies, and governmental departments that were established to assist the modern scientific management of the city.[20] Having caught up to other "sinful" cities, in Budapest there was a growing fascination and concern with the underworld by authorities and the population alike. Not surprisingly, the fascination, or rather obsession, with Budapest's sinfulness, similar to other capitals, was closely related to and reflected in the rapid growth of print media and the penny press that inundated the emerging metropolis.[21] Although always a step behind the popular press, the police joined the bandwagon of what seemed to be an unstoppable expansion of print media. The Metropolitan Police of Budapest not only established the official police journal *Rendőri Lapok*, to whose pages both Székely and Tábori were contributors, it also devoted sustained attention and resources to its public relations department. In some ways the collaboration of Székely and Tábori was inevitable. Their efforts were part of a transnational trend that saw a more sensationalist approach to criminality. Similar, for instance, to the publications of the *Österreichische Kriminal-Zeitung* (Austrian Criminal

Newspaper; hereafter ÖKZ) published in Vienna, Székely and Tábori's collaboration represented a productive intersection of the concerns of authorities and a growing general interest in the urban poor, the founding of an investigative journalism that was attentive to and fed public curiosity, and the profitability of sensationalist crime reporting.

Although the collaboration of a journalist and a policeman seemed odd to many at first, both Tábori and Székely had a strong conviction that journalism and police investigation could mutually benefit from working side by side. This was acknowledged by contemporaries such as *Pesti Hirlap*, a daily paper that praised them for setting an example of fruitful collaboration between journalism and the police: "Kornél Tábori and Vladimir Székely set an example for how a journalist and policeman need not quarrel and be in disagreement with each other. There are only benefits from them joining forces."[22] There was a long tradition of policemen serving as guides to and sources for reporters writing about social problems, but their partnership was unique because both men engaged in journalism and had genuine respect for each other's trade. Tábori and Székely were deeply committed to assisting Budapest's development into a modern, safe, and more manageable city. By responding to a growing demand for expert reporting on crime, they could transcend the mutual distrust felt by journalists and the members of the police for one another. In fact, extolling the benefits of partnership between the two professions remained a lifelong goal for both. As we turn to their serial publication, *Sinful Budapest*, it is remarkable how their style of writing and the particular way they shared scandalous facts about the less venerable side of the city dramatized the benefit of cooperation between the police and journalism. Their books became informative page-turners that served hungry readers across the country.

Székely and Tábori's idea about writing on same-sex sexuality had likely been directly inspired by investigative reports from the imperial capital, Vienna. To be sure, by the first decade of the twentieth century, there seemed to be an insatiable appetite for sex-themed publications. These were likely at least partially driven by high profile sexual scandals that had been taking place in Berlin and Vienna. The so-called Harden-Eulenburg affair, which involved members of Kaiser William II's inner circle, became one of the biggest homosexual scandals in continental Europe. The scandal broke out in 1907, when journalist Maximilian Harden accused Philipp, prince of Eulenburg, and Lieutenant General Kuno von Moltke of engaging in homosexual conduct.[23] The revelation that confidants of the kaiser were homosexuals (additional prominent figures were also accused of having homosexual tendencies) led to multiple trials. In the end, despite Harden being convicted of libel, Eulenburg's homosexuality was unquestionable. Moreover, in addition to tainting the kaiser politically, the drawn-out process of accusations of homosexuality by journalists and the counteraccusations for libel against journalists brought by aristocrats drove homosexuality into the limelight for the first time in Central Europe. Similar to the Oscar Wilde trial in 1895, the Harden-Eulenburg affair ignited a public discussion of homosexuality not only in Germany but across the whole continent.[24] The scandal was also widely reported in the Hungarian media. Irrespective of their political affiliation, papers reported on Harden's efforts to use homosexuality to smear the court of Kaiser Wilhelm II. Some of the daily papers such as the *Budapesti Hírlap* even sent its own correspondent to Berlin and published detailed accounts of the trials.[25] Thus, the ongoing scandal became a catalyst for a public discussion and a growing awareness of homosexuality across the Austro-Hungarian monarchy. This was particularly the case in Vienna, where, as Scott Spector points out, "the affair seemed at once so distant—So German, so Prussian—and at the same time, it could not help but raise questions about the possible existence of such activity in Vienna."[26] As Spector tells the story, at first the critics suggested that such immorality, "characteristics of Protestant Germans," would never occur in Catholic Austria. It wasn't too long, however, before an Austrian newspaper decided to put that assumption to a test. Starting in May 1907, *ÖKZ* published weekly reports on male homosexuality that exposed the extensive queer subculture of Vienna.[27] The *ÖKZ* was typical of the criminal/detective newspapers that sprang up across Europe during the late nineteenth and early twentieth centuries. The paper reflected the public's appetite for salacious details about an underworld that most would never have personal contact with. It is also telling that the former head police commissioner of Vienna, Ferdinand Lebzelter, initially edited the paper.[28] It is quite probable that Székely and Tábori both knew Lebzelter personally through their frequent travels to Vienna and contacts with international police personnel. It is also likely that they followed the *ÖKZ*'s coverage of the homosexual underworld of Vienna closely. This Viennese example provided a model for investigative reporting on sex that sparked immense public interest and was financially lucrative, something that Székely and Tábori would have noted. In 1908, the series *Bűnös Budapest* (Sinful Budapest) was born. With *Sinful Budapest* kicking off the series, the series included *The Secrets of Thieves* (1908); *Immoral Budapest* (1908); *Les Miserables and Villains* (1908); *Sinful Women* (1909); *Railway Thieves* (1909); and *Sinful Love* (ca. 1910).

THE QUEERS OF *SINFUL BUDAPEST*

Székely and Tábori's stories, which were first published in various dailies before they were sold in book form, became a national phenomenon. Overwhelmingly positive reviews and headlines appeared in newspapers across Hungary. Headlines such as "Real Life in Pest," "Secret Bohemians," "Queerness from the Streets of Pest," or "Behind the Scenes of Life in Pest" hinted at the main subject of their work.[29] As one daily newspaper stated, "Journalist Kornél Tábori and policeman Vladimir Székely introduce Budapest in a novel light in a new book series. The two authors . . . expose the criminals and the miserable, who are as stable and indestructible features of Budapest as the apaches [sic] [rascals] of the French capital."[30] While readers were introduced to the various shady elements of the streets of Budapest, the book reviews inform us that it was queer sexuality and especially the "knights of sick love" that were the most intriguing subjects. The daily newspaper *Magyar Nemzet*, for instance, declares,

> gloomy is the world of these buggers, but the authors' pen fills it with bright colors. The interest of the reader never languishes even for a second. This is a book that cannot be put down until it is avidly and with a fever of excitement read to the end. . . . Undoubtedly, the section that should expect the greatest interest from readers is the one which the authors devote to the perverts. Are they unfortunate or guilty? To this important question the authors do not provide a definitive answer, even though they thoroughly light up the souls of these people.[31]

Tábori and Székely's introduction of queers to readers in Budapest and in other major Hungarian cities was captivating enough that the subject became a topic of conversation of rich and poor denizens alike. So what exactly did the readers learn about queers from *Sinful Budapest*? And why did the stories about homosexuals garner such great attention when they appeared?

In the opening book of their series on the "real" Budapest, *Sinful Budapest* (1908), Tábori and Székely devoted a chapter to male same-sex sexuality entitled "A beteg szerelem lovagjai," literally meaning "The knights of sick love."[32] The title is suggestive of the authors' overall conceptualization of homosexuality. Here, just as in all previous as well as future references to same-sex sexuality, scientific perspective is thought to prevail.[33] As the authors remind us, "Modern science has already determined that homosexuals are not evil-doers, but rather unfortunate neuropaths, who belong in the sanatorium rather than in prison."[34] Seemingly straightforward, this sentence foreshadows the intricacies within Tábori and Székely's representation of same-sex desire, sex, and love. Homosexuals were not criminals. They required the attention of medical professionals rather than law enforcement. At the same time, references to homosexuals as "people with aberrant inclinations" were rooted as much within social as medical norms. Finally, their "unfortunate" status would not necessarily bar homosexuals from respectability. The expression the "knights of sick love" embodies the paradox inherent in the Tábori and Székely's representation of homosexuals. The Hungarian word *lovag*, or "knight," in spite of the different ways it might have been used, had a positive connotation. Regardless of whether it indicated one's social status or, what is more likely, a chivalrous man who courted a (wo)man, the meaning of the word had a much more positive association than most words that could have been used to describe homosexuals. The word *lovag* had no negative connotations. In contrast, "Beteg szerelem," translated as "Sick love," was much more in line with the Pan-European discourse on homosexuality, connecting same-sex desire and love to sickness and a visible symptom of urban decay.[35] The term "sick" in this context could be understood either as a medical condition, that is, nonnormative sexuality as a genuine incurable illness. Or it could specifically have referred to being sexually sick (i.e., perverted), which implied a moral question. Placing the seemingly conflicting words together, the phrase the "knights of sick love" expresses a rather ambiguous view that does not fall on either side of the spectrum. Rather, the expression points to a certain fluidity (or confusion) within the authors' representation of homosexuals. The negative subtext that equated queer sexual desires with perversion is present. But so too were moments that normalized same-sex desire and presented male homosexuals as decent men who, instead of women, courted other (decent) men. Characteristic of the early twentieth-century popular and expert discourses, Tábori and Székely's portrayal of same-sex desire, sex, and love reflected the messiness that surrounded the "essence" of same-sex sexuality.[36] The simple fact that the authors deemed the issue so important that they would grant it print space and comprehensive examination underscores two things: first, that same-sex sexuality was not simply a recognizable part of the Hungarian urban landscape, but something that, according to Székely and Tábori, needed attention, and second, that attention paid to it would generate readership.

The main focus of "The Knights of Sick Love" is not the innate queers, who act out of their true desires, but rather those who act out of greed and make their living by exploiting authentic homosexuals. It is the stories of young men who sell themselves to the "devotees of *paederastia*" that take center stage.[37]

> Those young pretty striplings, who entice ill older gentlemen just like female prostitutes would, fall into an entirely different category, . . . What drives these people is not perversion. Most could have a normal sexual life, in fact most do, aside from *paederastia*. Apart from having relations with men they often also have relations with night butterflies [prostitutes]. These men's pedophilia is nothing other than male prostitution, which at the same time inherently implies far more dangers than female prostitution. It also includes stealing and blackmailing on a grand scale.[38]

The authors' use of the word *paederastia* (Greek word for pederasty or "love of boys," which was assimilated into Hungarian without any changes) to refer to homosexuality was not a mistake. In fact, Tábori and Székely's conflation of homosexuality and sex between a young and old man was representative of a European-wide phenomenon. During the late nineteenth and early twentieth centuries, the word "pederasty" was used in many countries to denote men "who engaged in same-sex sexual activities."[39] Unlike some of the other words that contemporaries used for homosexuality, however, the word "pederasty" had unambiguously negative connotations; associating same-sex sexuality with vice and immorality.[40]

As they go on to present a detailed description of the dangerous queers, Tábori and Székely's use of the word parallels this wider usage of the term.

> Their clothes and behaviors are conspicuous. Their hair is done up, combed nicely, and they often grow it long. They have makeup on their face. They have a tight blazer, which surely is enticing. Their movements are easily noticeable. Their hands are full of rings. Their perfume can be smelled from a distance and they are experts at seduction. Such is the lead character of blackmailers. He is the hero of terrible tragedies, which take place in a few minutes, but just like general dramas of life, they hold their poor victims in horrible agony for months and years.
>
> Not one *buzeráns* [slang word for homosexual] works alone in order to maximize his earnings. Once having met and enticed his aberrantly inclined person at Elisabeth Square, City Park or one of the Baths and then having the act performed, the *buzi* [an abbreviated form of *buzeráns*] in love turns into a stringent businessman. He threatens the person with scandal and with going to the police and demands money. In the case of people who are well-off, he also accepts bonds.

Nevertheless, for the most part homosexuals work in groups and they know how to enmesh even healthy people, who are unfamiliar with the secrets of perversion, get into trouble for their inexperience. Within the criminal gang there are the following roles; the *buzi* entices the victim and the rest of the gang, often the head of the gang—dresses up as a policeman with one or two fake detectives. They often go to baths that specialize in the treatments of specific diseases [particularly those for venereal disease]. The group lie in wait for the *buzi* and the victim to be in flagrante and then "What an egregious atrocity!" The gang leader shouts. "Don't you feel ashamed of yourself to entice such a young gentleman?!" Then he turns to the "detectives, "Go on, take him to the police station." At this point the victim loses his mind. He asks, begs, and perhaps even cries; "What would the world and his family say?!" Then comes the shock. The head of the gang gets softer over time and eventually, for a significant amount of money, he lets the enmeshed dupe go. But often this is not the end of his ordeal. He will be blackmailed as long as the gang assumes he still has some money. At times, they can get 1000 Coronas [Austro-Hungarian currency] from well-to-do persons.

It is a clear fact: Once somebody gives in to the initial blackmailing, he becomes prey for the blackmailers and sometimes it is only through committing suicide that he can get rid of the criminal gang.[41]

Leaving their talent for sensationalist reporting aside for now, it is clear that the authors are less concerned with men who prefer pretty young men than with those who exploit people who cannot help their sexual inclinations. Similarly, the Metropolitan Police of Budapest placed blackmailers and criminal elements associated with homosexuality at the center of their attention. Considering the authors' intent in writing, which was to "offer protection against evildoers, aid the work of the vice police and to protect children," that Székely and Tábori were more concerned with such negative aspects of Hungarian turn-of-the-century same-sex sexuality is unsurprising.[42] What is more significant, though, is how Tábori and Székely's storytelling captures the semiotic codes of queerness of the time, both authentic and inauthentic alike. For instance, we learn about the telltale signs of inauthentic male queers as well as what sorts of features were considered to be desirable for queer men: men who had a particular way of moving their bodies and certain mannerisms, who dressed smartly in tight clothes with accessories like rings, and who even wore makeup. Their hairdos were slightly longer than the norm but meticulously coiffed, and they wore such heavy perfume that it could be smelled across a room. Besides their physical attractiveness, they were expert socializers who could even seduce heterosexual men.

As in the publications of Albert Moll or Magnus Hirschfeld in case of Berlin, *Sinful Budapest* provided some details about the basic geographies of queer subculture.[43] Like in cities across Europe and beyond, larger parks such as Városliget (City Park), and the recently finished Népliget (People's Park), which, with their lush vegetation, provided privacy even during the day, served as popular places, especially for men who had already found their sexual partners. For those looking to find sexual encounters, by the 1900s there were established cruising places in the busiest public areas in the center of the city. Elizabeth Square, with its green area in central Pest, offered avenues to stroll but also cafés to sit and observe. Similarly, the nearby Dunakorzó (Danube Embankment), which extended from the Széchényi Bridge to the Elizabeth Bridge, with its bustling pedestrian life, offered certain anonymity to homosexual men who could recognize each other. In addition, there were cafés, pubs, and bars that catered to a queer clientele. The pub on Teve Street and Minta Café on Dohány Street and the bar on Szövetség Street were nevertheless nothing like what we associate with gay and lesbian bars today. These establishments were discrete and avoided any unwarranted attention. Some of them like Minta Café could serve a heterosexual clientele in its front room, while catering to the queers in its secret backroom. The thermal baths were a staple and incredibly important site of Budapest's queer geography as early as the 1900s. Bathhouses in Császár, Rudas, Lukács, and Hungária all served as pickup places for seasoned homosexual men, as sites of voyeurism for the curious, and as places for the first same-sex sexual encounters for many. Finally, private homes of well-to-do men and women who hosted gatherings for vetted homosexuals played a crucial role in the emerging homosexual subculture, which in contrast to public and semipublic spaces, could provide a sense of physical and psychological safety away from the police, the public, and blackmailers.

Overall, the authenticity (and success) of *Sinful Budapest* rests on the position of Tábori and Székely as having been on the "inside" of the queer world. Both of them had been present at raids of homosexual establishments and the prosecutions of blackmailers and had visited the regular meeting places of homosexuals not only in Budapest but also in Vienna, Berlin, and St. Petersburg. We know that Tábori, at the invitation of his friend, the police chief of Berlin, had even attended homosexual balls in the German capital.[44] It is their intimate familiarity and personal experience with queer subculture, including its perilousness, that enabled them to produce a putative dialogue between the older authentic homosexual men and their objects of desire. The dramatic depiction of the torment of these unfortunate homosexual victims reveals not only the empathy the authors felt toward them but also how such a depiction could have cultivated sympathy for "authentic" homosexuals in their readers. Taking a step back, the content and tone of *Sinful Budapest* is indicative of a number of things: 1) by the first decade of the twentieth century, same-sex sexuality was seen as an inherent characteristic of Budapest, even when not discussed publicly; 2) that there was an extensive network of male (not just female) prostitution; 3) and perhaps most interestingly, that there were certain forms of nonnormative sexualities that were tolerated over others.

SICK LOVE AND THE SPREAD OF THE HOMOSEXUAL MENACE

It was not long after the publication of *Sinful Budapest* that Tábori and Székely published a second publication, *Beteg szerelem: Kragujevics bajtársai* (Sick love: Comrades of Kragujevics), which was entirely devoted to an examination of queer sexuality.[45] Tábori and Székely's motives for writing it were clearly mixed. Following the publication of their first books, they received considerable financial compensation and national fame as "the authors who finally showed what true life was really like in Budapest."[46] Once they had introduced queers to the greater public, it would have been a missed opportunity not to take advantage of the emerging market of interested readers for juicy stories about same-sex sexuality. But money and fame aside, it was Tábori and Székely's commitment to inform the public about the dangers that were present in the fast-growing city that was undoubtedly also a motivating factor. Specifically, the authors decided to take up the issue of homosexuality following the infamous murder trial of Spázó Kragujevics. The investigation and trial of the twenty-six-year-old law student from Budapest who robbed and murdered a businessman in Berlin and attempted to rob and murder another in Vienna received international attention. Kragujevics, who thanks to his family connections, good looks, and charming personality was a regular visitor at the homes of the well-to-do, supported his lavish lifestyle through befriending homosexual men of means and welcoming the overtures of "men with sick souls."[47] The prosecution of Kragujevics was a collaborative effort between the police forces of Berlin, Vienna, and Budapest. Despite Kragujevics's denials and a year-long investigation that held many twists and turns, ultimately Kragujevics was found guilty of stealing, fornication, murder, and robbery and was sentenced to

A Kereskedelmi Alkalmazottak Országos Egyesülete kirakatrendező szakosztályának budapesti kiküldöttjei, kik Lázár Mór szakoszt. alelnök vezetésével Berlinben, kirakatverseny tanulmányozásán voltak és a kereskedelmi minisztérium részéről 2000 korona államsegélyben részesültek. Felső sor : Gegner Viktor, László Andor, Vajda Salamon, Somogyi Miksa, Sik Gyula, Király Gusztáv, Komáromi Vilmos, Bálint Ármin. Alsó sor : Janovitz Soma, Lázár Mór, Spira Sándor, Fodor Vilmos.

Dittrich Jakab, a Kunz József és Társa vászonnagykereskedő czég üzleti szolgája, a kit negyven éves szolgálatának évfordulója alkalmából a kereskedelmi miniszter díszérmemmel, a czég értékes ajándékkal tüntetett ki.

Kragujevics Spázó, budapesti végzett jogszigorló, a ki Bécsben egy könyvelő ellen rablómerényletet követett el. Kragujevicset a berlini rendőrség két gyilkos merénylettel is vádolja. A bűn útjára tévedt fiatalember bűnügyét most tárgyalják a budapesti esküdtbíróság előtt.

és büntető hatóságokat is élénken foglalkoztatta a bűnügy, sőt a berlini rendőrség kiküldöttjei hosszabb ideig Budapesten tartózkodtak és segédkeztek az itteni rendőrségnek az adatok megszerzése körül. Ez a bűnügy most kerül főtárgyalás alá a budapesti esküdtbíróság előtt. Kragujevics arczképét itt közöljük.

Három bátorsági érdemjel tulajdonosa.

Domby Károly a kilenczedik huszárezredben volt őrmester. Vitéz katona, a ki három hadjáratban vett részt s vitézségével és bátorságával annyira kitűnt, hogy három alkalommal tüntették ki a bátorsági érdemjellel. Az első két kitüntetést 1864-ben a Schleswig-Holsteini hadjáratban vívta ki magának, melyen előbb mint közkatona, később pedig mint káplár vett részt. A harmadik érdemjellel 1866-ban tüntették ki, mikor az elsánczolt bécsi tábor előtt, Kronburgnál, Domby — kis szakaszával — megtámadta a sokkal erősebb ellenséget s sikerült neki a sánczot áttörni és mintegy kilenczven ellenséges lovaskatonát elfognia. A vitéz huszár most hetven esztendős s még mindig jó erőben van és a zalamegyei Tapolczán postaaltiszt. Ő Felsége Dombyt, a 70-ik születésnapja alkalmából, aranykoronás érdemkereszttel tüntette ki.

Főtárgyalás Kragujevics Spázó ügyében.

Kínos feltűnést keltett annak idején Kragujevics Spázó volt joghallgatónak, egy 26 éves fiatal embernek letartóztatása. A tisztességes családból származó ifjút, a kinek rokoni összeköttetéseinél, csinos külsejénél és megnyerő modoránál fogva sikerült itt Budapesten előkelő körökbe bejutni, súlyos bűncselekmények vádja terhelte, többek közt az, hogy Berlinben egy Engel Gyula nevű kereskedőt megölt és kirabolt. Bécsben pedig egy Reitz Ede nevű kereskedőn az ölést és rablást megkísérlette, de tettének véghezvitelében megakadályozták. A nyomozás sokáig huzódott, mert a bizonyítékok megszerzése nagy nehézségekbe ütközött. Úgy a ber-

Domby Károly, a 9-ik, Lichtenstein nevét viselő huszárezred volt őrmestere, a kinek mellét három bátorsági érdemjel diszíti. Kettőt 1864-iki Schleswig-holsteini hadjárat után, a harmadik nagy ezüst érdemrendet az 1866-ban vivta ki egy huszárbravurral. A vitéz huszár most hetven éves. Egyik képünk Dombyt jelenlegi arczképét ábrázolja, a másik mint fiatal

Figure 4. Spázó Kragujevics in *Tolnai Világlapja*, November 9, 1909, 2257. Image from Arcanum Digitecha.

twelve years in prison. Most of the daily papers in Hungary followed the case and provided detailed reporting on the investigations and trials. Since Székely and Tábori not only followed the case in the press but also personally reported on it, they had firsthand knowledge about the nature of the homosexual social world of Budapest that Kragujevics had gained access to. Regardless of whether Kragujevics was an authentic homosexual or simply a swindler who took advantage of them, his case influenced not only Székely and Tábori's views about homosexuality but also those of the larger public.

Inspired by the crimes of Kragujevics, *Beteg szerelem* portrays queer Budapest. The book's title, *Sick Love*, like that of their book chapter in *Sinful Budapest*, reveals the conflation of homosexuality as both a biological/medical and a moral issue. By the early twentieth century, this dual stigmatization became characteristic of Hungarian public opinion about homosexuality. Less sympathy for homosexuals was not a direct result of the Kragujevics's case alone. It was also a consequence of what Tábori and Székely saw as an epidemic rise of queers and of the particular ways in which homosexuality was spreading. In their own words:

> Love between men ought to be more substantially dealt with by defenders of public safety as well as of morality, because *this terrible fervor has been spreading* recently, and not only in Budapest but also in small places in the countryside. Five [or] ten years ago they only operated in bigger cities. But since then there have been organized associations and even clubs that have been set up by certain men and the number of homosexual men has been rapidly rising even outside of the capital.[48]

While writing their *Sinful Budapest* book series, the leading investigating Hungarian journalists became intimately familiar with the worlds of Budapest's inhabitants: the rich, poor, and middle classes and men and women alike. The passage above indicates that their time spent on the streets of Budapest made Tábori and Székely particularly concerned with two alleged aspects of homosexuality—the mounting visibility of queers and homosexuality's disease-like proliferation. According to the authors, homosexuality needed immediate attention for moral and criminal reasons. In its intention to raise awareness about the perils of homosexuality, *Beteg szerelem* also became the most informative account of contemporary Hungarian queer culture.

Tábori and Székely, inspired by the journalists, social reformers, and the altruistic social elite of London and other urban metropolises who "went slumming," embarked on operations to uncover the world of the underprivileged. According to their account, it was during these investigations that they discovered the world of homosexuals. "A few years ago—one of the authors of this book—spent weeks in masquerade among beggars, petty thieves and people of the like. During this time he was able to get to know the perverse people quite well."[49] The mission to expose the "knights and queens of sick love" emerged from the belief that only those people who came in contact with the homosexual community could have genuine knowledge about same-sex sexuality.[50] Instead of a medical perspective, however, *Beteg szerelem* took an investigative approach. Tábori and Székely mingled participant observation with techniques of sociology and sexual slumming. And who would have been in a better position than a policeman whose files were full of intimate details about homosexuals and a journalist who had firsthand experience of queer subcultures, not only in Budapest, but also in some of the major European cities? There could be no doubt that readers were in for a treat.

One of the dramatic stories retells the discovery of a homosexual establishment in the heart of Pest. We learn that Székely,

> during his time masquerading among perverse people, with another undercover colleague discovered a *buzeráns tanyát* [homosexual bar]. His partner was a rubicund, almost girl-like faced young lad, and the guests of the bar thought that he was with his *warme Schwester* [male homosexual friend], his "girlfriend." By the fourth time they walked into the bar, they were received very friendlily.... They saw such orgies in that bar that they lost their appetite for days. But their disgust gave place to anger when they realized that nearly every day there would be a new victim. Not just one respectable families' son was seduced this way.[51]

The incident the authors refer to most likely took place a few years prior, when following an anonymous tip the police discovered a homosexual establishment that operated out of "Modell Café and Canteen" in the center of Pest. At the time of the revelations in 1903, as well as at the time of the writing of *Sick Love*, it was the luring of the "young and respectable" that provided the impetus to denounce the homosexual bar and its nearby restaurant to the police. The police sent their own very handsome undercover detective, who in the words of Tábori and Székely, "proceeded to make a whole lot of homosexuals fall in love with him."[52] This tactic made gathering evidence easy. Within a few weeks, the police mapped the various homosexual operations that used the back rooms of the café as their hub, and the police busted both establishments. *Beteg szerelem* informs the readers—with a hint of sensationalism—that due to the "delicate details" of the raid, it refrained (as did other newspapers at the time) from "burdening their readers" with the specifics. In the subsequent analyses, however, we learn that quite a few respected gentlemen were exposed in the operation.[53]

But it is really the ways in which homosexuality supposedly spread and infected young men that the authors took issue with. To illustrate their point about how *this terrible fervor* spread, Tábori and Székely introduced the following dialogue between a young homosexual and a detective—who was most likely Székely himself—that the authors, allege took place at the police station following the police raid.[54]

DETECTIVE: How did you get to this foul place?
16-YEAR-OLD BOY: I was sitting at the Elisabeth Square and was studying to pass my fifth gymnasium exams. Then a gentleman came along who talked to me nicely and told me that he was a teacher and he could work with me on my studies. He invited me to his place . . . and then *it happened*.
DETECTIVE: And why didn't you tell this to your father, who is a respected merchant?
16-YEAR-OLD BOY: I was ashamed. And then I tried to avoid this man to no avail. He found me. First he begged me, then threatened me that he would get me arrested, at the same time he promised me great things. By the third time it was me who went to his place. By the end I ran away from home and I have been making my own living for three months.
DETECTIVE: Well, what a nice way of supporting yourself!
16-YEAR-OLD BOY: What can I do? Now, I cannot stop.[55]

Their message was clear: once one experienced a homosexual encounter, one would no longer desire heterosexual sex. This is what most concerned Tábori and Székely, who viewed same-sex sexuality, and particularly its effect on individuals and their greater community, as terribly detrimental. More specifically, they believed it would disrupt families and hurt the moral fiber of society. Their follow-up discussion about the sixteen-year-old makes this clear.

> The 16-year-old boy was very calm while talking about his sexuality and only got upset when the detective told him that his father would be noti-

fied of his whereabouts. Then his eyes swelled with tears as he shouted: "Please everything but that! It would be better if they thought I was dead. If you do not notify my parents, I will confess everything and swear that I'll never go around *schwesters* ever again."[56]

The boy was apparently caught six months later on a corner on the Pest side of the city. "He was standing like a female prostitute," with makeup on, waiting for customers. By then he was "worn out," an old *schwester*, and was making his money from pimping "like an old bawd." Tábori and Székely exhorted their readers to wonder, "How many young lads are ruined this way, physically and emotionally? People who fall into the abyss, have no power to get out."[57] Dramatic statements like this were just as likely to arouse readers' imaginations as they were to spark genuine reflection about the authors' concerns.

These excerpts also reveal the tendency of the authors to present homosexuality in an age-differential model, where one of the partners is significantly older.[58] Such a view was underwritten by increased concerns about youth and especially adolescent sexuality. Yet there was much more concern about young men in homosexual relationships with older partners than for young women in heterosexual relationships with older partners. Society tended to show much less concern about conceptualizing women as sexually mature above the age of fourteen than their male counterparts, and particularly those in homosexual relationships. Tábori and Székely's stories are representative of the ways in which young men were infantilized in order to be presented as victims of older male homosexuals. In the perception of authors and likely society at large, moreover, same-sex relationships, even more so than their heterosexual counterparts, were seen as unequal in terms of age and wealth. Whereas young women supposedly could fall in love or have sex with older men for their charms alone, that a young man might want to be with older men was generally believed to only occur when additional financial benefits or pressures pushed a young man into the relationship.

There was real anxiety about the rise of homosexuals and what that meant for the growing metropolis. Tábori and Székely's understanding of same-sex desire and homosexuality as a disease that spread with contact was at the heart of why they considered homosexuality a moral and a public health epidemic. Their increasing fervor against homosexuality could be interpreted as the authors' own attempt to avoid its contagion: after all, given their account, they heroically risked their own sexual souls to reveal this sinful state of affairs! Tábori and Székely were alarmed by the appalling social conditions in Budapest. Not unlike social reformers in London, Berlin, or New York, they believed that poverty and lack of adequate living space bred social and psychobiological diseases.[59] In this context, the spread and increase of same-sex sexual activity was seen as the embodiment of urban degeneration and signified everything that was wrong with modern Hungarian society.

Yet, closer attention to Székely and Tábori's actual representation of homosexuality reveals how their understanding of what homosexuality was and what it signified about the denizens of Budapest—and more generally about the city—could also be read differently. Their declaration that "even in the most normal human being exists some perversion or at least, the propensity for it" is a remarkable statement for its time, a time when European discourses on homosexuality were heavily infused with degeneration theories.[60] Their view that urban living and perversions were co-constitutive furthermore explains why *Beteg szerelem* portrays homosexuality as an effect, rather than a cause, of social problems.[61] Even as they sensationalize the spread and threat of queer desires, they portray homosexuals and queer subcultures as an inevitable part of modern Budapest. If anything, Tábori and Székely opine, authentic homosexuality should provoke our pity. And yet, while they call for pity, the ways in which they talk about the homosexuality of some of Budapest's respectable and renowned figures can also be read as evidence of Tábori and Székely's intention to normalize only certain types of homosexuality. Why else would they brag about how the ranks of homosexuals in Budapest included a number of widely known writers, a pianist, a millionaire Maecenas (patron of arts), and a famous actor?[62] They did not name these men, but considering the telling descriptions, it is likely that most of their readers could figure out whom they were referring to. The outing of well-known and beloved figures of Budapest was a proof that authentic homosexuality could go hand in hand with respectability and social stature. Tábori and Székely's sympathetic account of the Oscar Wilde scandal underscores this kind of empathetic and normalizing view of same-sex sexuality. In describing Wilde's story (whose sexual perversity we learn was "nothing" compared to some of Budapest's leading figures), the authors note that it was England's "brutish laws" that destroyed one of England's finest artists for nothing else but for *betegség gyötörte*, "suffering from an illness."[63]

Like the Budapest authorities discussed in chapter 1, Tábori and Székely's work distinguishes between acceptable and unacceptable representation and understanding of nonnormative sexuality. In their writings, there is a category of homosexuals who, while clearly far from celebrated, are depicted with empathy and given certain respect. Tábori and Székely do not question the existence or the legitimacy of certain queers or the "real knights" and define them as "respectable" against other forms of nonnormative sexualities. Such a portrayal resonates with both the discourses about the tolerance of respectable queers present in contemporary progressive and liberal circles and with the actual treatment of respectable homosexuals.[64] Surviving court records, which will be the subject of chapter 5, illuminate how authorities were selective in their policing of nonnormative sexualities. Often this meant that people with "legitimate and scientifically proven" desire for same-sex individuals could practice and live their chosen lifestyle in relative freedom.[65] But who exactly, according to Tábori and Székely, were those "respectable" homosexuals?[66]

They never explicitly defined it or used the word *tiszteletreméltó* (respectable) in their works. Yet, every time they talk about same-sex sexuality, there is a certain type of homosexuality that Tábori and Székely distinguish from the immoral, "degenerate," and criminal elements. Whether it is in the context of discussing Oscar Wilde, citing their experience in a Berlin homosexual party, or talking about "well-known" elite Hungarian homosexuals, there is a certain kind of respect that they evoke. In these cases, Tábori and Székely refrain from dwelling on the actual sexual nature of these individuals and instead focus on other aspects of their lives. If not necessarily putting them on even footing with their heterosexual counterparts, the journalists accorded men in this category respectability on the basis of their achievements and social standing. In doing so, they also advocated tolerance toward a type of homosexuality, which remained an elusive category and open to interpretation. This ambiguity was not necessarily a bad thing for queer men.

The relationship of class and respectable homosexuality in Tábori and Székely's writings was not always straightforward, however. Social class and wealth obviously mattered. For one, they enabled considerably more privacy and, thus, protected one's sexual life from the eyes of the law and from the public, a precondition of respectability. But in the authors' eyes, class and power could also enable the exploitation of poor men and the underprivileged. Consequently, higher socioeconomic status did not automatically mean respectability. Rather, the well-known Hungarian homosexuals of higher classes that Tábori and Székely mention are considered "respectable," not simply because of their class or social position, but also because of the work they did as members of society. In this sense, social class was neither necessary nor an inevitable component of respectable homosexuality. To be a respectable homosexual meant that one had to be both a model citizen in public life and a conscientious individual in one's private life.

THE WORLD OF TÁBORI AND SZÉKELY'S QUEERS

Thanks to the ongoing digitalization of contemporary newspapers and the possibility of data mining such sources, it has become possible to verify some of the stories about police operations in *Sinful Budapest* and *Sick Love*. Contemporary news reports provided some items about undercover busts and in rare instances about the entire undercover operation of the "homosexual squad." In terms of their description of the life of queer Budapest, however, there is very little historical data available to cross-check the authenticity of Tábori and Székely's writings. Keeping in mind that their intention was to raise awareness about the dark sides of homosexuality, we can read their analysis with a grain of salt. At the very least, reading *Sinful Budapest* and *Sick Love* helps us to imagine how the authors and the greater public perceived the situation of queers in Budapest during the early 1900s. For one, the number of homosexuals prior to World War I was supposed to be steadily on the rise both in and outside of cities. This is one of the few facts that can actually be verified by historical participants within the subculture. In a rare instance of a surviving homosexual voice from the 1900s, a homosexual man interviewed by forensic scientists seconded Tábori and Székely's observations.[67] In the man's own words,

> I would be very disappointed if somebody believed that "schwesters" are only in the big city and among the educated social strata. Someone like me who had travelled a lot, and someone who knows all regions of Hungary especially well, I can say from my personal experience that I had the opportunity to meet with schwesters not only in the larger cities, but often in small villages as well. And not one occasion did I see a schwester, who was a peasant.

By the early twentieth century, there was an increasing number of men not only in Budapest but also in smaller cities who formed their own identity as well as their social communities based on sexual preference. Moreover, homosexual men and men with queer sexual interest built a growing network that often cut across ethnic, class, and age differences. The most obvious place of networking was the homosexual association.

One of Tábori and Székely's more surprising findings is that by the first decade of the twentieth century, there was a formally established Hungarian homosexual association. Although not officially registered—it could not have been legally—our eager journalists state that the association in terms of its function resembled other registered associations.[68] The association was based in Budapest but soon had "offices" in a number of cities within the Hungarian kingdom, including Arad, Nagyvárad (Oradea), Kolozsvár (Cluj-Napoca), Pécs, and Székesfehérvár. The offices were in touch with each other as well as with the main office in Budapest. Aside from providing information about issues relating to homosexuality, these places facilitated the meeting and socializing of homosexual men.[69] By the turn of the century, there were also homosexual bars and cafés especially in Budapest that allowed queer customers to create communities as well as opportunities to find sex.[70]

Although there were no openly homosexual establishments, there were places that served as homosexual gathering places. These semiprivate places in the center of Pest tended to be quite restrictive in their accommodation of homosexual patrons. In general, it was those with professional jobs and social stature who were regulars at these establishments. Working-class homosexuals tended to carve out their establishments in the poorer suburbs and neighborhoods and, according to Tábori and Székely, were generally less discrete. As *Beteg szerelem* informs us, while the "better sort" of homosexuals certainly had wild parties in their clubs, it was the working-class *urning partik* (male homosexual parties) that apparently became infamous for being carnivalesque and out of control. There might have been wild antics and rowdy costume parties, yet most queers tended to be secretive and often met in private places. Although it might have been less interesting to readers looking for titillating entertainment, the great majority of homosexuals led mundane lives and concealed their (homo)sexual life outside of the queer community. For many, that queer community extended well beyond Budapest.

The homosexual community in Budapest was tuned in to the international information exchange about matters of homosexuality. Hungarian authorities were not the only ones who looked to the metropolises of Western Europe and the United States for inspiration and knowledge. By the first decade of the twentieth century, Hungarian homosexuals actively sought out information about their counterparts in some of the largest European cities. The did so in a variety of ways. Information on medical and legal aspects of homosexuality were circulated among members. News stories involving homosexuals were printed not only in papers in Budapest but also in smaller and regional publications. Those who could read most certainly could find access to the queer publications such as the ornate German publication *Der Eigene* (The Unique), the first homosexual journal published in Berlin.[71] They would have had access not only to *Der Eigene*, but also to the publications of French authors such as Andre Gide, Marcel Proust, and Jean

Cocteau who discussed homosexuality in their writings. According to Tábori and Székely, Hungarian homosexuals were particularly interested in following the latest trends coming out of the homosexual "Meccas" of Berlin and Paris. In addition, this period saw the explosion of pornographic catalogs that could be ordered through the mail. And, once they were in someone's possession, the catalogs could be circulated widely.[72] If mobile and financially secure, Hungarian homosexuals and people with queer desires could and did visit Berlin, Paris, or Vienna. As discussed in the previous chapter, Berlin and Vienna were especially important for Hungarian discourses on homosexuality. Like their medical counterparts, everyday language and references to homosexuality mostly arrived through the German language, initially without translation. During the last years of the 1900s, German terms such as *warme bruder*, *schwester*, and *urning* were the terms used by authorities and homosexuals alike. As prior excerpts attest, words like *buzeráns*, *warme bruder*, *schwester*, or *urning*, and, eventually, homosexual, were not only used in a pejorative sense but also as references of (self-)identification.[73] At the time of Tábori and Székely's writing, *schwester* (sister), which was also the dominant phrase used in Berlin, seemed to be the preferred term used among men who sexually desired and loved other men.[74]

"PARASITES OF PERVERTS": MALE HOMOSEXUAL PROSTITUTES

The most "treacherous" form of homosexuality and what most concerned Tábori and Székely was male prostitution. In *Beteg szerelem* we learn about a "whole army of *pervezek parazitái* [parasites of perverts]," who "made their living similarly to the female residents of bordellos."[75] The writings of Tábori and Székely and their conceptualization of different types of homosexuals must be understood in the context of prostitution and its unwanted and negative consequences. By the last decades of the nineteenth century, male prostitution had become a staple of Budapest's urban landscape. Unlike female prostitution, which had a long history of regulation in Hungary, male prostitution was never officially regulated. Given that sex between men was illegal, authorities initially saw no reason to specifically address male prostitution. Over time, however, although enjoying less "freedom" than women, male prostitutes carved out their own turf at a number of locales. Tábori and Székely explain that their most frequent workplace was a busy street, where prostitutes had their own routes and corners. The City Park and Elisabeth Square earned infamous reputations, but the promenade by the Danube and the Castle Gardens also served as "consulting places."[76] Male prostitutes also appeared at masquerade parties, at bars, and frequently in the city's many baths. As Budapest's bath culture expanded, receiving international praise and an increasing number of guests, so did the number of "knights of sick love" who frequented them.[77] Some male prostitutes would even offer their services in the love columns of various papers. Such was the case with the following ad published in the personals of a daily newspaper: "A handsome young, 18-year-old would befriend an energetic, well-to-do gentleman. Letters to the publisher under the motto, Night Eye."[78]

While despising most male prostitutes, Tábori and Székely made a distinction between the men who sold themselves for money but were strong enough to keep their "heterosexual manhood" intact and those who eventually joined the "perverts" permanently. They were much more tolerant and even sympathetic toward men who prostituted themselves purely for money than those who, like the sixteen-year-old boy discussed earlier, in the process also "became addicted" to men." By excusing some on the supply side of prostitution, the authors stood in contrast to the police and the courts, which were, like their counterparts elsewhere, harsher on the providers of sexual services. Describing female prostitution as a result of harsh living conditions and desperation, Tábori and Székely sounded more like social reformers. When it came to men selling their bodies in order to make ends meet, Tábori and Székely also blamed the demand side. They particularly blamed financially secure homosexual men who, instead of finding partners based on mutual interest, bought services of economically vulnerable young men, who only tried to make ends meet. In this instance, the words of historian Jeffrey Weeks are fitting, "The deviance of prostitution was supplementary to the 'deviance' of homosexuality."[79]

Tábori and Székely seemed to show a surprising amount of empathy toward soldiers who made some extra cash by sleeping with men who could pay for it. Military men (in and out of their uniforms) were fetishized within the homosexual subculture, and soldier prostitution was booming in bigger cities.[80] Budapest was no exception. There were cafés where "soldier-gallants" auctioned their services to the highest bidder.[81] But their acts were not considered indicative of their character. The notoriously low income that soldiers in the infantry received, "which was not even enough for a daily cigar," according to Tábori and Székely, left them ripe for becoming the "mediums of perverted gentlemen," whose love for those in uniform was well known.[82] The soldier prostitute was regarded as distinct from other male prostitutes because he possessed "mental toughness." Despite selling their sexual services to other men, soldiers were able to keep their own integrity as well as heterosexuality. Soldiers, moreover, presumably possessed not only an authentic (heterosexual) masculinity that they could periodically "trade," but also in their dealings with their clients had a fairer and more ethical core (than the rest of male prostitutes).[83] Tábori and Székely's view was not necessarily unique. Matt Houlbrook, in case of the British guards, for instance, showed how military men who were seen as embodiments of the traditional masculinity of the nation were also objects of queer desire and could engage in sex for money as "rent boys."[84] What was perhaps more unique in the case of Tábori and Székely was how soldiers, unlike the rest of men who prostituted themselves, were excused of their behavior. The highly respected social status of military men not only secured their presumed heterosexuality but also excused their homosexual transgressions. Similar to respected Hungarian citizens who happened to be homosexual, in the case of soldiers, sexuality took a backseat to social status.

In Tábori and Székely's muddled typology and econo-moral hierarchy of sinfulness, the lowest place was reserved to those who not only sold their sexual services in public but also subsequently blackmailed their clients. The authors made a distinction between male prostitutes who provided only physical services and those whose physical acts were accompanied by blackmail. As we have seen, their attitude toward men who worked as prostitutes to ease economic hardship could be sympathetic. In contrast, they saw those male prostitutes who were smart enough to make a living in other "decent" ways, but who chose to exploit those who by "nature's will" were attracted to their own sex, as the real problem that required attention. There is a graphic description of the so-called parasites of perverts who set up and then blackmailed men of stature. In this case, Tábori and Székely, like the authorities in general, blamed and disdained the supply side. These people, who contemporaries referred to as *mitmachers* (German word meaning "silent partners"), were considered to be "malicious, immoral, without a heart or soul, who capitalizing on the weaknesses of schwesters, blackmail them in every way possible."[85] They were, in the words of physician Ernő Moravcsik, "the real scum of humanity."[86] And as Tábori and Székely noted, "this is where the real danger of forbidden love lies."[87] It was not homosexuality that was dangerous, but rather its reverberations: the immorality and criminality that inescapably surrounded it.

Tábori and Székely's understanding and representation of nonnormative sexuality was highly gendered. The assumption that soldiers, in spite of engaging in sex with men, would retain their masculinity and virility was rooted in prevailing beliefs about the strength of Hungarian masculinity.[88] In contrast, women (most of whom were pushed into prostitution for economic reasons) lost both their femininity and moral purity after becoming prostitutes. Even if the authors pitied them, women who sold their sexual services were considered not just as embodiments of their own impurity but also of Budapest's and even of the nation's. Soldiers were neither considered the epitome of the decline of Hungarian virtues nor were they personally at risk of losing their own virility.[89] In Tábori and Székely's treatment of prostitutes, similar to that of the Metropolitan Police, the sex of the prostitutes was more important than the sex of their client. Selling one's sexual services and keeping one's respectability and decency intact was an unattainable pursuit for a woman. In the case of male soldiers who prostituted themselves, their supposedly virtuous armed service on behalf of the nation could still earn them respectability. The authors' lack of concern about the consequences of sex between men seemed to be shared by the military itself. As István Deák, in his seminal study of the Habsburg officers, notes, despite the fact that homosexuality must have been widespread in the army, "all in all, the military courts were not preoccupied with sexual crimes." He concluded that the army prosecuted homosexuality only if it involved nonconsensual sex, minors, or subordinates from the rank and file.[90] The uncontested masculinity and "heterosexuality" of soldiers (and most Hungarian men), moreover, seemed to be taken for granted, not only by authorities of the time, but also by historians.[91]

"LESBOS LOVE"

Although addressed less thoroughly, Tábori and Székely also wrote about women who "fall for Lesbos love."[92] The significantly less attention dedicated to female homosexuals in their work was representative of contemporary concerns about sex and understandings of homosexuality. In their portrayal, female homosexuality is presented as a more private and, therefore, a less dangerous matter than its male counterpart. Women, even of the lower classes, were more private and, space permitting, tended to conduct their affairs within the confines of home and other private spaces. Thanks to its secrecy, female homosexuality was presumably much less likely to pose a threat to the morality of the public and ultimately to the patriarchal structure of society. In addition, since homosexual acts between women were not criminalized, there was much less criminal and forensic scientific evidence to draw on. Consequently, the authors could (along with rest of society) claim that female homosexuality was more difficult to depict even though the number of lesbians in Hungary was apparently not insignificant. We learn, for example, that female homosexuality was prevalent among prostitutes. Tábori and Székely, who had access to the prostitution registry and were intimately familiar with most of Budapest's bordellos, declared that approximately 30 percent of Budapest's prostitutes were lesbians before posing the rhetorical question, "And who would have thought that the most rampant female same-sex love takes place among 'love's official priestesses'? Being sickened by too much sex with men, female prostitutes are inclined to turn to their own sex."[93] The idea of homosexuality being rampant among prostitutes because women had become sick (literally and figuratively) of men was widely shared by contemporaries.[94] Such a view was predicated on the belief that female homosexuality was much more likely to arise from nurture than nature. In an era when the possession of sexual desire was largely reserved for men and immoral women, having any sexual desire at all (let alone acting on it) rendered female homosexuality incompatible with respectability. It is only fitting, then, that Tábori and Székely discussed female homosexuality, or lesbos love as they referred to it, in the context of those women who were already attributed with possessing an active sexual drive: female prostitutes.

There is little to no discussion of authentic "respectable" female homosexuals whose sexual preference was congenital and who were in romantic relationships with other women. The exception is a short anecdotal account by a physician of an aristocratic woman who had for a long time lived with her female friend. The physician was summoned when the woman became ill from a serious neurosis. In Tábori and Székely's words,

> the physician observed in amazement the zeal and self-sacrifice of the friend in taking care of her. She [the friend] was almost transfigured by the patient's outburst. If the doctor touched one of the sore parts of the patient, she also shuddered. All sufferings of the patient were reflected on her own face: sleeplessness, loss of appetite was transferred from the ill patient to the healthy caretaker.[95]

These descriptions portray lesbianism as an unnaturally close bond between women that borders on pathological codependence. The authors note how in "lesbos love" women "were inseparable, and how they longed for each other and looked at each other with such tenderness."[96] Such descriptions, while they could imply a sexual intimacy, could also be read as depictions of intimate friendships without any sexual connotation. At a time when in their day-to-day life gender segregation was still the norm for the middle and upper classes, lesbianism was presented as an extreme on the continuum of homosociability. Just as in the case of homosexual men, such a conceptualization fit squarely within contemporary assumptions about gender.

Homosexual men's innate sexual drive (even if wrongfully directed) went unquestioned, while lesbians were depicted not as sexual beings but as having an unnatural amount of compassion toward other women. What historian of lesbianism Lillian Faderman has illustrated in *Odd Girls and Twilight Lovers* for the nineteenth-century US seems to resonate in early twentieth-century Budapest; outside of medical discussions, the idea of respectable, "healthy" women naturally desiring other women *sexually* was beyond what society could, if not necessarily imagine, at least openly discuss.[97] Tábori and Székely proved to be no exception.

As in the case of their male same-sex-desiring counterparts, when discussing women, Tábori and Székely payed particular attention to those "inauthentic" female homosexuals who posed the greatest danger to society: those who blackmailed and profited from women who were genuinely attracted to their own sex. Although their appearance was less noticeable and their activities more private, their methods of extortion from their victims were just as "cruel and sophisticated as their male counterparts."[98] This representation echoed the publication of Irma Nagy's *Sötét bűnök: Egy úrileány vallomásai* (Dark sins: Confessions of a young lady), which was published a few years prior. In this semipornographic book, the female protagonist, after emotionally wounding her male lovers at the end of the book, finds her happiness and erotic fulfillment in a relationship with a woman.[99] In both cases, the (homo)sexuality of these women was predicated on ulterior motives. Thus, what Sharon Marcus in Victorian England has illustrated was certainly true in the Hungarian context: it was not necessarily that either sensuality between women or intimate friendship was beyond the imagination of contemporaries. But it was associated with illicit women and certainly beyond what could be discussed in Hungary's "respectable" public and private spheres.[100]

Unless the person who was being blackmailed turned to the police, a rare occurrence, the reader of Tábori and Székely is informed, these stories were forever lost. One of the only ways these relationships could surface was when the relatives of a respectable woman filed a complaint with the police about "the overbearing and unhealthy influence of a female servant or a friend on their frail female relative."[101] Women who were blackmailed would rather have kept paying than have their reputation suffer. To conclude their succinct analysis of women, Tábori and Székely declared that just as in case of their male counterparts, blackmailing was an inevitable aspect of those female homosexual relations in which one-half of the couple had no real passion. And reinforcing their views about homosexuality, they conclude, "Same-sex sexuality is an illness but exploiting it is a serious crime."[102] What is notable in their portrayal is the way in which real lesbians appear to have very little control over their feelings and, indeed, over their lives. Within the authors' framing, the frail authentic female homosexual is juxtaposed with the rapacious servant or the greedy friend. Taking the words literally, female homosexuals of nobility are presented as weak and taken advantage of. In contrast to authentic male homosexuals of means who were portrayed as potential threats to young men, "true" lesbians of means were to be almost pitied as being hostages to their own ill desires, desires that would inevitably land them in the hands of extortionists. Whereas male homosexuals could be well-respected, successful men, Tábori and Székely seem to suggest that "abnormal" sexual inclination imprisoned women. Once women possessed sexual desire (in this case for other women), it overrode all other aspects of personality, background, and aptitude. Such representation signified a larger discursive change where, as Faderman and others have documented, romantic friendship and homosociability between women that had previously been considered devoid of sexual intimacy would increasingly become suspect.[103]

THE LASTING IMPACT OF TÁBORI AND SZÉKELY'S PUBLICATIONS

Sinful Budapest and *Sick Love* were both instant successes and remained popular books until the 1940s. Subsequently, they were abruptly forgotten and never mentioned or reprinted during the era of Hungary's postwar Communist regime. It is only in the last fifteen years that they have been "rediscovered" and both have been reprinted. *Sinful Budapest* is once again a staple item in bookstores. It is unlikely that there will ever be conclusive evidence to confirm the credibility of Tábori and Székely's accounts of queers. Besides the practical difficulties of validating their "facts," perhaps it would not even be a rewarding or useful exercise. Considering that Tábori and Székely wrote the only widely read source on Hungarian homosexuals and their culture, their observations, characterizations, and ideas about the "knights of sick love" became the reference and in a sense the "truth" about homosexuals for their contemporaries. It is also likely that their writings provided valuable information to people who wanted to seek and connect with queer and homosexual communities. Publishing the names of places and descriptions of locales where homosexual and queer activities took place would have been valuable to readers with an interest in such things. Exposing the queer world was at once a form of publicity, titillation, and invitation to readers and a danger to its existence. The paradoxical nature of this type of reporting is evident even within their texts. They narrated how their "discovery" led to the police subsequently cracking down on queer establishments and to arrests. But arguably, Tábori and Székely's influence was greatest in the dissemination of knowledge about nonnormative sexuality. In light of Tábori and Székely's extensive readership, their descriptions of respectable homosexuals and dangerous queers were crucial to circulating and popularizing such views to the greater public. Subsequent publications that discussed homosexuality prior to World War II undeniably resonate with Tábori and Székely's descriptions. Whether novelists like Gyula Krúdy and Ernő Szép or public intellectuals and doctors who published for lay audiences, the depictions of same-sex desire and homosexuals echo Tábori and Székely's portrayal.[104] These publications reiterate the representation of respectable homosexuals who other than being attracted to their own sex live respectable lives. Many of these publications also provided an even more humane representation of homosexuality, and some even openly called for its decriminalization. Tábori and Székely's representations of queer Budapest were both novel and at the same time also representative of Hungarian progressive circles that believed that homosexuals were an inevitable part of modern urban life.

At the same time of Tábori and Székely's writing for a popular audience, the decriminalization of homosexuality was openly discussed at meetings of the Hungarian national legal association. Two important lectures on homosexuality were delivered at sessions of the Hungarian Association of Legal Scholars in March of 1909. The intellectual roots or sources for these lectures likely lay within the concurrent legal debates around the reformation of penal codes in Austria and Germany. Austria, where both female and male homosexuality had been criminalized, published a new penal code in 1909 that simply recodified the ongoing legal practice.[105] In Germany, however, the government-commissioned proposal to extend Paragraph 175 to include the criminalization of female homosexuality elicited not just a legal but also a broad public debate.[106] The subsequent legal debate that took place in Budapest among Hungarian lawyers was undoubtedly inspired and informed by both the Austrian and German events. Yet, that these debates were taking place in the Hungarian context concomitantly also shows that support for the decriminalization of consensual homosexual relationships had significant homegrown support.

The lectures on homosexuality at the Hungarian national legal association are remarkable evidence of contemporary support for protecting respectable homosexuals.[107] The first of these lectures occurred on March 20, 1909, and was given by a physician, Ignácz Fischer. A neurologist and expert in forensic medicine, Fischer delivered a passionate paper entitled "Homosexuality and Its Forensic Contemplation" about why homosexuality should not be punishable by law.[108]

> I share the perspectives of Hirschfield, Merzbach, Näcke and Löwenfeld, and declare that homosexuality is not a psychical disorder, only an anomaly, where the sexual feeling desires an unnatural same-sex sexual fulfillment. But such desires do not make a person inferior in anything compared to those who exhibit and express heterosexual desires. . . . Just as we do not hold people with crooked noses or crooked legs inferior, we should not, and in fact it is not allowed to devalue those physically, whose sexual desires differ from the norm. Since we cannot change the law, or abolish it, we who are touched by the feeling that public sentiment is detrimental to these unfortunate, sexually different individuals, *it is our duty to inform the public, that in terms of intellect and ethical values, these people are fully on par with people of normal sexual orientation, and they provide no reason for contempt, let alone any punishment.*[109]

It is significant that Fischer's words, citing influential German medical and legal professionals, repeat the message and representation of respectable homosexuals expressed in *Sinful Budapest* and *Sinful Love*. As if responding to Tábori and Székely's attempt to enlighten people about "real" Budapest, Fischer is clear it is not respectable homosexuals whom city authorities and citizens should really be concerned about. Fischer's assertion that in terms of their intellect and especially their ethics, homosexuals were on par with any respectable citizen echoes the views of Tábori and Székely. Fischer's defense of respectable homosexuals was even more explicit, and his call for the education of the public about how homosexuals should be full members of Hungarian society went even further than Tábori and Székely's evocation. His is a truly remarkable stand: desiring one's own sex has no bearing on one's membership in the national community. Fischer's words, moreover, demonstrate how a strand of Hungarian authorities believed that granting respectable homosexuals equal legal rights was the "modern" way forward. Such differentiation between those "sexual abnormals" who were worthy of protection and those who were not foreshadows discussions in Weimar Germany over a decade later, where one set of homosexuals was recommended to be given new legal status, while another was to lose rights correspondingly.[110]

The second lecture took place at the next meeting of the Hungarian

Association of Legal Scholars. Zoltán Halász, a lawyer and legal scholar, delivered a lecture where, like Fischer, he made an earnest plea on behalf of the decriminalization of homosexuality.[111]

> A homosexual person is born as a homosexual, and who was not born as such, under no circumstances would he become a homosexual. I deem it necessary to highlight in opposition to those who want *pedarasztia* [sic] [in this context homosexuality] to be punishable on the basis of its physical contagiousness, the idea that without prohibiting and punishing homosexuality it will spread and gain followers. In contrast to this idea, I would like to remind people about the typical assertion by heterosexual supporters of the abolitionist camp [of the decriminalization of homosexuality] who argue that although they could imagine that under certain circumstances they would break every single paragraph of the Criminal Code, they could never imagine breaking Paragraph 241, that is the crime of male homosexuality.[112]

Halász's insistence that homosexuality was not "spreadable" actually challenged Tábori and Székely's view, and society's more generally, that exposure to same-sex sexuality could induce same-sex sexual desires. Giving voice to heterosexual defenders who argued that no heterosexual men would engage in homosexual acts reveals the existence of networks of advocates, many of whom were heterosexuals, who not only made shared arguments about homosexuality and why it should be decriminalized, but also about the deeply held social stigma that surrounded homosexuality. Given Halász's more favorable view of homosexuality, it isn't surprising that the legal scholar also believed that there was a category of homosexuals who were worthy of protection. He paints "normal" homosexual relationships between "authentic" homosexuals as a consensual relationship between adults based on love.

> An otherwise healthy adult person—fat or skinny—will never make a young child his sexually desired object. The matter is rather that just as a neurotically weak old heterosexual man could desire young girls, a *quad erectionem impotens* urning [in Latin: an impotent male homosexual] could similarly desire young boys. *But* a non-pervert homosexual adult would never desire a child; the mechanics of his own sexual desires will only work with physically matured men over a certain age who showed signs of physical adulthood.[113]

The message here is clear: otherwise "normal" individuals who happen to desire their own sex are neither a threat nor any different from their normal, heterosexual counterparts. Insisting that same-sex relations took place between two adult men, Halász's argument is representative of a paradigm shift that historian Gert Hekma argues was taking place within the sexual relationship between men across the continent.[114] Prior to the twentieth century, homosexual relationships tended to be unequal in terms of age, social, and economic position. In the twentieth century, they were increasingly between equals. In Halász's view, cross-generational sex—both hetero- and homosexual—is pathological. Sex between consenting men of similar age should be decriminalized and freed from taint of vice.[115] Halász believed that society and the state would be much better off spending their resources to combat sexual violence, exploitation, and underage sex, instead of policing sexual behavior between consenting adults.

Fischer and Halász both had a clear, more positive, and less sensationalist view of homosexuals than Tábori and Székely. Nevertheless, all four men upheld the notion of respectable homosexuality. Fischer and Halász, as a medical doctor and a lawyer, respectively, represented different kinds of authorities than Székely and Tábori, their police and investigating journalist counterparts. Yet, in some important ways, they each reflected the ways in which authorities and residents of Budapest were dealing with the city's rapid modernization and its complex consequences. Without denying their personal interests—in the case of Székely and Tábori monetary gain from the publication and sale of stories about the "knights of sick love"—these four men, by taking up the issue of nonnormative sexuality, were all genuinely invested in the betterment of the Hungarian capital. The ideas of Tábori and Székely, as well as of Fischer and Halász, and their growing concern about the spread of "sick love" were part of a much wider concern about the future of Budapest and the Hungarian race. Their interest in homosexuality took place within and alongside contemporary debates about contemporary social questions, such as poverty, social hygiene, and women's work more generally. Their representation of queer sexualities is consistent with contemporary accounts and historical works that portray a society filled with fears about the decline and composition of modern Hungarians. It also highlights the rapid growth of the city and sex trade, as bodies circulated more rapidly (geographically and intimately), and the inability of authorities to regulate these developments.[116] To all four commentators, and likely for many others in Budapest, queers seen as "inauthentic" (i.e., not biologically queer) and/or "immoral" (i.e., because they exploited others) were similar to the urban poor and prostitutes, the embodiments of Budapest's urban decline. Hungarian discourses that viewed queers as visible products of the emerging modern metropolis certainly borrowed from and imitated international discourses that saw homosexuality as a disease and negative consequence of urban modernity.[117] Yet, as the case of Tábori and Székely, along with Fischer and Halász, demonstrates, there was also an alternative discourse that was willing both to create and embrace a category of homosexuals.[118] The publications of Tábori and Székely and Fischer and Halász mattered because they endorsed and disseminated the idea of a category of "respectable homosexuals." Such distinction was predicated on the scientization of sexuality and a move away from religious morality and on an assumed proliferation of urban heterogeneity, a view which all of these men shared.

CONCLUSION

The publications of *Sinful Budapest* and *Sick Love*, while subsequently written out of Hungarian history, were the first widely read reports on queer sexualities. They were dependent on, and helped to fuel, both anxieties and fantasies about queer sexualities. Their representation of queer men and women was itself a testament to Budapest's place in the modern world. At the dawn of the twentieth century, Budapest was claiming its place within the European metropolitan network of sex. Tábori and Székely's writings demonstrate the historical existence of an extensive and vibrant homosexual culture in Budapest that predated the fall of the Austro-Hungarian monarchy. I argued that the specific circumstances in the early 1900s facilitated the arrival of the "Hungarian homosexual" in popular discourse: the liberal politics of an active, socially progressive intellectual segment, who believed in making Budapest into a modern (Western) metropolis; the rise of mass media and lax regulations; the presence of German discourses (medical, legal, and popular) of nonnormative sexuality; and a growing Hungarian sexual subculture of queer men.

Tábori and Székely's representation of same-sex relationship and desire reflected the elements of the various understandings of nonnormative sexuality that coexisted in European capitals at the dawn of the twentieth century. Their terminology and contradictory accounts of homosexuality were indicative of the confusion surrounding how to think and deal with people who genuinely desired their own sex. Ambiguity aside, Tábori and Székely, similar to the authorities, distinguished between "respectable"/authentic and immoral/inauthentic queers. Their publications offered an alternative conceptualization to the dominant view that homosexuality was simply a filthy and sick consequence of urban modernity. By creating a category of "respectable homosexuals" alongside their portrayal of "bad" queers, Tábori and Székely had an enduring impact on how their contemporaries and future Hungarians throughout the interwar years perceived and represented male homosexuals.

CHAPTER THREE

Rehabilitating "Sexual Abnormals" in the Hungarian Soviet Republic

On March 21, 1919, Hungary became the second country after Russia to declare a Communist-run Soviet (or Council) Republic, or Tanácsköztársaság. The reputation of the republic has had a fraught history. Already during its day, it was despised and blamed by many for its brutality and for Hungary's "mutilation," and for the Treaty of Trianon that led to the loss of two-thirds of the country's former territory. Such accusations became extreme immediately following the fall of the Soviet Republic and remained so throughout the interwar period. After World War II, with the onset of the Cold War and the establishment of Hungarian Communist one-party system, the revolutionaries of 1919 were rehabilitated and became national heroes. Since the fall of Communism in 1989, in yet another turnaround, the days of Tanácsköztársaság are considered a dark, and increasingly as a shameful, spot in Hungary's history. Historians outside of Hungary to a great extent also share this view.

During the brief five months of Communist rule, authorities, applying their revolutionary ideas to the justice system, established the Experimental Criminology Department of the Revolutionary Tribunal. The horrors of the Revolutionary Tribunal and politically motivated executions and sentencing are well known. Most historians stress the mass terror, ad hoc actions, and overall negative consequences of the Hungarian Communist revolutionary regime.[1] Without denying any of those claims, in light of recently emerged evidence, the meaning of the brief existence of the revolutionary regime needs to be rethought, in one broadly significant area at least. Shifting attention away from the Communists' bloody handling of political dissenters and toward their treatment of people who encountered the state courts for sexual nonconformity provides a strikingly different picture of Soviet justice. More specifically, the surviving documents of the Experimental Criminology

Department of the Budapest Revolutionary Tribunal speak not of the terror and political motivation, but rather of a serious effort to judge crime through the eyes of a comprehensive sociomedical approach, an approach that also incorporated psychoanalytical theories. The Communists' justice system did not simply attempt to correct the mistakes of the former bourgeois legal system of the Austro-Hungarian monarchy. Conceptualizing individuals as complex emotional, physical, and social beings, the experts of the Communists' justice system reworked the definition of crime. By combining some of the latest scientific approaches with a humanistic fervor, they also set out to transform society. The present chapter examines the Hungarian Soviet Republic's approach toward nonnormative (queer) sexuality through analyzing the Criminology Department and its methods in dealing with nonnormative sexuality. I draw on the archival collections of the Experimental Criminology Department of the Budapest Revolutionary Tribunal and of the National Criminology Institute, both housed in the Budapest City Archives. In addition, I rely on issues of *Proletárjog: A Szocialista Jogászszövetség hivatalos lapja* (Proletarian Law: The Official Journal of the Association of Socialist Lawyers), published during the existence of the Soviet Republic, that addressed and provided detailed accounts of the ideas, legality, and operation of the Experimental Criminology Department.[2] The chapter tells the story of a remarkable experiment of adopting a methodology in which the personal life histories of individuals became the center of understanding sexual crimes, as well as the basis of their rehabilitative rather than disciplinary treatment. Willing to consider sexuality as malleable and unfixed, and sexual history as an important determinant of people's action, courts in the Hungarian Soviet Republic instituted a novel approach to the treatment of nonnormative sexuality, not only within the Hungarian context, but also in the larger international scene. The Experimental Criminology Department's treatment of nonnormative sexuality was predicated on the genuine belief of the Hungarian Communist leadership that people had the potential to change and society could be fundamentally transformed. Reconstructing their efforts offers incredible details about the grand—albeit incompletely realized—vision of the Hungarian Soviet Republic to remake Hungarian subjects into Communist citizens. Committed to radical innovation in all spheres of life, Hungarian Communists granted psychoanalysis and more generally the social and human sciences a central place in this process. The relationship between the origins of psychoanalysis, Sigmund Freud, and fin de siècle Vienna is taken for granted. So is the connection between liberalism, social democratic politics, and the bourgeoning of psychoanalysis in Vienna and Berlin during the first two decades of the twentieth century.[3] A bourgeois clientele, a couch, and Professor Freud scribbling notes for his next publication are visual cues of the early history of psychoanalysis. But what happens when we shift from bourgeois Vienna to Communist Budapest, from Sigmund Freud to Sándor Ferenczi, and leave the couch for an exploratory laboratory? The serendipitously discovered single file of documents titled "Collection of Materials Concerning the Experimental Criminology Department" at the City Archives in Budapest offers an unexpected story about psychoanalysis in the hands of Hungarian Communists during the Hungarian Soviet Republic.[4]

One particular way the revolutionary Communist project was enacted is how the Hungarian Soviet state offered technologies of rehabilitation rather than instruments of punishment to men and women with nonnormative sexual desires. Whereas during the days of Austria-Hungary prior to 1918, the treatment of male homosexuality was a means to assess Budapest's place in the modern Western world, during Communism nonnormative sexuality was considered the "ill-fated by-product" of the bourgeois-ruled modern West. In contrast to the prevailing contemporary conceptualizations of homosexuality and nonnormative sexuality more generally as a medical condition and a deviant behavior, during the Communist dictatorship, "abnormal" sexuality was considered a condition that resulted from socioeconomic circumstance and personal psychological history. Reflecting the newfound influence of psychoanalysis, psychology, and sociology, for the first time the justice system placed psychoanalytical and psychosocial frameworks at the center of understanding sexual criminal behavior. Based on the surviving materials of the Experimental Criminology Department, this chapter reconstructs the ideas about and approaches toward sexuality without aiming to analyze their implementation in practice. The fragmented nature of available sources prevents an assessment of how far the Communists were able to succeed in implementing their vision. But even if there had been ample sources, it would be a less rewarding pursuit since the ephemeral existence of the Hungarian Soviet Republic, which lasted only about six months, would have unquestionably rendered the implementation incomplete and likely imperfect.

REVOLUTIONARY JUSTICE: THE ESTABLISHMENT OF THE EXPERIMENTAL CRIMINAL DEPARTMENT

Prior to 1918 Hungary's wealthiest aristocratic families ran the country, with an electoral system that essentially excluded a great majority of the population.[5] The Great War emboldened men and women alike, and there was a growing demand for change. Like in capitals across Europe, protests became commonplace in Budapest in the last two years of the war, as the political leadership could not diffuse social tensions stemming from lack of food and basic supplies.[6] The news of the fall of the Central Powers in the autumn of 1918 was a catalyst for change. As in Vienna, liberal and social democratic oppositions, in addition to ending the war, wanted comprehensive political reforms.[7] Their efforts, accompanied by a hungry populous and returning soldiers, culminated in the so-called Aster Revolution in October 1918. Named after the supporters wearing an Aster leaf, the leader of the revolution Mihály Károlyi, a progressive left-leaning aristocrat, supported comprehensive reforms to make Hungary a democratic nation.[8] Following the declaration of the Hungarian Democratic Republic on November 16, 1918, Károlyi became president, and the country's new government embarked on democratic changes. These developments were radical for most contemporaries; never before had Hungary been a republic, nor led by a social democratic party. Initially, Hungarian-speaking people in Budapest were hopeful; the war had ended, voting rights expanded, women got the vote, and large-scale land reform was in the making. All of this was occurring while victorious powers were deciding the fate of former empire(s) and the Romanian, Czechoslovakian, and Serbian armies were taking control of formerly Hungarian territories or fighting with the Hungarian Army. The broad social support that initially surrounded the establishment of the Democratic Republic did not last long. Amidst the increasing difficulties faced by the Károlyi-led government, the Communists under the leadership of Béla Kun rapidly mobilized and eventually, through a "second revolution" in March 1919, established the Socialist Governing Council, which proclaimed Hungary a Soviet republic. Within five months the country went from being part of one of the most prominent European monarchies to a democratic republic to the second Communist country in the world after Soviet Russia.

During the brief time (133 days) of the Communist revolutionary government, the new political elite instituted fundamental changes within Hungarian society. Hungarian Communists were committed to the essential restructuring and rebuilding of Hungarian society (as a step in achieving Communism worldwide) along Marxist-Leninist principles.[9] Aside from the separation of state and church and the achievement of universal suffrage, the Communists instituted radical changes within the structure of the arts and sciences and higher education.[10] As part of creating a socialist society, the Communists set out to radically transform social, medical, and public health care systems, beginning with the nationalization of all medical establishments and granting free health care to every working person.[11] The reorganization of society along Bolshevik principles also called for a new justice system. After the immediate suspension of the function of the "bourgeois" courts and the persecution of their personnel, the Revolutionary Council established the system of Revolutionary Tribunals.[12] Considerable attention of the new court system was aimed at "immediate dangers," hence political cases dominated the works of the courts. In these cases, the methods and decisions of the Revolutionary Tribunals were to a great extent politically motivated, most often lacked any legal protection for the accused, granted supreme authority to the council of judges, and ultimately led to hundreds of executions. Shifting the focus away from the politically charged cases, however, and looking at the so-called *közönséges bűnügyek* (ordinary crimes) provides a strikingly different picture.

The founding of the Experimental Criminology Department as a supplementary institute of the tribunal was itself a testament to a new Communist justice system that was to be based in scientific rationality and where scientific objectivity would prevail. The department was to provide "scientific opinions" about people who had been charged with nonpolitical crimes, with the understanding that the opinions would contribute to a more impartial and just treatment of the accused.[13] It was to operate as the model criminology institute for the future Communist justice system. As part of the official effort to "liquidate the old bourgeois legal system," pending and ongoing legal cases were transferred into the Experimental Criminology Department. Over the course of its existence, the department considered over three thousand cases.[14] In stark contrast to most contemporary reports and subsequent historical accounts of the Hungarian Soviet Republic that emphasize the politicization of each and every sphere of life, the Experimental Criminology Department was set up as a protected intellectual place of intense scientific work. The Communists, as the statutes of the Experimental Criminology Department of the Budapest Revolutionary Tribunal make clear, believed that the "institution was first and foremost a scientific institution" and that scientific work within the institution was predicated on intellectual freedom, "which is the basic precondition for all scientific work.[15] Providing "scientific objectivity" aside, the institute was envisioned as a laboratory for scientific creativity and research. But adhering to scientific rationality was not what made the department unique. It was the kinds of scientific approaches that the department embraced that did.

Communists granted new modern sciences of psychoanalysis, psychology, and sociology an essential place within the Criminology Department—a slap in the face of forensic medicine and more generally of psychiatry and neurology, which had been in charge of medical opinions and had conveyed considerable influence over the definition of crime as well as the treatment of the accused. On a purely ideological level, Hungarian Communists supported psychology, sociology, and psychoanalysis as revolutionarily virtuous in part because of their status as previously marginalized fields. As Sándor Ferenczi (1873–1933), the Hungarian psychoanalyst and close associate of Sigmund Freud, in his article "Psychoanalysis and Social Policy" in 1922 expressed, revolutionaries supported and gave institutional power to the previously marginalized (sciences) by principle: "revolutions are accompanied by a phenomenon, which is to say that revolutionaries out of principle tend to support new and radical—previously officially ignored—ideas and trends."[16] Medical establishment pre-1919 had castigated psychological sciences as "pornography dressed in scientific form" and their champions as evidence of the corruption and decline of bourgeois society.[17] Communists, eager to make a radical break with their predecessors, ironically turned to psychology. As part of their fundamental restructuring of the medical school and universities more generally, the Communists made Sándor Ferenczi, who along with Sigmund Freud was one of the most influential psychoanalysts of his time, the head of the world's first psychoanalytical department.[18] Thus, rather than in Vienna, Berlin, or London, it was in Budapest that Freud's theories were first granted official support.[19] In contrast to the customary depiction of psychoanalysis as a "bourgeois" science by both contemporaries and also historians of the period, the new evidence about the Experimental Criminology Department, along with Ferenczi's appointment and the institutionalization of psychoanalysis, illustrates the affinity between early twentieth-century Communism and psychoanalysis.[20] For both the social democratic and especially for the Communist leadership in 1918–19, the institutionalization of psychoanalysis into mainstream medicine was an affront to the Faculty of Hungarian Medicine, which had been notoriously hierarchical and categorically opposed to psychoanalytical approaches.[21] Psychology and sociology, which had been less castigated, also saw a rapid rise in their status.[22] Under Károlyi's social democratic government and particularly Kun's Communist rule, psychoanalysis, psychology, and sociology all received institutional support. Unlike in Bolshevik Russia, where psychoanalysis and experimental sociomedical theories were initially "tolerated as they could be justified as supportive of the revolution," in Hungary they were openly embraced.[23] In their aims to transform society, the Communist leadership granted a central role to the ideologies and approaches of these "new" disciplines.

The newfound importance attached to previously marginalized disciplines was a reflection of the genuine interest of the Hungarian Communist regime in facilitating cutting-edge scientific work.[24] The radical reforms, which brought fierce revulsion within existing and highly hierarchical establishments of universities, aimed to modernize and elevate Hungary's science and university education to be the best of the international elite.[25] Part of this aspiration included the integration of new "modern" areas of science that had been previously met with institutional and personal resistance. The Communists' empowerment of these new sciences was embraced by scientists regardless of their own political, often anti-Communist, beliefs.[26] Focusing on and investing purely in "scientific endeavors," reform-minded experts could minimize the "politicization" of their work and maneuver between different governments.[27] The case of Experimental Criminology Department attests to the foregrounding of science of authorities and individual scientists alike. Let's take a look at the work rules that were adopted at the Experimental Criminology Department.

> In order to regulate the freedom as well as to make the most use of each colleague's experience in the development of the Institute, the following guidelines should be respected:
> I. The sociologist and the medical doctor keep in mind that the given case should be treated *most thoroughly* with the *least amount delay* or wasting time.[28]
> II. The order and schedule of sociological and psychological examinations are determined based on the mutual agreement of sociologists and doctors who are assigned in the same group, and can be done at any time.
> III. The members of the Institute hold sessions on every Thursday at four o'clock with the heads of the sociologists and physicians presiding. The attendance is mandatory for all employees. The subjects of the sessions can be the following:
>   i. Motions for the work schedule and concerning the rules of organization
>   ii. Lectures
>   iii. Introductions of new ideas
>   iv. Critical and constructive comments[29]

The subsequent history of Communism in Eastern Europe should not prohibit us from taking these words at face value. The newly discovered documents concerning the Experimental Criminology Department, which contain the transcripts and reports of numerous lectures and seminars, overwhelmingly suggests that during its brief existence the Experimental Criminology Department was the home of intense scientific research and education.[30] If anything, the documents reveal an exciting working environment with intense intellectual labor. Consistent with employee work rules (ii) and (iii), we find well-known sociologists, psychologists, and psychoanalysts who lectured and talked about the latest international theories in the conceptualization of crime and the treatment of criminals.[31] It is important to remember that following five years of war, ongoing military action and severe economic hardship were present in Budapest in 1919, thus the establishment and operation of a scientific institution faced real and continuous difficulties. But even if the country was tormented socially, economically, and militarily, there were people, like Sándor Ferenczi and members of the Criminology Department, who believed that it was through continuing their medical and scientific work that they could most successfully survive the hard times and contribute to Hungary's stabilization. And it was such individuals who, often regardless of their personal political beliefs, earnestly believed in the scientific mission of Experimental Criminology Department and worked for it tirelessly during its existence.[32] The Experimental Criminology Department in many ways embodied Ferenczi's vision of a new justice system that would rely on psychoanalysis in order to protect society and reintegrate the offenders. In doing so, it created a unique experiment, albeit a brief one, where psychoanalysis was integrated into official approaches to the justice system.[33]

THE EXPERIMENTAL CRIMINOLOGY DEPARTMENT

Among the surviving documents of the close to three thousand cases that the Experimental Criminology Department considered during its brief existence, the case of Gyula Fekete provides some of the most illuminating insights into the Communist approach toward sexuality.[34] The thirty-five-old day laborer was supplementing his income by offering sexual services to men of means in various cafés in Budapest. In his eagerness to expand his customer base, Fekete approached a man who, unfortunately for Fekete, turned out to be an undercover police officer, which ended his business adventure. It was not the first time that Fekete was caught for soliciting sexual services, and as a recidivist his case landed at the desk of the Experimental Criminology Department. His previous charges for Paragraph 241, "unnatural fornication," of the Hungarian penal code under the Austro-Hungarian monarchy described him as a sexual degenerate, a truant, and a disgrace of society. In the eyes of the law, Fekete was a criminal for engaging in "unnatural" sexual acts and soliciting his sexual services. Fekete's actions were considered signs of his congenital homosexuality, which, following Krafft-Ebing's earlier theories on homosexuality, forensic scientists associated with hereditary degeneracy. Fekete's sexual acts were seen as particularly deviant since he had tended to have sex with men in public places. Finally, soliciting his sexual services in exchange for money and living off the payments of other men instead of seeking gainful employment, from the law enforcement's perspective, made Fekete especially despicable and a danger to society. Having been caught more than once, he had been considered a recidivist and been given increasingly longer prison sentences up to the one-year maximum. In addition to a prison sentence, following his releases he was sent back to his hometown and banned from Budapest. Had Austria-Hungary not fallen apart, Fekete would have likely spent the rest of his life in and out of the criminal system labeled as a degenerate, sexual deviant who, thanks to his congenital shortcomings, was doomed to continue to break the law and pose a moral threat to his surroundings.

In contrast to what would have happened in both pre- and post-1919 settings, Fekete, whose file following his arrest was transferred to the Experimental Criminology Department, was not simply trialed and jailed, but received a comprehensive evaluation and subsequent treatment in order to be rehabilitated as a productive member of the Hungarian Soviet Republic. During the time he spent at the Experimental Criminology Department, Fekete was analyzed by experts, according to whom Fekete had been traumatized by his childhood, hurt by structural inequalities, and needed rehabilitation. His files, along with the surviving documents of the Experimental Criminology Department, reveal a radical approach not only to sexuality but also to the Hungarian Communist aims of social engineering.

Upon his arrival at the Experimental Criminology Department, Fekete was evaluated through an interdisciplinary inquiry that was used for the assessment of all suspects referred to the institute, regardless of their crime. Fekete, like every other suspect, was cross-examined by a sociologist and a medical psychologist who ensured that the actions of the suspects would be considered in a holistic way. Teaming up a sociologist and a psychologist was an effort to use the ideas and methods of these new sciences to treat criminals. Antal Neumann, one of the medical experts at the Experimental Criminology Department, in an article titled "The Role of Medical Psychologists in the Justice System" published in *Proletárjog*, the official Communist law journal, illuminates the specific logic behind paring a sociologist and psychologist: "Today, when we have understood the possibilities of our unconscious life, and the centrality of our unconscious acts in shaping our conscious self . . . it is no longer the criminal act that matters, rather the motives and personality of the person who committed it."[35] Consequently, the author opined, "the accused stands in front of the sociologist as a social being, while in front of the psychologist as an individual."[36] Instead of the immediate details and milieu of the crime that authorities would have been concerned with prior to 1918, in the new era, the examinations were to focus on the intimate personal histories and contextualize them within the social history of the person's community.[37] Previously, moreover, the primary intention of a medical forensic expert—who had almost always been a psychiatrist—was to locate biological and innate abnormalities to explain criminal behavior. In contrast, within the Experimental Criminology Department's assessment, theories of sociology, psychology, and psychoanalysis were all integrated in order to assess each individual and map the potential ills and harms of their social and psychological histories. In so doing, the institute hoped to "accurately" evaluate people's motives and judge their actions. The assessment consisted of a comprehensive examination of the person's personal, familial, professional, and socioeconomic background. In addition to inquiries about people's socioeconomic background, there were questions on the development of personal relations and sexuality, including childhood memories, family relations, personal relationships with friends and colleagues, and also romantic love and sexuality. The following is the questionnaire and basic instructions that the staff of the Criminology Department used to assess people whose cases were transferred from the Communist courts.

Environmental/Background Case Study [Környezettanulmány][38]
I.
1. Questions concerning the father, mother, grandparents, siblings:
   Has any of them had a history of neurosis, suicide, alcoholism, drug addiction, abnormality in their character, eccentricity, criminality, or being a genius?
2. Questions about the circumstances of the suspect's birth and childhood:
   Was he/she born "normally"? At the expected time? Which child was he/she? How old were his/her parents at his/her birth? Were his or her parents drunk at the moment of conception? Did he/she have any childhood diseases especially spasmodic, jittering ones? Whose milk did he/she have and for how long?
3. Physical and emotional disorders in childhood:
   Gigantism or dwarfism, rickets, hydrocephalus . . . bedwetting at

night, excessive shyness, initial criminal activities, stealing, lying, torturing of animals, alcoholism, excessive fantasizing, who did he/she sleep with, for how long? What kind of relationship did he/she have with his/her parents, siblings and friends?
4. The sketching of the early childhood milieu:
 The parents' relationship toward each other and to their child: excessive rigor, excessive love; the intelligence of the parents, social and economic background; the child's disposition to humor, when did he/she start walking, speaking? Did he live in a village or in a big town?
5. Primary schooling:
 Where, how did he/she study? How many times did he/she change his/her schools, why?
 How many years of schooling does he or she have? How did he/she behave with his/her teachers and with his classmates? In what subjects was her/she particularly strong or weak at?
6. The time of first sexual feelings:
 When? early—late; for women, the time of their first period; physical abnormalities; noticeable paleness, obesity, persistent headaches
 Emotional abnormalities: changes in personality/character, general nervousness, introverted, aggression, masturbation, propensity for sin, signs of neurosis
7. Questions regarding adolescence/puberty:
 Economic, social circumstances: question, reasons of choosing a profession, evolution of his/her personal/love/sexual life; alcoholism, criminality, intellect, books, knowledge, social life, work life, discipline; worldview/political, religious, social, conflicts with his/her environment, physical health, emotional problems, separation from parents' influence/environment, attempts of suicide, vagrancy, etc.
8. From adulthood to the present:
 The expressions of his/her instincts: sexuality, circumstances of marriage, abnormalities, unjustified outbreaks of temper;
 Intellectual capabilities: his/her knowledge base, interests;
 Emotional life: likes, dislikes, within and outside of the family, noticeable mood swings; neurosis, suicide, lues and other sexually transmitted disease, alcoholism, drug addiction, criminality, eccentricity, or being a genius, character[39]

>   Circumstantial factors: standard of living, food, personal achievements in terms of socioeconomic status; with women, the number of pregnancy, number of birth, and number of abortions
>
> II
>
>   The immediate milieu of the crime . . .⁴⁰

A closer look at the questionnaire makes it clear that the novel approach of the Communists toward understanding and treating criminals did not mean abandoning the belief in the biological roots of crime. Questions about the mental and physical health of parents, for instance, underscore how the Communist approach also supposed a link between criminal behavior and biological abnormalities, which they were certain, just like their counterparts of the liberal Austro-Hungarian era, could be detected through "scientific" examination. In accordance with the transnationally accepted criminal discourse and practice of the day, the questionnaire thus opened with the medical family history, in order to determine the presence of assumed biologically inherited traits such as neurosis, suicide, and alcoholism, which would indicate that the suspect had been biologically predisposed to criminal behavior.[41] Additionally, throughout the questionnaire, we find questions that bear the marks of connecting crime to innate and biological attributes. For instance, inquiries on physical abnormalities and alcoholism both confirm how the new Communist regime continued to rely on biological determinism when assessing crime. What recent research on the relationship between Communism and eugenics has revealed in other East-Central European countries was also true in the Hungarian setting: Communist ideas could comfortably coexist with eugenic beliefs in hereditary and biological traits.[42] It was not only the class and political enemies of socialism who were denied membership in the Hungarian Soviet Republic. It was also people who were seen as biologically unfit to serve the Hungarian and international cause of the proletariat. Those deemed mentally ill, suffering from a severe case of "degeneracy" and unable to live self-sufficiently, were to be placed in institutional care.[43] From the very top of the leadership down to the level of professional experts at the Experimental Criminology Department, Hungarian Communists embraced Social Darwinism and eugenic ideas about the need to protect the health of the Hungarian nation. In their plan to bring about socialism, weeding out the eugenically unqualified was part of the Communist plan.

But in the case of the great majority of people, who were deemed biologically "normal," as in the case of Gyula Fekete and "sexually abnormals" more generally, the Experimental Criminology Department was granted freedom to assess and to configure the most fitting approach to rehabilitate the individual.[44] "Criminal psychology and sociology had proven that in the majority of cases, criminals have no biological abnormalities."[45] The incorporation of psychology and sociology meant it was the psychological and sociological factors that came to weigh the heaviest in the assessment of individuals. By being grounded in psychological theories, the majority of questions on the Experimental Criminology Department's questionnaire represent a break from biological theories of crime. And this is where the novel approach of the Experimental Criminology Department most visibly manifests itself. Instead of looking at hereditary origins, the intent of the medical team was to uncover the evolution of the emotional histories of the accused in order to map the mental and emotional traumas and conflicts that could have caused criminal behavior. Unlike approaches that looked for a somatic, physiological explanation for "abnormal" and criminal behavior, the experts at the Experimental Criminology Department assigned crucial importance to the examination of psychological behavior and the emotional and sexual histories of the subjects. Sigmund Freud's idea of assigning meaning to behavior was taken to heart.[46] Following the lead of Freud and Sándor Ferenczi's Budapest Psychoanalytical School, the experts considered the psychological motives behind people's criminal (or abnormal) behavior as the only way to truly understand their actions. While Ferenczi's exact relationship to the department is unclear, his influence on the department is unmistakable. In the eyes of the medical experts of the Communist regime, criminal behavior could serve as a mere symptom of underlying psychological disorder(s). More specifically, the "abnormal" or criminal behavior of a person, regardless of his or her age, was seen as a manifestation of early developmental problems, most often resulting from traumatic experiences within the family.[47] For that reason, questions on the questionnaire about emotional disorders in childhood, early childhood milieu, and primary school experience (questions 3–5) all aimed to detect those moments in the suspect's early life that indicated instances and ruptures when he or she diverged from what was understood as the "appropriate" and "normal" path. Instead of seeing it as innate and biologically predetermined, crime was seen as the consequence of "improper" personality development. Whereas prewar European practices wanted to isolate, medicalize, and treat individuals for diverging from normative behavior as "sick," the Experimental Criminology Department's approach focused on identifying the root of abnormal practices. Rather than *individuals*, it was *practices* that were "sick" or at fault for causing nonnormative behavior. And such an interpretation could open the possibility not just to "forgive" and reintegrate people into society but also for the complete remaking of individuals.

The socioeconomic background of suspects was also given an important consideration. As a number of questions on the questionnaire reveal, such as those pertaining to the suspects' standard of living, food, achieved success within the person's socioeconomic status, and of course their profession, the Criminology Department assigned great significance to people's background. While psychologists examined the conscious and subconscious emotional worlds of the accused, sociologists studied their physical and social environments. As Fekete's case study illustrates, the experts assigned a pivotal role to people's environment both in their understanding of a person's sexuality and in their evaluation of the person's (criminal) acts. Together, the sociologist and the psychologist were responsible for evaluating the degree to which people's socioeconomic environment contributed to a person's emotional being and, consequently, to the given criminal act. Unlike the Revolutionary Tribunals, most of which operated and practiced justice along political and class affiliations, the records of the Experimental Criminology Department do not contain evidence of using political beliefs and socioeconomic background as "sufficient" evidence of people's crimes.[48] To the contrary, evidence suggests that the Experimental Criminology Department's experts actively avoided having to use political or class affiliation as scientific evidence. However, while people were not punished for their anti-Communist beliefs and capitalist and bourgeois backgrounds, when the suspects came from the "materially exploited lower classes," their class background was always a mitigating factor in the assessment of their crime and usually led to a more lenient punishment.[49]

Intrinsically connected to the Experimental Criminology Department's psychosocial approach was the systematic examination of the sexual feelings and sexual history of the accused. Psychoanalysis in particular ascribed a fundamental role to sexual history as a reflection of people's character development. Questions ranging from the time of first sexual feelings (question 6) to the detailed history of people's sexual life (question 7), which encompassed both physical and emotional relationships, reflected the significance that the experts of the Experimental Criminology Department assigned to sexual experience. The experts studied if, when, and how exactly the suspects exhibited "abnormal" sexual and emotional behavior, which they connected to the working of the unconscious, which they believed regulated human behavior.[50] Along the lines of psychoanalytical views, nonnormative sexual behavior was understood not as a symptom of degeneration, but rather as the manifestation of the incomplete or abnormal development of an individual's natural sexual drives. The quest was to locate the point of departure from "normal" development.

Like everyone else, Gyula Fekete was cross-examined along the lines of the structured questionnaire. We learn about his immediate family:

> His father, who is 75 years old, is an alcoholic, rough and impatient character. The suspect's mother only married him because of the parental pressure. . . . They never lived a happy family life, his father mauled his mother and would even kick her. . . . His mother gave birth 9 times, 6 of them are still alive today, three children died in their childhood.[51]

This was followed by a character analysis of the siblings and some additional family members. Moving on to Fekete's early childhood, we learn about his physical and emotional struggles as a child and, thanks to Fekete's father, about the abusive milieu of the Fekete family:

> he was too timorous as a child, was afraid to stay by himself, and so he slept with his mother, and when he became older he slept on a couch next to his mother's bed. He was very scared of his father, since he was a rude man who would hit him often for no reason. His siblings did not like him and chased and teased him constantly.[52]

Eventually, we are presented with the analysis of Fekete's first sexual encounter and sexual awakening:

> He was 13 years old, when he watched how a female servant was having sex with a young man. She was a pretty girl. Fekete told the girl that she had to also have sex with him, otherwise he would tell everyone about the man the girl had sex with. The girl gave in and within a few days Fekete had his first sexual encounter with her, which was repeated a couple of times. Soon the girl became ill and moved to another place in the countryside. Around the same time Fekete saw another boy masturbating, which he also tried. And since he found it pleasurable and he had no girl acquaintances, he continued to masturbate.[53]

Soon we learn about Fekete's first homosexual encounter:

> There was a civil servant who rented a room at the house where Fekete was staying. He invited Fekete to his room and asked him to suck his

penis. Initially, Fekete was apprehensive, but since the clerk paid him some money he ended up doing what he was asked to do. He sucked the semen drops, and then washed his mouth. A few days later the clerk invited Fekete to his room again. He lay down and had Fekete lay on top of him and they would suck each other's penis until ejaculation.... The man lived at the house approximately for a year and the "relationship" [sic] between him and Fekete continued until the men left.⁵⁴

And for the rest of the case study, we get a detailed description of Fekete's sexual history, which included both men and women. He moved to Budapest when he was still in his teens and soon found himself among homosexual men, often of high stature as well as soldiers and military officials.⁵⁵ He was caught a number of times by the police and always sent back to his hometown in the countryside where he could never stay more than six months, so he would go back to Budapest. The last time, on May 26, 1919, he made an offer to a stranger who ended up being the secret policeman who turned Fekete in to the district headquarters of the red guards. He could not account for the motive of his action; by his own account, he was led by his sick inclination.

These surviving records provide a window into a forgotten history of queer existence in Budapest. Budapest was a hub for queer sexual activity, and men who desired men could count on finding them in the city's known queer-friendly meeting places: baths, certain squares, the City Park, and restaurants, like Hungaria, where Gyula Fekete mingled with men of high stature. Taken at face value, Fekete's case study suggests that homosexuality was not limited by class or profession. Fekete's admission of having sexual relationships with high-ranking military officers and also socializing with them in semipublic places is a testimony to the existence of homosexual subcultures that even reached the military. At the same time, without actual voices like Fekete's, it is difficult to ascertain how men who had sex and loved other men thought of themselves. Fekete's quoted statement, according to which his sexual life was "driven by sick inclination," suggests that by the late 1910s the medicalized discourse of homosexuality and conceptualizing homosexuality as an illness was embraced by some homosexual men even in the lower classes. Alternatively, or simultaneously, it could also mean that homosexual and queer men believed that framing their sexual behavior in negative medical language could potentially help in mitigating their punishments.

Turning to the medical opinion on Fekete's case, the last surviving document in his file begins to provide insights into Hungarian Communist ideas about sex and sexual abnormalities. The medical opinion explains Fekete's "abnormal" homosexual behavior as "acquired and situational" and on the whole as a result of his personal psychological development.

> His father was a drunkard, and F suffered a head injury at the age of 7. His schooling was sporadic and he could not write or read properly. His knowledge base is quite limited. . . . He is aware of his limitations and in fact, he tends to over exaggerate them.
>
> As for the motivations for his perversion, he gave various reasons during his examination. In part this was due to him being in a psychologically agitated state and also, him not knowing what would help his release.
>
> His genitals are well developed along with the secondary sexual marks. It is likely that he was coerced by an older man during his younger years. In fact, he received money for his perversion during his younger years when he was in all respect "*non compos.*"[56] Later, due to his mental weakness, using his sexual services as a means to earn money became standard. Which is also understandable considering without any money and being mentally weak he could not have gone to women. [In other words, he was too poor to buy a prostitute or marry a woman.]
>
> Although he is aware of the criminality of perversion, in terms of his criminal offense he has to be considered *non-compos*. Without any medical attendance there is no expected improvement.[57]

From the detailed descriptions of his parents to his upbringing and encounters with men, the medical opinion focuses on Fekete's personal history. Rather than trying to fit him into a medical category or pathological type, the experts focus on the specific and individualized (psychological) reasons why he became homosexual. The experts do not label him as a criminal, nor do they label him as a homosexual. Instead, they conceptualize his (abnormal) sexuality as a result of his troubled psychological development and disadvantaged socioeconomic history. Stressing the effects of early childhood experiences and their role in developing homosexuality, moreover, reveals not only the integration of socioeconomic and psychological factors but also the influence of psychoanalytical explanations. The influence of psychoanalysis is embedded in the ways in which experts analyzed Fekete's emotional motivations and their origins and, ultimately, aimed to "get to the suspect's unconscious."[58] The psychology expert stressed how the early childhood development of Fekete deviated from "normal" childhood, which in turn helped to explain some of his "abnormal" sexual behavior later in life. Just as significant was the experts' reliance on socioeconomic and class backgrounds. As they stated in their opinion, it was the economic hardships that Fekete had constantly struggled with throughout his life that served as the most important "causal" factor of his homosexuality. Ascribing nonnormative sexuality, and particularly homosexuality, to one's socioeconomic situation was a distinct feature that set the Experimental Criminology Department's approach apart from both the pre–World War I era and the interwar years.

As situational as the medical opinion makes Fekete's sexuality, the Communists, similar to the previous liberal regime, believed that there were some "authentic" homosexuals and thus also some "inauthentic" ones.[59] Yet, as the case of Fekete demonstrates, in cases where they thought innate biological homosexuality was not present, the experts argued that homo- and nonnormative sexuality was the result of environmental and psychological factors. In the majority of cases, where there was "evidence" suggesting acquired homosexuality, the Criminology Department could prescribe therapy in order to "heal" and reintegrate people as heterosexuals. Such was the case with Fekete, whose concluding medical opinion stated, "with medical therapy the suspect could 'heal' [i.e., become heterosexual]."[60] Mirroring the teachings of Freud and Ferenczi, the Criminology Department granted unprecedented power to "talk therapy" and to tending to people's psyche.[61] Believing that through proper psychological help, a suspect could become normal (heterosexual), the experts psychosociologized sexuality rather than medicalizing it. To reiterate, sexuality was not necessarily a pathological, innate biological issue, as the dominant medical discourses of the day (and of the interwar period) claimed, instead the Experimental Criminology Department understood it as both social (shaped by one's physical, social, and cultural environment) and individual (unique to a given person based on his or her experiences). This in turn suggested that, in most instances, homosexuality was treatable using psychological treatment and social interventions. The shift in the conceptualization of sexuality, on the one hand, explains how consensual homosexuality and other nonnormative sexualities could go unpunished. On the other hand, the novel conceptualization of the Experimental Criminology Department opened the possibility of reintegration to society. This was precisely the intent of the Communist leadership and the driving force behind the establishment of the Criminology Department. Instead of locking up people for abnormal sexual activities, the Communist justice system offered an alternative: by providing emotional and psychological assistance as well as work, people charged with sexual crimes could be "healed" and reintegrated into society.⁶² As the official legal journal of the Communists declared, the mission of the department was to "reform and focus on prevention instead of giving out barbaric punishments."⁶³ In cases where psychological help would not be enough, people would be placed in a *gyógyintézet*, literally a "healing institution" (as opposed to medical institution), specifically designed for criminals.

SEX AND THE HUNGARIAN SOVIET REPUBLIC

So how did the approaches of Experimental Criminal Department fit within the ideas of Hungarian Communists about nonnormative sexuality and more generally the Hungarian Soviet Republic's approaches to sex? The evidence is limited, but there are solid clues that suggest that the Communists imagined a society where sexuality would have been no longer a taboo, people cohabited based on love, men and women were equal, and female and male prostitution vanished. The experience of World War I in terms of the mass mobilization of men, wartime sexual activities, and prolonged homosocial environments was no doubt important in shaping the Communist ideas. One of the first laws the Communists intended to pass was the secularization of marriage and liberalization of divorce laws. The age of consent for marriage was lowered from eighteen to sixteen years for men and from sixteen to fourteen years for women.⁶⁴ In accordance with Bolshevik ideology, the new marriage law was only meant to be transitory, "as a step in building socialism," where the institution of marriage would become obsolete as free unions between equals would take its place.⁶⁵ As Zoltán Rónai, the commissar of justice, noted in the Communist daily, "of course this [marriage law] is only temporary, a transition towards the law of the emerging socialist society. The closer we get to the economic and intellectual emancipation of women, the faster the legal institution of marriage will lose its significance."⁶⁶ Until socialism was reached, Hungarian Communists looked to the Bolshevik Code on Marriage, the Family, and Guardianship of 1918 and, in a radical move, made marriage a civil institution based on individual rights and equality between men and women.⁶⁷ Divorce could be granted based on the request of either of the spouses. In a stroke of a pen, these changes swept away the historical power of the churches and the patriarchal basis of marriage. No longer needing the blessings of the church, individuals were granted unprecedented agency to decide whom they wanted to marry and if and when they wanted to divorce and potentially remarry. These were radical ideas for most Hungarians, especially in the rural areas, where religious norms reigned. As a result of these Communist policies, in peasant communities across Hungary, the Communists in Budapest were seen as not only preachers of but also as practitioners of free love.[68]

To facilitate these sweeping changes required public discussions not just about marriage but also about sex and sexuality. Or rather, sex had to be talked about differently from how it had been talked about. What Michel Foucault poignantly observed about Western European societies from the seventeenth century onward resonated with Hungary: from the late nineteenth century, sex and sexuality became part of mainstream public discourse.[69] But discourses of sexuality were medicalized and moralizing, with an explicit intent of pointing out the dangers of having sex outside of the married bedroom. Thus, apart from the officially banned pornographic publications, sex was discussed first and foremost in the context of vice and deviance, namely, prostitution and venereal diseases.[70] Many of the Communists believed that it was time for a new approach.[71] Contrary to the prudish "bourgeois" norms, and against the "antiquated" teachings of the church, they believed sexuality had to be discussed in a way that, on the one hand, aided people's understanding of sexually transmitted diseases, while, on the other hand, allowed for a discussion that was free of shame and acknowledged some of the positive aspects of human sexuality. Instead of "anti-"sex education that centered around fear and intimidation about the potential dangers of untamed sexual passion, the new approach of *szexuális felvilágosítás* (literally meaning sexual enlightenment, adopted from the German *Sexual Aufklärung*) would aim to normalize sexuality.[72] Such ideas seemed to motivate George Lukács, who under the Kun regime served as the deputy people's commissar of education, in instituting a revolutionary sex education program in schools.[73] For all students above fourteen years old, sex education was to be a weekly phenomenon, where they would learn about and become comfortable with their own bodies and sexuality.[74] And while the initiative was short-lived, it nevertheless suggests that many Hungarian Communists believed that a novel approach to sexual discourse was an important endeavor in the larger Communist goal of transforming society. Promoting public discussion on sexual matters was crucial for promoting sexual health and curbing rates of venereal diseases, which during the war climbed to unprecedented levels.[75] In this regard, the Communists only aimed to find more successful ways than the previous political regimes to positively influence public behavior. What was more radical is the way in which Communists understood the potential of liberating discussions around sex. In some ways, concomitant to early Soviet approaches that utilized discourse around sex as a tool of popular mobilizing for bringing about socialism, the aim of normalizing talking about sex was seen by Hungarian Communists as an important tool for bolstering the Communist cause.[76] Many within the Communist Party believed that liberated discussions around sex could play a pivotal role in the process of secularizing the population and, not least, in lessening the power of parents over their children. In contrast to prevailing notions of limited, individualized, and private discussion about sexual matters, the idea of a more popular and public form of sex education was indeed a radical proposal.[77] In actuality, instituting mandatory sex education, along with the new marriage and divorce law, met serious local opposition especially in rural areas and stirred disagreements even within the Kun government. As in the case of Bolsheviks in Russia, there were competing ideas among Hungarian Communists on the precise function and role of sexuality in Communism.[78] And like during the 1920s in the Soviet Union, peasants were highly antagonistic toward the "Godless" Communist attempts to secularize and collectivize sexuality.

In terms of policies regulating sexuality, Hungarian Communists were far from advocating free love. Quite the contrary. Frances Bernstein and Dan Healey have argued that sexual enlightenment in Bolshevik and Soviet Russia became ultimately not about pleasure and sexual fulfillment but rather about a scientifically managed heterosexual reproductive monogamy for the collective.[79] This seemed to resonate with the aims of the Hungarian Communist leadership in 1919. Their stress on the importance of sex education and a healthy relationship to one's body went hand in hand with advocating monogamous relationships between two healthy adults as part of building socialism. The same marriage law that granted equal rights to men and women also proposed that marriage would be restricted to people who were deemed physically and mentally healthy.[80] As we already saw in the case of the Experimental Criminology Department, Hungarian Communists embraced eugenic ideas (both positive and negative) about the necessity to protect the future of Hungarian *faj* (akin to race, but more inclusive, which in the conceptualization of the Communist could include anyone who was culturally Hungarian, regardless of one's supposed biological/racial background).[81] In their vision, the foundation of socialist society was a healthy proletariat. Accordingly, the improvement and protection of the health of the Hungarian *faj* became the guiding principle behind the policies of the Hungarian Soviet Republic. On the one hand, by making marriage and remarrying easier, along with granting full rights to illegitimate children, the Communists encouraged the reproduction of healthy Hungarians. On the other hand, by making health a precondition of marriage, they actively discouraged the reproduction of people deemed unhealthy. Sexual health explicitly became a must if one intended to marry. Being diagnosed with a sexual illness prohibited a person (male or female) from marriage, and if the illness was transmitted to another, the person could also face criminal prosecution.[82] To facilitate the medical examination prior to marriage, the Communists planned to institutionalize universal premarital screening. Had they stayed in power, they would have done it fifteen years prior to the Nuremberg Laws (1935) in Nazi Germany and more than two decades prior to Marriage Law of 1941 that effectively established it in Hungary.

At the same time, Communists believed that most sexual deviants could be rehabilitated into the future Hungarian society. Shifting the blame away from the people who engaged in prostitution and queer sexual practices, the Communists' policy makers and jurists faulted capitalism and argued that nothing less than the transformation of society was necessary before male and female sexual deviancy could be extinguished. This did not mean that in the transitional period to socialism they would not address sexual deviants. Despite attempts by female sex workers to form their own union during the early days of the Soviet Republic, it was clear that there was to be no place for "members of the oldest profession" in the new Communist society. From a Communist perspective, female prostitution had been conceptualized as a harmful by-product of capitalism that similarly to marriage would cease to exist once society matured to socialism.[83] In the interim—basically during the existence of the Soviet Republic—women who sold their sexual services were seen as remnants of the old order and victims of parental negligence. As one report noted, "These unfortunate creatures all still live in the old ideology and believe—as in the previous system—that they could only get prosperity, bread, nice clothes if they sell themselves."[84] Prostitution wasn't just seen as a vestige of the bourgeois moral order. It was also seen as a public health risk. Considered a root cause of sexually transmitted diseases, the Communists stepped up the policing and prosecution of female prostitution. However, unlike previous political systems that also persecuted female prostitution, the Communists believed in the reeducation and ultimately the rehabilitation of women as productive members of society. "It is the aim of the new social order that even those [female prostitutes] who used to live according to the old capitalist mindset get used to and learn that the communist society respects the working hands above all things and that prosperity can only be achieved through work."[85] As gravely concerned as they were about the health risk that female prostitution posed, the Communists genuinely believed that female prostitutes could be reintegrated into the future Communist society. Whereas previous and future political systems wrote off prostitutes as lost causes for society, the Communists were ready to invest in their reeducation.

When it came to male nonnormative sexual practices, the Communists seemed much less concerned. As long as men were free of sexually transmitted illnesses and engaged in consensual sexual activity, even if they sold their sexual services the Communists saw no reason to be concerned. Simply stated, the Communists seemed much less bothered about the potential short-term effects of male prostitution and male homosexuality. In the Communist view, male same-sex activity did not pose any significant danger to the new order. As *Proletárjog*, the official legal journal, declared, "Perversion between men needs not to be punished, unless it impedes on personal autonomy, because this act, from the perspective of the health of our '*faj*,' poses no danger for the public. In this case, we are faced with nature's aberration, which from the perspective of *faj egészség* [*faj* health] makes no sense to criminalize."[86] In accordance with their international socialist and Communist counterparts, Hungarian Communists considered authentic homosexuality as an innate condition that instead of being punished should be tolerated. And while the short life of the Hungarian Soviet Republic disallowed the codification of a new criminal law, based on the surviving records it is clear that the Communists intended to decriminalize consensual male homosexuality two years earlier than when homosexuality would be dropped from the Soviet criminal code.[87] Thus, legally speaking, the Communists went further to protect male homosexuals than any of the political regimes pre- and also post-1919 until the decriminalization of homosexuality in 1961.

In contrast to male homosexuality, which received both legal and sociomedical attention, there is no surviving evidence to suggest that there was any discussion—legislative, public health, or sociomedical—that concerned female homosexuality. In terms of their lack of attention to female homosexuality, the silence within Communists' publications on sex between women was in part due to the fact that female homosexuality had not been criminalized in the previous Hungarian criminal code. Consequently, since the Communist law was to continue the previous legal precedent, there was no need for any discussions. That there had been no ongoing criminal investigations of female homosexuals on the basis of their sexual behavior also explains why we found no discussion of female homosexuality in the cases of the Experimental Criminology Department. But the silence about female homosexuality was also an effect of the Communists' assumption that female homosexuality and female homosexuals were insignificant in terms of the threat they posed for public (sexual) health and, thanks to their low numbers, to the reproductive capabilities of the Hungarian Soviet Republic. A look at the Communist approach to female prostitution makes it apparent that the tolerance of female homosexuals had much more to do with their supposed inconsequentiality than a genuine acknowledgment of their inherent biological (homo)sexual drive. It also demonstrates that while the Communists granted formal equality between the sexes, when it came to policing sexuality, like their pre-1918 counterparts, they continued to apply a double standard.

That the Communists prioritized the policing of female sexuality over male sexuality, including homosexuality, was not new, nor were the arguments on behalf of decriminalization of consensual homosexuality. What was new in the Communist approach was the degree to which they thought to protect consensual male homosexuality as well as how they dismissed the effects of male prostitution. "At any rate, if a man prostitutes himself, from the perspective of society this has nowhere near the dangerous consequences than if a woman does it."[88] There are no contemporary records that provide a more comprehensive explanation behind why the Communists thought male prostitution posed far less danger; a few reasons were likely. Sex between men did not preclude healthy children with a woman. Amidst the upheaval of the war and prisoner-of-war camp life, the separation of men and women across the home and war fronts made sex between men less problematic than between female prostitutes and men. From a public health perspective, it was assumed (wrongly) that sexual diseases would be much more likely to be transmitted and spread via female rather than male prostitution. Consequently, female prostitutes, by exposing men—current, potential, and future fathers—to sexually transmitted diseases endangered not only the men themselves, but also the family and, ultimately, the future of Hungarian society. In contrast, sex between men, in the eyes of the Communist authorities, did not require punishment because the act itself did not endanger the biological health of the society. From an ideological perspective, despite being exploited by men, female prostitutes' work was considered non- and unproductive. Men's sex work was not seen as full-time work. Instead of referring to them as "male prostitutes," the reference to "men who prostitute themselves" suggests that despite selling sex, men could presumably still preform additional "productive" work. More leniency toward male nonnormative sexuality aside, as the conclusion will demonstrate, official approaches to homosexuality and more generally nonnormative sexualities were far from inconsistent with the approaches of the Experimental

Criminology Department. And in the long run, nor were they necessarily promising for queer men and women.

CONCLUSION

This chapter argued that the work of the Experimental Criminology Department of the Hungarian Soviet Republic represents a radically different approach to sexuality. It was an approach that centered on a psychosocial analysis and the examination of suspects' personal and sexual histories. Thus, rather than focusing on a given crime and its circumstances or motives, the experts of the Experimental Criminology Department looked to the "background study" and the intimate personal histories of individuals. This was a method and perspective that had not been the case previously, nor would it be after the brief existence of the Communist regime. The thorough examination of the suspect's family history and the consideration of the emotional and sexual feelings of individuals attest to the centrality that sexuality, psyche, and socioeconomic circumstance played in both the assessment of crime and the treatment of suspects. Having incorporated ideas from psychoanalytic, psychological, and sociological theories, experts considered same-sex sexuality and nonnormative sexuality more generally to be primarily "situational." Importantly, akin to most psychoanalysts, the Communists also believed that there were "authentic" and biologically innate homosexuals. When a case was deemed to involve an "authentic" homosexual, the Communists planned to protect them, as long as they were productive members of society who engaged in consensual sexual activities and did not spread sexually transmitted illnesses. But apart from those deemed "nature's aberrations," sexuality was considered fluid and not innate. The opinions of the Criminology Department experts reveal how, in their medical approaches to sexuality, experts regarded and explained sexual crimes and nonnormative sexualities as symptoms of unresolved traumas from people's pasts. Consequently, nonheterosexuality or nonnormative sexuality was overwhelmingly conceptualized neither as an innate condition nor necessarily as an immoral or criminal act. Implicit in this conceptualization was the belief that since sexuality was "situational," sexuality could be changed and abnormal sexuality could be "healed." There were three reasons why such a distinctive approach came about.

First, the Experimental Criminology Department's conceptualization and treatment of nonnormative sexuality was intimately tied to the Hungarian Communist leadership's aim to radically reform society and the belief that people were malleable. (Its fate was also tied to the Communists. As soon as the Communists were driven out, the department was dismantled.) The ultimate goal of the Communist leadership was to create a socialist society and, thus, confidence in the malleability of human beings was essential. Hungarian Communists aspired to transform Hungarian subjects, even unruly ones, into Communist citizens. Looking at the trajectory of Communist politics, these ideas and approaches foreshadow the practices of Communist parties across Europe during the coming decades. The intent of building socialism and creating Communist subjects that would come to characterize the Soviet Union and eventually China and the Eastern Bloc during the 1950s was already present during the Hungarian Soviet Republic in 1919.[89] As this chapter demonstrates, ideas around sexuality embodied this Communist vision. Echoing Communist authorities' aspiration to transform people into Communist subjects, the experts of the Experimental Criminology Department believed that the majority of "sexual deviants" could and should be rehabilitated into a heteronormative lifestyle.

Second, the presence of novel Communist principles within the justice system was instrumental in making environmental factors solely responsible for sexuality, which ultimately enabled homosexuality to go unpunished. If we place the study of nonnormative sexuality within the non–politically charged ordinary crime cases of the Hungarian Soviet Republic, we gain significant insights. The records of the Experimental Criminology Department, and particularly the case study of Gyula Fekete considered in this chapter, bring to light a principle of the Communist justice system that stood in contrast to the liberal justice system of the Austro-Hungarian monarchy and the future courts of the conservative Horthy regime. Specifically, unlike any other justice systems, during the brief Communist rule in 1919, nonnormative sexuality and even violent sexual crimes could go unpunished as long as they did not directly pose a threat to or endanger the "Dictatorship of the Proletariat." Underpinned by the Communist legal philosophy, "even if a deed might fall under a paragraph of the existing criminal code, but it poses no danger to the Dictatorship of the Proletariat, the person who committed the deed cannot be considered guilty of a crime," the Experimental Criminology Department did not have to consider punishment for people with queer sexualities.[90] The same logic that was used to allow the prosecution of anyone deemed an "enemy of the Dictatorship of the Proletariat" on its flipside allowed formerly criminalized behaviors to go unpunished.

Third was the institutionalization of formerly marginalized sciences—a process closely linked to both Communist ideas of justice and of reforming society. In part because of the genuine interest of the Communist regime in establishing cutting-edge scientific work and partly because of the strong connections between Communists and the new sciences, the emerging professions of sociology, psychology, and psychoanalysis could endorse the Communist vision. The Communist leadership embraced these three sciences and bestowed upon them a central place in the justice system. These new sciences became the means to enact scientific judgment and the primary tools for the successful reintegration of those who were deemed curable. Together, these aspects of the Hungarian Communist rule contributed to and facilitated the different approach of the Experimental Criminology Department, which was radical in its understanding and treatment of nonnormative sexuality, not only within the Hungarian context, but also in the larger international scene.

It is crucial to consider the implications of the Communist approach to sexuality for homosexuals and for nonnormative sexuality more generally. The Communist approach was radical, not only in its rehabilitative and social approach to nonnormative sexual crimes, but also because of the allowance it made for Communist subjects to be not strictly heteronormative. According to the Communists, engaging in consensual same-sex activity did not necessarily harm the health of the Hungarian society. As long as they were otherwise productive workers and were healthy (free of sexually transmitted illnesses), homosexual and queer men for the first time could legally fulfill their sexual desires. However, such recognition and protection of homosexuality would have been short-lived. Paradoxically, the same ideological underpinnings that in the short run fostered a more lenient approach toward those that previous political systems regarded as sexual deviants, in the long run would have imposed much greater penalties for nonnormative behavior. Even though the Communists believed that there were innate homosexuals and queers who could not be rehabilitated at the time, over the course of turning Hungary into a socialist society, according to Communists' logic, the socioeconomic and personal circumstances that enabled homosexuality for the majority of people would wither away. Believing that sexuality for the great majority was fluid and that it was the wrong social and socioeconomic environment along with unfortunate family dynamics that *caused* homo- (and nonnormative) sexuality was a short respite for homosexuals. Such an understanding of sexuality, although it offered a temporary relief as it made homosexuality not punishable, in the long run likely would have prohibited the idea not only of "respectable" homosexuality but the very notion of homo- and nonnormative sexuality. This, as chapter 6 will demonstrate, would have had disastrous implications for homosexual men and lesbians once the Communists got a second chance. Following the (re)establishment of Communist dictatorship after World War II, homo- and nonnormative sexuality would become not simply antithetical to socialism but also a threat to national security that warranted harsh punishment.

Ironically, in the long run, in terms of queer sexualities, and most certainly "respectable" homosexuality, the Communist approach thus would have offered much less space than both the previous and subsequent political systems. The liberal justice system during the Austro-Hungarian monarchy, even though it criminalized male homosexuality, in practice was actually quite lenient. By only punishing public homosexual behaviors that involved other criminal activities or disturbed the public, the liberal justice system not only offered a considerable space for urban homosexuals but at times even active protection. Similarly, the next two chapters will demonstrate how, following of the collapse of the Hungarian Soviet Republic and the consolidation of power in the hands of Admiral Horthy, the interwar political system, in its treatment of homosexuality, adopted the prewar liberal practices. Not only did the conservative authoritarian political regime continue the practice of the pre-1914 authorities, but by its self-imposed silence around homosexuality, it in fact facilitated a growing homosexual subculture.

CHAPTER FOUR

Peepholes and "Sprouts": A Lesbian Scandal

The organization of counterrevolutionary forces called the Whites was already taking place during the days of the Hungarian Soviet Republic (March 21–August 1, 1919).[1] The militant anti-Communist forces gathered around Admiral Miklós Horthy in the southeastern Hungarian town of Szeged. Upon the withdrawal of Romanian forces in November of 1919, the counterrevolutionary army entered Budapest.[2] Even before it arrived in the capital, the so-called White Terror began. The retaliation against Communists and their alleged sympathizers was incredibly brutal. Without formal trials or any attempt of judiciary intervention, counterrevolutionary forces targeted Communists, socialists, leftist intellectuals, and Jews. The exact number of people who were executed or imprisoned is still debated. Recent scholarship estimates that between one and two thousand people were killed, while tens of thousands were imprisoned.[3] In addition, tens of thousands of people fled the country to escape retaliation.[4] Amidst the brutal attacks and executions, which Admiral Horthy and his close echelon endorsed, the counterrevolutionary forces established tight control over the country. Horthy's personal connection to, and the personal involvement of, many of his political leaders in the White Terror set the tone for the establishment of a repressive conservative political system.

By March 1920, the new Hungarian political order was in place. Hungary became a constitutional monarchy without a king. Admiral Miklós Horthy, as regent, assumed many of the king's privileges, which he made use of until his abdication of power in 1944.[5] Between 1920 and 1944, Hungary was a rightist country with authoritarian measures, ruled by a competing old conservative right and a new radical right. Three months following the consolidation of Horthy's power, Hungary's new "mutilated" borders were granted legality by the Western powers. The signing of the Treaty of Trianon in June 1920 brought about the greatest disaster in Hungary's history since it's defeat by the Ottomans in 1526.⁶ It was a political, economic, and social catastrophe that affected all Hungarians. The country lost 67 percent of its pre–World War I territory and 53 percent of its prewar population and a significant share of its industry. Even without counting the non-Hungarian population, it is estimated that about 3.2 million ethnic Hungarians found themselves stranded outside of Hungary's new borders. Hungary entered World War I as part of one of the prominent continental powers and finished it as one of the most battered. At the onset of the war, Hungary was one of the most ethnically diverse countries in Europe; following the Treaty of Trianon, it became one of the most, if not the most, homogenous. In 1914, Hungarians comprised barely 50 percent of the population of approximately 20.8 million. In contrast, in 1920 less than 10 percent of Hungary's population, which now stood at 7.9 million, was non-Hungarian.⁷ The new, conservative leadership had no choice but to sign the treaty, but by doing so it also renounced its validity from the onset. The renegotiation and revision of the treaty became a foundational goal of the Horthy regime.

In sharp contrast to any of the previous political regimes since 1867, the counterrevolutionary forces under the aegis of Admiral Horthy established their rule based on two principles: Christian nationalism and irredentism.⁸ In contrast to the immoderate liberal times prior to the Great War and the "horrifying deeds" of the social democrats and the Communists in 1918–19, Horthy and his conservative government wanted the new Hungary to be firmly grounded in conservative ideology. The ideology was simple: "anti-Bolshevism, historical values, positive Christianity, order, authority, and opposition to Jewish influence."⁹ The conservative political vision, which since the late nineteenth century has emphasized that Hungary's future lay in the strengthening of (ethnic and religious) purity, became the rule of the land. Now in power, conservative politicians also made sure that they would face no political opposition. In addition to the retaliation against the Communists and their sympathizers, the institution of censorship in the media, art, and politics and the passing the first postwar anti-Jewish law in Europe were the hallmarks of the Horthy regime during its initial years of the 1920s.¹⁰ Unlike neighboring Czechoslovakia, France, England, and Weimar Germany, which all held multiple political discourses during the 1920s, conservative nationalism went unchallenged in Hungary. Having ousted or annihilated proponents of Communism, social democracy, and liberalism, the Hungarian elite was united in their belief in Christian conservatism and irredentism.¹¹

But what did such extreme nationalism and Christian governance mean for the understanding and treatment of nonnormative sexualities? How would the view of homosexuals change from their former status as symbols of Hungary's modernity during the Austro-Hungarian monarchy and as malleable Communist subjects who could be rehabilitated as productive heterosexual members of the Hungarian Communist society? The present and the following chapter will aim to answer these questions, albeit using very different case studies. While the next chapter will provide a comprehensive overview of the legal prosecution of homosexuality between the two world wars, this chapter examines a single case, interwar Hungary's most notorious sex scandal, which implicated that the country's leading women were homosexuals. The names of Oscar Wilde, Radclyffe Hall, or even Prince Eulenburg need no introduction; their place for historians of sexuality is forever secured. In this chapter, however, I turn to an individual of international reputation and contemporary prominence whose scandal of female homosexuality—despite its high political stakes, juicy bedroom details, long line of distinguished witnesses, and extensive press coverage—was until recently largely forgotten.

Why, despite being a national sensation at the time, the charges of female homosexuality did not damage Hungary's two most prominent conservative women of the interwar period is one of the main questions this chapter sets out to answer. In so doing, it reveals the reasons for a continuing tolerance of certain queer sexualities under the conservative Horthy regime. An analysis of the highly charged political circumstances of the scandal aside, the "shocking" details of the trial also offer a rare view of contemporary conceptualizations of female (homo)sexuality. The chapter examines how newspapers, legal and medical experts, the protagonists, and their servants expressed and negotiated their understandings of female same-sex sexuality. Placing servant voices center stage within concurrent legal and medical discourses, the chapter illuminates a strong presence of a vernacular, highly gender-, class-, and geographically specific understanding of homosexuality. And while there were clear continuities in the conceptualization of homosexuality from the pre-1919 era and there were urban-rural differences in the language of female homosexuality, I argue that neither country folk nor sophisticated urbanites could imagine female homosexuality outside of a strictly heteronormative framework.

THE PARTICIPANTS AND THE OUTBREAK OF THE SCANDAL

The political and social implications at stake in the divorce trial of Count Rafael Zichy (1877–1944) and his wife, Eduardina Pallavicini (1877–1964), along with the fame of the implicated third person, Cécile Tormay (1875–1937), made a scandal inevitable. Cécile Tormay and Eduardina Pallavicini were two of the most influential, politically active, and publicly visible women of the reigning conservative regime during the interwar period. In the eyes of many people in the interwar years, Cécile Tormay represented the "Great Saving Soul" of "Mutilated Hungary." For most Hungarians as well as foreigners, she was known as the writer of *Bujdosó könyv*, or *An Outlaw's Diary*, an internationally acclaimed book about the evils of Communism.[12] Her work was alleged to be an account of Tormay's personal experience of the horrors of the so-called Aster Revolution following World War I and the subsequent short-lived Soviet Republic of Hungary.[13] While writing in the first person, the book spoke on behalf the Hungarian gentry and privileged classes whose former existence and power was wiped away by the Communists. It also represented those across the class spectrum who blamed Hungary's as well as their own decline on the Jewish community. Considering the prevailing fears of the ruling classes across Europe about the spread of the "Communist Menace," it is easy to see why Tormay's book was so well received not only in Hungary but abroad as well.[14]

Tormay, who had been recognized as a literary writer for *Emberek a kövek közt* (People between the stones; 1911) and *Régi ház* (Old house; 1915), with *An Outlaw's Diary*, changed genres and also became political. Much more like her male counterparts and perhaps even more so than most of them, in *An Outlaw's Diary*, Tormay was openly expressive of her political views. The book begins with the fall of the Austro-Hungarian monarchy and the establishment of an independent Hungary. The following is a short excerpt where Tormay describes her feelings, while standing in front of the Hungarian parliament when the establishment of the Hungarian Democratic Republic was announced publicly on November 16, 1918:

> It is to our everlasting shame that no single Hungarian rose to choke these words. In the Hall of Hungary's parliament Lenin's agent could unfurl at his ease the flag of Bolshevism, could blow the clarion of social revolution and announce the advent of a world revolution, while outside, in Parliament Square, Lovászi and Bokányi, accompanied by Jászi [all three were Jewish], informed the people that the National Council had proclaimed the Republic. On the staircase Károlyi made another oration. Down in the square, Landler, Weltler, Preusz and other Jews glorified the Republic—there was not a single Hungarian among them. That was the secret of the whole revolution. Above: the mask, Michael Károlyi; below: the foreign race has proclaimed its mastery.[15]

As the excerpt reveals, Tormay despised both the social democratic government and especially the subsequent Communist rule as alien to Hungary and to "true" Hungarians. In fact, no excerpt can sufficiently reflect the extent to which the two volumes of *An Outlaw's Diary* are full of blatant anti-Semitic, antiliberal, and anti-Communist views. Tormay's rants against Jews and Communists and the detailed description of their horrible misdeeds were accompanied by her narration of an emerging Hungarian resistance and the sacrifices made to reclaim Hungary for Christianity. The story of counterrevolutionary forces as the true representatives and heroic saviors of the nation assured that once Admiral Horthy and the conservative forces secured control over the country, the book would gain literary success and its writer cultural and political prominence. With the restoration of conservative power in Hungary in 1920, Tormay's celebrity was unsurpassed. She remained one of the most visible and intellectually recognized Hungarian female figures who also achieved considerable international attention until her death in 1937. In 1923, the year of the scandal, Tormay became the editor

Figure 5. Photograph of Cécile Tormay. Image courtesy of Magyar Tudományos Akadémia Könyvtár és Információs Központ Kézirattár és Régi Könyvek Gyűjteménye.

of the most important conservative literary journal, *Napkelet* (Eastern Sunrise), which she directed until the end of her life. Neither before nor since would a woman lead a conservative journal in Hungary. In addition, Tormay was nominated for the Nobel Prize in literature twice (1936 and 1937), and following the death of Marie Curie in 1934, she was selected for membership in the Committee of Intellectual Cooperation of the League of Nations.[16]

The other woman involved in the scandal, Eduardina Pallavicini, was from a distinguished aristocratic family that had considerable influence over Hungary's internal affairs. Eduardina's father, Eduard Pallavicini, was the director of the Hungarian General Credit Bank, vice president of the National Hungarian Economic Association, and a member of the upper house of the Hungarian parliament. Eduardina Pallavicini had a high public profile; among other things she was the president of the National Association of Hungarian Catholic Women's Associations and the deputy chair of the Hungarian Red Cross.[17] Along with Tormay she was one of the founders of the Hungarian Literary Society, which was established in 1922 in order to combat "soul destroying literature" and was instrumental in the launching of the society's literary journal, *Napkelet*, which was to counter the influence of *Nyugat* (West), the most prominent Hungarian liberal literary journal.

In addition, she was active in the Hungarian literary world in her own right, as an editor, a translator, and a writer. Pallavicini's translated works included the life of Michelangelo (1926) and the selected works of Mussolini (1927). She was the managing editor of the *Catholic Women's Journal* (1926–33) and later the editor in chief of *Women and Girls* (1933–44), a monthly publication. Her own publications appeared in *Napkelet*, and she was also the coauthor of a number of books. In sum, Pallavicini was not only a member an established powerful family, but as a leader of social and cultural organizations, she possessed considerable clout in Hungary's political affairs. Pallavicini, similar to Cécile Tormay, belonged to Horthy's closest political and cultural circle and along with Tormay used her various positions to bolster Horthy's conservative, Catholic, and irredentist political stance.

Pallavicini's husband, Count Rafael Zichy, who initiated the divorce and the ensuing scandal, came from one of the noblest Hungarian families, which had been prominent in Hungarian history since the thirteenth century. Members of his family had served in the highest economic, political, and cultural positions. Considering his family's long-standing cultural, economic, and political influence, Rafael Zichy, who was himself a member of the upper house of the parliament, possessed a visible presence among Hungary's well-to-do.[18] The potential divorce of a Pallavicini and a Zichy represented not only an estrangement between two of Hungary's most powerful aristocratic families but also an open infringement of one of the central tenants of the conservative Horthy regime: the sacrosanct status of marriage. Thus, though news of bickering aristocrats was not a novelty for Hungarians, the divorce case ignited both serious power struggles among the political elite and provided endless entertainment to people on the streets of Budapest and its surroundings.

It was the sexual nature of Count Zichy's 1923 divorce petition that ensured both its immediate notoriety and its scandalous place in the public eye for years. Reports on and about homosexuals, or the "knights of sick love" as some contemporaries referred to men who had sex with other men, had been present in the press since the late nineteenth century. With the explosion of the penny press and daily newspapers, there were more opportunities for sensational stories as well as semiofficial reports about same-sex affairs, such as the trials of Oscar Wilde. However, Hungary had not yet had a high-profile case or scandal about homosexuality, much less lesbianism. Only one earlier incident held a similar potential for scandal—the homosexual escapades of Colonel Alfred Redl, the chief of Austria-Hungary's military counterintelligence, who after being exposed as a double agent committed suicide in 1913. Allegedly, it was Redl's homosexuality that Russian military intelligence could exploit, and by having blackmailed him, they acquired critical classified information about the Habsburg monarchy's military for over a decade.[19] Following his death, Redl's treason was soon exposed. However, for the most part, the Habsburg monarch, Franz Joseph I (1848–1916), thanks in large part to the military hierarchy, was able to strategically prevent the more intimate details of the Redl scandal from going public. Thus, for instance, most Hungarian newspapers made no mention of his homosexuality.[20] For that reason, the case of Count Zichy's divorce suit showed much more resemblance to the Eulenburg scandal and the inability of Kaiser Wilhelm II to limit public knowledge of Eulenburg's homosexual relationship with Moltke. The head of the Hungarian state, Admiral Horthy, must have been as eager as the kaiser and the monarch had been previously to prevent a scandal. After all, it was his beloved friend and ally, "the greatest Hungarian woman," Cécile Tormay, who was implicated. Horthy's failure to do so in large part was due to the political and social consequences of the ten turbulent years that separated the Redl and Zichy events. In particular, two factors contributed to more intense public coverage of the Zichy-Tormay case: a less controlled professional press who found ways to publish news of the trial and the triple impetus that Zichy, Tormay, and Pallavicini (the accused lover of Tormay) collectively represented as three of Hungary's most prominent and politically powerful families and individuals. Paradoxically, the tight censorship that was initially imposed on the media following the fall of the Hungarian Soviet Republic during the initial days of the new conservative regime by 1923 had given way to less government oversight. As long as the press refrained from publishing articles that "affronted the Regent [Horthy]'s or the parliament's authority or jeopardized the country's foreign policy, security and external relations," the press could enjoy considerable freedom.[21] Since the divorce and consequent libel case threatened none of these explicitly, the press could find a way to publish even the most salacious details of the case. That all of the people involved were prominent and well-known public figures, moreover, secured the attention of the press and guaranteed an attentive readership.

THE PUBLIC REVERBERATIONS OF THE SCANDAL

On October 30, 1923, Count Zichy filed for divorce based on charges of *termèszetellenes*, an "unnatural" relationship between his wife and Cécile Tormay.[22] Although sex between women was not criminalized in the Hungarian penal code, it was legitimate grounds for divorce under the civil code.[23] Citing an illicit homosexual relationship as the cause for divorce most likely would have generated wide interest no matter who was involved. The passionate and visible role these women played in the (re)building of Christian and conservative Hungary, however, caused the case to become a national sensation overnight. Screaming headlines such as "Today the Court Begins Hearing Juicy Episodes of the Most Scandalous Aristocratic Legal Suit in Decades" appeared in papers across Hungary.[24] The fact that neither the divorce suit nor the subsequent libel case was open to the public posed little obstacle; all major newspapers, even conservative ones, provided extensive commentary on the scandalous details that leaked out of the courtroom. As one report from the daily newspaper the *8 Órai Újság* (8 O'clock News) stated, "Despite the fact the libel case is tried behind closed doors, it can be safely stated that likely on a daily basis the entire city is informed about the testimonials and statements. We all know that typewritten reports are circulating around city, which were even distributed in the parliament."[25] And the news of the "Bickering Aristocrats," as many of the headlines initially labeled the case, did not stop at the outskirts of the capital. The rumors about the case rapidly spread across the country.

Contemplating the likelihood of a sexual relationship between Tormay and the Countess Zichy would have certainly intrigued contemporaries. The count's sexual affairs with other women and a longtime love affair with one woman in particular appeared to many observers as his ulterior motive for instigating the scandal. "The origins of this entire case began years ago when Count Zichy was introduced to a woman whose beauty was renowned in the capital. Until then the Count and the Countess had no marital problems," stated the *Pesti Hírlap* (Gazette of Pest), and for most papers and likely for most readers, Count Zichy's longtime affair with a famously beautiful woman seemed a believable justification for seeking divorce.[26] To learn about the infidelity of male aristocrats and their occasional attempts to divorce their wives for younger women would have not been new nor necessarily interesting for contemporaries.[27] This is evident even in the papers' generic and matter-of-fact references to the count's infidelity. Statements such as "The Count grew cold towards his wife ten years ago, and for years he had been thinking about a divorce in order to marry someone else" were regurgitated in most papers.[28] In contrast, hearing about an allegedly sexual relationship between two well-known women certainly would have offered a fresh topic for scandal-hungry readers. The report of another daily paper *Esti Kurir* (Evening Courier) attests to the complete fascination that readers had for the case, "In the past few decades there has seldom been a criminal suit in Hungary that has generated such great interest as the case of Count Zichy Rafael and his fellow culprits."[29] And while the papers had to carefully play with words when discussing female, and especially respectable female, sexuality, to the horror or delight of many people the case of Countess Zichy and Tormay introduced a new and scintillating topic. Regardless of their disbelief, horror, or fascination about the possibility of a homosexual relationship between the two women, contemporaries were consumed by the news.

It was not simply the women's status and visible public life that made their potential romantic relationship interesting; it was their specific status as two of the most influential women who spearheaded the new conservative social order that added to the case's sensationalism. In the post–World War I era, contemplating the actual nature of the relationship between the two women was the first public opportunity for a recognition and discussion of female homosexuality.[30] The heyday of liberal times in Hungary were over, but the establishment of a conservative regime did not mean that either the ideas or the experience of the flapper and modern womanhood escaped Hungary.[31] An increased visibility of women taking on public roles was apparent especially in Budapest.[32] Tormay and Countess Zichy, who would have certainly not thought of themselves as representatives of the New Woman, were in many ways beneficiaries of female emancipation.[33] Both women were involved in various social and cultural organizations and were much more politically active than women of previous generations. At the same time, in spite of the "modern" ways these two women lived (e.g., one was single, and both took public roles), Tormay's and the countess's politics and gender views were unapologetically conservative. Therefore, instead of the New Woman, they were much more representative of a kind of "conservative modernity."[34] That is, Tormay and Pallavicini took on modern ways to pursue their conservative political goals: through leading various national organizations, they actively propagated the reinstitutionalization of traditional gender order and the redomestication of women.

The two women founded the National Association of Hungarian Women (MANSz) in 1918 and took on organizing Hungarian women to fight Communism. Tormay's *An Outlaw's Diary*, which by the time of the trial made her a legendary icon, dedicates significant space to document how she and her dear friend Baroness Eduardina Pallavicini founded MANSz and organized female resistance during the days of the Hungarian Soviet Republic. According to these two women, women in Hungary until World War I enjoyed a sheltered and fulfilling life in the home. The destruction of war and especially of Communist rule ended that tranquility. But in contrast to the war and the subsequent democratic and Communist regimes that mobilized women outside of the home, in the conservative counterrevolution, Hungarian women were asked to fight from within their home.

> Our country has never suffered greater distress than now, and, as we sat there, we all knew that the women would respond to our call and would sow the seed of the counter-revolution. Not at meetings, not in the market-place, but in their homes, in the souls of their men exhausted by the hardships of war, men who are down-hearted to-day but who, to-morrow, will not dare to give the lie to (fail) women who believe in their courage.[35]

Unlike Tormay, who was unmarried and had a visible public profile, and even unlike Pallavicini, who even though she was married lived a very active public life, Hungarian women were supposed help to reclaim Christian Hungary first and foremost by providing moral support to their husbands at home. Similar to right-wing and conservative women's movements elsewhere of the interwar period, under the leadership of Tormay, MANSz prescribed the role of women in society as complementing their husbands in the private domestic sphere, supporting patriotism, and above all, living by Christian principles.[36] Tormay and Pallavicini's vision came to shape not only the Hungarian national women's movement, and its auxiliary organizations, which by 1921 had over a half million members, but also the official rhetoric on womanhood throughout the interwar period.[37]

No wonder then that Count Zichy's charges of a homosexual relationship between Tormay and Countess Zichy created such scandal. There were many people who would have felt outrage about the women's hypocrisy. In their view, that conservative leaders who campaigned against sexual decadence and immorality would be having an illicit sexual affair made the Hungarian proverb "he preaches water but drinks wine" more than fitting. But there were probably many more people who, because of the two women's conservative views, would have been hesitant to believe anything that would have implicated them. So, even though it was precisely the accusation of female homosexual relationship between Tormay and Countess Zichy that caused sensation, their very honored position within society also made many question the validity of such claims. Not least, when it came to (the denial of) sexual and romantic liaisons, contemporaries were much more likely to believe the words of upper-class women than their male counterparts. Nevertheless, even if most people would have sided with the women, the divorce and subsequent libel suit provided a platform for a broad spectrum of Hungarian society to reflect on female homosexuality outside of the professional fields of law and medicine.

THE LEGAL SUITS

Count Zichy appealed for divorce on two legal points. First, based on Paragraph 76 of the Marriage Law of 1894, which explicitly stated that divorce could be requested by someone whose spouse committed adultery, or *természet elleni fajtalanság* (unnatural fornication). While the Hungarian criminal code only criminalized sex between men, according to the marriage law sex between two women could still serve as grounds for divorce. This was a direct accusation that required proof. Count Zichy had no firsthand knowledge about his wife's alleged sexual relationship with Cécile Tormay, but in his case, he alleged that the servants did. Second, the appeal of the count invoked clauses *a* and *c* of Paragraph 80 of the marriage law and claimed that his wife's behavior and actions had intentionally violated their marriage contract and also that she had led an immoral life. In order to support those claims, the count testified that his wife was "cold, unkind, derisive and exhibited a desire to be authoritarian. In front of their children, servants, and strangers she strove to undermine his authority and respect; disagreed with and countered his intentions in regards to the education of their children."[38] According to the count, this often led to his public humiliation. He also stated that Countess Zichy was a lavish spender. Finally, he stated that instead of the "normal physical relations" of a married couple, the countess demanded "mutual *digital manipulation* combined with masturbation like coitus."[39] This assertion was made to illustrate that Countess Zichy preferred hands to penises, with the implication that she could only have learned this from being sexually active with another woman. In this case, the preference of sexual position and a particular way of receiving pleasure was supposed to prove the countess's homosexuality.

The subsequent divorce and libel cases that stretched between 1923 and 1927 were both tried in three different courts and involved nearly one hundred witnesses ranging from the cream of the Hungarian aristocratic elite and medical doctors to numerous servants. Each of the three courts denied Count Zichy's appeal for divorce.[40] Despite the fact that Eduardina Pallavicini did not want to divorce her husband and they remained married until the count's death in 1944, in 1924 Cécile Tormay and the countess sued the count and four servants for lying under oath and libel.[41] The criminal libel suit was also tried in every court possible; in each decision the count and the servants were found guilty, and in 1927 all were sentenced to jail.[42] Almost a hundred years later, the only materials that survived—from what would have been no doubt a colossal documentation trail—are the decisions and sentencing of the courts and the testimonials of the servants. None of the minutes, expert opinions, nor testimonials of prominent witnesses survived. With that in mind, the rest of the chapter is less concerned with a comprehensive reconstruction of the trials.[43] Instead, it aims to reconstruct contemporary discourses on female homosexuality.

THE SERVANT VOICES: LANGUAGE, SOCIAL GEOGRAPHIES, AND THE "SHE-MAN"

The servants' testimony became central in the divorce suit because the granting of divorce eventually hinged on whether or not there had been a sexual relationship between Countess Zichy and Cécile Tormay. And as the only eyewitnesses willing to testify, the servants became the key players in the divorce trial. The male and female servants of the Zichys and of Cécile Tormay—József Walter, Ferencné Poszlik, and Mária Zeisler—were far from shy about describing the personal relationship of the two women.[44] Unlike notorious male homosexual scandals like the Cleveland Street affair (1889–90) or the Oscar Wilde trial (1895), where servants were looked on as participants in rough trade and male prostitution and whose testimonials were accordingly suspect, the servants in the Zichy case were initially seen as the "bearers of the truth" and key witnesses.[45] Although ultimately, they were discredited and sentenced to prison for libel. Whether or not we believe in the authenticity of their claims or question the motives for their depositions, the surviving servant testimonials offer a rare opportunity to recover how people serving the rich thought of female homosexuality. The ways in which the servants used language to explain the relationship between the two women is particularly useful in shedding light on how female homosexuality was conceptualized outside of the medical, legal, and urban worlds during the 1920s. Focusing on both "how" and "what" the servants said will be equally valuable.

What exactly did the servants say they saw, heard, knew, and thought?[46] According to the courts' interpretation, the two women, although acquainted for almost a decade, became very close following the Communist revolution. Cécile Tormay would spend extensive time at the Zichy residence in Budapest as well as at the family estate on the countryside. It was during this period that the servants started gossiping about the "unnatural" closeness of the countess and Tormay. This information eventually found its way to the ears of Count Rafael Zichy, who by 1922, welcomed any news that could help him get a divorce. Having been informed about the strangely intimate relationship between his wife and Cécile Tormay, the count ordered the porter and longtime servant József Walter to spy on the women. When this effort did not lead to the results he had anticipated, the count arranged to have holes drilled through the ceilings of the countess's bedroom, their daughter's bedroom, and the guest bedroom. Moreover, to make sure nothing would be missed, the count arranged for microphones—a cutting-edge technology at the time—to be installed in the chandeliers. The porter spent months spying on the women through the peepholes and recorded his observations. These, along with the observations of the rest of the servants, stood at the heart of the divorce case and were the primary subject of the criminal suit.

The servants presented a gender-based understanding of sexuality where both the sexuality of women and their relationship were conceived within a framework of traditional gender norms. Regardless of the women's biological sex and self-representation as women, in the accounts of the servants, Tormay assumes a masculine role, and the two women are depicted as a "heterosexual" couple. The countess appears as the feminine, passive, and subservient female. No matter her intellectual abilities and powerful personality, both of which come through clearly in the trial records and letters to her husband, her marital status and role as the mother of five assured that the countess was presented as feminine. Cécile Tormay, who had never married, did not have children, worked as an independent writer, and led a traditionally "male" life, was portrayed as a masculine Casanova and a male rival to the count. The servants' stories, which they claimed either to have seen or heard through the "servant network," painted Tormay as having a notorious appetite for and success with women, including making physical advances to female maids and having other intimate relationships with women of high social classes. Aside from proposing that Tormay's behavior was known to the social elite, the testimonials also depict Tormay as a considerable threat to the husbands of her various love interests. The cook, József Walter, in particular, portrayed Tormay as a lady's man, who successfully infiltrated aristocratic families and even prompted the men of these families to take action. From Walter's sworn testimony, we learn that

> a while back Tormay wanted to creep into the D. family as well, while Count D. was not around. When Count D. arrived back from Budapest to the train station, he rode in his coach home. And on the way he asked his coachman whether there was any news or any guests at the estate. The coachman told him that Tormay was visiting to which the Count ordered him to turn around went back to the station and telephoned home and told the maid the following: "report to the Countess that Tormay must leave immediately, because if I see her there I will shoot her."[47]

In addition, we learn that while Walter served at the house of D.T., D.T.'s mother, Gy. B., received regular visits from Tormay. The cook went on to tell the servants at the Zichy palace that the friendship of Tormay and Gy. B. became so intimate and private that when Tormay was present, only one maid was allowed to enter Gy. B.'s room, where the women were spending time. And even then, only when they specifically requested food. The son of Gy. B. did not like the intimacy of that friendship. The cook believed the son had suspected something, because when he saw or heard of Tormay's arrival he exclaimed in front of the servants, "Tormay is coming, watch out or she will fuck somebody!"[48] The cook's recollections did not end there. Since the rest of Gy. B.'s family had become aware of Tormay's nature and wanted to stop her visits, the family arranged a game while Tormay was present. Tormay's prize was veiled, and when she pulled off the veil, she found an electric toy monkey, which was playing with its penis. On the foot of the monkey there was an engraved sentence that read, "the monkey plays with its pe . . . [sic] the way Tormay plays with her own pe. . . . [sic]." According to the cook, after this, Tormay stopped visiting Gy. B.'s.[49]

As outlandish as these stories must have seemed to contemporaries, the servants' conceptualization of the nature of Tormay and Countess Zichy's relationship, and why it seemed "unnatural," actually adhered to strictly normative ideas. The servants perceived Tormay's behavior as unnatural because she was transgressing gender norms and acting like a man. It did not matter that Countess Zichy herself transgressed gender expectations; she, similar to Tormay, led an active public life and her intellect was known to be far superior to her husband's. According to people around her, she had a dominant personality, yet the servants constructed her as the fragile female and presented the women's relationship in a "heteronormative" framework. In so doing, the servants turned Tormay into the male figure. Or rather in the servant's imaginings, Tormay became more like a person of the "third sex," even if they were unaware of that designation found in the language and categories of sexologists.[50] The servants did blame the countess for her coldness toward the count. They pointed out some of her "odd" behaviors, such as making her daughter give up her bedroom, which was right next to the countess's, whenever Tormay stayed over. One could argue that they faulted her for not fulfilling her womanly responsibilities. Yet, the servants never demonized her sexuality, nor was her heterosexuality questioned. That the countess's sexuality was never questioned illustrates the protective shield that performing gender normativity, in this this case the "passive" female, could offer in same-sex relationships during the interwar years.[51]

It is not surprising then that the countess appears as the jealous wife or lover who cannot bear the sight of competition. As one of Tormay's maids recalled, "once I was present when a woman . . . on the phone was inquiring when she could see Tormay. The Countess was present and said to Tormay impetuously, 'I do not want you to see her' at that point Cécile Tormay took the Countess's hand and kissed it."[52] The same maid also told the notary that she had knowledge of the fact that Tormay had been frequently visited by Countess Vay, who was "well-known for her perverted inclinations."[53] According to the maid, Countess Zichy was jealous of Vay and did not allow Tormay to receive her or go to see her. However, on one occasion when Countess Vay came to see Tormay, Countess Zichy was also there, and a servant had to tell Vay that Tormay was not at home. Vay wanted to go into the salon to write a few lines for Tormay at which point Tormay locked the door from inside.[54]

THE CURIOUS APPEARANCE OF VAY, OR "D'ARTAGNAN"

The appearance of Sarolta (Charlotte) Vay (1859–1918) is interesting for a number of reasons. Sarolta, or rather Sándor (Alexander), as she referred to

Figure 6. Drawing of "Comtesses Sarolta Vay" by Wiener Tagblatt.
Image courtesy of the Welcome Collection.

herself, had been dead for years. This clearly would have been a blow to the authenticity of the maid's story! Nevertheless, the seemingly strategic mention of Vay and the reference to her "well-known perversion" is a testament to the extent to which Vay had become infamous in popular discourse by the 1920s. Vay, born female but raised as a boy by her eccentric aristocrat father, eventually assumed a male identity as Sándor (and D'Artagnan was his pen name).[55] He became a national sensation when he ran off with a woman, and they legally wed.[56] It is more than likely that the maid (along with the rest of the servants) had been informed and heard about Vay's scandalous divorce trial and, consequently, about the confusion around her/his biological sex.[57] Clearly, although many were literate, the servants would most likely not have read Richard von Krafft-Ebing's or Havelock Ellis's extensive studies on the sexuality of Vay. Their work described Vay as a congenital sexual invert and essentially as a prototypical lesbian.[58] Nevertheless, medical experts and sexologists aside, in understanding Vay's gender many people went along with Vay's self-identification as a man who until his death lived his life as part of the male gentry of the Austro-Hungarian monarchy.[59] Vay's story had even become part of popular culture, mostly thanks to Gyula Krúdy, the prolific writer and journalist who incorporated Vay into some of his novels such as *Hét bagoly* (1922), as well as writing some articles that specifically addressed Vay's eccentric life. According to Krúdy, there was a time "when even the sparrows on the Hungarian pea fields were talking about Vay."[60] The testimonial of the maid makes it clear that the servants had heard of Vay, and perhaps they (the ones that could read) might have even read either Vay's own writing or something about her by Gyula Krúdy.[61] Fabrication aside, the appearance of Vay in the maid's story suggests that by the 1920s ideas about nonnormative sexualities were circulating even in the broader popular culture.[62]

Conceptually speaking, the appearance of and particular reference to Vay points to certain fluidity of female masculinity. The Vay story certainly complicates the servants' portrayal of Tormay. In terms of gender representation, Vay, while referred to as a *she*, is presented as the pursuer and masculine subject. This is, in a sense, not surprising considering Vay's well-known male identification. However, apart from the Vay story, it is Tormay who is portrayed as being masculine, with the servants going out of their way to emphasize her strong masculine characteristics even vis-à-vis her male counterparts. Unlike in the portrayal of Tormay's relationship to the countess, in which Tormay appears as the sexual transgressor and as the antithesis of "ladylike" and "feminine" behavior, in the account of Tormay's relationship to Vay, the maid transforms Tormay into a "lady" and, thus, the pursued rather than the pursuer. Rather than seeing these different (re)presentations as contradictory, I would argue that they speak of early twentieth-century understanding of queer female gender and sexual expressions that were based in the combination of a premedicalized and presexualized view of female relations. The key to understanding the different gender representations of Tormay, whose physical appearance and clothing certainly did not transgress contemporary gender norms, is to look at the specific ways in which people perceived her in her intimate friendships and relationships. She was imagined as masculine when she was seen as being the one in charge, while she was represented as feminine when she was pursued and acted "ladylike." Thus, her perceived masculinity, and the understanding of female masculinity in 1920 Hungary, had much less to do with Tormay and women's physical appearance per se and much more to do with the particular *role* that a woman in a relationship was perceived to play. Consequently, at an age when most women, especially of the middle and upper class, conformed to dress codes of femininity, it was women's assertive personality, male-like confidence, and male-like conduct of their interrelationships with women and men that could be seen as threatening gender norms.

The servants' description of homosexuality illuminates the persistence of an older, premedicalized language to name and perhaps even conceptualize female same-sex desire and love. The following conversation, which allegedly took place between two maids, one of which was leaving the Zichy estate to work somewhere else, provides a window into the servants' understanding of female homosexuality.

> Maid S: Thank God that I can leave . . . because I wouldn't have tolerated what the Countess and Tormay were doing. Then K [the other maid] laughed at S tauntingly, and asked her what exactly it was that she would not have tolerated? Maid S: "that Tormay was such a woman who loved the Countess in a way like a man did."
>
> Then K asked again: "what do you mean?" To answer this S told K that Tormay was a *csira* [sprout] and that she knew this for certain. Then K asked what a *csira* was, because she had never heard of it.
>
> S told her that "the Countess and Tormay are living as husband and wife."[63]

Apart from her apparent distaste, it is maid S's use of the word *csira*, literally meaning sprout (a young plant growth such as a bud or shoot), to describe Tormay that is particularly intriguing and revealing. The word itself came from a regional dialect of Heves County, northeast of Budapest, and had been used to refer to a person who had both male and female sexual organs.[64] In fact, around 1900 we still find the word *csira* interchangeably used with the word "hermaphrodite." By 1910 the latter term became the exclusive word used not just in the medical but also increasingly in lay language to describe people (who would be labeled as intersexual today).[65] Consequently, the maid's use of the word *csira* is evidence of the persistence of an older, premedicalized language for expressing "abnormal" sexualities. Thinking about the literal meaning of the word "sprout," it seems reasonable to propose that the maid's language reflects a conceptualization of sexuality that was grounded in nature. What it also indicates is that during the 1920s, people living in rural areas, especially those who were illiterate or had no access to newspapers, had still not been exposed to medical and sexological terminologies. Furthermore, the fact that maid K had no idea what the word *csira* meant in the context of sexuality also points to the existence of regional and dialectical variation in the expressions associated with nonnormative sexualities still being present in the 1920s. Regional differences in the language used to express different sexualities would have been particularly apparent during the immediate post-Trianon years and throughout the 1920s, when ethnic Hungarians, often with very different local traditions, arrived from the territories of former Austria-Hungary to the new and significantly smaller Hungary. Finally, the conversation between the two maids offers a concrete example of how ideas about sexuality circulated between servants from different regions within the borders of pre-1918 Hungary—by word of mouth.

The maid's use of the expression *csira* also draws attention to the absence of the language, and one might add of the concept itself, of a female homosexuality that was not strictly based on a traditional gender model or on a physiological difference. Calling Tormay a "sprout" and saying she loved the countess "like a man" (along with the tendency of male servants and male members of the upper class to attribute a penis to Tormay) suggests that in order for the servants to conceptualize and articulate the "unnatural" sexual relationship between two women, one of them had to have a penis.[66] That is not to say that penetration was the only act that the servants would have considered sexual or "unnatural." Rather, by presenting the two women within a heteronormative—an active masculine and a passive feminine—framework, the servants made their assumed sexual relationship legible. The porter, the main witness who was in charge of peeping through the ceiling holes, for instance, recorded a number of "suspicious," read sexual, activities between Tormay and the countess that took place under the covers.[67] But often, when he was describing what he saw taking place between the two women, he would directly compare the actions of the women to those of a heterosexual couple. Though the porter himself never used the expression, he was describing female homosexuality or tribadism, which he understood *not* as a heterosexual relationship but as a "heterosexual-like" sexual encounter between two women. Statements such as "they [Tormay and the countess] were moving the ways in which a man and a woman would be moving" or "Tormay has a bigger dick than a male does" bring to light the limitations of the porter's and, more generally, of the servants' language and likely conceptual framework of nonnormative female sexuality.[68] This was the case not just for those who spent most of their time outside of the city, but also for those male servants who, having lived in Budapest, were at least familiar with vernacular expressions of male homosexuality. Regardless of the extent and differences of their exposure to nonnormative sexualities, the servants conceptualized and expressed Tormay's sexuality similarly—as a "she-man." Consequently, in as much Tormay could be seen as a *buzeráns* (homosexual), she was also portrayed as having male gender expressions as well as male body parts. Of course, one can speculate about whether the perception of Tormay as essentially a "she-man" had any validity. If she indeed had male sexual organs, the servants' portrayal becomes self-explanatory. If, on the other hand, we treat their depiction of Tormay as a conceptual tool, their inability to construct female homosexuality as something outside the heteronormative model becomes all the more apparent. Thus, unlike the medical and legal discourses on female same-sex sexuality that by the 1920s constructed at least a distinct vocabulary in order to express sexual desire between two women, the servants' understanding suggests that the "love that dared not to speak its name" actually had neither a name in everyday Hungarian nor a concept of its own.[69]

Based on the servants' testimonials, it seems that women and men of the upper classes responded to and dealt with Tormay's "perversity" differently. While the woman-Casanova, Tormay, agitated husbands and drew angry reactions, women were more understanding and accepting of Tormay's allegedly masculine characteristics and same-sex sexuality. The accounts of servants portray angry male relatives and give us a sense that it was men more generally who could not stomach Tormay and the countess's relationship. In contrast, women seemed to be more comfortable with nonnormative sexuality. A story from one of the servants underscores this point. He gives an account of a lunch that took place at the Zichy palace in the absence of Count Zichy. Explaining how "at a table during a family lunch one of the guests, Countess X, pointed to the chair of Count Zichy and said to Tormay: 'Cécile, sit here, this place actually should be yours.'" Thus, a servant interpreted Countess X's words as expressing her acceptance and in a sense respect for Tormay's place as head of the Zichy family.[70] Overall, the difficulty of making sense of same-sex sexuality between women outside of the heteronormative framework cut across class, gender, and even urban and rural divides. The dearth of language for expressing female homosexuality was not confined to the servants, a fact apparent in the contemporary news coverage of the case. Along with ordering the trials to be closed, the courts initially tried to limit what papers could report on the case.[71] Nevertheless, most papers were able to tell the gist of the story and made it clear that the authorities' intention of keeping the scandal off the streets was utterly unsuccessful. The censoring of intimate bedroom details aside, the newspaper coverage had a difficult time expressing female same-sex sexual desire and female homosexuality. Using "friendship" in quotation marks or expressions such as "the ink would not be able to handle the nature of the charges," the representation of female homosexuality remained vague, ambiguous, and, at times, even threatening. It is not necessarily that people of the time were unfamiliar with same-sex love and sex between women but that the language to express it and ideas of "lesbianism" and what exactly it entailed were, for many, unintelligible. This, as we will see, was also true for the courts and legal discourse more generally.

LEGAL BATTLES OVER DEFINING FEMALE HOMOSEXUALITY

The surviving Civil and Criminal Court records also offer a window into legal and medical discourses on female homosexuality in Hungary during the 1920s. The following description is from Count Zichy's legal petition for divorce that details how the alleged homosexual relationship developed between his wife and Tormay.

> The defendant [Countess Zichy], who according to herself is one of our country's most beautiful souls, and who cultivates great admiration for intellectual excellence, was undoubtedly fascinated by Cécile Tormay's literary talent, and even more so by her fame and far-reaching wonderful literary success, powerfully suggestive oratorical skills, organizational talents, and unquestionable prestige—which she enjoys mainly among women. This wonder and admiration was the instigator of further psychological processes. This admiration and amazement was requited by a kind friendship and in the pleasure, which is similar to the delight of a sower—who sees the springing of his sowing, but also to the pleasure of the conqueror, who sees enemies at his feet.[72]

It was Tormay's intellectual brilliance and charisma that initially enticed the countess. The account paints Countess Zichy as starstruck, while Tormay was the active pursuer. As the count's appeal goes on to explain, "This admiration, this veneration, this bowing before the preeminence of intellectual spiritual power is itself the passive component within the relationship of the two women."[73] For the count's legal team then, female homosexuality is a transformation from (a passive) intellectual and emotional admiration to physical devotion. "This spiritual devotion then gradually, or less gradually, skidded into the world of corporeality. And considering that even the most conventional contact between two women—counter to men's—is not without its physical moments, over time as the inhibitions gradually faded, the power of instincts grew and eventually came to prevail."[74] According to the count's appeal, considering the fact that women in their friendships were much more physically expressive than their male counterparts—that is, they kissed, hugged, and embraced each other as part of their friendship—once there were romantic feelings involved, a sexual relationship could come about more easily. It is when the emotional and spiritual connections had come to full bloom that female homosexuality "emerged."

The lower courts categorically refrained from taking a stand on what female homosexuality might—legally speaking—entail. So, in all three courts in the divorce suit, through extremely circuitous processes, every single accusation except *tribádia* (tribadism; the contemporary legal definition of female homosexuality) was dismissed.[75] If proven, it would have served as the only legitimate reason for granting a divorce. Consequently, not only the outcome of the divorce, but also of the subsequent criminal suit, rested on the substantiation of a sexual relationship between the two women. Every single one of the courts found the accusation of tribadism unsubstantiated. The lower courts in the divorce case did so by invoking the "sitting at the same table" principle.[76] The courts argued that because the count continued to dine with his wife even after he had been informed of her alleged sexual encounters with Cécile Tormay, he could no longer bring suit for past occurrences on "moral grounds." The sheer fact that the count did not halt his regular routine of eating with his wife, the court reasoned, proved that the charges of tribadism could not have been possible, because "having considered the personal character and social status of the plaintiff [Count Zichy], it is impossible he would have continued to keep up with his regular contact with his wife had she committed such a thing."[77] The verdict went on to state that it was "inconceivable" that a married partner who was "convinced of his partner's sexual misconducts" would have "continued to have the same regular contact with her unless he had forgiven her."[78] According to this contradictory reasoning, since the count did continue to dine with the countess, he had most certainly forgiven his wife for acts that had taken place. Either way, since Count Zichy continued to dine with his wife, the nature of the women's relationship was ruled irrelevant, and the possibility of divorce was gone. With this line of reasoning, the lower courts essentially refrained from taking a stand on what legally constituted tribadism. Without having to actually define it, the courts marshaled evidence to corroborate all the reasons why the countess and Tormay could not have been sexually involved. The reasons for the courts' reticence and difficulty in defining female homosexuality were likely twofold. The judges were either confused about how to define and interpret female sexual acts or they simply overlooked extramarital sex, even if it was homosexual and the perpetrator was a female, because of their reverence for domesticity and the necessity of upholding the sanctity of marriage.

It was only the highest court, the Royal Curia, which explicitly addressed sexuality and considered the implications of same-sex sexual encounters for women. In contrast to the opinion of the medical experts, who defined female homosexuality in a much broader and more inclusive way, according to the Curia *only* sexual acts could define a "perverse" (homosexual) relationship between women. The Curia, by going beyond the narrowest interpretation of male homosexuality under Paragraph 241 of the Hungarian penal code, resoundingly rejected medical opinions and declared that only absolute proof of sexual acts served as a legitimate reason for divorce. As stated by the Curia,

> The opinion of medical experts in which they argued that ... homosexual acts could manifest themselves in acts as simple as hugging, cannot be accepted in the legal decision of the divorce appeal, because such acts alone do not fulfil the conditions that would justify granting a divorce as stated in §76 of the Marriage Law. According to the Curia, *unnatural fornication* as a legitimate reason for divorce stated in §76 of the Marriage Law is only justified if one's *sexual instincts are satisfied* outside of marriage through unnatural [perverse], indecent, and immoral fornicating acts.[79]

Thus, unlike male perversion, which according to legal interpretations could encompass a variety of sexual acts that imitated "normal" (heterosexual) sexual acts, in this rather ambiguous ruling the Curia defined female sexuality in its most-narrow sense—equating it to penetrative sex. Furthermore, the Curia's statement that female homosexuality existed only "if one's sexual instincts are satisfied" must have been as intriguing for contemporaries as it is for a historian today. Would a proof of orgasm have been necessary to prove female homosexuality, and how could the courts determine that? Deciding that acting on one's same-sex desire was only definitive as long as it led to sexual satisfaction, the legal decision came to depend solely on the proof and verification of sexual (satisf)action between the countess and

Cécile Tormay. The burden of proof for this satisfaction lay on the servants' testimonials.

CLASS AND THE COURTS

The servants' position as low-status dependents assured that the courts' rulings, in both the divorce and subsequent libel case rejected the authenticity of their testimonials about an alleged "perverse" sexual relationship. Considering the prominent position of the upper social classes in interwar Hungary, it is not surprising that the denials of these high-status women, along with that of their enlisted aristocratic witnesses, seemed more credible than the reports of the servants.[80] To fully grasp the court's ruling and eventual dismissal of the servants' testimonials, however, we must remember the effects of Communist rule in which the proletariat and in general the under classes overnight gained the upper hand over their former employers and social superiors. The position of servants during the days of the Soviet Republic had potentially been particularly powerful as they could have, similar to their proletariat counterparts, claimed power over their noble or gentry employers. In actuality, this was most often not the case. The great majority of servants stayed loyal to their employers. Since they were often more religious than those they served, they shared with the nobility feelings of distrust toward Communists and, frequently, Jews.[81] Nevertheless, during the turmoil that followed World War I, servants became suspect and their loyalty questionable. Cécile Tormay in *An Outlaw's Diary* expresses the loss of trustworthiness in servants as a result of the "Dictatorship of the Proletariat." Describing the novel position of servants within the houses of their "no-longer possessors," she writes, "Class hatred has established spies and watchers in all the houses of Budapest: the secret agents of the new power are to be found in every house: they watch, blackmail, and report."[82] By painting the servants as untrustworthy and dangerous, Tormay foreshadowed the depiction of servants in *Édes Anna* (*Wonder Maid*), one of the most popular Hungarian novels of the interwar period.[83] But while Dezső Kosztolányi's *Édes Anna*, a tale about a servant girl who ends up killing her masters, also portrays the complexity of the master-servant relationship and their codependency, Tormay's representation of the situation of the servants remains much more black and white. According to her, servants were selfish, only cared about themselves, and if it benefited them, would have not hesitated to sell their souls to the devil. When the judges of the courts formed their opinion on the testimonials of the servants, it was Tormay's representation that the courts embraced; servants were out to take revenge on the higher classes.

Class bias becomes even more evident if we note that the courts did not stop at the consideration and rebuttal of the actual facts in the servants' testimonials. Rather, they went on to destroy the servants' overall credibility. According to the rulings, the subservient position of the servants made them not simply susceptible to outside influence (notably from Count Zichy and gossip), but it also tainted the servants' perception and even their eyesight. In the opinion of the judges, the disenfranchised position of the servants basically discredited the validity of their claims. The influence of class becomes even more blatant if we compare the courts' treatment of the servants with Count Zichy's. In spite of tearing his case apart, throwing his infidelity into his face, and trying him in Criminal Courts for defamation, the courts treated Count Zichy very differently than they did the servants. Zichy's social status and what that implied in terms of intelligence, consciousness, and credibility was never fundamentally challenged. He might be deemed selfish and written off as acting out of passion, but his words were never discredited as those of a lesser human being.[84] Consequently, while initially it was their intimate relationship and insight that made servants proxy for evidence, ultimately their unique position within the world of the elite also served as a vehicle to discredit them. Finally, the most explicit evidence of class-specific standards of the Hungarian justice system lay in the different degrees of punishment meted out for similar offenses. Even though the higher courts upheld the lengths of the punishment for the servants in the criminal libel suit, they significantly lowered the punishment of Count Zichy.[85] Initially, the Criminal Court sentenced the count to a year and a half in prison, then the Royal Court of Appeals lowered it to ten months in prison, and, subsequently, the highest court, the Royal Curia, lowered the count's sentence to only fourteen days in the lightest form of confinement.[86]

Having repudiated the credibility of servant testimonials, the courts had a clear mission to redeem and reinstate Hungary's two most important female patriots. In their verdict the judges made it unmistakably clear both how they perceived and how they wanted people to remember this scandalous legal suit.

> On one hand, there stands a person driven by an irresistible passion, who would not even hesitate or feel remorse for a committing crime and living an utterly selfish life. While, on the other hand, there are two intellectually and ethically high standing people who have been making important

contributions to the betterment of the public, whose ethical purity has not been the least bit overshadowed by this case.[87]

The courts' decisions constructed a black-and-white interpretation of an evil but noble man, Count Zichy, while simultaneously creating a vision of virtuous women, Cécile Tormay and Countess Zichy. Despite the fact that homosexuality was supposedly central to the outcome of the legal suits, in the end the courts successfully wrote nonnormative sexuality out of their rulings. In regard to the intimate relationship of the two women, including their nights spent together, the Criminal Court concluded that

> it was the most necessary and certainly most understandable and natural progression that in their common and passionate pursuit for public good, with such an extraordinary spiritual talent and leading such sophisticated lives these two women would increasingly become more intimate with each other in their private life.[88]

The court's interpretation of the relationship between the two women as an intimate friendship that was necessitated by their joint passion to rebuild Hungary basically excluded the possibility that any aspect of their relationship was sexual. As a result, the jurists did not have to consider the medical (or any other) perspective that could have offered a different interpretation. Testimonials by medical experts and the servants that could have stigmatized female friendship as tribadic were discarded. Instead, the court reaffirmed friendship between women as a pure and asexual form of romance. Unlike in the case of Radclyffe Hall's *The Well of Loneliness*, where the courts in condemning lesbianism explicitly acknowledged the existence of sexual relationships between women, the courts in Budapest refused to entertain the possibility of sexual intimacy between two respectable women. In presenting romantic female friendship above all as asexual, the courts ignored the forces of stigmatization of romantic female friendship that, as scholars in various contexts have shown, were, by the interwar years, internationally apparent.[89] With this decision the court also assured that the issue of female homosexuality would be recloseted in legal discourse. Not until World War II would female homosexuality again become subject of a legal discussion.

STRATEGIC DEPLOYMENT OF MEDICINE

While the courts eventually rejected the opinion of medical experts, the language used to describe (homo)sexuality and the involvement of the medical establishment throughout the case demonstrates the influence that medicine had in legal attempts to define sexuality by the 1920s. In the surviving references to medical opinions, we see the presence of both a biological view of homosexuality (that stressed the innateness of homosexuality) and psychological explanations that argued for its situational nature. The coexistence of biological and psychological explanations of homosexuality point to continuities in medical personnel as well as ideas from both the Austro-Hungarian era and the more recent Communist rule. Although the legal definition of homosexuality as a specific act was upheld (even if unintelligibly), it was clear that by the 1920s homosexuality could no longer be determined by a single physical act. Homosexuality had become something more than just sex between people of the same sex. The conceptualization of homosexuality became muddier and heavily reliant on contemporary sociomedical and psychological theories. And since there seemed to be no agreement among medical experts as to what specific evidence was necessary to determine "female homosexuality," both the plaintiff and respondent could deploy the crème de la crème of the medical establishment to prove their cases. Three of the most distinguished medical experts on sexuality testified as forensic experts on tribadism. Doctors Ignácz Fischer, Ödön Németh, and Gusztáv Oláh were internationally renowned professors, all received their education during the last two decades of the monarchy, traveled widely, and worked with some of the most influential psychiatrists and neurologists of the time, such as Jean-Martin Charcot in Paris (who among many others also tutored Sigmund Freud). Fischer was one of the early advocates of the decriminalization of homosexuality, and during the debate about homosexuality in the Hungarian national legal association in 1909, he made a passionate appeal on behalf of the respectable homosexual community. The presence of these experts on both sides of aisle makes it apparent that medical opinions were to play a central role in determining the outcome of the case.

The medicalization of sexuality and the contradictory understandings of female homosexuality were both apparent in the court proceedings. For instance, in the divorce trial, Countess Zichy and her lawyers, even as they denied all charges, felt a need to make the case that sexuality and sexual acts could not be seen as "rational and intentional deeds" and therefore did not classify as crimes against nature.[90] Then they went on to argue that tribadism could not be a legitimate reason for a divorce because "according to medical opinions tribadism is an unintentional and an impulsive act resulting from congenital brain or rather nerve malfunction, and to grant divorce the law required purposefulness."[91] In another similarly telling instance, the jury, assuming that there were physical signs of homosexuality (such as an enlarged labia or the growth of a beard), asked the husband whether during the time of his marriage he had noticed any abnormalities in the physique of his wife. Last but not least, the court in the divorce case pointed out in its ruling that "tribadism is an uncontainable instinct."[92] Again, the percolation of medical theories—however mutually contradictory—into legal discourse is legible on multiple registers.

Alongside medical approaches that stressed inborn and biological reasons for homosexuality, a careful reading of the sources also reveals the presence of discourses on sexuality that were based in psychological explanations. This is evident, not only in the medical opinions that the courts cite, but also in the ways in which the different courts themselves made their arguments to justify the "uncommonly close" friendship between the two women. For instance, in the divorce suit, the Royal Curia argued that it was understandable that Countess Zichy "would have developed an intimate relationship that was deeper than usual with her lady friend. . . . considering the fact that her husband had broken off his married life with her, [and that she was] devoid of marital love and intimacy."[93] Arguing that intimacy, both psychical and emotional, was important and a basic component of human relations, the Curia applied a psychological explanation for why and how two women could have become so close. Countess Zichy, who had been married and, therefore, in the court's eyes, had been both physically and emotionally intimate, was going through a withdrawal following her husband's departure. In such an emotional and psychical void, the Curia argued, it was perfectly normal that the countess opened up to Tormay, who, by being attentive and present in the countess's daily life, could fill the gap that Count Zichy had left. Rather than denying the abnormality of the two women's relationship, by psychologizing it the Curia ultimately ended up normalizing it. The most outrageous example of reliance on nonbiological explanations of female homosexuality is the count's claim that his wife preferred to be satisfied by a hand rather than the "normal" way, that is, by a penis. According to this line of reasoning, being exposed to and consequently "taught" about lesbian sex explained the queer sexual preference of the countess. Since the exposure to nonpenetrative sex could turn someone into a lesbian, the argument followed, there had to be a direct link between a particular way of being pleased and homosexuality.

In the absence of the actual testimonials of the medical experts, it is difficult present a more comprehensive account of where the various ideas on sexuality originated and who introduced them on behalf of the different players. What these surviving documents along with contemporary medical publications do suggest is that the medical establishment and doctors in

Budapest during the conservative Horthy regime continued to be informed by, and (selectively) applied, the latest theories of European sexologists and psychiatrists. Despite the power of medicine, it is obvious that the courts and the parties involved all used and applied medical and psychological discourses on sexuality selectively, citing these ideas in ways that made their particular case most convincing. This is most apparent when we read the opinion of medical experts who contended that "the details of the depositions of three (servant) witnesses (about Countess Zichy and Tormay), if factual, were clear indication of tribadism and those acts described by witnesses would be most certainly the consequences of homosexual acts, and that tribadism is nothing other, than an irresistible instinct."[94] Other than the plaintiff, no one was ready or willing to fully accept this position and its possible consequences. In the end, the courts came to utilize medical and psychological arguments to reject the possibility of a sexual relationship between the two women. As the Royal Tribunal stated, "there is not the slightest chance that the respondent [Countess Zichy], who had a normal sexual life with the plaintiff, who gave birth to five children, and was at an age when her sexual desire was lessening, would have committed unnatural fornication."[95] While the courts would have likely refrained from making the same claim had the person in question been a man in his midforties, in the case of the countess, medical theories on female sexual desire served to basically dismiss Countess Zichy as a sexual being. In so doing, the courts also killed the possibility of her homosexuality. Thus, even though legal perceptions on sexuality were littered with medical and psychological ideas, the courts and people who brought cases before them were strategically selective in their utilization.

CONTEMPORARY FAME AND FUTURE OBLIVION

Taking a step back, it is clear that neither the divorce nor the criminal libel suit was aimed at directly attacking or defining female homosexuality. Analyzing the Zichy-Tormay case, it seems indisputable that the "accusation of lesbianism was not an end in itself but a means to another end, political or personal in nature."[96] In this case, the unsuccessfully pursued end was to acquire a divorce and, perhaps to a lesser degree, discredit some of Hungary's most important political figures. Despite the stronghold that female respectability held in interwar Hungary, it would have been in the best interest of the interwar political leadership to clear Cécile Tormay's and Countess Zichy's names. As is often the case, the question of sexuality in this case was deeply political.

By the mid-1920s, conservatism in Hungary was deeply entrenched; with the historically rooted aristocracy continuing to control politics and keeping in check (and often strictly censoring) the Communists as well as the radical right.[97] The influence of the upper classes in decision making and the frequent bias of the courts toward the well-to-do was of course far from unique to Hungary. Yet, the trials also reflected a gradual movement away from a society ruled solely by the old landed aristocracy toward a more complex society, where the old nobility had to share power with the middle and lower-middle classes.[98] The political power and influence of members of the high aristocracy, for instance, the Zichys, were increasingly challenged by the Hungarian gentry (represented by people like Tormay). In this milieu, the divorce and subsequent libel case of Count Zichy and his wife and Cécile Tormay represented a power struggle within ruling political circles, with the outcomes, on one hand, pointing to the strength of Admiral Horthy and, on the other hand, to the continuing class bias of the legal system. The ruling of the courts, which ultimately placed all fault on Count Zichy and his servants and denied the possibility of a sexual relationship between the two women, was evidently a kick in the teeth to Count Zichy. It was also a disappointment to those who would have liked to see a more transparent justice and court system.[99] Initially, the political nature of the case was confined to Count Zichy's attempt to use his political capital to influence the court. Events took an unexpected turn when the regent, Admiral Horthy himself, got involved. Then, the political opposition and marginalized social democrats picked up the case in order to expose the corrupt nature and hypocrisy of the political system.[100]

There are indications that the decisions made were influenced by some of Hungary's highest political forces. The diary of Páter Zadravecz, who was the bishop of the Hungarian military between 1920 and 1928 and a close friend of Admiral Miklós Horthy, provides the most explicit and direct evidence of these maneuverings. In his *Secret Diary of Father Zadravecz*, the former bishop recalls the time when Horthy ordered him to intervene with the judges and make sure that Count Zichy would lose on all accounts.[101] According to Zadravecz's diary, on the day that the Criminal Court announced the verdict in the libel case, Horthy personally told the bishop that it was his own personal intervention that decided the case: "I held today as my most triumphant day because today that scoundrel Rafael Zichy was sentenced for a year and a half in prison for slander. This verdict comes only as a result of my forceful personal intervention. The minister of the interior himself questioned whether the court would even announce Zichy guilty. . . . But I put the pressure on."[102] Zadravecz's diary also speaks of a special relationship between Tormay and Horthy.[103] The admiral and Tormay did in fact share some history and remained close until Tormay's death in 1937. Born into gentry families, both of them were in some ways outsiders to the world of Hungarian high aristocracy, and similar to many of its historical members, they remained outsiders regardless of their achievements. They both benefited from the Aster and Communist revolutions, and their stars began to rise on the day of Horthy's arrival to the "Sinful City," as they both liked to refer to Budapest.[104] Tormay was one of the people who welcomed "the Admiral on horseback," and their alliance proved beneficial for both. Horthy held Tormay in the highest regard and had a direct role in making her the first female editor in chief of the most prestigious literary journal of the time, *Napkelet*. As the celebrated writer of *An Outlaw's Diary*, Tormay remained loyal to Horthy, and throughout her active public life as the president of MANSz, she propagated the official Christian nationalist conservative doctrine.[105]

At the end, the political views and self-fashioning of Tormay and Countess Zichy as conservative Catholic national patriots, in tandem with their relentless denial of same-sex desire, and last but not least their importance for the political leadership of interwar Hungary, ensured the outcome of the trials. On a more general level, the successful lobbying of Horthy and the mostly undamaged respectability of Tormay following the case signified the political shifts of interwar Hungary, where the former historical aristocracy was slowly losing power vis-à-vis the petit bourgeoisie and gentry.

Just as importantly, it is likely that the disappearance of all sensitive materials relating to the charges of homosexuality from the court records (including witness and expert testimonies) was no accident. While there is no definitive evidence as to why, out of the files of the divorce case, the testimonies of the main actors and experts as well as of the witnesses were destroyed, it was undoubtedly in the best interest of the interwar leadership to make sure that almost no evidence implicating the two women survived. And this is important especially since the court essentially based its ruling not on the opinions of experts but rather "on the common [contemporary] view of life."[106] In light of the fact that the documents of witnesses' and experts' views suggested that the countess and Tormay could have been sexually involved and that Tormay was a homosexual, that they would have been destroyed under the conservative illiberal regime is far from surprising.

Famous "homosexual" trials elsewhere, notably of Oscar Wilde or Radcliffe Hall, that at the time shamed and condemned alleged homosexuals, were also an important step in creating a language and wider knowledge of the sexually marginalized. The Zichy-Tormay case did not create a more

Figure 7. Statue of Cécile Tormay, 1939. Image from Metropolitan Ervin, Szabó Library, Budapest.

precise language nor did it seem to lead to a wider understanding of homosexuality. Dirtying the names of Hungary's two most important female spokespersons for the reigning conservative regime was neither desirable nor safe for most contemporary Hungarians. And although contemporary papers did say that the case had "surely given the wrong ideas to young women," the case's legacy as a part of the history of (homo)sexuality has yet to be claimed. The courts' intention of "clearing and restoring the name of Tormay and Countess Zichy" stood the test of time. After forty years of Communist silencing of bourgeois and aristocrat voices, Cécile Tormay only reemerged in the 2000s, precisely in the image the interwar courts would have wanted her to appear.

CONCLUSION

There has been a concerted effort to rehabilitate the Horthy era and frame it in a positive light since the 2010 landslide victory of Fidesz and meteoric rise of the Hungarian far-right party, Jobbik, both of which ran on and continue to promote "anti-West" platforms.[107] As part of this effort, the conservatives and far right happily (re)embraced Tormay as Hungary's ideal patriotic female figure of the past century. All of Tormay's books have been reprinted, with *Bujdosó könyv* (*An Outlaw's Diary*) claiming a cult following. In March 2012, a statue was erected in Budapest, commemorating her as one of the "Greatest Hungarian Women." The same year the Hungarian Ministry of Education was seriously considering including Tormay in the new national educational core curriculum. While that effort failed thanks to criticism from all corners, and Fidesz eventually stopped publicly supporting Tormay's rehabilitation, she continues to be a hero for supporters of conservatives and the far right alike.[108]

What was perhaps most surprising about the rehabilitation of Tormay was not that conservatives and especially the far right found her (along with many other interwar figures') anti-Semitic, irredentist, and traditionalist gender views and strong nationalist sentiments appealing and timely. Rather, what was surprising was that they did so without considering, or in fact in spite of, the details of Tormay's personal life, which represented everything conservatives and the far right were advocating against: namely, a strong independent woman, who never married or had children, worked in a male profession, and (as all historical evidence points to) was also a woman who desired those of her own sex. Thus, while Tormay's writings and public work were well suited to stand for advocating a family-centered vision and traditional gender norms, her personal life fell noticeably short from the twenty-first-century conservative and far-right ideologies. Yet, despite a seeming discordancy between Tormay's personal life and the political platform of her twenty-first century revivers, she was unconditionally embraced. In part, we can account for this by simply pointing out how both the right and the far right claimed ignorance or dismissed questions about Tormay's personal life as irrelevant or a smear campaign by the political opposition. Focusing exclusively on her literary works and public persona, moreover, made both Tormay's gender and her sexuality irrelevant to their goals. It was in fact precisely because they ignored Tormay's sexuality and gender that Tormay was able to become a usable figure. By disregarding that she was a woman, she could occupy male (literary and public) spheres, and by ignoring her (nonnormative) sexuality, she could stand for all women and speak for patriarchal policies and views.

Like their far-right and conservative historical counterparts in Hungary and elsewhere, for Jobbik and Fidesz an abstract conservative female figure could serve, not only as a spokesperson for, but also as a representative of, their ideal nation.[109] Through her literary works that portray traditional and complementary norms for men and women, Tormay has come to symbolize not only Hungarian women but also the Hungarian nation. As it turns out, upholding Tormay's vision of traditional gender norms as ideal and inspirational while at the same time deeming Tormay's actual personal life irrelevant became a conservative trademark. In their approach to sexuality, twenty-first-century Hungarian conservatives and far-right politicians followed in the footsteps of their interwar counterparts. Ironically, the politics and discourses that fashioned the silencing of same-sex sexuality in Tormay's lifetime, which will be examined further in the following chapter, have also proven to be the most enduring agents of silence in the historical memory of interwar (homo)sexuality. As a result, both the interwar and the Fidesz-led illiberal systems could rally around individuals whose personal and sexual life was outside of these regimes' espoused ideals of heteronormative, family-centered social life.

Finally, as for Tormay's sexuality, the case's legacy as a part of the history of (homo)sexuality has yet to be claimed. On one hand, strict contemporary silencing by the Horthy regime and the subsequent silencing of nonnormative sexualities by the post–World War II Communist regime pose a considerable (although by no means impossible) obstacle to reconstructing and interpreting the sexuality of Tormay. On the other hand, the fact that even the LGBTQ community has not embraced Tormay is in no small part due to Tormay's politics. Tormay's anti-Semitic, fascist, and irredentist beliefs until recently made her too controversial to be commemorated as a foremother for Hungarian lesbians.

CHAPTER FIVE

Unlikely Allies: Queer Men and Horthy Conservatives

In 1932 there was a murder case in Budapest whose cold bloodedness and brutality captivated denizens of the city. The victim was a wealthy restaurant owner who, through an intermediary, paid young men (often soldiers) for sex. The murderers, three soldiers from the nearby barracks who had had sexual relationships with the victim before deciding to rob and kill him, were eventually tracked down using the homosexual registry.[1] The reporting on the case in the papers followed the pattern of the conservative interwar years where discussions of homosexuality emerged only around scandals and murder cases. Breaking with an otherwise general silence around homosexuality, a number of newspapers reported on the case. In their discussion of the murder, the papers used a rather vague language that glided over the homosexual orientation of the respectable victim. In line with the reporting pattern, the respectability of the victim demanded the intentional silencing of his queerness. While not directly addressing the case, the right-leaning journal, the *Város* (City), used the (mostly unreported) details of the case and published a long diatribe against homosexuals in the city. In doing so the journal provided a rare public acknowledgment of queer Budapest as well as its toleration by the conservative regime.

> The fact is that unless these people [homosexuals] violate public decency or cause a [public] scandal, they can do whatever they want in private homes. The police, even if they do know about a case, cannot do anything . . .
> It is well known that in the heart of the capital there have surfaced several casino-like establishments, which have been running their [homosexual prostitution] business almost completely in the open. In Budapest

the "love agents" of the sodomite criminals of Paris, Berlin, and the [French] Riviera have set up their latest and most disgusting industry . . .

The brutal and unforgivable passion takes its victims from both sexes approximately the same degree. . . . Nevertheless, it is a known fact that among women the organization is much tighter and more mighty. They do their business in the uttermost secrecy and there are no traitors among them.²

This excerpt echoes the finding of the previous chapter. While during the interwar era Hungarian authorities might not have had a clear definition of female homosexuality, people were aware of women having sex with other women. But female homosexuality, which was not criminalized, remained largely outside of the radar of the police, jurisprudence, and the authorities in general, who were, first and foremost, concerned with heterosexual and, increasingly by the 1930s, male homosexual prostitution. Not only was love between women not prosecuted, but there also seemed to be an unspoken consensus on the part of leading voices that "whatever we do not talk about does not exist." Officials and social commentators alike feared that open discussion of female homosexuality would introduce the idea of Sapphic love to innocent women, hence it was not up for public discussion. When female homosexuality entered the public eye, as it did in the case of Tormay and Pallavicini, the conservative Horthy regime deliberately minimized and attempted to silence the conversation. Such an approach to female homosexuality took place within a political and social climate in which the subsequent conservative governments prescribed a particular role for Hungarian women. Moreover, as this chapter will further elaborate on, during the interwar years, the authorities policed and prosecuted nonnormative female behavior, particularly prostitution, to a much greater degree than the more liberal governments had done during the Austro-Hungarian monarchy. Thus, even though female sexuality became more regulated and policed, female homosexuality never became an openly discussed issue and was not prosecuted throughout the interwar period. Female homosexuals were ignored by law enforcement and society alike.

But what about male homosexuality during the 1920s and 1930s? How did the authorities approach male homosexuality during an increasingly conservative era? In terms of the regulation of same-sex sexuality, the previous chapters illustrated that Hungary, closely following Paragraph 175 of the German penal code, had criminalized sex between men in 1878. Paragraph 241 of the Hungarian penal code criminalized sexual both acts between men and bestiality as *természet elleni fajtalanság*, "unnatural fornication," acts for which the resulting punishment was up to one year in the least severe form of incarceration. Paragraph 242 made nonconsensual acts of "unnatural fornication" punishable up to five years in prison, with the potential of life imprisonment if the act caused the death of the plaintiff. However, just because there were concrete laws on the books regarding male homosexuality did not mean that they were necessarily enforced. As the first two chapters illustrated, between 1878 and the end of World War I, the Budapest Metropolitan Police practiced modern scientific management by establishing a homosexual registry and tracking male homosexuals. But being labeled and registered as homosexuals did not mean legal action for most of the men in question. The novel approach of the Communists discussed in chapter 3 to decriminalize and rehabilitate homosexuals as heterosexuals in 1919 proved short-lived. During the interwar years, in contrast to nonnormative female sexuality (prostitution), the conceptualization, regulation, and treatment of male homosexuality shows remarkable continuities from the pre-1918 period. Unlike the case of religious or ethnic minorities, there were no new or further discriminatory laws against male homosexuals, nor were the existing regulations more thoroughly enforced in the case of homosexual men. Despite the growing influence of the radical right and rapidly increasing membership and visibility of far-right elements following the onset of the economic depression in 1929, throughout the 1930s, as the excerpt from *Város* hints at, homosexuals were neither used as scapegoats nor treated more punitively.

Why would a conservative political system that set out to (re)establish "Christian morality" as the foundation of the Hungarian national community tolerate male homosexuality? Why would a system, which, among other things, introduced the first anti-Jewish laws in the postwar period, protect male homosexuals at a time when most European countries were increasingly prosecuting them?[3] Why did this conservative authoritarian regime that made restoring and protecting the (heterosexual) family a cornerstone of its ideology not target its homosexual minority? Moreover, during 1920s and 1930s, even the right-wing elements remained conspicuously silent about Budapest's sizeable homosexual minority. Why and how could this be? What factors produced such a seeming anachronism—a highly conservative state that tolerated nonnormative sexuality? And finally, what were the limits of this tenuous relationship as seen through the lens of law, culture, and public health? Grappling with these questions is the aim of this chapter. The answers are, of course, not straightforward. In fact, only the complicated interplay of various factors can together explain why, despite the turmoil of 1918–19, the abandonment of liberalism, and the establishment of an arch-conservative regime in 1919, the new era did not bring a change in the treatment of nonnormative male sexuality. The upheavals following World War I; the political, social, and economic consequences of the Treaty of Trianon; a particular understanding of postwar masculinities and male sexualities more generally; a focus on the heterosexual transmission of venereal disease; and a carryover of a lenient rehabilitative medical approach to homosexuality, all in conjunction with one another, facilitated the unique coexistence of conservative governance and male homosexuality. I contend that the particular gendered dynamics of social regulation extended to homosexuality, which paradoxically allowed a certain kind of male homosexuality to coexist with and within conservatism.

SEXUAL AND MORAL ORDER OF THE HORTHY REGIME

To understand why an increasingly conservative Horthy regime continued to tolerate homosexuality requires looking at the effects and consequences of World War I, particularly in the context of gender politics. As the last chapter illustrated, the conservative Horthy regime set out to restore order in every sphere of life. There was a concerted effort to curtail liberalization, in all spheres of life. This was especially the case in Budapest, which had been the vanguard of Hungarian modernity and the hotbed of liberal and progressive attitudes. It was no accident that, upon entering Budapest, Admiral Horthy named the capital "Sinful Budapest," and the new conservative government set out to rid the city of its "filth" and "immoral" elements.[4] Thus, after the Horthy regime had punished the political opposition and had driven many people into exile, it turned its attention to cultural and social elements that were undesirable for the new Christian Hungarian national community. The restoration of traditional gender norms and the policing of public sexual morale were at the heart of the efforts by consecutive governments to cleanse Budapest.

In stark opposition to the approach of the Democratic and Communist governments, as well as of the policies of the Hungarian governments during the dual monarchy, the interwar leadership saw the reestablishment of traditional gender norms in Budapest as essential for Hungary's ability to move "forward." While Budapest, as "the center of sin," received considerable attention, the conservative leadership in a close collaboration with—and often through—all Christian churches also targeted the rural areas. One of the top priorities during the interwar era was to reverse the demographic decline and attack the so-called *egykézést*, the growing family practice of having only one child.[5] Enjoying its newfound power, the Catholic Church took the lead in taking concrete steps to propagate the importance of conservative gender and sexual norms in both private and public spheres.[6] In the name of Christianity, both religious and government authorities propagated gender-specific roles as the foundation of new conservative Hungarian society.[7] Whether through sermons, school curriculums, or organizations closely linked with the Catholic Church, men and women were educated about their intended social role. The following description of the contours of the desired moral order, where valorous Hungarian men are paired with and supported by virtuous women, comes from a contemporary publication entitled *My Way around the Stork's Nest* (1923), a directive on sex education for educators and parents.

> The Treaty of Trianon will be sanctified by the Hungarian children's room, and our nation's great prayer that it will be our sons who will say the saving, liberating and glorifying "Amen." Therefore, the primary aim in our education is to educate good mothers, and make our sons to be men, not babies whom were taught to be tender, fearful or arrogant, or to exhibit excessive modesty and cringing incompetence. If the homes of our children are aware that our daughters should not be educated for the public and outside world that is shallow, and would not allow them to satisfy society's need for glamour and decadence; but rather aim to educate our daughters to be good mothers and housewives, while in our sons improve their self-worth, work ethic, self-sufficiency, patriotism, strength, and character, than despite our dreadful present, we can expect our resurrection, regeneration, and a great and prosperous future.[8]

Following World War I, all participating countries, regardless of the nature of their political governance, attempted to (re-)create heterosexual families and advocated pronatalist policies.[9] In "mutilated" Hungary, however, pronatalism and the raising of as many healthy Hungarian children as possible had an added significance. In the wake of Hungary's territorial losses thanks to the Treaty of Trianon, the raising of a new generation of men and women was seen literally as the prerequisite of territorial revision and the country's resurrection. To succeed men and women of the new generation had specific roles to play. Underpinned by Christian principles, women were to be good mothers and housewives, while men would become physically, mentally, and morally tough. Horthy era politicians prescribed the ideal nineteenth-century bourgeois social structure: a pious and patriotic male head of the household with the purity and health of the family (and the happiness of the husband) as a wifely responsibility. This was true even as wifely duties in the private spheres were increasingly "professionalized," which in the post–World War I era required the learning of modern housekeeping skills, to complement male breadwinning in the public sphere.[10]

Virility and the moral strength of Hungarian men, moreover, were propagated, not only as crucial foundations of the new conservative order, but also as essential prerequisites for Hungary's revisionist aims. The experience of World War I prompted the Hungarian elite to focus on the physical strength of its men.[11] As a defeated country, the national army was restricted to thirty-five thousand soldiers, and conscription was not introduced until 1939. Nevertheless, from the 1920s onward, the Hungarian authorities systematically manipulated administrative and bureaucratic procedures in order to recruit and train soldiers.[12] For example, the establishment of the "Levente law," and the consequent "Levente movement," essentially mandated the physical education of men between the ages of twelve and twenty-one.[13] From 1924 onward, the Levente Associations ensured that all young Hungarian men, even those who were not in school, received physical training. In addition, authorities were particularly active in supporting the Hungarian Boy Scouts Association, Magyar Cserkészszövetség, whose numbers rose during the 1930s. The development of the physical strength and virility of Hungary's future soldiers was seen as the cornerstone for the new conservative education system built on a Christian moral foundation.[14] There were also a number of concrete steps taken to impose conservative sexual ethics. Ignoring statistics about the prevalence of premarital sex, the Catholic Church's teachings of abstinence prior to marriage, the dangers of masturbation, and the consumption of pornography were the dominant messages of the day.[15] In the name of moral and sexual purity, the government made the media more accountable for their content. Thus, the formerly liberal press, one of the least censored in Europe prior to 1914, became significantly more conformist by the 1920s.[16] The authorities also stepped up the prosecution of midwives and doctors providing abortion services.[17] In so doing, they punished those women who sought abortion and those men and women who thought to provide them, without addressing either the role of male partners or the larger socioeconomic issues that made women seek abortion in the first place. The most illustrative efforts of the conservatives to cleanse Budapest of its former sexual decadence were the empowerment of the police to regulate public morality and the reform of prostitution.

In 1927, the protection of public morality was elevated to an issue of national security. In a sweeping order, the Ministry of Justice granted the police the right to prosecute anyone deemed a threat to public morality.[18] As the following excerpt from the preamble of the circular titled "Protection of Public Morale" illustrates, the conservative approach to public morality was a clear departure from the pre-1918 era: "the protection of public morality, that is to ensure that the behavior of individuals within public/social life would always meet the prerequisites of good morale and good taste is one of the most important tasks of authorities and especially of the police and public safety."[19] That law enforcement was tasked with "the raising of the morale of the street and more generally of public spaces" was a clear departure from the mission of Metropolitan Police of Budapest during the Austro-Hungarian era. Whereas pre-1918 the goal of the police was to mitigate the ill effects of the fast-growing metropolis, in the interwar era the police were seen as an important force for social change. In a dramatic shift from the pre–World War I era, when the police were responsible first and foremost to protect denizens, police were now mandated to uphold and propagate conservative moral order.[20] In a remarkable extension of their reach, moreover, the police were granted the power to prosecute anyone whom they deemed to have violated accepted (conservative) norms of public behavior. The police could intervene and stop any cultural performance (dance or play) or event from taking place if any parts of it or any performance within or during it was deemed to offend "appropriate morals."[21] Simply uttering a word or making a gesture in public that the police deemed "offensive to public morality" could land someone at the police station with a charge of a misdemeanor. The same ordinance also made it a criminal offense for a man to address uninvited, make a proposition to, or harass a *tiszteletreméltó* (respectable) woman in public. Last but not least, the ordinance criminalized same-sex sexual solicitation between men in public as well as "all behaviors appearing to be as such, i.e. intrusive solicitation, following, improper mannerisms."[22] The intention of the order was clear. The conservative leadership made a concerted effort to police public morale and its citizens. The purposeful vagueness of what counted as "offensive" behaviors could not only be used to intimidate people but also as a means to take action against potential opponents of the regime.

The comprehensive reform of prostitution enacted in the same year also had a dual purpose: reduce the visibility of immoral elements and gain greater oversight over the denizens of Budapest. According to the Ministry of Justice, the reform was needed to protect public morality, public health, and women.[23] The police was reassured of its total oversight over the institution of prostitution. They had been in charge of the mandatory registering and biweekly medical examination of female prostitutes since the late nineteenth century. Now, they were also in charge of determining every detail about who could be a prostitute, where they could work and live, and how they could offer their sexual services. According to the new ordinance, every woman who wanted to register had to be interviewed by the vice police with the intention of using the interview to dissuade women from entering the profession. Once registered, the new ordinance provided some additional protection to female prostitutes against abuse. Since the new regulation eliminated pimps and the profiteering middle men by revoking all brothel licenses, prostitutes were less vulnerable.[24] Ultimately, however, the ordinance placed the fate of the registered prostitute in the hands of the police. At any moment, they could decide that a woman with her either private or public conduct did not comply with or follow the extensive requirements outlined in the sixty-paragraph-long ordinance, which could not only lead to the loss of her license, but also land her in prison, and as an unemployed person ban her from Budapest.

The new regulation of prostitution was a clear break from the past and reflected the Horthy regime's belief that brothels and prostitution had been responsible for destroying the moral fiber of Hungarian society. Conservative authorities, like their pre-1918 counterparts, did not necessarily seek to end prostitution immediately. They were aware of the extent to which it was ingrained in the fabric of Hungarian society. However, there was a clear change in which police and city officials in the interwar era talked about and consequently approached prostitution. According to new official discourse, prostitution was no longer seen as a "necessary evil," nor necessarily as a consequence primarily of urban poverty, but rather, increasingly, prostitution was portrayed solely as a product of immorality. Of course, none of this was new. But unlike previous explanations that alongside immoral aspects stressed poverty and argued that in most cases it was destitution that drove women to prostitution and economic and social factors that made men to be consumers of it, the conservative rhetoric equated prostitution with lack of morality. In the new conservative order, anyone associated with prostitution—both male purchasers and female sellers of services—was portrayed as an immoral element who posed a health and moral risk to society and the future of Hungary. Following the establishment of the Horthy regime's punitive regulations to (re)establish public morality, one would imagine that homosexuality and people on the homosexual registry would have experienced an increase in prosecution. However, as the rest of chapter will argue, this did not seem to be the case.

THE LIFE OF K, A HUNGARIAN HOMOSEXUAL DURING THE INTERWAR YEARS

A Hungarian queer or homosexual memoir from this period is yet to be discovered, and, as I acknowledged in the introduction, writing on the history of queer Budapest without the unmediated voices of the actual queer people certainly has its limits. While there is no homosexual memoir or autobiography, we do at least we have a sustained discussion of a single anonymous individual, whom I will call K, whose life experiences were recorded by a Hungarian physician, Zoltán Nemes Nagy, during the 1930s. Nemes Nagy actually published a case study of K in his 1933 book *Catastrophies of Love Life*.[25] K was a patient of doctor Nemes Nagy during the first years of the 1930s.[26] As a sexual pathologist and practicing physician with a specialty in sexual "dysfunctions," Nemes Nagy's account of K is most certainly biased, as it highlights K's "peculiar" sexual nature, and, first and foremost, it does so in a publication about so-called sexual pathologies.[27] The placement of K's story in a book, which discusses all that could go wrong with love, positions K's homosexuality as a "tragedy." Despite the inherent biases of Nemes Nagy's account, when read against the grain, it provides a valuable window into Hungarian homosexual life in the first three decades of the twentieth century. Thus, building on Nemes Nagy's description, in the following I am going to contextualize K's story within contemporary Hungarian history. As we will see, K's experiences illustrate how homosexual men could live and conduct their lives relatively freely in Budapest throughout the 1920s and 1930s, and yet it also gives us a darker picture of what being registered on the homosexual registry and feeling the contempt of society could be like for an individual in this era.

Like the great majority of inhabitants of Budapest and most homosexuals in the city, K was born and raised in the countryside and moved to Budapest in his late teens. When World War I broke out in 1914, K and millions of others enlisted to fight for the Austro-Hungarian monarchy. The horrors and the outcomes of the war are well known.[28] What is less frequently discussed is how, for certain men, being in the trenches and eventually, being prisoners of war with thousands of other men, offered opportunities for diverse sexual experiences. According to Nemes Nagy, K was one of those men who actually found, even amidst the gruesome circumstances of the war, something positive. Namely, the fulfillment of his sexual desires. This was particularly the case during K's time as a prisoner of war in Russia, where, as Nemes Nagy explains, "K, as an experienced homosexual, faired pretty well."[29] In

K's "words," being an experienced homosexual and being on "friendly" territory (meaning an all-male environment), he could pick and choose with whom he wanted to have sexual encounters. Many men who had been at war for years and often not seen women for extended periods of time became more open, and at times eager, to have sexual experiences with other men. In Nemes Nagy's presentation, K, although aware that many men only acted because of their forced and prolonged sexual abstinence, was glad to offer his services and overall appreciated his experience in the POW camp.[30] Nemes Nagy's account of K's experience corresponds to other representations of homosexuals across Europe who had fought in World War I.[31] According to these accounts, amidst horrid conditions, both the war and, for those who were captured alive, the prison camps offered a strange, almost bittersweet, opportunity to men who had been living a clandestine homosexual life. It is impossible to know the prevalence and/or extent to which sexual activities between men were present in the different armies and on different fronts during the war. K's story and the official Hungarian reports published after the war nevertheless suggest that sexual encounters were common between Hungarian soldiers.[32] Nemes Nagy's account of K's wartime experience also helps us to see why, during the interwar years, the Hungarian authorities came to blame World War I for turning a record number of Hungary's finest men into homosexuals.[33] In the authorities' opinion, the prolonged homosocial environment of the war, not only had facilitated homosexual contact for men who already knew they preferred their own sex, but had also introduced many other men to the idea and practice of same-sex sexuality. This could not have been totally wrong, since, following the war, Budapest, along with most major European cities, experienced an unprecedented increase of the visibility of male homosexuality.[34] Although no official data about the number of homosexuals exists, various authorities estimated that the number of homosexual men (those who were "authentic") were around fifteen thousand by the 1930s.[35]

HOMOSEXUAL MEETING PLACES IN INTERWAR BUDAPEST

Following his war experience, which, in spite of his sexual "successes," also put him through incredible physical and emotional hardships, K returned to Budapest. The Budapest K returned to, however, was a very different city than the one he had left at the onset of the Great War. Hunger, demoralization, and a fear of terror affected the poor and rich denizens of Budapest alike. Yet, despite all of the destruction, the loss of men, and the economic hardship, people in the city of Budapest in the 1920s possessed "a relentless fever of wanting to have a good time." Residents, young and old, new and previous, were making the most of the rapid reestablishment of Budapest's entertainment industry.[36] K, like most of his counterparts, was ready to start his life again, and also to make use of his now extensive sexual knowledge. And they could do so in a city whose population saw a rapid growth, quickly surpassing the prewar era numbers. By 1925 Budapest's population stood around 1,300,000.[37] Thanks to a large influx of immigrants and demobilized men, the city was full of men. In this environment, K, "with his now solid homosexual experience and skill set," could pursue his homosexual lifestyle with confidence.[38] What George Chauncey in the context of New York describes as living a double life was certainly true in the case of homosexuals in Budapest.[39] Men like K could blend into heteronormative public and professional places while also live an exciting homosexual lifestyle. Using his finely tuned ability to recognize homosexual men, K identified potential sexual partners everywhere: on the streets of Budapest, in restaurants, in business meetings.[40] We learn that, having met and chosen a partner, there were a variety of options where men could go to have sex. Budapest during the 1920s, unlike Berlin, Amsterdam, or Paris, did not have a lot of openly homosexual public establishments. A 1921 article from *Detektív*, a police journal, echoes the city's comparably less visible public homosexual culture.

> The position of Budapest, for example, compared to Berlin, is relatively fortunate because those with sick inclination [homosexuals] at least are not inclined to be in the public as much they are elsewhere. Only those in the know recognize the strangely behaved men on the streets, their secret meeting places, their cafés, where they usually gather in mass.[41]

That the police took pride in the fact that homosexuals were less visible in Budapest than in Berlin during the days of the Weimar Republic is notable. However, their choice to compare Budapest to Berlin (the homosexual capital of the 1920s) can be viewed ironically as well. While clearly inferior to Berlin at the time, as we learn from K, there were plenty of options in Budapest for male homosexuals if they wanted to cruise or pick up men in public and semipublic places. In fact, the prewar queer geography of the city swiftly resumed its former contours following the end of the war. The City Park, People's Park, Elizabeth Square, and Danube Promenade, along with the Emke corner, continued to serve as meeting places for the seasoned and novice homosexual men alike.[42] There were also new popular cruising areas on busy squares in downtown Pest, such as the Berlin or Kálvin Squares. Moreover, the expansion of existing previously small baths such Széchenyi and Gellért into spacious grand public baths and the building of new baths such as Dandár not only enhanced Budapest status as a bath capital but also exponentially expanded its queer geography. In addition, we learn that once men "became a couple," they would often go hiking in the hills of Buda or on some of the smaller and more secluded islands on the Danube.[43] Overall, Nemes Nagy's narration of K's extensive and colorful homosexual experiences during the 1920s and the early 1930s parallels the police and medical reports from the 1920s, which emphasized the significant rise and greater visibility of male homosexuals in Budapest.[44] Even if it were not necessarily visible to "untrained" eyes, K's life attests to an extensive Hungarian homosexual network and elements of a growing homosexual subculture.

Nemes Nagy's accounts of K and the other case studies of homosexuals that Nemes Nagy published surprisingly speak very little about either the policing of or the social stigma around homosexuality. Considering that male homosexuality was a criminal activity, punishable by up to a year in prison, it is interesting that K's life story hardly touches on the burdens that he, or other homosexuals, faced at this time. Yet, even if K's life was, according to himself, "quite diverse, exciting, pleasant and moreover, happy," examining the details that Nemes Nagy provides about his life more closely helps to contextualize his experience within post–World War I Hungarian history. It also reveals some of the difficulties that living as a homosexual could pose.[45] In particular, K's story provides evidence of the painful economic hardships that people, regardless of their sexuality, had to face both following the war and again during the 1930s. The economic hardships that characterized Budapest from 1916 until the mid-1920s and again following 1929 cannot be overemphasized.[46] Unlike, for instance, in New York, where most working gay men were able to live on their own, in Budapest crowded living conditions meant that privacy remained a privilege of the middle and upper classes.[47]

At the same, high unemployment, and an increase in violence all imposed a tremendous burden not just on the inhabitants but importantly also on the Metropolitan Police of Budapest.[48] This helps to explain why K in his account seemed relatively unconcerned with the police. Because the police were primarily concerned with keeping violent and dangerous criminals at bay during the first half of the 1920s (especially after the world financial crash in 1929), most Hungarian homosexuals were never charged. Even if the police had greater oversight and a mandate to fight immorality, amidst the economic and social realities that plagued Budapest during the interwar era, the prosecution of homosexuality remained a low priority. This helps to explain how K, although he had thousands of homosexual encounters for

Figure 8. Emke Kávézó. Source: Magyar Nemzeti Múzeum Történeti Fényképtár gyűjteménye.

over a decade (until 1933), managed to avoid any contact with the police. As K's stories demonstrate, men having consensual sex with other men, especially if practiced in private, continued to be of little interest to the police, whose priorities were the reduction of violent crime and theft.[49]

THE POLICE AND HOMOSEXUALS IN INTERWAR BUDAPEST

When K was finally arrested and registered by the police, it was on an occasion in which he cross-dressed as a woman, which, according to Nemes Nagy, he occasionally liked to do. During a night out with two German men who believed K was a woman, K found himself in a violent brawl in a hotel room once the men discovered that he was a man. After the police had taken all three of them to the station, K had his name placed on the homosexual registry, and the police filed a misdemeanor against him.[50] He was released without being charged and resumed his life, but he became much more careful about the ways in which he conducted his sexual liaisons. K's experience with the police, as well as with the legal system, is indicative of new trends in the surveillance and prosecutorial practices of the Horthy era Hungarian state. The fact that he was registered and then eventually released without a charge is representative of the approach of authorities during the interwar era. The police under the conservative Horthy regime continued to register

Figure 9. Two men standing at Duna Strandfürdő, 1929.
Courtesy of Fortepan/Péter Balassa.

men who were caught or thought to have sex with other men. In fact, K was among the approximately 3,500–5,000 homosexuals that by the early 1930s were on the registry, a considerable increase from the pre–World War I era.[51] The surviving documents of the interwar period, moreover, demonstrate how the police squad dedicated to homosexuals was actually quite active in tracking down and registering homosexuals and men who had sex with men. Previously, the police had focused more on the so-called inauthentic homosexuals, those men who often demanded some sort of compensation for their services. During the 1920s, the squad also began to register the so-called authentic homosexuals. The registry itself became more "sophisticated" and, from the mid-1920s, contained additional personal information about male homosexuals, including their exact work position, personal histories, educational background, and female names.[52] From the mid-1920s

Figure 10. Two men embrace outside of Budapest, 1943.
Courtesy of Fortepan/Márton Kurutz.

onward, the police were also actively filing charges against homosexual men who were caught for crimes other than homosexuality. This reflected, on the one hand, the conservative regime's aim to "clean up" and rid the "sinful" capital of its criminal and illicit elements and, on the other hand, the increasing ability of the Metropolitan Police of Budapest to police public spaces. Whether they caught people engaging in same-sex sexual activity or apprehended people who were involved in some unlawful activity who also happen to be homosexuals, homosexuals faced greater likelihood of being arrested and prosecuted.

Yet, as evidenced by K's experience, the attitude and actions of the police did not necessarily become more punitive or lead to criminal convictions for men who had sex with men. Unfortunately, there are no surviving written police memos about internal police orders with regard to homosexuals during the interwar era. Apart from surviving medical and legal records, what we do have that speaks directly to the behavior of the police comes from interviews with homosexuals, which were collected during the 1980s and 1990s.[53] According to these oral histories, during the interwar era, an officer

Figure 11. Three men sitting at Duna Strandürdő, 1929.
Courtesy of Fortepan/Péter Balassa.

Figure 12. Two men sitting on a bench, Duna Strandfürdő, 1929.
Courtesy of Fortepan/Péter Balassa.

Figure 13. Two men at Római Part, 1929. Courtesy of Fortepan/Péter Balassa.

named Czar was heading the "homosexual squad," "about whom nothing bad was said in the pages of homosexual fables."[54] Officer Czar (who does appear in the court records) was lenient and even defended some homosexual men during this era.[55] The policing of sexuality might have been more intense, but the police continued to show leniency for, not only "authentic" homosexuals (those who were thought to have acted out of their innate desire for their own sex), but also toward a wide range of men who engaged with nonnormative sexual activities. The relatively lax approach had limits, however; the squad became more punitive if the acts were nonconsensual (including sex with boys under twelve years old), were accompanied by additional unlawful acts, or disrupted the public order. In the eyes of the police, for instance, K's queer sexuality became a problem only when he misled two other men and also caused a public scene. Homosexuals who did not commit any crime other than that of their desire for their own sex continued to be left alone and, at times, were even protected by the police.

Figure 14. Dunakorzó/Danube Promenade, 1940. Courtesy of Fortepan/Gali.

Apart from run-ins with the police and the risk of criminal prosecution, which loomed over homosexuals, a careful reading of K's account points to their vulnerability to blackmailing and to the social stigma that surrounded homosexuality. K had experiences with both of these. Although Nemes Nagy does not address it explicitly, it is still clear that K knew that society thought of men like him as "abnormal" and sick individuals. While we never know how K actually felt about his own sexuality, according to Nemes Nagy, he referred to his own sexuality as "sick" and shared society's view that homosexuality was "abnormal." It is also evident that K had to be careful and was not open about his sexuality with most people. He never picked up lovers at his workplace and kept his relationships very private. The fact that, in spite of his discreetness, he was, at least on one occasion, reported to the police for "unnatural fornication" also illustrates how vulnerable homosexuals were to potential ill-wishers and blackmail. The last thing that we learn about K is that he was thinking about leaving Budapest in order to sta-

Figure 15. Széchényi Bath, 1930. Courtesy of Wikimedia Commons/Pesti Napló, 1850–1930, ajándék album.

bilize his finances. Ironically, the same economic hardship that could shield men like K from the attention of the police could also lead to them having to leave "queer Budapest." Following the great financial crisis, K lost his job as a manager in a clothing salon. According to Nemes Nagy's account, since K was not able to find a new job and could not obtain any money, he actually began thinking about leaving Budapest. Even though the thought of having to be with a woman "terrified him," he was seriously considering marrying a female hotel owner from the countryside, whom he met in Pest. The woman fell in love with him and proposed to marry him. Although we don't know K's ultimate fate, if this scenario happened, K would have left Pest and moved to a small town in the country. While moving to the countryside could make sense economically, in terms of pursuing a homosexual lifestyle it was most often thought as a kind of social death. Within the new borders of Hungary following the Treaty of Trianon, Budapest remained the only sizeable city that could offer both anonymity and a sizeable homosexual network.[56] Having to leave Budapest meant the suspension of queer social and often sexual activities. Regardless of whether or not K, like countless other homosexual men, ended up marrying and living with a woman, K's life story offers at least a partial window into the history of queer Budapest. As the story of K highlighted, the experience of World War I and prison-camp life was an important chapter in the history of Hungarian male homosexuals. His experience also reveals how it was much less the political changes following the war than the eventual economic hardship that became the most influential factor in shaping his (homo-) sexual experiences.

HOMOSEXUALITY AT THE BUDAPEST CRIMINAL COURTS

Following the establishment of the Horthy regime's punitive regulations to (re)establish public morality, one would imagine that homosexuality and people on the homosexual registry would have experienced an increase in prosecution. However, this did not seem to be the case. K's experience with the legal system shows how being charged even repeatedly with unnatural fornication under Paragraph 241 often did not lead to convictions. Nemes Nagy's recounting of K's encounter with a local judge in his hometown in the countryside reveals an unexpected insight into how legal authorities could treat homosexuals with empathy and even aid them with information. Once, even before K moved to Budapest, a local judge had followed K walking down the street dressed in female clothes and wearing makeup, which he admittedly liked to do occasionally. Following his public promenade, the judge summoned him to admonish him for his behavior. Having told K he should not behave queer in public, the judge proceeded to talk to K about homosexual meeting places in Budapest where K could find people like himself. The fact that it was a judge, an important representative of law and order, who informed and, in a sense, educated K about how to navigate his queer sexual life was certainly not the norm.

At the same time the surviving records on judicial treatment of homosexuality support K's experience in terms of providing a fair trial and a lenient application of the law. Drawing on the surviving records of cases of "unnatural fornication" that included Paragraph 241 (consensual) and Paragraph 242 (nonconsensual) homosexual acts at the Budapest Criminal

Courts, it is possible to reconstruct some of the major trends in the legal treatment of male homosexuality.[57] Following the enactment of Article 1895, XLIV, unnatural fornication cases in Budapest were tried at the Budapest Royal Criminal District Courts with the Budapest Royal Criminal Court serving as the so-called court of second instance, or Appeals Court.[58] The legal treatment of male homosexuality that emerges from the surviving documents from the Royal Criminal and District Courts during the interwar years suggests a legal approach that defies conservative rhetoric. The incomplete records of District Courts make it difficult to provide anything but estimates of the overall trends in terms of prosecutions. The Criminal Court indexes, which are almost intact, do suggest that from the reestablishment of the justice system after the fall of Hungarian Soviet Republic and its Revolutionary Tribunal system from 1920 to 1940, the number of cases that were appealed ranged from ten to sixty-one.[59]

Table 6 shows Criminal Court cases of homosexual acts (crimes against nature) in Budapest under Paragraphs 251 and 252 of the 1878 Hungarian penal code.[60] But even if we had complete records of unnatural fornication cases from the period, it would likely not provide us with a full picture, since homosexual men could be and in fact were prosecuted for crimes other than homosexuality. As police captain József Vogl estimated in 1929, "about one third of homosexual men come into conflict with the Penal Code."[61] Between 1926 and 1929, there were about six hundred people from the homosexual registry who were prosecuted for misdemeanors and crimes.[62] Men were prosecuted for stealing, bribery, and petty crimes as well as for libel and perjury. "Unnatural fornication" charges were, however, pressed in cases of sex with minors (boys under eighteen) and in cases of nonconsensual sex. In both of these cases, the accused, if proven guilty, faced harsh punishment.[63]

During the entire interwar period, the number of cases in which people were reported to the police for their alleged homosexuality or their alleged same-sex sexual affairs/relationships remained relatively small. As K observed, it was unlikely that a homosexual person would approach and make a sexual advance to a stranger, unless they were certain that the person understood and was open to the idea of homosexual encounters. Reading through the court documents, we only find one or two cases in which someone was charged with attempted homosexual activity. Another reason for the low numbers of Paragraph 241 charges had to do with the fact that many people who could have informed the police about homosexuals did not do so for their own personal benefit. In fact, the greatest danger homosexuals in Budapest faced was those criminals who used their (often intimate) knowledge of people's sexuality and sexual practices to rob them or to blackmail

TABLE 6. Criminal Court cases

Year	Criminal District Courts	Criminal [Appeals] Court
1918	7	5
1919	7	1
1920	10	*
1921	16	1
1922	25	3
1923	35	6
1924	61	5
1925	48	6
1926	27	10
1927	41	13
1928	40	9
1929	37	8
1930	*	7
1931	9	5
1932	33	5
1933	*	9
1934	*	7
1935	32	6
1936	35	8
1937	24	7
1938	32	8
1939	3040	6
1940	40	6
1941	62	3
1942	56	2
1943	*	7
1944	*	1
1945	5	2

* Index volumes are missing or incomplete.

them for their silence. While the police would register a homosexual man and they would therefore have a police record on file, the consequences of being robbed or blackmailed were significantly worse.

When and how were people actually prosecuted in the courts for "unnatural fornication"? The Criminal District Courts tended to pursue the charges of homosexuality on the recommendations of the public prosecution office.⁶⁴ In general, men were apprehended by the "homosexual squad" in public venues, lavatories, city parks, and public baths, where men would engage in what were considered to be "unnatural" acts, ranging from having sex with another man to the "inappropriate" touching of another man's genitals. Similar to most countries that criminalized male homosexuality, different Hungarian courts and legal scholars had varying understandings of how "unnatural fornication" should be defined.⁶⁵ Nevertheless, considering that, in most cases, throughout the entire interwar period, there were no arguments between the judges, the defense, and the public prosecutors about the parameters of "unnatural fornication," it is likely that there was a tacit understanding within the judicial system about what actions would fulfill the conditions of "unnatural fornication." This is supported by the fact that, between 1918 and 1940, those accused of "unnatural fornication" rarely contested the charges on the basis of "not meeting the criteria of Paragraph 241." It seems highly likely that the police only filed charges against those men who had incontestably committed acts of "unnatural fornication."⁶⁶

In the great majority of cases during this period, charges were made against working-class men and men with low social and economic status. Overwhelmingly, these men were born outside of Budapest, mainly in rural areas and in small towns. They had all moved to the capital for work. Almost all of them performed some form of manual labor.⁶⁷ Not surprisingly, men with the means to conduct their sexual encounters in private were greatly underrepresented. In terms of marital status, about 80 percent (or four out of five men) were unmarried.⁶⁸ Most men were Roman Catholic, as were most of the Hungarian countryside. Along with Catholics, Jewish men were slightly overrepresented among the accused.⁶⁹ The ages of the men varied between seventeen and the mid-sixties, with the majority being in their twenties and thirties.⁷⁰ In sum, most men who were accused of homosexuality between 1918 and 1940 were of rural origin and, similar to their international counterparts, in their twenties and thirties, working class, and unmarried. As such, the nature of the prosecution of queer men in Budapest highlights a transnational urban pattern during the interwar era, where young working-class men were disproportionately overrepresented in cases with charges of homosexuality.⁷¹

During the 1920s the charges for consensual public homosexual acts ranged from a financial penalty to a few weeks in the lightest form of confinement. Considering that according to the penal code if the accused were found guilty of "unnatural fornication," the punishment was up to one year, it is noteworthy that the courts rarely assigned a sentence of more than ten days or more than a few weeks for consensual sex.[72] In fact, if men had no prior criminal history, in the majority of cases, the courts often suspended the punishment. The rationale behind this leniency was that the courts expected that "it would have a positive effect on the accused and would deter him from repeating the same deed again in the future."[73] As a result, first-time offenders often received only probation, in which case the penalty was most often a fine. Considering that most people were working class, this could still be a hardship. If they could not pay, if they repeated offenses, or if they were charged for multiple sexual acts with multiple people, the punishment ranged from a week to a few weeks in *fogház*, the lightest form of confinement.

By no means did the public prosecutor's office always have its way. In approximately 15 percent of the cases, the courts dismissed the charges of "unnatural fornication" for lack of sufficient proof.[74] This was true in both the 1920s and 1930s. Judges were fully aware that an accusation of homosexuality placed men in a vulnerable position. Thus, unless the judges were fully convinced that "unnatural" acts between two (or more) men indeed had taken place, they were reluctant to pursue a charge of Paragraph 241. Being charged with homosexuality tainted one's public image, and the judges knew all too well that it was much easier to make accusations of "unnatural deeds" than prove them untrue. The surviving documents speak of a legal process that reflects a conscious effort on the judges' part to protect people until they were unquestionably proven guilty. Fully aware of the social stigma around homosexuality and the power of accusation, it was rare that the courts would pronounce someone guilty of Paragraph 241 based on a single witness.[75] The courts not only questioned the authenticity of independent witnesses but also even interrogated and at times dismissed police reports and the testimonials of detectives, if they thought that they were unconvincing or inadequate to prove the charges.[76]

Despite the definite political turn toward a more authoritarian conservatism and right-wing politics throughout the 1930s, the Hungarian legal system, at least on second degree, actually tried fewer cases for the charges of "unnatural fornication." After Black Tuesday in 1929 and the subsequent world economic crisis and depression that characterized the first part of the 1930s, the number of "unnatural fornication" charges actually declined, while the crimes associated with economic destitution, like stealing or solicitation, saw an enormous rise.[77] Similar to the 1920s, during the 1930s many homosexuals were charged for petty crimes, but not for being a homosexual. Although it is difficult to verify the exact numbers, according to contemporary medical, police, and legal sources, the police prosecuted criminal homosexuals with renewed vigor. The homosexual registry was expanding and had a subdivision for male homosexual prostitutes. Yet, the judicial treatment of homosexuals did not change.

Unless the minors were prostitutes (in which case both men were prosecuted), having consensual sexual encounters with men under the age of eighteen was considered a more serious offense.[78] The most severe sentences were reserved for men who had sexual encounters with boys under the age of twelve. In this instance, similar to adult men who had nonconsensual sex with other adult men, people were charged with Paragraph 242 "nonconsensual sex between men."[79] Minors could not "consent" to sex—unless they had already had sex enough to be "ruined." In the eyes of the authorities, forced sexual encounters damaged men not only physically but also morally. This was especially the case with men who had not reached full psychical and emotional maturity. According to the courts, nonconsensual "unnatural fornication" caused "moral decay" in young men. Defined in this way, the physical, emotional, and moral violation of men and particularly young men through forced homosexual sex harmed not just the individuals against whom the crime was committed but also the greater community. Thus, in the context of minors and nonconsensual sex, the courts considered homosexuality to be a relevant additional criminal factor. Because the harm was done to men, homosexuality was seen as weakening Hungary's manpower and, hence, Hungary's future. Last but not least, during the 1930s men were charged with Paragraph 241 in cases also involving theft and bribery. About one in five cases of "unnatural fornication" during the 1930s involved theft.[80] The cases, which often involved more than two men, centered around stealing, while homosexuality was usually a facilitator of the crime and always a secondary consideration of the courts. The theft generally happened during a homosexual encounter or within the context of longer same-sex relationship that took place usually between a man of reasonable means and a poorer man. In these instances, the person who suffered was still charged with Paragraph 241 but received a lenient punishment. In contrast, the punishments for theft were much more severe.[81] Overall, reading the case records of the 1920s and 1930s suggests that the judicial treatment of male homosexuality was remarkably stable throughout the interwar years. This is true in terms of the conceptualization of male homosexuality, which remained similarly murky when it had to be defined by precise physical actions, and also in terms of the legal system's lenient prosecutorial attitude toward homosexuality. The courts gave the accused the benefit of the doubt and, even when found guilty, gave out relatively mild sentences. The legal procedure and legal opinions on male sexuality continued to uphold a lenient attitude about nonnormative male sexual behaviors that were not seen as an endangerment to others or as harmful to the public morale.

MALE HOMOSEXUAL PROSTITUTION IN BUDAPEST DURING THE INTERWAR YEARS

A look at male prostitution neatly accentuates the discrepancies between the rhetoric and the intent of the conservative interwar governments and the actual situation on the ground. The publications of Kornél Tábori and Vladimir Székely discussed in chapter 2 revealed that male homosexual prostitution, by the turn of the century, was a staple component of Budapest's urban landscape. Not necessarily visible to an "unfamiliar" eye, but, as the journalists told their readers, the "knights of sick love" had a considerable supply of men who would offer their services. At the time of writing in 1908, Tábori and Székely hoped that paying more attention to the factors that drove (even) men to prostitution would help reduce the harmful effects of the practice. But even Tábori and Székely, who not only established the investigative journalism of the Budapest underworld, but were also probably more familiar with male homosexuals than most of the police, could not have imagined the exponential expansion of male homosexual prostitution that took place in Budapest in the 1930s. As K's experience demonstrated, Budapest, similar to bigger cities across Europe, experienced a visible increase in male homosexual prostitution.[82] Indeed, we learn from Jenő Szántó, a practicing chief medical doctor, that "perhaps there is not even a single bar or a busier café, where we would not occasionally come across a male prostitute."[83] Szántó, who evidently had a working relationship with the police and was a regular contributor to *Népegészségügy* (Public Health), the official public health journal published by the Ministry of Interior, and other medical journals, gives, perhaps, the most comprehensive official account on male prostitutions during the interwar period. Szántó's articles also provide a rare window into the minds of Hungarian professionals and bureaucrats whose job it was to make Budapest a healthier urban metropolis. His position—as a doctor who was involved both in research and in the treatment of both nonnormative sexuality and sexually transmitted illnesses, and as an inside participant of the police department—makes Szántó uniquely suited to provide essential insights.

In his 1934 article entitled "The Issue of Male Homosexual Prostitution," Szántó states that, "in the confidential registry of the Metropolitan Police, there had been 1695 individuals until May 1932, of whom we can

TABLE 7. Registered male prostitutes (1,695)

Occupation*	#	Occupation	#
Factory worker, day laborer, house servant	241	Pupil (46), university student (23)	69
Merchant, salesman	194	Hairdresser, barber	44
Private officeholder, factory owner, landowner, property owner	58	Upholsterer, decorator, painter	46
Civil servant, civil worker	33	Artist, actor	9
Tailors (both for men and women)	124	Butcher, slaughterer	30
Ironworkers, chauffeurs	180	Engineer, architect, chemist	2
Waiters, bartenders,	80	Nurse, masseur	6
Carpenters, masons,	109	Artiste, dancer	17
Gardener, digger	128	Musician	14
Baker, cook, confectioner	53	Textile worker, weaver	19
Shoemaker	86	Bookbinder, printer	7
Manservant	48	Soldier (incomplete data)	7
Jeweler, artificer, optician, photographer	82		

* Szántó, "A homosexualitásról, különös tekintettel a budpesti viszonyokra," Bőrgyógyászati, Urológiai és Venereologiai Szemle, no. 2 (1933): 828.

safely conclude that they were prostitutes because, by their own admission, it was monetary reasons that had driven them to the male homosexual crowd."[84] In registering these people, he informs the readers, the police used a special label, the word *érdek* (interest in) to differentiate them from other homosexuals in the registry. Subsequently, Szántó presents detailed statistical breakdowns of the male prostitutes in terms of their socioeconomic background, occupation (table 7), and age.

One of the interesting things about this categorization is how, according to the police, none of the male homosexuals were "unemployed" or perceived as "full-time prostitutes." Rather than assuming that the police believed that none of these men worked as full-time prostitutes, it is more likely that the occupations listed on the registry referred to the occupational background and qualifications of the men, rather than their actual occupation. Most of the 1,695 male prostitutes came from the lower classes and, according to Szántó, sold their sexual services to men for similar purposes as their female counterparts, that is, for money. At the height of the Great Depression, unemployed men and men with low salaries turned to prostitution in order to supplement their income. Most male homosexual prostitutes were in their twenties, as Szántó, referring to his homosexual sources, explains "prostitutes over thirty were considered superannuated." He also notes that the actual number of juvenile male prostitutes was far greater than the registered number (sixty-four) in 1932.[85] The reason for the low number of juvenile registries lay in the attitude of the police. "Out of humanitarian reasons, the police postpone the registering of youth until there is no hope left for these young people to amend their life and leave this kind of lifestyle."[86]

Szántó's publications expose the inherent contradictions of the authorities' treatment of male sexuality. To begin with, the physician reminds us of "the double moral standards, which burden male homosexual activity as immoral and a perversion, while ignoring female homosexuality with a smile."[87] Szántó's observation highlights a general aspect of interwar Hungary, namely, that, culturally, there was a continuing acceptance of men visiting female prostitutes and, to some extent, of male same-sex sexual encounters. However, in contrast to the regulation of female prostitution, where the conservative regime enacted stricter laws and regulations, Szántó points out, there continued to be no regulations directly dealing with male prostitution.[88] While this was not necessarily the case, since the 1927 Protection of Public Morality Ordinance did address same-sex soliciting and made it a petty offense (punishable up to fifteen days detention and eighty-pengő fine), Szántó was overall not wrong.[89] Female prostitution regularly drew the attention of lawmakers, public health and city officials, and the larger public, but there are no public records on male prostitution in either the parliamentary memos or in the memos of the city council. Paradoxically, then, even if female prostitution was more accepted socially, the consequences of growing conservatism actually imposed much greater burdens on female prostitutes.[90]

The conjunction of the cultural acceptance of female prostitution with the increasing regulation and policing of female sexuality created a situation in which many male prostitutes fared better than their female counterparts. Szántó aptly illustrates the gendered dynamics of social regulation that were a central feature of the Hungarian and more generally of the European state during the interwar years.[91] He believed that women who were registered as prostitutes by the Vice Squad of the Budapest Metropolitan Police were humiliated and disenfranchised by the process. In contrast, he argued that this was not case for the treatment of male prostitutes. In his words,

> While the regulation puts a burdensome and humiliating shackle on female prostitutes, it does not concern itself with male prostitution. Thus, it is almost impossible to re-integrate oneself from female prosti-

tution into respectable society, but for those burnt out male homosexual prostitutes, with the help of their well-to-do friends, the door is wide open to become a successful and respected member of bourgeois society.[92]

This is, of course, a sweeping generalization and unquestionably minimized the difficult circumstances with which male prostitutes had to contend. Nevertheless, Szántó was right to point out that the conservative Horthy regime's drastic change in the regulation and policing of female prostitution placed all those women who sold their sexual services in a difficult position. At the same time, evidence attests that female prostitution continued to prosper and remained widely accepted (most certainly by male members of society) as part of life.[93] The culture continued to accept men seeking female prostitutes and in general thought nothing less of these men. In fact, masculinity continued to be reinforced by visiting so-called butterflies of the night. Whereas femininity was forever tainted by involvement in prostitution, and the chances of a woman having a decent life following her sex work were slim. In contrast, Szántó believed that those men who sold their bodies, even if society—overall—considered their trade to be more shameful, often had, in the long run, better prospects in life. Szántó argued that male prostitutes fared better than their female counterparts because their male homosexual customers would be much more likely, willing, and able to assist them than the heterosexual male customers would be able or inclined to help female prostitutes. As historians of sexuality in other contexts have shown, the illicitness and social stigma around male homosexuality facilitated a structure within homosexual prostitution that was often more "egalitarian" and communal than within female prostitution.[94] Being marginalized by their own sexuality, many men who paid to have sex with other men were protective of their former (paid) lovers. Szántó also noted that the same authorities that had passed draconian regulations for female prostitution in the 1920s simply avoided the question of male prostitution and deferred its treatment to the police.

Not being directed (or bound) by myriad regulations, it was up to the police to decide how to deal with male prostitution. Following the establishment of the conservative regime, the police did indeed attempt to make some changes. They began registering men as male homosexual prostitutes, and, according to the surviving sources, their number in the registry increased exponentially from 1,696 to 1,932.[95] The squad specializing in homosexual crimes monitored the most frequented pickup places, and those who were repeatedly caught were charged with "loitering with intent" and sent back to their place of origin in the countryside.[96] However, by and large, the police and the "homosexual squad" continued the pre-1918 practice, according to which, while all men who were caught with other men (both prostitutes and homosexuals) were registered, the majority of them did not get prosecuted unless their action disturbed the public, was nonconsensual, or involved blackmail. The case of K also seems to suggest that, although homosexual men dreaded being registered, being on the male homosexual registry (even as a male prostitute) entailed fewer negative consequences than was the case for female prostitutes. Szántó, writing in 1934, certainly believed this was the case and maintained that the male registry, in sharp contrast to the female registry, "was not accompanied by the same degrading obligations and it also did not impinge on the civil rights of the individual."[97] Rather than stripping individuals of their human dignity, Szántó continued, "the sole purpose of the registry was so the police could get to know the prostitutes and, if necessary, track them." In this way, the police were more successful in knowing where soliciting was taking place and were better placed to separate notorious pimps and panders (who recruited from the young and innocent) from those who were soliciting out of desperation.[98] Overall, according to him, tracking, rather than punishing, allowed the police to inquire about more details of male prostitutes and also helped to dissuade those men who were not authentic homosexuals from the trade.[99] No police memos or internal orders remain to substantiate Szántó's claims further. Nevertheless, the existing evidence corroborates that the police only concerned themselves with a particular type of nonnormative male sexuality, which explains why a considerable segment of male prostitution could remain unregulated and, according to Szántó, relatively undisturbed.

CONSERVATIVE SEXUAL ORDER AND ITS GENDERED IMPLICATIONS

In order to arrive at a more comprehensive answer to why male homosexuality could be tolerated under an increasingly conservative political system, we have to consider the contemporary understandings of male sexuality. As much as the conservative regime set out to raise the morale of men (along with women), the members of the police and the criminal legal system, and of course the medical establishment, were painfully aware that the majority of men, regardless of their sexual orientation, fell short of living by the creeds of Christianity. Equally important was the experience of World War I, which left many men not only physically, but also psychologically, damaged. Even before the war ended, psychoanalysts and psychiatrists were actively involved in the treatment of "shell-shocked" men.[100] Following the war, there was both concern and anxiety, which was present in most of the countries that had fought in the war, about the reintegration of these men into civil society.[101] Postwar violent behavior was understood to be a consequence of men experiencing unprecedented brutality at the front, as well as experiencing the harsh conditions of prison camps. Sources attest to the fact that many men who came back suffered, not only from what we would today call "posttraumatic stress disorders," but also from sexual "dysfunctions."[102] That many men had a difficult time readjusting themselves to civilian life and heterosexual relationships is evident. And it is against this background that, in Budapest, the actions of the police in terms of male homosexuality make more sense. Nonnormative male sexual practices could be overlooked or at least looked upon with the understanding that the experience of World War I had deeply unsettled the masculinity and "normal" sexuality of men. Szántó himself openly acknowledges that most men were not living up to the state's expectations and that they were not able to, even if they had tried. "There are very few men, whose sexual life would at all times and in all respects, meet the requirements of religious ethics. . . . In terms of sexual life, we cannot talk about normal and abnormal, otherwise two-thirds of the men would have to be labeled as pathological."[103] We can only speculate about the specific basis upon which Szántó made his claim. It is most probable that he used the term "pathological" in a broader sense, encompassing medical and psychological "abnormalities," as well as moral shortcomings. Reading Szántó's statement from this perspective, he basically argues that two-thirds of Hungarian men failed to fulfil the medical and/or cultural prerequisites of Hungarian manhood. Consequently, the fact that, during the interwar years, the police continued to play a practical role by recognizing the de facto status of existing sexual morals, while protecting public morality, should come as no surprise.[104] Wishing homosexuality would go away was one thing. But perceiving and accepting that homosexuality and even homosexual prostitution was an integral part of modern urban life was another thing entirely. These aspects were far from being mutually exclusive and were simultaneously present throughout the interwar years.

In spite of the Horthy regime's attempts to make the urban population (re)absorb traditional religious sexual ethics, we also find that the idea that the fulfillment of sexual desires was an important factor in an individual's health was also present. By the 1920s and most definitely by the 1930s, the idea that sex and sexuality were central in determining individual and societal health and character had been making its way, not only into popular culture, but also into the thinking of the regulatory authorities. Szántó's articles demonstrate that the idea that engaging in sex and pursuing sexual satisfaction was one of the driving forces of human existence could be part of the official language of the public health officials and the police, but not the politicians. Accepting that men were inherently sexual served to legitimize the de facto existence of female prostitution, and also served as an excuse that could be used to explain forms of male sexual behavior, even outside of the monogamous heterosexual relationship. No other issue highlights the de facto acceptance of men being active sexually better than the campaign against syphilis and venereal disease, which intensified during the interwar years. While rhetoric could still praise abstinence and sexual monogamy, authorities were also pragmatic about sex education and the need to provide necessary information about causes, treatments, and cures of sexually transmitted illnesses.[105] In turn, the conceptualization of sexuality as a central component of human life, along with the understanding that homosexuality was an innate condition, could justify the protection of homosexuals. Although Szántó might have been unique in his frank statement that "the church from its high ground can demand self-restraint, but the great majority of male homosexuals could not bear to be excluded from experiencing the most basic manifestation of zest for life," he most certainly was not the only one who made sexual satisfaction (hetero or homo) an imperative for human existence.[106] It seems that even those who opposed homosexuality as an immoral and perverse deed admitted that the sexual drive was fundamental in shaping human behavior. While conservative voices pointed to modernity and urban decadence as the root causes of sexual immorality, they too acknowledged the power of sexual drive.[107] From that position, it was not difficult to conceptualize that, in a modern society, individuals should be entitled to fulfill their sexual drives as long as it did not harm others. As the first two chapters illustrate, the notion of individual sexual rights had been present both in the discourse and in most of the practices of Hungarian authorities prior to 1918. In this regard Szántó's approach to (homo-) sexuality was not novel:

> We must facilitate these [homosexual] people so they can fulfill their instinctual desires although, only as long as they do not harm or endanger the rights of the individual or the collective, and as long as they do not impinge on the interest of the state, and as long they do not offend the moral view of the majority with outrageous behavior.[108]

Yet considering the conservative climate, that Szántó could unreservedly say in the official publication of the authorities in 1934 that the sexual activities of two adults, within four walls, behind closed doors, based upon consent and mutual understanding are nobody else's business is quite surprising. Szántó's subsequent assertion, according to which engaging in homosexual acts does not impede the interest of the state nor offend the moral view of the majority, is even more surprising. And it was not he alone who made his argument.[109]

Authorities, like many of their European counterparts, continued to uphold two important assumptions about homosexuality from the prewar era: that there was a category of "authentic" or constitutional homosexuals, "who simply could not help their sexuality," and second, that most people could develop a desire for their own sex in certain environments.[110] Police and public health officials of the interwar period, to varying degrees, embraced the idea that, developmentally, people were on a spectrum of sexuality. Such a conceptualization could foster the continuing acceptance of "authentic" homosexuality on the basis that "authentic" homosexuals were born with their homosexuality and had no ability to change.[111] According to contemporary views, however, most were not innate homosexuals but rather *acquired* their homosexuality and thus were deemed "pseudo-homosexuals." And it was the process of acquiring homosexuality that, first and foremost, concerned the authorities. This idea particularly underwrote concerns about the fragility of youth sexuality. As Mark Cornwall demonstrated in the context of German youth movements in the newly formed Czechoslovakia, there was an acknowledged coexistence of nationalist aims and homosocial environments; for Hungarian authorities the homosociality of interwar youth movements was a cause of concern.[112] As in the case of the pre-1918 era, the concerns over the (hetero)sexuality of youth and in particular of young boys are evident in the fear of the contagiousness of homosexuality. Even as they advocated moral and sexual purity, single-sex organizations such as the Hungarian Boys Scouts or Levente Associations could be seen as susceptible to homosexual activities. Safeguarding youth and their supposed fragile (hetero)sexuality from the prey of authentic homosexuals remained a top priority.

The few extant interwar literary representations of homosexuality echo the fragility of heterosexual masculinity as well as the deep concern with protecting the youth. Sándor Márai's 1930 novel *Zendülők* (The rebels) and Antal Szerb's 1937 *Utas és holdvilág* (Journey by moonlight) both portray the thin line that separated the presence of homoeroticism among young men—assumed to be platonic and therefore harmless—from homosexual desire, understood as an aberration.[113] While Szerb's *Utas és holdvilág*, a novel about a young bourgeois man on his honeymoon to Italy, portrays homo- and more generally nonnormative sexuality on a more symbolic register, Márai's *Zendülők* is a much more tangible representation of how, as a consequence of World War I and the absence of strong male figures, male sexuality could be corrupted.[114] *Zendülők* tells a tale of four teenage boys who, in a small town during the last days of World War I, rebel against the adult world—by despising, lying to, and even robbing adults. It paints a picture of a society where boys and young men, in their unwillingness to face the real world, fail to become real Hungarian men (able, masculine, heterosexual, etc.). The boys, as a contemporary reviewer of the novel notes, "lost faith and confidence in the turbulent and dangerous world of adults, [and] did not desire to enter the spiritual sphere of adulthood, but instead hid in its infantile greenhouse, clinging spasmodically in lifestyles of childhood, as they would to a huge mother in a thousand-chained skirt."[115] The boys, whose heterosexual awakenings are repressed while their friendships are erotically charged, become infatuated with Amadé, an actor in a local theater, whose feminine allure masks his homosexuality. The story culminates with the town's Jewish pawnbroker (whom the boys meet following one of their robberies) taking advantage of the boys' gullibility, with the help of a homosexual actor. Having made the boys inebriated in the empty theater, the pawnbroker and the actor entice them to enact a homosexual "play," which Amadé participates in while the pawnbroker secretly watches. The trope of Jewish sexual perversion aside, the novel's ending reflects fears contemporaries held about the slippage among male adolescence between "childishly delicate eroticism in a platonic sense of the word" and the potential for homosexuality.[116] Ultimately, *Zendülők* is a manifestation of the perceived fragility of heterosexual manhood especially during adolescence.

Like in Márai's novel, for authorities, having homosexual encounters did not necessarily mean that one would become a homosexual. There were many reasons why men could engage in sex with other men: men who sexually engaged with other men could be seen as suffering from the posttraumatic experience and replicate the homosocial experience of the war; economic hardship and necessity could also drive men, who having had the experience with homosexuality during the war, could sell their services to other men. In these cases, with the deterrents of being registered and a financial penalty, the police and legal authorities believed that men and their sexuality could be rehabilitated.[117] At the same time, the authorities' focus on the prosecution of "real" criminal elements among homosexuals, people who stole, used force, had sex with the underage or blackmailed, also left "authentic" noncriminal homosexuals with a considerable space to conduct their homosexual affairs.

The issue of sexually transmitted diseases in relation to homosexual men can provide an additional piece to the puzzle. During the interwar period Hungary had one of, if not the, highest rates of venereal disease in Europe.[118] While there was not a day that the papers did not talk about venereal disease in connection with female prostitution, with some notable exceptions male homosexuals were conspicuously absent from public or official discussions.[119] Considering the high rates of syphilis and gonorrhea, the lack of acknowledgment of the prevalence of sexually transmitted illnesses among male prostitutes and their clientele was a notable shortcoming of the Hungarian authorities. The conservative regime could talk about male and female sexuality in the context of heterosexual sexual relations, but same-sex sexuality did not enter the discourse, official or unofficial. Even those few public health documents that raised the issue of male homosexuality in the context of sexually transmitted diseases did so in passing. During the interwar years, the widely accepted idea that sexuality was fluid meant that people's sexuality was considered malleable. Most people, according to reigning interwar ideas about sexuality, acquired their homosexuality through exposure to homoerotic ideas and homosocial environments. Hence, even as Catholic and more generally Christian sex education materials considered homosexuality as sinful and to be avoided at all cost, the last thing officials, the spokespersons of conservative, Catholic ruling classes, and even the far-right elements or the small more liberal opposition and their media outlets wanted was to mainstream discussion about homosexuality.[120] One contemporary judge and legal scholar opined, "in their approach to homosexuality public authorities must be extremely cautious and discreet so they will not cause a public scandal in instances when the deed (homosexuality) would have vanished without a trace in the filthy den which it came from."[121] The notions that "what is not discussed does not exist, and the less we talk about it the better" were shared across the political and social spheres during the interwar years. Strengthening the morality and virility of men could go hand in hand with the acceptance of men's fragility in both of those areas. And this goes a long way toward explaining why containment through silence came to be a defining feature of the conservative Horthy regime's approach to male homosexuality.

EUGENICS AND THE INFLUENCE OF NAZI GERMANY

As Marius Turda and János Gyurgyák and most recently Attila Kund have demonstrated, Hungary had a strong tradition of eugenic thinking of its own that cut across the political spectrum.[122] Present since the late nineteenth century, the loss of World War I and the Treaty of Trianon brought eugenic ideas into mainstream discourse. Imbued with antisemitism, race scientists, politicians, and public intellectuals called for the regeneration of the Hungarian nation that would protect as well as strengthen Hungarian *faj*.[123] Members of the *fajvédők*, the so-called race protectors, became vocal in their support for the application of eugenics to protect the Hungarian race during the 1920s. Aided by race biologists and selectively applying biological racist theories, they called for both positive and negative eugenic measures, to protect and promote healthy non-Jewish Hungarians while curtailing the rights and reproduction capabilities of those deemed unhealthy others. However, it was not until after the worldwide economic depression in 1929 began and the subsequent rise of the Nazi Party that eugenic ideas and racial biology came to be explicitly considered arguments for controlling homosexuality. Certainly, eugenic ideas in regard to sexuality had been gaining influence prior to the arrival of Hitler and the establishment of the Nazi regime.[124] Eugenics ideas from Nazi medical and public health worlds as well as Nazi racial laws served as boosters for the proposals of the *fajvédők*. They further legitimized the *fajvédők*'s aims for the purification of the Hungarian race, which in their view, while destined for greatness, could only live up to its potential by weeding out both foreign and unhealthy Hungarian elements.[125] In terms of eugenic ideas about homosexuality, which in general received scant attention, attitudes of the race protectors reflected the pan-European discourse on homosexuality at the time, with most commentators condemning it as a form of degeneration or "mental weakness."[126] Despite that eugenicists and supporters of race protectors agreed that male homosexuality was dangerous for the health of Hungarian race and should be eliminated, their rhetorical rants never materialized into actual policy or legal recommendations.[127] Put differently, at the same time eugenic and Social Darwinist ideas were increasingly present in public discourse, their influence and, especially, the implementation of negative eugenic measures remained curtailed well into the 1930s. As in the case of Italy and Catholic nations more generally, the legalization of negative eugenic measures was prevented first and foremost by the Christian churches.[128] Consequently, Hungarian authorities prosecuted abortion and prostitution with a vengeance, but the sterilization of "defectives" and, more generally, the legalization of discriminatory measures based on physical, mental, or sexual grounds were unimplemented. Overall, along with the propagation of conservative sexual ethics, there was a general silence on the question of homosexuality. Considered by most as a mental or biological shortcoming, many medical and legal authorities, as well social critics, tended to agree that the public's exposure to same-sex sexuality, like pornography, whether through literature, journalism, or court reporting could actually ignite "abnormal" sexual fantasies and therefore contribute to the spreading of homosexuality. Even the otherwise sensational liberal press, which periodically covered stories about people with nonnormative gender and sexual behavior, did so in a subdued manner.[129]

The radical right (national-socialist and fascist political parties that were united in their antisemitism, anti-Bolshevism, and their commitment to the restoration of Hungary's pre-Trianon borders) also shared the idea that more discussion of homosexual relationships, even if condemning, would do more harm than good. Unlike conservatives, the radical right parties were staunch believers in negative eugenics and regularly called for the implementation of measures to "purify" the Hungarian nation from its "undesirables." Yet, they remained silent on homosexuality, and there are no records of them openly discussing the issue. In a rather surprising way, the Hungarian radical right followed the rest of society: with an ostrich policy, burying their heads in the sand. Hungarian men needed to be valorous and ethnically pure, but based on a survey of the major radical right daily publications of the 1930s, it seems that the radical right either took Hungarian masculinity and heterosexuality for granted or, similar to the police and conservative justice system, was more willing to ignore certain nonnormative male behaviors.[130] Articles frequently stressed the "exceptionality" of Hungarian males—especially of the peasants—in terms of their spiritual strength but remained silent on their sexual behavior.[131] The silence of the radical right becomes most pronounced vis-à-vis their ever increasing outspokenness in the promotion of eugenic measures to solve the so-called Jewish question, where aggressive anti-Semitic propaganda played a decisive role in the future direction that authorities took in regard to dealing with the Jewish minority.[132] In sharp contrast, staunch conservatives, far-right ideologues, and right-wing populists were conspicuously silent about male homosexuality. There is little trace of their having called attention to the perils of homosexuality or naming it among the causes of social ills and especially the implementation of negative eugenic measures.[133] This is particularly telling in light of the homosocial environment of the mostly exclusively male spaces of the radical right parties. While there is no evidence of the type of homosexual culture that existed within the German SA (Sturmabteilung, or storm troopers), just as in the case of single-sex Hungarian youth movements there was an obvious tension between extoling male camaraderie and exclusively male spaces and assuring the rank-and-file members' hetcroscxuality.[134]

The meteoric rise of Hitler and the Nazi takeover of Germany was closely followed in Hungary, and the institutionalization of racial and eugenic policies in Germany was welcome in many conservative and all radical right circles. From conservative to radical right Hungarian publications, Nazi policies of promoting positive and negative eugenic measures received commendations.[135] During the Röhm Putsch, or the Night of the Long Knives, the media briefly broke its silence on homosexuality and reported on the decadent and "disgusting" (homo)sexual habits of SA chief of staff Ernst Röhm, citing it as an inevitable cause of his downfall.[136] In terms of Nazi sexual politics, however, the media, including the newspapers of the radical right, remained silent about the events that followed the Night of the Long Knives. Sticking to their policy of not talking about homosexuality did not necessarily mean, however, that leading medical and governmental circles had no knowledge of the establishment and aims of the Reich Central Office for Combatting Homosexuality and Abortion. The debates at the Hungarian legal association in 1936, for instance, and subsequent legal publications demonstrate that the applicability of negative eugenics ideas in "dealing with" homosexuality was openly discussed.[137] Indeed, there were medical and legal debates that explicitly considered the possibility of introducing sterilization for the mentally and physically disabled and for homosexuals.[138] But even though Hungarian politicians and authorities were informed about the Nazi intentions to apply negative eugenic measures and prosecute homosexual behavior, they refrained from openly considering their application in the Hungarian context.[139] There were two main reasons for this. For one, regardless of their ever-growing appeal, negative eugenics was seen as a messy affair. As respected Hungarian legal scholar Pál Angyal expressed in 1936,

> We Hungarians should be extremely cautious about the measures of negative eugenics, because we could less afford [than Germany and populous states more generally] the luxury to thin/rarefy our ranks, for an idea, whose advantage today looks very dubious and uncertain, about the alleged promise of fewer but superior Hungarians.[140]

Therefore, living in "mutilated Hungary" and being obsessed with the declining numbers of the Hungarian population, Hungarian authorities were hesitant to adopt negative eugenic measures until they were convincingly proven "scientific" and delivered the promised results. Simply put, there were too few Hungarians to thin their ranks. The second reason had to do with the fear that the legalization of sterilization (and negative eugenics more generally) would lend itself to abuse. Angyal and other leading legal scholars believed that the institutionalization of negative eugenics into criminal law was both unwarranted on legal grounds and carried an inherent danger by providing a means to penalize individuals for political and ideological reasons.[141] Consequently, in spite of the unquestionable appeal of Nazi eugenic politics within pro-Nazi circles and increasing political pressure to implement Nazi eugenic measures, conservative authorities continued to reject the validity and usefulness of negative eugenics, including the sterilization of homosexuals.[142] Not only was sterilization off the table, but unlike in the case of Paragraph 175 of the German penal code, there was also no change in the Hungarian penal code in terms of the definition or the punishment of same-sex sexual acts.[143]

CONCLUSION

Having surveyed the opinions of Hungarian authorities and social critics on male homosexuality and male nonnormative behavior more generally, a couple of distinct features emerge. Budapest's image in the eyes of governing conservatives as the "Sinful City," in opposition to the perceived purity of the countryside, in many ways served as a self-fulfilling prophecy.[144] As the experiences of K evinced during the interwar years, the capital of now "mutilated" Hungary remained an urban metropolis that continued to have a decadent side. Ironically, amidst growing conservatism male homosexuals experienced a growing subculture and some "queer-friendly" establishments. The coexistence of a nationalist Christian conservative regime and a visible and acknowledged homosexual presence in the Hungarian capital was, above all, the result of the social and economic aftermath of World War I and the Treaty of Trianon, which ensured that the police and authorities in Budapest were overwhelmingly concerned with ensuring safety, security, and public order. In this respect, policing or prosecuting consensual male homosexual activity, especially when conducted in private, was low on the police agenda. Furthermore, the Metropolitan Police, while continuing to register homosexuals as well as male prostitutes, only pressed charges in certain instances: if sex was not consensual, took place in public, involved a minor, or in cases of additional ulterior motives such as bribery or theft.

Greater policing of male sexuality was neither necessarily detrimental for certain homosexuals nor implied greater prosecution. In wanting to assure future strength (moral, physical, and numerical), interwar Hungarian governments, similar to many of their European counterparts, increasingly made "normal" sexuality a prerequisite of citizenship. This was part of a greater process of state intervention into people's lives that did not stop at the bedroom.[145] The highly gendered notion of "normal" sexuality was accompanied by a highly sexed and gendered policing. As this chapter has demonstrated, the ways in which authorities in Budapest, for instance, approached and handled male and female prostitution embodied how the conservative state channeled much greater resources into policing female and especially nonnormative heterosexual female sexuality. Authorities did not ignore nonnormative male sexual and especially homosexual behaviors in public. In fact, during the interwar years, the Metropolitan Police increased the policing of homosexual activities. However, they did so in a specific way. They differentiated between, on the one hand, "authentic" men who, even if not innately homosexual, nonetheless engaged in homosexual activities because of their sexual inclinations and, on the other hand, those men who only engaged in or were associated with homosexual activities for truly immoral reasons with ulterior motives. Even though there was an increase in the policing of male sexuality, "authentic" homosexuals could paradoxically benefit from the increased presence of the state. By focusing more closely and imposing harsher measures on the exploiters of authentic sexual otherness (blackmailers, thieves, etc.), while continuing to not prosecute and by and large "ignore" consensual homosexual activity in private, the Hungarian authorities actually continued to protect and thus partially normalize a form of male homosexuality during the 1920s and 1930s.[146]

Perhaps one of the most perplexing findings about the interwar period and particularly the 1930s is the extent to which homosexuality continued to be on the back burner even for the radical right elements. Many historians have demonstrated the success that Hungarian radical right politics could achieve by influencing the ruling conservative elite. This was particularly the case in terms of the so-called Jewish question, where aggressive anti-Semitic propaganda played a decisive role in the direction that authorities took in regard to dealing with the Jewish minority. In sharp contrast, staunch conservatives and far-right ideologues and right-wing populists were conspicuously silent about homosexuality. We find no trace of these groups being openly addressed or becoming scapegoats for social ills. Why this was the case I believe has to do with an understanding of sexuality and particularly male sexuality that was shared along the political spectrum. As this chapter argued, there was a genuine belief (on the part of the authorities) that human sexuality was fluid, and hence, people that were malleable. Such an understanding of sexuality explains why there was no public discussion and official acknowledgment of (female or male) homosexuality. The authorities believed that public exposure and official acknowledgment of the extent of homosexual activities in Budapest would have only exacerbated the problem by inviting the curious and those who possessed the possibility of becoming homosexuals. The radical right also shared the idea that more exposure to and talk of homosexual relationships, even if condemning them, would have done more harm than good. In this way, they followed the rest of society: with an ostrich policy, digging their heads into the sand. Hungarian men needed to be strong and ethnically pure, but it seems that the radical right either had some concern about the strength of Hungarian masculinity and heterosexuality, or similar to the police and justice system of the conservatives, was more willing to excuse certain nonnormative male behavior.

Paradoxically, the belief in sexual malleability can also explain the lenient treatment of homosexuals at the courts and of the authorities more generally. To be sure, there was no uniform or one-way treatment and certainly there were many homosexuals who were treated harshly. Based on the surviving documents, however, it seems that the judiciary's treatment of homosexuals overall remained fair and impartial throughout the 1920s and 1930s. This is significant in light of the fact that, compared to both the Communist rule in 1919 and the liberal Austro-Hungarian era, the conservative regime was overall much more punitive in dealing with crime and behavior that was hurting Hungary's "moral economy." Yet, men who had sex with men were treated no harsher than prior to 1920. Whereas crimes such as stealing and cheating were considered serious moral crimes and were treated harshly, consensual homosexuality between adults continued to receive a merciful treatment. According to the courts, if one was an "authentic" homosexual, even if the person was considered "unnatural," his homosexuality was looked at as something that was not a moral or personal failure. The courts considered inborn homosexuality something that needed to be tamed and controlled, but in most cases, they did not consider imprisonment a desirable "treatment." In contrast, when proper male sexuality could be "redeemed"—that is, when according to the experts and authorities, men were not "innately" homosexual—the courts considered men, especially in the cases of first-time offenders, as "savable." In these instances, the courts believed that these men could be (re)educated despite having engaged in homosexual activities. Amidst increasing conservatism and the apparent potency of eugenic ideas among some of the governing elites, when it came to sexual crimes and especially to homosexuality, people were judged and treated as individuals who could be "saved." As long as the possibility existed that masculinity and "normal" male sexuality could be restored, Hungarian men were granted a second chance. As the next chapter demonstrates, it was not until Hungary's entry into the war in 1941 and the rapid rise of Nazi influence that homosexuality became irreconcilable with the idea of national community.

CHAPTER SIX

The End of a Precarious Coexistence: The Prosecution of Homosexuals

Hungary's entry into the war in April of 1941 marked a turning point in the official treatment of homosexuals. The Anschluss, on March 15, 1938—the annexation of Austria into Nazi Germany—and Germany's unambiguous move toward war in 1938-39 triggered the radicalization of Hungary's politics.[1] Within less than a year, the Hungarian fascist party, the Arrow Cross, became a mass party with over three hundred thousand members.[2] Despite the fact that Hungary did not "officially" become fascist until 1944, from 1939 onward the parliament as well as informal politics became heavily influenced by Nazi ideas.[3] The ruling old conservatives were certainly united in disliking the rapidly growing Hungarian radical right movements. Yet, many of them sympathized with Nazi Germany as they saw Hitler as the only possible ally that would lend support to Hungary's claims to its pre-Trianon territories.[4] Between 1938 and 1941, the alignment with Nazi Germany led to the revision of the Treaty of Trianon, whereby Hungary regained some of its pre-1918 territories.[5] The resulting official and popular fervor from the return of the Felvidék (Upper lands) made Nazi Germany and fascist Italy staunch allies in the eyes of the people and political parties alike. Their highly militaristic and spectacularly enacted nationalism served as a great inspiration not just for the Hungarian radical right but also, increasingly, for the governing conservatives. But riding the wave of territorial gains came with other ideological implications; now Nazi racial policies also came to be seen as the best model to follow. The time had come for those on the right and the radical right of Hungarian politics, who had until then been unsuccessful in lobbying for the introduction of racial as well as eugenic measures, to "protect and strengthen" ethnic Hungarians. The result was that subsequent laws and policies significantly expanded the boundaries of what acts constituted sexual deviancy.

Hungary's entry into the war in 1941 brought significant changes that led, not only to the mass mobilization of Hungarian men and eventually the entire population, but also to a change in perspective about who was worthy of full membership in the Hungarian national community. Under the Bárdossy government (April 1941–March 1942), the Hungarian leadership was openly pro-German and supported the German invasion of the Soviet Union in June 1941. On the domestic front, Hungarian governing authorities came to embrace the idea that the survival of the Hungarian nation depended on the purity of Hungarian race.[6] With the enactment of anti-Jewish laws, the previously porous boundaries of respectability and membership in the Hungarian *faj* became much more restrictedly defined. Or it is perhaps just as accurate to say that Hungarian authorities became first and foremost more explicit in defining who did not belong to the national community. This was true not just in terms of race and health but also of sexuality.

The present chapter traces the end of the precarious coexistence of the tolerance of homosexuality and the Hungarian state from Hungary's entry into World War II to the establishment of the Communist dictatorship in 1948. With Hungary's entry into the war in 1941 and the rapidly rising influence of Nazism, homosexuality became irreconcilable with the idea of national community. That homosexuality and homosexuals became more systematically targeted was intimately tied to the expansion of the modern Hungarian state. By the outbreak of the war, state apparatuses, including the police and bureaucracy, were extensive and highly functional. However, it was following World War II and the establishment of the Communist state that for the first time a Hungarian state came to systematically prosecute homosexual men. Recently accessible court documents suggest that until the decriminalization of "unnatural fornication" in 1961, homosexual men were seen as the enemies of the Hungarian state and, consequently, were relentlessly prosecuted. Moreover, there are reasons to believe that homosexuality and sexuality more generally became an important tool in the hands of the Communist State Security organs. Despite the end of Stalinist repressive rule, and the decriminalization of homosexuality, homosexuals continued to be registered and the Hungarian State Security apparatus continued to use homosexuality for nefarious means: as tool of blackmail, to frame people, and as a way to turn people into informants.

EXCLUDING HUNGARIAN JEWS AND BANNING SEXUAL RELATIONS

The war brought sexuality to the forefront of public discussions and justified state intervention in the most private aspect of people's lives: their sexuality. To be sure, the Hungarian radical right and conservative press, similar to their Austrian and German counterparts, had demonized both male and female Jewish sexuality throughout most of the interwar era. Well-to-do Jewish men were portrayed as social climbers who, with their money, married themselves or their sons and daughters into "real" Hungarian families while their lower-class counterparts were painted as men who exploited innocent Hungarian women and girls.[7] Jewish women were portrayed as highly sexual and frequently as madams of parlors where they, like their male counterparts, exploited Hungarian women.[8] In the radical right papers' depiction, Jewish immorality posed an insurmountable danger to Hungarian women, especially to the morally pure young women from the countryside. With headlines such as "Village Girls in Massive Numbers Are Becoming Loose Women in the Tiny Offices of Budapest," radical right publications blamed Jews, especially Jewish women, for taking advantage of gullible Hungarian peasant women and turning them into prostitutes.[9] The image of the immoral and sexually deviant Jew was accompanied, increasingly more piercingly, by calls to enact anti-Jewish measures to protect the Hungarian race.[10] It was only following Hungary's formal joining of the Axis Powers in 1940, however, that governing authorities also came to see Jewish sexuality as something that needed to be quarantined. As Hungary's entry into the war on the side of the Axis became inevitable, Jewish sexuality was officially made deviant in 1941.[11]

While the first anti-Jewish laws were passed before the outbreak of the war in 1938, it was the so-called third Jewish law in 1941 that came to explicitly address sexual relations and sexuality. Between the May 1938 annexation of Austria by Germany and August 1941, the Hungarian government enacted a series of anti-Jewish laws that, emulating the Nuremberg Laws, defined Jews as a "racial" rather than a religious group.[12] These *zsidótörvények* (Jewish laws) severely limited and eventually prohibited their participation in the economy, civil service, and professions, and finally the so-called third Jewish law in 1941 prohibited intermarriage between Christians and Jews. Moreover, based on the Law for the Protection of German Blood and German Honor, Article XV of the 1941 law also criminalized sexual relationships between Jewish men and "respectable" Hungarian women.[13] In noted contrast to the initial Nazi laws, however, while the law prohibited sexual relationships between Jewish men and non-Jewish Hungarian as well as non-Jewish foreign women, Hungarian men could continue to form sexual relationships with Jewish women without punishment.[14] The double standard in the treatment of male and female sexuality once again prevailed—female sexuality was rigorously policed while authorities turned a blind eye to many male sexual practices. As we have seen in the previous chapters, regulating women's "appropriate" sexual behavior and enforcing female respectability was a central feature of the Horthy era. That women who had sexual intercourse with Jewish men risked contaminating the Hungarian race was also not a novel concept. Only its legal codification was new. The enacting of the Hungarian law of race defilement along with the news coverage it received, however, brought all women, irrespective of their class, under scrutiny. Even simply being seen in the company of Jewish men could threaten non-Jewish Hungarian women's moral and sexual respectability.[15] In the name of safeguarding the racial health of Hungarians, moreover, the 1941 law also introduced mandatory premarital health screening.[16] The screening, which originally had been conceived as a floodgate to the spreading of venereal diseases and tuberculosis, quickly became seen as a mechanism of imposing racial purity as well as a preventative eugenic measure.[17] While there was no new legislation that explicitly addressed homosexuality, concomitantly to the enactment of eugenic and gendered anti-Jewish laws, authorities stepped up the prosecution of male homosexuals.

TREATMENT OF HOMOSEXUALITY DURING WORLD WAR II

Until 1941 Hungarian authorities refrained from openly attacking or changing their approach toward homosexuality. The judicial and prosecutorial approach to male homosexuality between 1935 and 1941 did not change. The number of charges under Paragraph 241 (unnatural fornication) did not rise nor did the legal definition of homosexuality become more comprehensive.[18] The evidence from the Criminal Courts suggests that governing authorities did not adopt the repressive Nazi policies toward homosexuals. Unless the person was considered Jewish, homosexuals, and men who had engaged in sex with other men, were not specifically targeted, nor were they prosecuted more vigorously. Moreover, homosexuals continued to be left out from the rhetorical tirade directed against the "polluting" elements within the Hungarian *faj* (race) that were becoming part of public discourse writ large and, especially, of the discourse of the radical right. Following the outbreak of World War II, radical right publications openly called for the quarantining (and the eventual expulsion) of Jews and Roma, as well as the hereditarily ill.[19] The elimination of what were seen as the deplorable consequences of a liberal capitalist worldview—single men and women, childlessness, prostitution, pornography and loose morals, alcoholism, gambling, and selfish decadence—was a dominant trope in public discourse. It is against this backdrop that a continuing silence about homosexuality gains added significance. In spite of the ever-louder denunciation of racial and social ills, which came to encompass a progressively longer list of things, homosexuality never explicitly became a target.[20] Until Hungary's entry into the war, homosexuals remained outside of the reach of the increasingly authoritarian state as well as of the diatribes of the radical right.

Although the Hungarian state was likely not as methodical as Nazi Germany, by 1942 the systematic oppression and stripping of rights from the Jewish, and increasingly the Roma, population also began to encompass homosexuals.[21] Hungary's entry into the war in April of 1941 was a turning point in the official treatment of homosexuals. There is no surviving evidence of official orders or policy change in the form of new laws or amendments that directly addressed the treatment of same-sex acts.[22] Yet, looking at the indexes of Criminal Court records of Budapest reveals a significant increase in the number of charges of homosexuality. In contrast to the previous thirty to forty cases per year, in 1941 there were sixty-two cases and in 1942 there were fifty-six cases in which people were charged with homosexuality.[23] Considering that by this time a significant portion of men between seventeen and fifty years of age were conscripted to the Hungarian Army, this increase becomes all the more striking.[24] In 1941 and 1942, the prosecution of male homosexuals intensified. Moreover, as a recently resurfaced document exposed, similar to Nazi Germany, Hungarian officials began to consider using the homosexual registry to identify and then intern men for use as forced laborers.[25]

The most explicit evidence that homosexuals became targeted by the regime comes from the Military History Archive.[26] The subject of the document is an official request by the head of the State Security Centre of the Ministry of Interior to the Ministry of Defense to conscript the registered homosexual individuals of Budapest into forced labor service.[27] The letter stated, "The State Security Centre requests that the registered homosexual individuals (living within greater Budapest) be conscripted into a compulsory labor force within the military."[28] The Ministry of Defense denied the request on the grounds that based on their sexuality alone, homosexuals could not be considered "unreliable and unpatriotic to the nation," which was the legal charge under which Jews had been conscripted into forced labor.²⁹ At the same time, considering homosexuals as reliable, according to the response of the Ministry of Defense, "would have required that they would be conscripted into the fighting units," which in his mind "was an absolutely undesirable solution."³⁰ In the eyes of military officials, having homosexuals serving in or around the fighting units was a terrible idea. The Ministry of Defense argued that membership in the military was an honor, and "the conscription and placement of homosexuals into a form of military service would hurt the morale of the impeccable soldiers on the front by making it seem like fighting was a punishment."³¹ The response unequivocally stated that the military was not a punitive institution, and, therefore, the "homosexual issue" was a police and administrative matter, not a military one.

The military's refusal to set up homosexual labor battalions, then, should also be interpreted in the context of the self-understanding of the military. The military leadership rejected the idea that the military could be regarded as a criminal institution because it viewed itself as an institution of honor and physical excellence. Such self-perception explains why the military refused to conscript on political grounds (i.e., there were no socialist or Communist group conscriptions) and until 1944 explains why there were no separate Roma or homosexual detachments. Those men considered morally and physically ready to fight, whether Roma or homosexual, were conscripted into the regular army where they fought until the arrival of the Nazis in March 1944. The only notable exceptions were the Jews, whom the military held too unreliable to provide with arms. That Jewish men were required to serve in labor battalions while homosexual men were not was a clear manifestation of how the military's antisemitism trumped homophobia.

Yet it is also clear that during World War II the fears and concerns about homosexuality reached new heights. Authorities and particularly the military leadership were aware that sex between men took place in homosocial environments, like those created by military service and prisoner-of-war camps. For that reason, preventing known homosexuals, even if they were able and willing to serve within the military, was seen as a crucial step in protecting the "strength" of the army. The few surviving documents addressing homosexuality and the military support this point of view. For instance, in responding to the Ministry of Interior about conscripting homosexuals into the military, the Ministry of Defense argues that in the presence of homosexuals, "the generally young soldiers fighting on the front would face deterioration."³² The fear of "authentic" homosexuals spreading homosexuality among young soldiers was even greater than the potential benefits of their service. The experience of World War I, and particularly the knowledge that a long-standing war facilitated sexual activity among soldiers, called for preventative measures for the healthy and punitive measures for those "diseased with same-sex desire."[33]

The fear of healthy soldiers' degeneration and heightened attention to its prevention was also embedded in an anxious desire to attest to Hungarian greatness. It was one thing to declare the superiority of the Hungarian race and that "Hungary was a military nation," but proving it was an entirely different matter.[34] The conservative and radical right publications' portrayal of the fighting Hungarian soldier as the bedrock of the future Hungarian empire underscores how, in the eyes of pro-Nazi circles, the outbreak of World War II, at the same time as being an opportunity to reclaim Hungarian territories, was also seen as a chance for Hungarian men to proclaim their manhood and masculinity on an international scale. Yet, as scholars have repeatedly underscored, the Hungarian Army was ill equipped and unprepared for a sustained war.[35] Nor did most Hungarian men seem too keen to prove their assumed superiority. As historian Cecil Eby notes, "In the streets of Budapest the dominant reaction to the war was apathy."[36] According to Eby not even the staunchest supporters of the rightists were eager to volunteer to join the army. His summary of the general attitude is telling: "It might as well as have been news of war on the moon. Probably the average citizen . . . felt that it was good riddance to both if Germans and Russians were killing one another, but that there was no reason for Hungary to pitch in."[37] Even Hungary's foremost military ally, Germany, agreed that Hungarian forces were poorly prepared.[38] In sum, Hungarian virility was under siege even before Hungary formally entered the war. In this atmosphere, for pro-Nazi authorities who were fast attaining more power both in the government and the military, eliminating elements that threatened the (already precarious) strength of Hungarian manpower became paramount. This view is expressed in the words of an officer, according to whom, "it would be undoubtedly convenient if these, from the nation's perspective, unreliable [homosexual] elements would decay."[39]

However, the open attack on homosexuality that pro-Nazi leadership called for also raised problems for the old conservative leadership who were acutely aware that there were homosexual officers in the rank and file of the Hungarian Army. The response of the Ministry of Defense to the Ministry of Interior provides a revealing cue. At the end of their long reasoning as to why the conscription of homosexuals to military service within explicit "homosexual battalions" was undesirable (in 1942), the representatives of the Ministry of Defense state that "finally, it must be pointed out that among those [registered homosexuals] who had served in the military there would be, in fact there will be [homosexuals] who have attained military rankings and medals."[40] Here, the Ministry of Defense voices concern that calling people up from the homosexual registry would expose, not only the presence of homosexuals within the army, but potentially also that there were homosexuals in ranking military positions. Such an explicit acknowledgment of homosexuals in the military by a colonial general, the head of Hungary's armed forces, reveals the difficulty that old conservatives faced.[41] By 1942, old conservatives who had coexisted with the idea and presence of homosexuals were under increasing pressure to fall in line with Nazi ideology and practice.[42] Consequently, even as the prosecution of homosexuals outside of the military intensified, the army continued to resist making homosexuality a factor in assessing a soldier's ability to fight, let alone creating a punitive homosexual unit. For the military, the potential singling out and persecution of homosexuals seemed more of a distraction from directing all available resources to the fighting of Hungary's enemies. The change in the conceptualization of homosexuality as irreconcilable with the national community came once such pragmatism was swept aside by zealous ideologues who declared total war.

THE ARROW CROSS AND SEXUAL DEVIANTS

Although in December 1942 the Ministry of Defense denied the request to establish a homosexual labor battalion, the fate of the 995 registered homosexuals whose names were on the list (contained in the original memo) is uncertain. Were homosexuals and queer men on the homosexual registry of the Budapest police, similar to Jewish men, conscripted into forced labor battalions later in the war? Ultimately, did the arrival of the Nazis in March 1944 and the establishment of the Hungarian Arrow Cross rule in October 1944 lead to an organized attack on the homosexual community? Since the registry itself disappeared, there is no way to track the fate of the individuals who were on it.

Hungary's alignment with Nazi Germany was never unanimously accepted among the political leadership, and once the tides began turning in the war, Admiral Horthy appointed the more pro-British Miklós Kállay as prime minister (March 1942–March 1944). Kállay, who did not change the composition of his government and therefore its mostly pro-Nazi personnel, from 1943 worked behind the scenes to make a separate peace with the Allies and get Hungary out of the war.[43] The Germans became aware of his intentions, and in March 1944, while Horthy was summoned to meet Hitler in Austria, German units occupied Hungary. Kállay was dismissed, and the uncompromisingly pro-Nazi Döme Sztójay (March 1944–August 1944) was made to be the new head of the government. With Romania switching sides in the war and now fighting on the side of the Allies, Horthy became desperate to get Hungary out of the war. He appointed Colonel General Géza Lakatos de Csíkszentsimon (August 1944–October 1944), who was tasked with pulling Hungary out of the war. Amidst the approaching Soviet forces and impending victory by the Allies, on October 15, 1944, Horthy, on a national radio broadcast, announced Hungary's armistice with the Allies, which Hungary had signed four days earlier in Moscow. The German forces and their Hungarian supporters, who had been aware of Horthy and Lakatos's attempt, acted fast, and by kidnapping Horthy's son, forced Horthy and the Lakatos government to resign. The time had finally come for the Hungarian fascist party, the Arrow Cross. Ferenc Szálasi, the leader of the Hungarian Arrow Cross Party, was sworn into office as prime minister. The Arrow Cross regime announced total war and set out to mobilize the entire Hungarian population to defend Hungary from the "Bolshevik menace."[44] The Soviet forces proved unstoppable, yet the Arrow Cross's leadership remained fanatically steadfast not only to hold out militarily but also to create a new *Hungarista* society. It was to be a social revolution engineered by eugenic ideas and ultranationalism. It was within this context that homosexuals came to be seen as undesirable and incompatible with the Hungarian race.

While the disastrous fate of Jewish and Roma people during the German and Arrow Cross rule is well documented, we can only speculate as to what happened to men on the homosexual registry.[45] With the arrival of the Arrow Cross Party, Hungarian authorities came to embrace that the survival of the Hungarian nation depended on the total purity of Hungarian race. Racial and eugenic theories were to be applied to every member of the Hungarian nation. During the brief and chaotic period between October 1944 and April 1945, when Ferenc Szálasi and his Arrow Cross Party ruled over Hungary, they formulated some of the most illiberal family laws in modern history.[46] Similar to fascist and national socialist parties across Europe, the Arrow Cross Party believed in the centrality of the family to the nation and propagated rigidly traditional gender norms. But it also went much further by proposing a radical plan for the "Hungarian empire" that would have made the state the sole arbiter in deciding who could marry, who could stay married, and who would be sterilized based on a curious mix of eugenic, racist, moral, Christian, and mystical arguments.[47]

In its proposed Family Law, the Arrow Cross introduced severe limitations on people whom, based on their racial, physical, or social classification, the state deemed unworthy of membership in the national community. While for the ethnically "pure" and physically healthy Hungarians, it made childbearing the precondition of marriage and citizenship in the future Hungarian empire, the law prohibited marriage among different races: Hungarians, Jews, and Roma as well as between people deemed physically unhealthy.[48] According to the law, moreover, the state could also intervene in a marriage and annul it if the marriage produced no children or if the state decided that for whatever reason it did not live up to the expectations of the *Hungarista* empire. As a result, the category of sexual deviants expanded exponentially. Outside of heterosexual procreative sexual relationships between biologically healthy ethnically pure Hungarians, anyone was a suspect. For instance, "loose" women and single young men who did not fulfill the expectations of the state were to live in state-funded rehabilitative institutions.[49] That men were also to be held accountable for not fulfilling their duty of being married, contributing children to the empire, and caring for the next generation meant that the Arrow Cross broke with previously held gendered regulations. In the *Hungarista* empire, men and women were both expected to be monogamous, married, reproductive, and caring parents. If of a fertile age, those who were nonmonogamous, or unmarried, or not having children were not only chastised in rhetoric but faced actual material punishment and, in the cases of some, mandatory incarceration at rehabilitation centers.[50] But it was those who the Arrow Cross state deemed "sexually deviant" that were to face the harshest treatment.

Through a radical expansion of previous racial and eugenic laws, the Arrow Cross state introduced compulsory sterilization and castration laws to deal with deviant sexualities. For the first time, forced sterilization was to be institutionalized for Jewish and Roma men who had sexual contact with ethnic Hungarian women, for people with hereditary physical impairments, and for all social deviants with identifiably hereditary traits (i.e., alcoholism and other addictions that were thought to be innate).[51] The introduction of the sterilization of Jewish and Roma men was an extension of already existing anti-Jewish and anti-Roma regulations. The sterilization of people with supposedly hereditary physical and social traits was also an extension of the Arrow Cross's rhetoric of the interwar era. In both of these cases, the Family Law "only" expanded and followed through with previously expressed policy recommendations and ideas of the Arrow Cross. Notably, however, this was not the case with homosexuality.

It was within the context of total war and total societal makeover that the Arrow Cross broke with the interwar status quo and tolerance of homosexuality. Once in power, the Arrow Cross broke with their own previous stance of official silence and willful ignorance about homosexuality and made homosexuals incompatible with the new Hungarian empire. The proposed new Family Law addressed homosexuality explicitly and homosexuals were named to face harsh punishment. According to the proposal, "people burdened with abnormal sexual instinct" (homosexuals) were to be castrated along with "men and women with non-healing sexual diseases who repeatedly passed on their diseases" and "Jewish and Gypsy men who repeatedly had sexual intercourse with non-Jewish or non-Gypsy [Hungarian] women."[52] The institutionalization of such a humiliating and irreversible procedure meant that by late 1944 the proposed fate of Hungarian homosexuals in terms of their physical punishment came to parallel—if not exceed—their German counterparts.[53] By explicitly addressing "abnormal sexual instincts," the Arrow Cross broke with its previous stance on being silent about homosexuality. They also broke with decades of continuity in tolerating homosexuality. In their effort to create a eugenically healthy national body, the Arrow Cross embraced the harshest measures. Gone were the barriers that the Catholic Church and conservatives had erected against negative eugenic policies in the past. And despite the fact that there is evidence that in his personal opinion Szálasi continued to show little concern about homosexuality, he and his leadership were nevertheless intent on introducing draconian measures to deal with it.[54] While stigmatized and forced into rehabilitation centers, men and women who sold their bodies, were nonmonogamous, or avoided their responsibilities at home or work were perceived as curable; homosexuality was not. According to the Arrow Cross's Family Law, homosexuality was not only an incurable disease that required quarantine but also a disease that needed to be eradicated. The Arrow Cross's intent to eradicate homosexuality shows remarkable parallels to the goals of the Hungarian Soviet Republic. While driven by conceptually different models of homosexuality (the Communists believed that it was unfavorable socioeconomic circumstances while the Arrow Cross favored eugenic hereditary arguments), both of these regimes aimed to remove queer sexualities from the Hungarian body politic.

The intended sanctioning of castration, moreover, meant that regulations dealing with homosexuality were to be amended for the first time since the criminalization of male unnatural fornication (homosexual acts) was codified in 1878. Amending the punishment (a maximum of one year of incarceration) to include castration aside, the language of the Family Law suggested that the charges of homosexuality could now apply to both men and women. Specifically, the use of the word *emberek* (people) instead of *férfiak* (men) when referring to "abnormal sexual instinct" meant that for the first-time charges against homosexual acts encompassed both men and women. Based on the inclusiveness of the Family Law, even if there is no surviving evidence of a proposed Arrow Cross's penal code, it is very possible that had they stayed in power the Arrow Cross would have criminalized sexual acts between women. Taking it a step further, by providing no clear definition of what constituted "abnormal sexual instincts," the category could potentially have included not only male and female same-sex sexual acts but also essentially any nonprocreative sexual acts. Consequently, irrespective of the social, physical, and emotional realities of the raging war that by November 1944 involved the entire country, in envisioning the contours of the *Hungarista* empire, the ideologues of the Arrow Cross expanded the category of sexual deviants to include anybody outside of a heterosexual procreative sexual relationship between biologically healthy, ethnically pure Hungarians. Sexual deviance had never been so inclusive nor had it ever been more gender neutral.

The implementation of the Arrow Cross's Family Law most likely never took place since the situation by November 1944 was totally chaotic. The Soviet forces were advancing, and Budapest was under a siege by the end of December. The advancing Soviet forces soon forced the Arrow Cross leadership to evacuate to Sopron (in West Hungary), abandoning Budapest and leaving it in the hands of subordinate officials and raging Arrow Cross guards.[55] And while the ensuing administrative chaos and the siege of Budapest did not stop the Arrow Cross guards from imposing a reign of terror and murdering thousands of Jews, it is difficult to imagine that the Arrow Cross regime would have had the administrative capability of tracking down homosexuals and, more generally, people deemed sexual deviants.[56] The feasibility of the implementation notwithstanding, the Family Law represented the final nail in the coffin of the precarious coexistence of tolerated homosexuality and the conservative political system. As I have argued, there were multiple factors that kept homosexuality out of the public discourse throughout the 1930s. The existence of the homosexual registry, which left nonpublic homosexuality relatively alone, the gendered policing of sex that treated nonnormative male sexuality more leniently, the problematic existence of homosexuals within the military, and the conceptualization of sexuality as fluid that led to the fear of spreading same-sex sexuality all contributed to a self-imposed public silence and a willful ignorance on the part of the authorities to openly address homosexuality. Even as the Nazis came to power and Hungarian politics shifted further to the right, the silence around homosexuality continued throughout the 1930s, while the policing and judicial treatment of homosexuality remained remarkably stable. What finally brought changes in the treatment and understanding of homosexuality and sexual deviancy more generally was entering World War II on the side of Nazi Germany. It was not until pro-Nazi governments and the Arrow Cross leadership decided that the state had the right and duty to regulate and manage the most intimate sphere of life—the bedroom—that the precarious balancing act between homosexuality, silence, and toleration ended. By explicitly addressing nonheterosexual sex and institutionalizing castration, the Arrow Cross broke with the decades of silence in public discourse that surrounded homosexuality. Ultimately, the Arrow Cross was unable to translate policy into practice. Ironically, once swept aside by the Soviet forces, it was the Arrow Cross's supreme enemy, the Communists, who would have both the time and the resources to carry out the first state-sponsored comprehensive prosecution of Hungarian homosexuals.

HOMOSEXUALITY IN COMMUNIST HUNGARY

Between 1949 and 1989, the People's Republic of Hungary was a Communist, authoritarian state under the ultimate control of the Soviet Union. The initial period, the so-called Rákosi era (1948–56)—named after Mátyás Rákosi, the general secretary of the Hungarian Communist Party, who had been referred to as "Stalin's best pupil"—imposed terror and repression on anyone who dissented from the official Stalinist line.[57] In accordance with Stalinist practices, the Hungarian Communist Party set out to destroy (at times literally) all who were seen as posing a danger to the Communist system, based on their real as well as alleged political, social, economic, and moral opposition to Communist principles.[58] While the political and social repression of the regime has been well documented, the regime's repression of sexual minorities has not been analyzed. But how did the Communists think about and approach sex and, in particular, homosexuality? The rest of the chapter documents the Communist efforts to prosecute homosexuals with the intention of reeducating them into the strictly heteronormative socialist society.

The Red Army reached the eastern borders of Hungary in September 1944, and Soviet forces reached the outskirts of Budapest by late October and the siege of the city began in December. The battle for Budapest, one of the longest and bloodiest city battles of the Second World War, ended with the German and Hungarian surrender to the Soviets on February 13, 1945.[59] Having lost Budapest, most remaining Hungarian forces soon surrendered or left with the retreating German forces. Hungary's postwar fate had been determined even before the provisional Hungarian government concluded an armistice treaty with the Allies on January 20, 1945, and while fighting was still going on in the western part of Hungary. In October 1944 Stalin and Churchill came to agreement about what the postwar sphere of influence would be, putting Hungary in the Soviet sphere.[60] In addition to having Soviet "supervision," the Treaty of Peace that Hungary was forced to sign with the Allies on February 10, 1947, restored the country's territory to its pre-1938 borders, essentially reaffirming the borders established in the Treaty of Trianon after World War I. As a consequence of the war, Hungary suffered a colossal human and territorial loss. It was a total defeat. The direct actions as well as the complicity of wartime Hungarian governments resulted in the death of 450,000 Hungarian Jews and tens of thousands of Hungarian Roma. Moreover, approximately 150,000 civilians and 300,000 soldiers perished during the war.[61] In addition to the staggering human loss and hundreds of thousands of prisoners of war, the country was also structurally devastated: 80 percent of Budapest's buildings were damaged and almost half of the country's communication and transport infrastructure was destroyed, along with most of the country's food supply. And yet from hindsight, it is also clear that despite or perhaps even because of these terrible circumstances Hungary experienced a brief moment between 1945 and 1948, when once again, similar to 1918, democratic changes seemed possible.

Notwithstanding agreeing to the presence of the Red Army and Soviet oversight, the Allies, similar to other countries in the Soviet sphere, were in support of the establishment of a democratic government. Most Hungarians also seemed to favor a radical break with previous political governance. The postwar Hungarian political parties, the Smallholders', the social democratic, the Communist, and the National Peasant parties, initially all agreed to a multiparty system that they believed was essential for what was to become a sovereign independent Hungary. The first democratic elections in November 1945 were won by the Smallholders' Party, who created a grand coalition with representatives from each of the four parties.[62] Under their leadership, on February 1, 1946, Hungary became a republic. The granting of universal suffrage and the separation of legislative, executive, and judicial powers were representative of a genuine attempt to establish the pillars of a democratic political system. But difficulties were present from the beginning. The country was physically, financially, and emotionally devastated, the reconstruction was slow, and both urban and rural residents faced daily hardships and the lack of basic necessities.[63] Political cracks were also apparent. Initially both Smallholders' and Communist parties tried to reinforce their own positions within the coalition and gain new ones. Most importantly, as the contours of the Cold War solidified, Hungary's fate was sealed. Thanks to its geopolitical importance for the Soviet Union, the democratic government of the Second Republic of Hungary stood little chance. With the elimination of the Smallholders' and Peasant parties and the forced merger of the social democrats into the Hungarian Workers' Party, the newly named Communist Party became the sole political party. By 1948 the Hungarian Communists, with the backing of the Soviet Union, systematically eliminated not only the multiparty system but increasingly all political opposition.[64] Hungary's second experiment with democracy formally ended in 1949 with the establishment of the People's Republic of Hungary.

SEXUALITY IN 1950s COMMUNIST IDEOLOGY

As recent scholarship has demonstrated, gender and sexual equality were embraced as crucial goals for building socialism in the new state-socialist Eastern Bloc. And even if the original goals of true gender and sexual equality and the withering away of the family were abandoned and pronatalism policies became the law of the land during the late 1950s and 1960s, the work of Sándor Horváth, Agnieszka Kościańska, Kateřina Liškova, and Josie McLellan, among others, has demonstrated that, over the four decades behind the Iron Curtain, heterosexual liberation was to varying degrees embraced by state-socialist authorities and denizens alike.[65] In Hungary, the Constitution of 1949 declared equality between the sexes, the 1952 Family Law introduced "no fault divorce," where either spouse could initiate divorce, and it also guaranteed equal ownership rights. Formal equality before the law, the liberalization of divorce, and eventual legalization of abortion in 1956 were incredible landmarks in the emancipation of women. This legislation, by the late 1950s, also led to Hungary having one of the highest divorce and abortion rates in the world. It was against this background that there was a return to conservative sexual policies, which centered on the family and the idealization of motherhood.[66] Thus, in contrast to Western European and North American democracies, where sexual conservativism during the 1950s was predicated on supposed differences between the sexes and the (re-)relegation of women to the private sphere, in Hungary and the Communist Eastern Bloc more generally, sexual conservatism was reintroduced following the backlash to the institutionalization of gender equality and women's integration into the workforce.[67]

During the onset of the Communist rule, the commitment to gender equality and an increased attention to nonnormative sexualities went hand in hand. The same zeal that the Communists invested in creating gender equality on the road to socialism was applied to creating a socialist society based on heteronormative sexual practices. Gone were previous Communist ideas that celebrated sexual freedom and freedom of sexual expression.[68] One could marry someone of the opposite sex for love, and if one fell out of love, divorce the person and then marry again for love. But one could not engage in extramarital sex or have children out of wedlock. Whereas official propaganda shunned adultery and nonmonogamy as counter to socialist ethics, they declared war on what they, in terms of sexual practices, thought of as the true impediment to the advance of socialist society: "unnatural fornication," or queer sex. As we saw in the case of the Hungarian Communists in 1919, in the long run, socialism was thought to be incompatible with homosexuality, which according to the socialist concept of progress, "would automatically disappear as an outdated remnant of oppressive vice and social malaise."[69] What had remained only a long-term goal and utopian concept during the brief existence of the Hungarian Communist dictatorship in 1919 would become a concretized plan of action in the newly established People's Republic. In contrast to 1919, when homosexuality, considered a psychosocial condition, would have been decriminalized until homosexuals could be "healed" from their misaligned sexual object choice, the post–World War II Communist regime took a much firmer stand against homosexuality and homosexuals. Considered a "class enemy" that, according to new Communist leadership, reflected both the moral and physical degeneracy of the former ruling capitalist classes, homosexuality was made antithetical to a socialist way of being. Homosexuality was not only antithetical to idealizations of masculinity and the moral strength of the working class but was also seen as a potential source of contamination for them. As a consequence, sex between men came to be prosecuted with a never-before-seen vengeance in Hungary.

The Communists, who denounced fascism as a reactionary ideology in the hands of capitalists that aimed to crush the working class, prosecuted people who held positions in the former Horthy and Arrow Cross regimes.[70] Hungarian Communists repeatedly emphasized the inhumanity of fascist Horthy and Arrow Cross policies.[71] And yet as historians continue to point out, the Communists in many ways continued what Hannah Arendt in *The Origins of Totalitarianism* labeled as the dehumanization of people that began in the Horthy regime and reached unprecedented heights during the Arrow Cross rule.[72] The executions, torture, show trials, hard-labor camps, and an increasingly comprehensive surveillance system under Communist rule, albeit justified from a different ideological position, represented the continued strengthening of the power of the state over individuals.[73] The treatment of homosexuals is a clear demonstration of how, despite positioning itself ideologically as the antithesis of fascism, in actuality the Communists were comfortable continuing some of the same discriminatory actions that were put in place by their political and ideological nemeses. More significantly, once in power and enjoying a fast-growing police and surveillance system, the Communist justice system during the so-called Rákosi era (1948–56) became the first to systematically prosecute male homosexuals.

Based on available documents from the Criminal Courts of Budapest and the minutes of party meetings, it is clear that from the late 1940s through the mid-1950s, homosexuals were seen as unreliable elements who were incompatible with the emerging political system. Within the newfound realities of one-party authoritarianism and its rapidly expanding bureaucratic powers, the Communist Party used the already-existing and fast-growing homosexual registry of the police to cleanse queerness from its ranks. Starting with their own ranks, homosexuals or those simply suspected as such were purged from the Hungarian Workers' (Communist) Party. As the minutes of the meetings of the Hungarian Workers' Party of Budapest made clear, "Homosexuals do not belong to the party." Consequently, if discovered to have been caught for homosexual activities or registered on the police's homosexual registry, Communist Party members were expelled without the possibility of an appeal.[74] And it was not just male members who were affected. Despite the fact that the Communist penal code did not go into effect until 1962, and according to the existing penal code female homosexuality was not criminalized, the Communist Party seemed equally unsympathetic toward female homosexual members. Women who were accused of carrying on a homosexual lifestyle or having had homosexual encounters, such B. Jánosné, were expelled from the party for leading a "homosexual and immoral life."[75] Reflecting the puritanical standards of Communist parties across the Eastern Bloc, Hungarian party membership required a pure private life, where a homosexual lifestyle was grounds for immediate expulsion.[76]

The fierceness of the Communist drive to cleanse themselves of homosexuals was in part due to sexual prudishness and to the lingering view that associated homosexuality with immorality as well as with congenital abnormality. But during the initial years of the Communist dictatorship, homosexuals were also hunted down thanks to a general paranoia that existed among Communist members about the perils of enemies within. Ironically, paranoia about spies and invisible enemies made homosexuality suspect (albeit for different reasons) in both the capitalist and Communist blocs. While in the West homosexuals were associated with leftist ideas and hence suspect of being Communists, in the Communist Bloc they were seen as product of bourgeois (im)morality and suspected of Western influence.[77] The Communist takeover of Hungary, similar to most countries in Stalin's newly acquired satellite states, was brutal and took place against the majority's will. Early on, the Communist Party and its rapidly swelling political police, the State Security forces, conceived of anyone who deviated even slightly from socialist norms as a traitor and a potential enemy.[78] In the eyes of Communist authorities, one's relationship to socialism was assessed on a continuum. Most important during the initial years following the establishment of the one-party system was a person's political commitment. Consequently, from the Communist perspective, assessing political attitudes or one's "ideological whereabouts" was the primary determinant of people's reliability. However, thanks to a high level of insecurity and paranoia about the infiltration of "the enemy" that was fueled by the onset of the Cold War, any behavior that deviated from the supposed socialist norms could be a sign of ideological nonconformity. In this context, homosexuality could be seen as the manifestation of capitalist bourgeois ideological orientation, literally the enemy within. But even when it was not explicitly seen in connection to the (capitalist) enemy, or considered proof of a politically hostile attitude, homosexuality was considered a compromising factor for more than one reason. For one, it could be seen as an "inclination" that was inherently antisocialist. In an era when anyone who was not fully on board with living according to socialist principles was considered an enemy, simply having a homosexual inclination could make one an enemy of socialism. Homosexuality, moreover, was seen as a liability for blackmail that could potentially undermine one's ideological and political allegiance to the Communist cause. Thus, even those homosexuals who were committed to socialism could not be trusted. As a result, during the time when the Communists were not only adamant about preventing the contamination of socialism but also about the reeducation of Hungarians into the beliefs of socialism, the elimination of homosexuality was seen as a necessity.

CRIMINAL PROSECUTION OF HOMOSEXUALS IN THE BUDAPEST COURT SYSTEM

During the 1950s countries on both sides of the Iron Curtain saw a rapid rise in the prosecution of homosexuals.[79] Like elsewhere in the Eastern Bloc during the Stalinist years, homosexuality in Hungary was prosecuted not simply as a crime against morality but a crime against socialism.[80] In contrast to the relatively lenient sentencing of previous political systems, which usually entailed paying fines rather than going to prison, under the charge of *természet elleni fajtalanság* (unnatural fornication), or homosexual acts, under Paragraph 337 of the provisional Socialist Criminal Law, the Communist courts handed down prison sentences to men with "perverted" sexual inclinations. The approximately eight hundred cases involving charges of "unnatural fornication" at the Budapest Criminal Court (that served as the Appeals Court) between 1949 and 1962 suggest that, under the new Communist system, while the legal terms of the criminalization of male homosexual acts remained unchanged, the prosecution of homosexual men intensified to an unprecedented level. From 1949 until 1955, the courts openly expressed abhorrence toward sex between men (even if consensual) on a moral as well as ideological basis. Across the cases references to homosexual acts as *undorító* (disgusting), *minden épérzékű embert mèltán felháborító cselekmények* (acts worthy of the outrage of every healthy minded person), and *a szocialista társdalom értékeivel ellentétes* (antithetical to norms of socialist society) are abundant.[81] Homosexuality, as Jennifer V. Evans, in the context of the GDR, illustrated, was also antithetical to "new socialist manhood," which consisted of "masculinity, class consciousness, and moral integrity."[82] Understood as a danger to a socialist way of being (for failing to embody socialist masculinity and socialist morality) and hence a danger to society, the courts, having verbally shamed the accused, also handed down serious punishments to even first-time convicted "homosexuals."

In most cases the police arrested men who had sex with men after having caught them in public areas of Budapest. In the rapid rebuilding of Budapest, the long-established bathhouses, such as Széchényi, Hungária, Király, and Lukács, continued to serve as meeting places for homosexual men. There were also the public urinals at Nyugati and Keleti train stations and on frequented public squares such as Deák or Petőfi, where men sought and solicited other men for sex. Finally, there were a few establishments such as Tejvendéglő (Milk Pub) and Népbüfé (People Buffet), both on Marx Square (today Nyugati Square), or the Sörszanatorium (Beer Sanatorium) on Lenin Boulevard (today's Erzsébet Boulevard) that were frequented by homosexual men. All of these places were closely monitored by the police and were where most of those men who were prosecuted were arrested. According to available court records, the great majority of the defendants for Paragraph 337 landed in court thanks to police who caught them just before, during, or soon after having had a sexual encounter with another man in these public and semipublic places.[83] In a minority of cases, people were caught after having been denounced to the police by men they had made a proposition to (i.e., relatives of younger homosexual men reported the older partner in the hopes of "rescuing" their loved one) and by zealous Communist informants who wanted to expose sinful and antisocialist behavior. Once arrested by the police, many men would face pretrial detention before going in front of a three-panel judge.

In accordance with the Constitution of 1949, the judiciary, along with all other branches of government, was politicized, and appointments to the courts were made contingent on the approval of the Communist Party.[84] While the revision of the new criminal code took over a decade, in the interim the existing criminal law was changed via a number of codifications by the Ministry of Justice. Most importantly, following along the lines of Soviet criminal law, criminal acts were no longer codified as acts that were committed only against the law but rather as acts that also posed a "danger to society." Accordingly, sex between men was now considered an act that was directly endangering the well-being of socialist society.[85] Specifically, as a panel judge on the court of first instance opined, "the deed [sexual acts between men] poses an increased social danger, because such acts do not only destroy the morality and willpower of the offender, but they also lead to the deterioration of their physical strength. . . . In our building of a [socialist] society, the spread of these crimes would result in a decrease of production and this illness affects our youth as an infectious disease. This must be prevented at all cost."[86] Homosexuality and, more generally, acts of queer sex were antisocial on an ideological level because they constituted a roadblock to the building of a socialist society. They continued to be seen as a biological as well as a psychological threat that could spread among the young. In the eyes of the Communist authorities, these reasons warranted a firm response by the state.

In terms of what counted as unnatural fornication, the courts applied the existing law in its widest possible interpretation. As a court decision from 1953 explained, "any kind of fornication between men, even if does not resemble the natural sexual intercourse—the penetration of male sexual organ into the rectum—since it aims to satisfy the sexual desire in unnatural way, fulfills Paragraph 337. Contrary practice [of the application of the law] can be considered obsolete."[87] As an opinion of a lower court from 1952 adds, the legal practice of limiting the fulfilment of unnatural fornication to acts that resembled sexual intercourse between a man and woman "was the judicial practice of the capitalist system prior to liberation."[88] In contrast to the capitalist legal practice, the same opinion continues, "the socialist justice system takes communist morality as its foundation. For that reason, anything that is contrary to natural sexual life . . . is considered to be a crime of unnatural fornication."[89] Similar to East Germany and other state-socialist countries in the Eastern Bloc, even as Hungarian Communist courts tried to differentiate themselves from the previous "bourgeois capitalist" courts by alleging that "in the capitalist system the charge of unnatural fornication only applied when the act caused physical harm or death," their actual interpretation of the law was more similar than different.[90] As we have seen, by the 1930s courts and the police were in agreement that unnatural sexual acts between men—in whatever form and shape they had taken place—fulfilled the conditions of unnatural fornication. In a rather similar manner to the interwar judicial practice, it seems that whenever the police charged men with unnatural fornication post-1949, as long as it was proven to be true, the courts did not question whether or not their actual sexual acts fulfilled the crime. However, unlike in the interwar era when the courts served as a check on the potential abuse of power by the police, the courts under the newly established Communist rule rarely pushed back against the charges of the police.[91] Instead, they served as an extension of the police and State Security. One illustrative manifestation of this relationship is the courts' reaction (or rather the lack thereof) to complaints made by defendants of police intimidation. Reading the depositions and accounts of the defense in the court records of Paragraph 337 cases, there is a steady stream of references to police abuse and to intimidation of men to confess to having sexual encounters with other men.[92] Yet, the courts rarely if ever took up the issue.

With the blessing of the courts, the police could arrest and bring charges against men based on a mere suspicion of a suspect having had an intention to seek "unnatural" sexual satisfaction. Thus, in addition to having more police personnel to monitor the public areas of Budapest, the judicial expansion of the category of unnatural fornication was an important precondition of the astronomical rise of court cases involving homosexuality. Prosecuted in much greater numbers, the majority of men caught up in the judicial system (similar to their counterparts throughout the first part of the twentieth century) tended to be younger, working class, and born outside of Budapest. Having established the crime of "unnatural fornication," and underscored the "danger of this crime to socialist society," in determining the punishment the courts focused on the circumstances of the crime and on the accused's relationship to work and society at large. If the sexual acts were a one-time consensual act between two adult men who were similar in age, with no criminal history, and who possessed solid jobs, the courts showed a certain amount of leniency, especially on the second instance. In these cases, when men "sincerely admitted to the charge and showed remorse for having committed the crime," the lower courts would sentence these men to anywhere from one month to a year of imprisonment, and if appealed, in certain cases the Appeals Court suspended the prison sentences for three years. If there was a criminal past, a "fascist" or "capitalist" background, multiple charges, a significant age difference between the men, lack of a confirmed job, or if there was solicitation or coercion involved, the courts handed down prison sentences often with additional financial penalties. In these cases, if appealed, the Appeals Court was much less likely to lessen or suspend the sentence. The harshest punishment was reserved for older men who sought out young boys. In these cases, the minimum sentence was one year, which the Appeals Court often raised.[93] And even if the individual treatment of various Criminal Courts of "unnatural fornication" could vary in terms of the severity of punishment, the judicial approach to homosexuality during the initial years of Communist rule was unequivocally the harshest since homosexual acts were criminalized in 1878.

THE COURTS AS TRANSFORMERS OF SEXUAL ORIENTATION

Paradoxically, even as homosexuality was being prosecuted at an unprecedented level during the initial years of the Hungarian's People's Republic, homosexuality was also approached as a habit or inclination that could be changed. That even one's sexual orientation could be changed was in line with the commitment of the Communist leadership to transform Hungarian society into a socialist people's republic.[94] The fundamental reorganization of Hungarian society along Stalinist principles and the transformation of law, education, and cultural norms were all aimed to assist the comprehensive reeducation of Hungarians into socialist citizens.[95] The courts were to play an important role in the transformation of individuals and society. In this context, that courts would believe that they could change people's sexual preferences becomes less surprising. Even if the courts acknowledged that people could have homosexual inclinations that were not their own fault, they also believed that individuals possessed the power to change their homosexual inclinations. Disgusted as they were, from the court documents it is also evident that early on the courts genuinely believed that with the *megfelelő* (appropriate) punishment they could not only steer men away from having sex with other men, but actually help to transform them into proper socialist citizens. At the same time as they acknowledged homosexual inclination as an innate phenomenon, the courts believed that in addition to medical help, sport and physical work could "relieve and ultimately do away with" homosexual behaviors.[96] The role of the courts was thus not simply to punish and discourage but rather to instigate individuals to actively work on changing their sexual preference.

In hindsight the homophobia, prudishness, and naivety of the Communists is glaringly obvious, but the treatment of homosexuals during the initial years of state-socialism has to be contextualized within the widely prevalent grand and optimistic conviction that it was possible to fundamentally change society. Surely, getting rid of any social vestiges of capitalism would initially require force, but it would set society on a new path, opined early state-socialists. During the initial years of the 1950s, the Communists, like their 1919 counterparts, believed in the malleability of human character and considered the zealous (re)education of the Hungarian people to be a social responsibility. The following opinion of a lower court from 1953 is illustrative of the grandiose expectations that Communist judges held about the power of individuals to change: "Despite the fact that the defendant was fully aware of his [homosexual] inclination, apart from seeking medical help, he did nothing else in order to halt his [homosexual] activities. He did not experiment with playing sports or engage in physical activities, he did nothing to redirect his [sexual] desires, or to stop seeking contact with other [homosexual] men and their friendship."[97] Put differently, individuals were supposed to do everything within their power to change their behavior, in this instance their sexual behavior. In the early years of Communist rule, party officials and appointees, like the judges, genuinely believed that with medical help and personal determination individuals could "cure" themselves of homosexuality. In cases where there was not enough will on the part of individuals, the courts would "help" by providing strong disincentives. These included imprisonment for up to three years, a substantial fine, the possibility of being banned from living in the city for two years, and a permanent note in one's *erkölcsi bizonyítvány* (the moral certificate that was required to hold a job), along with being tried in public. All were intended to ensure that people shed their homosexual urges. The courts took their duty to reeducate homosexuals seriously.

Whether it was men who were caught cruising or soliciting for sex in front of a public urinal or homosexual men who were in a monogamous relationship who were turned in to the police or older men who were caught enticing young men in one of the many bathhouses of Budapest, the courts saw their role in homosexuality as an agent of transformation. In their treatment of homosexual men and men who were prosecuted for having some sort of sexual contact with other men, the judges repeatedly emphasized how the punishment of these men was required for a dual purpose: to protect society by coercing the defendants to "refrain from committing a similar crime" and also in order to "re-educate the defendants."[98] The few testimonials of defendants and/or their associated court references that survived show the disconnectedness from and insensitivity of judges to the situation of homosexual men, especially those who were caught and charged repeatedly for "unnatural fornication." These men, who by their own admission never felt attracted to the opposite sex, only had sexual contact with adult men, and some of whom even confessed to having tried to change their ways continued to face judges. They tended to show up repeatedly in the court of the first instance that dismissed these people's pleas and remained unwavering in arguing for the need to change their behavior. The failure of transforming the homosexual desires of these men into desires for women is not just glaringly obvious to historians reading these records, but was also obvious to those contemporaries who dealt with cases involving charges of homosexuality. And even if judges on the Appeals Court were more sympathetic to the pleas of men who were caught, it was not until after the Hungarian Revolution of 1956 that there was a significant change in how the courts approached consensual homosexual acts.

POST-1956 AND THE DECRIMINALIZATION OF HOMOSEXUALITY

The political and social consolidation following the Hungarian Revolution in 1956, which eased the grip of the state over society, also brought about changes in the judicial treatment of sex between men. The Hungarian Revolution in 1956 was initially an attempt to introduce reforms within state-socialism. It turned into a revolution for Hungary's independence and was promptly crushed by Soviet forces. The years immediately following the revolution were ones of retaliation and terror. From the late 1950s, however, the Communist leadership decided to appease the population by allowing limited economic privatization and greater personal freedom to Hungarians than was held by most of their counterparts within the Eastern Bloc. During the Kádár era (named after János Kádár, the general secretary of the Hungarian Communist Party between 1956 and 1988), the new regime introduced what came to be known as "goulash communism," or as *fridzsider szocializmus* (refrigerator socialism). This concept referred both to the rapidly growing access to consumer goods such as refrigerators and television sets that used to be considered luxury items and to the fact that strict totalitarian state control was replaced by a milder form of authoritarianism.

In the second half of the 1950s, then, courts became more lenient as authorities no longer required people to believe in socialism and medicine began to claim much greater authority over the understanding and management of nonnormative sexualities. Although the number of charges remained high even after 1956, there was a distinctive change in the outcome of the charges. Some of the lower courts continued to hand out imprisonments, but the Appeals Court began to systematically overturn lower court sentences in favor of suspended custodial sentences and monetary fines. In the case of consensual sexual acts between two adult men, the penalty no longer involved incarceration but rather a fine. This reflected the resignation of the courts and of the authorities more generally to the fact that imprisoning homosexual men did not help to "eradicate" homosexual desire (in fact, as the records show, judges noted the opposite effect). Concomitant to this shift in the legal landscape was a shift in the medical conceptualization of homosexuality. Instead of social deviancy and antisocialist behavior, homosexuality was now considered primarily as a medical pathology.[99] As long as men fulfilled their socialist duties, first and foremost by contributing to the building of socialism through their jobs, the courts increasingly framed sex between men as a medical condition. This was especially the case with the Appeals Court, which in general tended toward lighter punishments in keeping with the belief that socialist justice needed to be tempered with humanism. Thus, a typical opinion on consensual sex between men would emphasize how "men, who otherwise normally fulfilled their work duties, committed their crime [unnatural fornication] because of their illness, warranted a fine rather than imprisonment."[100] This marked a shift from emphasizing the moral danger that homosexuality posed to socialism to an emphasis on the innateness of homosexual desire that in certain *akaratgyenge* (weak-willed) men could not be stopped but which in and of itself did not threaten socialism. As an opinion from 1960 stated, "according to the established practice of the Metropolitan Court, unnatural fornication committed consensually between two adults, poses only a very slight danger to society."[101] Such changes in the conceptualization of homosexuality were embedded in the post-1956 political leadership's approach to society. Gone was the belief and determination to make people true believers of socialism and transform society. As General Secretary János Kádár put it, "whoever is not against us, is with us." The intent of the Communist leadership was to keep the status quo, not reform society. Homosexuality, like other formerly antisocialist behaviors, became tolerated as long as it was kept private and outside of the public sphere where it could not be politicized or seen as a threat to socialist norms.

It was this ideological shift of the Communist leadership, which no longer aspired to transforming people into model socialist citizens, that enabled the decriminalization of consensual homosexual acts in 1961 (which went into effect in 1962). In doing so, state-socialist Hungary and Czechoslovakia, which legalized consensual homosexuality at the same time, became the first countries to do so in the Eastern Bloc (with the exception of Poland, which following its post-WWI independence did not [re]criminalize it), and they did so before West Germany, England, and most states in the US.[102] While the actual request to delete homosexual acts from the socialist criminal code, which was being drafted at the time, came from a self-described homosexual in 1958, that homosexuality was indeed removed from the criminal code was a result of a confluence of forces.[103] There is no direct evidence to support it, but the fact that an individual petition was taken up and led to the creation of a special committee to study the issue of homosexuality indicates that there was internal support within the Communist judiciary leadership to support decriminalization. Even if not openly acknowledged, it was clear that the courts could not transform sexual orientation. A result of this realization was the growing scientific perception of homosexuality as an innate, unchangeable, and in most cases nonspreadable biological condition.

In March 1958 the Health Scientific Committee of the Ministry of Justice, which was tasked to evaluate and assess the benefits of incorporating the latest medical advancements into the criminal code, created a "Neurology Expert Committee" to review issues regarding homosexuality, medicine, and criminal law.[104] The committee, comprised of some Hungary's leading psychiatrists, discussed the factors that supported the continuing criminalization of homosexual acts as well as the reasons why decriminalization might be warranted. The conversation followed a pattern similar to professional medical and legal discussions in previous political systems. Following a historical and medical overview that detailed the legal approaches of other countries as well as the discussion of leading international medical theories on homosexuality, the discussion turned more specifically to the Hungarian context. With their references to, not only Magnus Hirschfeld, but also Alfred Kinsey, Alfred Binet, and Konrad Lorenz, the experts clearly demonstrated that, despite being on the east side of the Iron Curtain, Hungarian medical professionals were up to date on Western medical theories on sexuality.[105] While the format and questions considered during the 1958 discussions resembled previous legal and medical discussions, the conclusions were remarkably different. In a marked contrast to the 1909 and 1936 discussions about the nature of homosexuality, experts no longer believed that homosexuality was infectious and therefore required quarantining. In their medical opinion, doctors argued that homosexuality did not pose a danger to the health of society because homosexuality was not "spreadable." According to their final opinion, since "healthy heterosexual inclination produces natural aversion towards homosexuality," homosexuality generates "aversion, disgust, and does not entice followers."[106] This statement, imbued with contemporary medical understandings of homosexuality that framed homosexuality as either an arrested development on the path to "healthy" heterosexuality or as a deviation that will not stick once one has experienced heterosexual sex, was far from new.[107] But by 1958 there seemed to be a general agreement among doctors that the most likely outcome of homosexual exposure was disgust rather than allure.

There was a candid acknowledgment of the prevalence of premarital and nonprocreative sex. Men and women had been having plenty of nonprocreative sex even before that time. By the late 1950s, however, there was an increasing acceptance that sexually active heterosexual people were actively using forms of contraception (abortion, the rhythm method, and condoms). The committee pointed out that it would be highly hypocritical to punish homosexuals on the basis of engaging in unreproductive sex.[108] This line of reasoning echoed the findings of the British Wolfenden Report of 1957, which, in its recommendation to decriminalize homosexuality, made the same parallels between nonprocreative heterosexual sex and homosexual acts.[109] In both cases there was also a distinction made between consensual private acts and "scandalous" or nonconsensual sex. In this sense, the Hungarian case of decriminalization of homosexuality was part of conceptual shift in Western sexual morality. The legalization of consensual adult homosexual sex in the case of Britain (and Western countries more generally), as Dagmar Herzog notes, represented "the ascent of legal concepts and moral values of *consent* and *privacy*."[110] While in Hungary and Czechoslovakia decriminalization was ultimately justified on medical grounds, there was also a clear acknowledgment of consent and privacy as legitimate moral and legal concepts.

Finally, perhaps the most crucial consensus that the medical profession arrived at was that homosexuality was not only incurable but also almost impossible to suppress by punishment. Although not an unanimous view, since, for example, the president of the Neurology Committee, Dr. Gyula Nyirő, stated that homosexuality was neither congenital nor incurable, by the late 1950s, most Hungarian physicians viewed homosexuality as a congenital abnormality that required neither punishment nor treatment.[111] As the succinct recommendation from the committee to decriminalize consensual homosexuality states, "Neither the prison, nor the prison hospital can be used for treating homosexual abnormalities."[112] That prisons were hotbeds of homosexual activity had been long known. We can recall how in the interwar years judges would point out that prison sentences were ineffectual in the suppression of homosexuality. That prisons were counterproductive in fighting homosexuality was becoming ever more apparent amidst the unprecedented levels of incarceration of homosexuals that had been ongoing since the establishment of the Communist dictatorship. The futility of incarceration in fighting homosexuality aside, by the late 1950s, Hungarian physicians increasingly came to believe that there was no "magic bullet," hormone therapy, or other treatment that could "cure" homosexuals and turn them into heterosexuals. That did not necessarily stop homosexuals from trying to be cured nor prevent some medical professionals from trying to cure them, but as evidenced by the experts' opinion from 1958, the mainstream medical profession was painfully aware of the futility of medical "cures" for homosexuality. In fact, ultimately, the decriminalization of consensual homosexuality was justified by its medical incurability. In its legal comments on the new penal code, the Ministry of Justice stated that since "even the most elaborate therapy rarely achieves the desired result [heterosexuality]," indications were that homosexuality was a "biological phenomenon." In light of this, the Ministry of Justice opined that "the criminalization of homosexuality would be incorrect."[113] The decriminalization of homosexuality, then, was largely a result of the medicalization of sexuality and, in particular, the medical pathologizing of homosexuality. In this process, similar to what Vera Sokolova and Kateřina Lišková describe in the case of Czechoslovakia, Hungarian sexologists (who were overall not as progressive as their Czech counterparts) played a crucial role in shaping discourses on sexuality. As Sokolova highlights, while, following decriminalization, Czechoslovakian sexologists "actively challenged the picture of homosexual subjects as (only) deviant and sick," in Hungary, with a few notable exceptions, sexologists and the medical community treated homosexuals as medically sick until the end of state-socialism.[114]

Apart from these clear differences from earlier eras in terms of medical and legal opinions, there were also some clear continuities. Blackmail continued to occupy a central place in the discussions about the pros and cons of decriminalization of consensual homosexuality. Similar to prior attempts to decriminalize homosexuality, advocates of decriminalization emphasized the negative effects of blackmail, which remained a threat with very real legal consequences while homosexuality was criminalized. In fact, "the wide possibility of blackmail" was a major consideration in favor of decriminalization.[115] The protection of youth also remained a paramount concern across eras. Some of the most heated arguments within the medical community and later among legal experts took place around determining the appropriate age of consent in homosexual relationships. In the initial proposal that was put forward to the medical experts in 1958, the age of consent was eighteen years of age (similar to Czechoslovakia). There were also suggestions that would have set the age of consent (for both hetero- and homosexual relationships) to be sixteen years of age. That, at the end, the law that was adopted raised the age of consent of homosexual relationship to twenty years of age for both sexes, while leaving the age of consent for heterosexuals at fourteen is revealing. For one, the difference in ages of consent for hetero- and homosexual youth reflects how ideas about the fragility of youth and in particular the malleability of sexuality in adolescence were even more strongly felt post–World War II than during the interwar years. Such a difference in consent age was characteristic of a concern for protecting adolescents and young men and women that was true in countries on both sides of the Iron Curtain.[116] Despite the fact that experts were no longer concerned about homosexuality being contagious, they considered having homosexual sexual experiences at a young age deeply traumatic and possibly irreversible in terms of one's sexual orientation. In this sense, the age difference highlights the inherent contradiction in both medical and legal opinions. If homosexuality was indeed a biological phenomenon and only affected those who were biologically wired to desire their own sex, there would have been no need to have a different age of consent for homosexuals. That there was a different age of consent reveals the double standard authorities held. It was a similar need to protect young people that was used to justify the criminalization of female homosexuality under twenty years of age. Ironically, what did not materialize under the brief and chaotic Arrow Cross rule was finally put in place by the Communist justice system. For the first time since the first modern Hungarian penal code of 1878, sex between women became a criminal offense, and homosexual women, like their male counterparts, could be charged with up to three years in prison if they had sex with people under twenty years of age.[117]

By raising the age of consent to twenty years irrespective of sex, the new penal code did not just hold same-sex sexual relationships to a different set of "standards" than heterosexual relationships. The introduction of a special clause about "perversion against nature conducted in a scandalous manner" (which could carry a sentence of up to three years in prison) also provided additional legal means for the authorities to press charges against homosexuals.[118] The differing ages of consent and the elusiveness of the definition of "scandalous manner" provided the grounds for the police to continue to keep those accused of homosexual practices under close control. Thus, even as it decriminalized consensual homosexuality, the new penal code granted considerable power in the hands of police to prosecute or, perhaps more crucially, to continue to have the possibility to prosecute homosexual men and women. Finally, as the next section demonstrates, the decriminalization of homosexuality and the significant easing of authoritarian control over the population that took place during the 1960s did not lead to the abandonment of the homosexual registry. Far from it.

THE UTILIZATION OF THE HOMOSEXUAL REGISTRY BY HUNGARIAN STATE SECURITY

Although registering homosexuals had been part of the Metropolitan Police's duties since the beginning of the twentieth century, the homosexual registry became systematically utilized by the state for the first time during the Communist years. While the actual registry itself might never resurface, there are a number of documents from the Communist era that provide both quantitative and qualitative information about the contents of the registry and its use during this era. One striking example is from the recorded minutes of the Neurology Committee. During a meeting in March of 1958, as physicians were debating the decriminalization of consensual homosexual acts, one of the active members, a Dr. Pál Juhász, referred to the homosexual registry and noted that the Budapest Metropolitan Police had approximately eighty thousand men registered on it.[119] Considering that during the mid-1930s the number of registered homosexual men was less than five thousand, the increase in registration is truly astronomical. Even if we keep in mind that the registering and prosecution of homosexuals intensified following Hungary's entry to World War II in 1941, it is almost inconceivable that amidst the war the number of registered men could have climbed by the tens of thousands. Although there are no criminal records remaining from the period immediately following the war and up to 1948, it is also unlikely that amidst the desperate need to rebuild the city and the prosecution of fascists and Arrow Cross members for their crimes during the war, the registering of homosexual men would have been a high priority for authorities after the war. Therefore, it is most likely that the exponential increase in efforts to register and prosecute homosexuals in Budapest, and likely across Hungary, occurred after the consolidation of Communist power in 1948.

The documents at the Historical Archives of the Hungarian State Security (ÁBTL), the Hungarian equivalent of the Soviet KGB and East German

Stasi, illuminate how homosexuality was not only more vigorously prosecuted than ever before but also that homosexuality and sexuality more generally became an important tool in the hands of the State Security organs during the 1950s.[120] Although according to archivists, there are no *available* official records of the actual homosexual registry under the Communists (they have either been destroyed or continue to be kept as part of the still inaccessible documents of the State Security organizations), there is still plenty of evidence that confirms that the registry continued to be utilized. Based on a "strictly confidential" instruction note on the criminal registries from 1958, it is clear that, in addition to the homosexual registry of Budapest, by the mid-1950s there was also a national homosexual registry.[121] From a secret internal State Security directive, moreover, we also know that the registry held "every person whose homosexual inclinations have been confirmed by police." In addition to detailed personal information, including pictures, nicknames (both male and female), and people's "preferred types of fornication," the registry contained information about the person's circle of friends, with special attention given to those who also engaged in homosexual behavior.[122] That the registry came to include not just personal information on homosexual men but also information on their (homosexual) acquaintances under Communist rule is far from surprising. In a growing police state that depended on informants and spies, queer sexual orientation became an ace card in the hands of State Security personnel. The homosexual registry must have continued to expand thanks in part to the enlarged police apparatus. As court records demonstrate, in addition to the police patrols that became a permanent feature of public spaces across Budapest, the police also placed undercover agents in known homosexual meeting places: public baths, parks, and toilets, as well as restaurants, pubs, and eateries. In addition to undercover police agents, homosexual men could also be reported to the Vice Department of the police by informants and State Security agents.

Following the decriminalization of homosexuality, outright repression and prosecution might have been over, but surveillance most certainly was not. Despite the fact that consensual homosexual acts were no longer criminalized, the homosexual registry continued to be used even after 1961.[123] As trial records, references from the records of the State Security Archives, and anecdotal evidence attest, intelligence services continued to use homosexuality and the registry as a means to control people through blackmail and turn them into informants. The social stigma attached to homosexuality and the fear of being outed made homosexuals easy prey for State Security agencies. Although queer sex might not have been considered a sin or criminal offense, in the minds of most people homosexuality continued to be associated with abnormality. While there are no surveys of public opinion from the 1960s, based on in-depth interviews conducted by sociologist László Cseh-Szombathy with homosexual men during the late 1970s and early 1980s, it is clear that we cannot overestimate the impact of negative stigma held toward homosexuality, which men reportedly found incapacitating even as late as the 1980s.[124] For example, while reflecting on the general attitude toward homosexuality, one interviewee said, "if it [homosexuality] is brought up, it is evident that a *buzi* [fag] is not a human being. And it [homosexuality] is also associated with criminality."[125] Not only did the decriminalization of homosexuality not bring social acceptance but the actual easing of censorship led to a greater stigmatization of homosexuality as a pathological and a deviant condition. Thanks to the general medicalization of sex in public discourse, all nonnormative sexual behaviors, and homosexuality particularly, became pathologized. Occasional references made to homosexuality on state television and in newspapers portrayed homosexuality exclusively as a medical aberration—often accompanied by various crimes. A male homosexual was also portrayed as explicitly feminine, as "not a real man."[126] In contrast to lesbians, who were still considered to be women, the portrayal of male homosexuals reflected the strict boundaries and insecurities of heteronormative scripts of Hungarian masculinity that Communists had cultivated.[127] Such portrayals had a lasting effect. At the end of Communism in 1989, sexually desiring one's own gender was considered first and foremost as "sick," a medical aberration, by a majority of the Hungarian people.[128]

Given the existence of entrenched cultural homophobia, the resulting internalized shame, and the fear of being outed, the Communists could use people's homosexuality to pressure them into informing on their acquaintances and loved ones. The Ministry of Interior's "strictly confidential" training manual for the recruitment of informants from 1957 opens a window into how the state utilized sexuality and in particular homosexuality in its policing of the Hungarian population. The manual was written to aid in the training of State Security agents' efforts to recruit informants at all levels and circles of society. Despite liberalization during the Kádár era, Hungary functioned as a police state, where State Security remained the most feared and powerful agency.[129] Besides the directives and textbooks of the agency, there are actual work files that offer clear evidence of how the state used both homo- and heterosexual sexual encounters to blackmail individuals. In the recruitment training manual from 1957, we learn that out of the three different ways people could be recruited—appealing to patriotism, through compromising facts, and via playing on the material interests of people—

homosexuality was a widely used category of compromising information. The manual went to great length to explain how to successfully recruit someone using compromising facts. "During recruitment based on comprising facts, the potential agent candidates should not be aware of the purpose of the true nature of state security interest in them, until they themselves bring up the issue of clandestine cooperation."[130] Through presenting the incriminating evidence, the goal was to make the potential candidates paranoid about the extent to which their "secret" was known and potentially could be used against them. And eventually it was to make them realize that the only way to ensure that their secret, that is their sexual orientation, would not be made public was to cooperate fully with the State Security Service. According to the manual, it was in cases in which the candidate was willing to do anything to stop compromising information from being leaked that recruitment was most likely to be successful.[131] While heterosexual affairs were also incriminating, it was homosexual relationships that were especially valuable findings for State Security. Once someone agreed to be an informant, the recruited person was given a pseudonym, and their information was filed within the elaborate informant database. There were a number of different ways in which recruits were used. For instance, a person who was of interest to the political police needed to be trailed in order to gather information for the creation of a *környezet tanulmány* (social inquiry report). The agents who trailed them might realize that their target frequented a bar that was a known meeting place for homosexuals. First, State Security would cross-reference the person under surveillance with the police's homosexual registry. Sometimes this provided additional information about the person's sexual preference. Second, the team assigned to the case would request an agent who would "fit in" with the milieu of the bar. And, thus, the activation of a recent recruit would begin.[132] But perhaps in more than any other area, homosexual informants served the Communist authorities in their fight against religion.

HOMOSEXUAL AGENTS IN THE COMMUNIST WAR ON RELIGION

Homosexual agents were key players in the Communist efforts to loosen the hold of religion and the church over the Hungarian population. According to Marxist-Leninist ideology, there was no place for religion in socialism. From the moment Hungarian Communists secured their one-party based dictatorship, they aimed to discredit and lessen the power of all religions and, first and foremost, the influence of the Catholic Church. Indeed, the process of limiting the power of religious institutions began even before the Communists came to power.[133] Thanks to the nationalization of large property holdings, the Catholic Church lost most of its land, and the second largest denomination in Hungary, the Calvinist Church, lost almost half of its estates. By 1952 all religious institutions had to give up what remained of their property. Once their dictatorship was firmly in place, the Communists waged an all-out war against religion. They nationalized schools and banned all religious orders (most of which were Catholic) and religious youth organizations. To bring the largest churches to heel, the Communists forced changes in church leadership, through manipulation, show trials, and imprisonments, most famously of the Hungarian prelate Cardinal József Mindszenty.[134] The new leadership, which owed loyalty to the Communists, signed agreements with the People's Republic. By the end of 1948, the Calvinist, Unitarian, Lutheran, and Jewish leaders signed an agreement that allowed them to continue to have a few religious schools but restricted them from interfering with the Communist Party's secularization project. The Catholic Church held out the longest in resisting such compromises. Considering that at the end of the war approximately 70 percent of Hungarians were Catholic, the fight against the Catholic Church was seen as a critical step on the road to socialism. The intimidation and draconian regulations that cut the Catholic Church off from its assets payed off. With no property, little income, and without the means of communicating with the Vatican, Hungarian Catholic leaders signed an agreement with the state in August of 1950. In return for its support of the People's Republic, the Catholic Church was guaranteed meager financial support from the state and was granted the right to continue to operate eight secondary schools.[135] To further subjugate the churches to the party's will, a State Office of Religion was established, based on the Soviet model, in 1951. Its official function was to oversee the relationship between all religious organizations and the state. In reality, however, like elsewhere in the Eastern Bloc, its unofficial function was to control, censor, and limit the reach of the churches. From that point on, all major appointments of personnel and any administrative decisions had to be preapproved by the State Office of Religion. Finally, to make sure nothing would fly under the radar of the party, the office worked closely with State Security to monitor activities of both any remaining churches and former religious orders.

Despite the political thaw following 1958 and the significantly curtailed power of the churches, party leadership remained deeply suspicious of organized religion, and especially of the Catholic Church. In 1960 there was an organized campaign to further damage the reputation of the Catholic leadership and to diminish any remaining influence of the church. Rather than bringing political charges against the Catholic Church, however, the party pursued morality charges. At the time when, thanks to show trials and state retaliation following the 1956 uprising, people were fully aware that Communist charges of "antidemocratic" activities were politically motivated and fabricated, in the eyes of the masses the exposure of moral crimes was more believable than political crimes. Bringing to light the homosexual affairs of priests and nuns proved to be an exceptionally captivating way to do just that. From the notes of the Department of Propaganda and Agitation (APO) of the Central Committee of the Party (following 1956, named the Hungarian Socialist Workers' Party), we know that there was a concerted effort between various state organizations to use homosexuality as a means of alienating Hungarians from the church. The APO's action plan, titled "Exploiting the Homosexual Affairs of Catholic Priests," from 1960 explained that "one of the weakest points of the Catholic Church is that the majority of priests are homosexuals. We [the party] have not exploited this enough, even though with religious people, the homosexual affairs of priests, especially those associated with youth, are very effective [in discrediting the moral standing of the church]. Using homosexual affairs is also an effective way to expose and deactivate reactionary priests."[136] The action plan went on to detail how incriminating information should be used: as a means of intimidation, as a way to create internal divisions within the church, and as a means to influence public opinion even prior to the official trials of individual priests.

Homosexual informants of the State Security Service produced much of the incriminating evidence that allowed Communist officials to build their cases against priests and other church officials. As files of Operation Black Raven and Operation Apostles show, informants provided extensive evidence about homosexual activities that took place at church hierarchy levels ranging from that of the highest leadership down to the local parishes.[137] Once the target was identified, State Security operatives would proceed in the following way. First, the person under surveillance was cross-checked with the police's homosexual registry. A homosexual agent would then seek to contact the accused in order to gather incriminating evidence. Once there was evidence of homosexual activity, State Security would bring the individual in and press them for additional information on homosexual contacts. Evidence of homosexuality could also be used to blackmail, not only the person himself, but also people within the leadership of the Catholic Church. It was not only in the best interest of the religious personnel themselves to keep their sexual life out of public eye but also in the interests of the Catholic leadership to limit the damage that the publicizing of priests' homosexual affairs could inflict on the church's reputation. Officers at State Security thought about how to inflict the most damage to the church, whether it was by bringing someone to trial or turning them into informants. Thus, homosexual affairs of religious personnel were not always prosecuted. State Security carefully selected which priests would go on trial for "unnatural fornication." Unlike most cases involving homosexual acts, which were closed to the public, the trials of religious figures were always open to the public and, in fact, were widely publicized. Whether it was priests, monks of the Cistercian order, or former Benedictine nuns, the State Security built highly public cases around the homosexual affairs (and often homosexual affairs with youths) to demonstrate to the nation how the entire Catholic Church was rife with immoral sexual practices. Whether the charges were real or fabricated, homosexual informants played a crucial role in providing explicit evidence through which Communist authorities could destroy the moral standing of respected religious figures, as well as blackmail them into cooperation. The surveillance and use of homosexuality as a means to blackmail and damage the moral standing of religious institutions continued until the fall of Communism.

CONCLUSION

As this chapter demonstrates, Hungary's entry into World War II and the establishment of the Communist dictatorship in 1948 brought a definitive end to the tolerance of homosexuality and the official silences that had surrounded it. With the rising influence of Nazism and its ideologies, especially under the Arrow Cross regime, homosexuality became irreconcilable with the idea of national community. Driven by concerns about the racial and eugenic health of the Hungarian population, homosexuality came to be characterized as a burden on the national community—one that required state intervention. With its plans to castrate homosexuals, the Arrow Cross would have introduced the first major changes in the official treatment of homosexuals. However, since Hungary lost the war and the Arrow Cross government never had the opportunity to implement their proposed policies, their legacy in terms of homosexuality has remained largely theoretical. Following the end of World War II, it was the Communists who, after they secured dictatorial powers, had the institutional capabilities to, not only systematically purge homosexual men and women from their ranks, but also prosecute homosexual men at an unprecedented level. For the first time, homosexuality was denounced not only on a medical and moral basis, but also on an ideological basis. In the Stalinist, repressive Rákosi era, homosexual men and women were portrayed as the enemies of socialism.

The prosecution of homosexuals was intimately tied to the goal of transforming Hungarian society into a socialist state. It is no coincidence that at the same time as the Communists intended to make gender and sexual equality the pillars of the new socialist society, homosexuality was thought be curable. By prosecuting and handing down prison sentences to thousands of men, the Communist justice system also believed in the possibility of transforming homosexual men into acceptable socialist citizens. In this sense, the early 1950s finally saw the implementation of the long-held hopes for the possibility of changing sexual orientation that were discussed during the brief rule of the Communists in 1919. And it is also not a coincidence that the abandonment of changing (homo)sexual orientation coincided with the abandonment of radical gender and sexual politics and, more generally, of the hope to fundamentally transform society. Homosexuality was decriminalized just as conservative gender and sexual politics were reembraced. The same reinvention of the private sphere and the family as building blocks of state-socialism that underwrote decriminalization of homosexuality also enacted a structural impediment for homosexuals. Making marriage the prerequisite for individual privacy, along with a sustained shortage of apartments in Budapest, created a situation that was increasingly burdensome on heterosexual men and women. For homosexuals it effectively eliminated the possibility of privacy.

Adopting the view of the congenital nature of homosexuality became a convenient way to deflect from having to acknowledge the failure of socialism to transform sexual orientation. It also ensured the stigmatization of homosexuality as a pathological illness. Thus, the decriminalization in 1961 of consensual homosexuality for those over twenty years of age did not lead to greater societal acceptance. In the long run, it exacerbated public homophobia. Moreover, Communist authorities continued to exploit homosexuals via blackmail and forced them to become informants for the State Security organization. And for many men and women, the choice to comply had lasting effects well beyond the democratic changes of 1989. It is not difficult to see why following 1989 for most who experienced being blackmailed, working for the Communist secret service became a subject best left behind. But the silencing of nonnormative and homosexual experiences of the state-socialist era also played into the hands of those who were critical of the newfound liberalization of sexual morality.

EPILOGUE

Queers and Democracy: The Misremembering of the Queer Past

By the first decade of the twentieth century, Budapest had a vibrant queer culture, especially for men. Thanks to the rapid expansion of the city in a relatively confined space, along with lax enforcement of laws regulating sexuality, Budapest had a growing public sexual culture, with an increasingly visible queer presence. The formation of homosexual culture in Budapest was tied to and informed by transnational and in particular Austrian and German discourses, events, and cultures of homosexuality. There were established places in the city for men, and to lesser extent women, who desired their own sex and wanted casual sexual encounters or to socialize. Many of those places, such as the baths, the City Park, and the promenade on the banks of the Danube, remained remarkably stable parts of the city's queer geography throughout its turbulent history. While far from the limelight of mass media or official attention, queers were increasingly legible to authorities and denizens of the city alike—and they remained so throughout the first four decades of the twentieth century. In fact, as this book argues, it was precisely the official unwillingness to acknowledge homosexuality that facilitated the coexistence of homosexuals and different political systems. Despite a conservative turn, Budapest continued to accommodate a homosexual culture that by the 1930s numbered homosexuals in the tens of thousands. Homosexuals could navigate the city with relative ease, especially if they conformed to normative gender roles in public. It was only the aftermath of World War II and the establishment of the Communist one-party system that sent queer men and women back into the closet, so to speak, from where they would not reemerge until the 1980s. Such a trajectory, on one hand, places Budapest within now considerable scholarship on urban histories of homosexuality that emphasize the visibility and toleration of homosexual cultures during the first part of the twentieth century.

The extended period of backlash against homosexuals and the invisibility of their culture throughout most of the state-socialist era, on the other hand, is not just a reminder of the nonlinear progression of the history of (homo)sexualities, but also of the crucial role the Communist one-party system played in shaping the trajectory of Budapest's and more generally of East-Central European histories of homosexuality.

Throughout the twentieth century, Hungary experienced radically different political systems. Yet, these regimes shared some fundamental assumptions about homosexuality. They believed that while there were some congenital homosexuals, the majority of homosexuals *became* homosexuals. In their view, homosexuality was akin to a communicable disease. And regardless of their political stance, subsequent Hungarian authorities, like many of their transnational counterparts, ascribed to a similar practice: imposing silence on homosexuality, which they believed was an essential element in stopping the spread of the "disease." Disagreements about the roots and causes of same-sex desire aside, there was a tacit agreement among public officials and politicians, fueled by fear that talking about it, even if only to condemn it, would inevitably ignite same-sex desire in some people. The collective silencing around issues of homosexuality cut across political and ideological divides. Outside of law enforcement, medicine, and the legal profession, the subject of homosexuality was taboo. The deliberate silencing of nonnormative sexualities that characterized political regimes prior to 1945 also produced erasures of contemporary sources that would have indicated the presence of homosexuality. This was clearly the case with the scandal around Cécile Tormay's (founder of the National Association Hungarian Women) homosexuality during the 1920s. The news of the trial of Tormay and her alleged lover were suppressed at the time, and most of the legal documents were subsequently purged. That consecutive regimes kept the homosexual registry and its records secret is only the most conspicuous evidence of the great length to which multiple regimes went in order to limit contemporary and future discourse on queer sexualities—to literally rewrite the past. Their efforts were largely successful. Unlike Berlin, Paris, London, and Vienna, but similar to other East-Central European capitals, the historical existence of queer sexual culture in Budapest has, until very recently, not been acknowledged, either in public memory or in historical scholarship.[1]

That subsequent authorities were invested in silencing, both during their respective times and also retroactively by confiscating, keeping, or destroying relevant documents, becomes especially important in light of the history of the Communist years. The fact that following the establishment of the Communist dictatorship post–World War II, sexuality, and especially homosexuality, became an important tool for the Communist Party in the surveillance of the Hungarian population can provide a reasonable explanation as to why sources on homosexuality, like the homosexual registry, continue to be (and go) missing. If homosexuality was used for blackmail and as a means to turn people into informants for the price of keeping their sexuality "secret," both homosexuals and the Communist Party were odd but invested bedfellows in concealing information about their tacit agreement. Thus the Communist period between 1948 and 1989 is an important contributor to the historical silencing of queer sexualities in Hungarian (and more generally in East-Central European) society.[2] By escalating prosecution of (especially throughout the 1940s and 1950s), continuing surveillance of, and censoring knowledge about homosexuality over the course of four decades, the Communist government overrode the memory and experience of both the interwar and pre-1918 periods that accommodated a visible queer sexual culture.

By creating a doubled shame, stigmatizing homosexuality as a pathology and as a tool of collaboration with the Communists, the Communist period also actively discouraged people from accounting for their queer past after the fall of Communism. Considering that according to some of the latest estimates, out of ten million Hungarians, approximately two hundred thousand people served as informants and that as many as one in ten Hungarian people at some point in time were informants, the use of homosexuality as a tool of State Security is unsurprising.[3] What is more interesting are the reasons why since the end of Communism and establishment of democracy in 1989 there has been no acknowledgment of the use of sexuality as a means of turning people into informants. In contrast to the considerable and continuous official and public interest in exposing former collaborators and informants for the Communist state, there has been little to no acknowledgment or interest in the role of sexuality played in making people spy on their friends, acquaintances, and families. For understandable reasons, the Catholic Church, whose personnel, both men and women, were especially implicated, has also chosen to remain silent on this issue. In short, even if the post-1989 democratic era has granted the freedom and certain protections to the queer community that in previous eras would have been unimaginable, the legacy of the Communist era has encouraged self-censorship and silence on both individual and institutional levels.[4] Such a legacy has been instrumental in assisting the more recent backlash against the queer community, which I would argue fits squarely within the last major turn of the history of Hungarian homosexualities in which the long history of coexistence between illiberal governments and queer sexuality has shattered.

The perpetual silencing and lack of visibility during Communism resulted in a collective misremembering about the past. According to this popular idea, which ironically unites both the young LGBTQ communities and their harshest adversaries, queer culture came about following 1989 on the both the wings of liberal democracy and capitalism. Two relatively recent accounts illustrate post-1989 attitudes toward Hungary's LGBTQ sexual minority and its relationship to Hungary's political past. The first has to do with Jobbik, the radical right nationalist political party (currently the third largest party in the parliament).[5] Inspired by Russia, in 2012, a member of the Jobbik Party submitted a proposal to the parliament to criminalize the "promotion of sexual behavior disorders," defined as the encouragement of homosexuality (along with transsexuality, bisexuality, and pedophilia).[6] According to the party's explanation, the amendment of the Hungarian criminal law was necessary in order to "protect public morality and the mental health of the younger generations."[7] While the amendment never passed and Jobbik has not submitted any proposals since, the party has continued to be vocal in inciting homophobia and anti-LGBTQ sentiments. Most recently, the party protested the legitimacy of the annual Pride Parade, stating:

> For Jobbik, it is unacceptable that certain groups [LGBTQ] impose their own queerness on the majority of society, and that the majority of society should be obliged to endure such deviant exhibitionism. . . . To protect the majority of society and minors, when Jobbik comes to govern it will find the way to legally ban this provocative, offensive and counterproductive [Pride] march.[8]

In Jobbik's vision, queer people are invaders who, with events like the Pride Parade, offend the sensibilities of the silent heterosexual majority of Hungarians. Such a negative attitude toward the queer community, which also totally overlooks the societal wide homophobia and structural discrimination that queer people face on a daily basis, has not been limited to the radical right party. Since 2010, when the conservative Fidesz gained a supermajority in the parliament, it has attacked the rights and recognition of sexual minorities.[9] According to both Fidesz and Jobbik, the visibility of homosexuals represents the perils of neoliberal capitalism and, more generally, liberal democracies. In their interpretation, too much freedom and Western-style capitalism have been the main causes of the perceived rise of (homo)sexual subcultures. Queers in public are not *just* propagating decadence, but, in the eyes of the pronatalist right-wing parties, queers (by not reproducing) are literally destroying the future of Hungarian society. And such perspectives are not limited to Hungary but widely shared across the former Eastern Bloc.[10] Implicit in this view is the notion that homosexuality and homosexuals arrived to Hungary after 1989.

A brief look at the Hungarian LGBTQ community's perspective of itself shows that, even if militantly disputing their conservative and far-right critiques, most members of the sexual minority share the view that it was *only* following the end of Communism and the establishment of democracy that homosexuals could become more visible members of the national community. Accordingly, since the 1990s representatives of LGBTQ organizations have generally declared that the growth and visibility of the Hungarian queer community took place as a result of liberalization of laws and public attitudes.[11] The recent documentary *Hot Men Cold Dictatorship* (2015) that recounts the gay experience during late state-socialism, while pioneering in its efforts to document the social and cultural history of Hungarian gay subculture during Communism, also reiterates the assumed connection between liberal democracy and sexual freedom. The implication here is that prior to the arrival of democracy, there was *no* Hungarian gay movement, nor was homosexuality visible in previous political systems.[12] Without histories of sexualities of the past to contest this idea, this distorted view has served as a ground for portraying the existence of sexual minorities as the negative consequence of democratization while providing the queer communities with no basis to counter these arguments. Historians, by reinserting the histories of nonnormative sexualities, have the opportunity to play an important role in debunking the arguments of the far right and also provide usable (hi)stories for the LGBTQ communities. My hope is that *Queer Budapest* is a step in that direction.

ACKNOWLEDGMENTS

This book would not have been possible without the generous help of Hungarian archivists, scholars, and members of the LGBTQ community. Special thanks to archivists László Nagy, András Lugosi, and Mihály Szécsényi at the City Archives of Budapest, and Géza Vörös at the Historical Archives of the Hungarian State Security, all of whom were indispensable in locating materials for my research. Scholars in Hungary—Anna Borgos, Rudolf Paksa, Hadley Rankin, Gábor Szegedi, Eszter Timár, and Háttér Társaság—provided many important insights and helpful suggestions along the way. I owe a great intellectual and personal debt to Judit Takács for her generosity in sharing her research data and for her collaboration. I deeply benefited from and enjoyed our conversations on the history of Hungarian sexualities. Thanks go as well to Örs Somfay, whose love of studying and learning from the past first sparked my interest in history, and whose research assistance with Arcanum was foundational to this project. I wish to thank Bryn Mawr College, the European University Institute, Rutgers University, and the Andrew W. Mellow Foundation for supporting the research and writing of this book.

Unbounded thanks to Paul Hanberbrink for reading this manuscript in its entirety and for an ongoing investment in and support for my intellectual growth. I am extremely grateful to Belinda Davis, Melissa Feinberg, Seth Koven, and Dagmar Herzog for their incisive insights, support, and generosity; each of them made crucial interventions at various stages of the project and have been instrumental in the evolution of my work. In addition, special thanks to Seth Koven for his fierce encouragement. The work of Mark Cornwall, Dan Healy, Josie McLellan, Agnieszka Kościańska, Kateřina Lišková, Keely Stauter-Halstead, and Nancy Wingfield on Eastern European histories of sexuality has been, and continues to be, a great inspiration. Alix Genter,

Allison Miller, and Svanur Petursson have provided important intellectual comraderie, support for my project, and friendships at Rutgers University. Thanks also to my students at Bryn Mawr College, the European University Institution, and Rutgers University for their curiosity, insights, and dedication to learning about the past. Their unrelenting aspiration to question established historical narratives as well as learn about and recover marginalized histories has served as a source of creativity and motivation.

I was fortunate to have the opportunity to workshop and receive feedback on different parts of the manuscript during my tenure as a Max Weber postdoctoral fellow at the European University Institute and as a Penn Humanities Forum regional fellow at the University of Pennsylvania. I would like to thank the members of the Philadelphia Area Modern Germany Workshop for welcoming me and offering helpful suggestions in the later stages of the manuscript. Their annual gathering has become an integral part of my intellectual and collegial life.

I feel exceptionally lucky to have landed at Bryn Mawr College, an institution where I have found such extraordinary colleagues and friends. I am particularly grateful to the members of my department—Ignacio Gallup-Diaz, Madhavi Kale, Kalala Ngalamulume, Elly R. Truitt, and Sharon Ullman—for their collegial support and mentorship. I am also indebted to Alison Cook-Sather and Jamie Taylor for their guidance. Thanks to my junior faculty cohort—Martin Gaspar, Yan Kung, Susanna Fioratta, Adrienne Prettyman, and Maja Seselj—for providing a necessary balance with regular activities of leisure. Special thanks to Bethany Schneider, Kate Thomas, and Elly R. Truitt for their culinary magic, intellectual support, and friendship. I am indebted to Alix Genter for her skilled editorial work on my introduction, to Jessical Linker for her help with creating a map of queer Budapest, and to Linda Gerstein for reading early drafts of the manuscript. Deep thanks to Priya S. Nelson, the late Douglas Mitchell, and their team at the University Chicago Press for shepherding this book through publication. I am grateful to Mark Reschke for editing the entire manuscript.

Many far-flung friends have helped me bring this book to fruition. I thank Lyuba Bakalova, Paige Bowie, Jessica Dosch, Joanne Gregorio, Jessie Hempel, Shannon McKenzie, Nicole Melch, Natalie Neusch, and Jen Stoody for their curiosity about my research. Whether it happened while running races, walking to and from yoga, traveling together, conversing over happy hour drinks, or sitting on the ski lift, responding to their questions and queries about "the most important takeaways from my research" became a deeply helpful part of my writing process. Members of the csipet csapat in Hungary—Vera Csermely, Judit and Kati Zsedényi, Viki Senkálszky, Anita

Vékhely—and Fruzsi Réczey in Brussels: thank you for the past twenty years of friendship and encouragement. I would not be here without you.

Special thanks to my family for all their emotional, intellectual, and financial support. I am grateful for József Farkas, Ann Isenberg, Miles Gurtler, Emő Fülöp, Szofi Kurimay, Anne Montgomery, and Brendan Hart. Mary Lee Sargeant has offered continuous support, encouragement, and interest in my work. I am forever grateful for her insightful feedback and the countless times that she has read and meticulously edited my work. To my grandmother and my late grandfather: words cannot express my gratitude for your unconditional love and respect for humanity. Thank you to my mother, Magdolna Krasznai, and my father, Tamás Kurimay, for supporting me as I set out on the road less traveled. Their work ethic and productivity have and continue to serve as an inspiration. My sister, Dóra Kurimay, has offered unrelenting support and regular reminders that finishing this book was all about my mental game. To Karcsika and Brooke: Your arrivals have not made the completion of this book any easier. And that is an understatement. But it has certainly forced me to be more efficient than ever. Finally, this book would have not been possible without the support and partnership of Bridget Gurtler. I am forever grateful for her patience and her steady encouragement all the way through to the finish line. She has seen this project evolve from its inception to the end, and she has read, edited, and commented on this manuscript more times than I could count. Thank you for being my copilot, never ceasing to find laughter, and for showing me that life is better lived with the glass half full.

NOTES

INTRODUCTION

1. Soma Guthi, *Homosexuális szerelem (Tuzár detektív naplója): Bűnügyi Regény* (Budapest: Kunossy, Szilágyi és társa Könyvkiadóvállalat, 1908). Italics are mine.
2. Guthi, 6–7, 12, 159–60.
3. While Budapest's "bigger sister," Vienna, definitely remained more significant in the production of nude and sexual images, Budapest was also gaining momentum, although officially the publication of these images was illegal. On the public image of sexual culture in Vienna, see Scott Spector, *Violent Sensations: Sex, Crime, and Utopia in Vienna and Berlin, 1860–1914* (Chicago: University of Chicago Press, 2016), 17–73. At the turn of the century, there were 930 pubs, 249 cafés, 87 restaurants, and 426 small cafés in the city. In addition to bordellos, prostitution was present in many of these establishments as well as in local baths and hotels. Judit Forrai, "Kávéházak és kéjnők," *Budapesti Negyed: Lap a Városról* 12–13, nos. 2–3 (1996): 120.
4. "Budapest erkölcse," in *A Budapesti Leányvásár Titka*, ed. Jenő Kostyál (Fritz Ármin könyvnyomdája: Kostyál Jenő, 1902), 3–4.
5. Following the Compromise of 1867, Hungary readopted the 1848 regulation of the press. By contemporary standards this granted great freedom and protection of speech. From the 1880s Budapest had a rapidly expanding commercial press. For instance, in 1870 there were about eighty different publications in Budapest. By 1900 there were 384 publications. Dorottya Lipták, "A családi lapoktól a társasági lapokig: Újságok és újságolvasók a századvégen," *Budapesti Negyed* 16–17, nos. 2–3 (1997): 47.
6. The word "sinful" soon became an umbrella term for critiquing the capital for its cosmopolitanism, non-Hungarian elements, and lax mores. For a theoretical discussion of the relationship between fascination with sex and the actual lived experience of sexual culture, see Spector, *Violent Sensations*, 1–17.
7. Géza Buzinkay and György Kókay, *A magyar sajtó története I.: A kezdetektől a fordulat évéig* (Budapest: Ráció, 2005), 152–74.
8. Sándor Szatmáry, *Nagyvárosi erkölcsök: Budapest sexuális élete* (Budapest: Országos Laptudósító, 1908), 12–15. Italics are mine.

9. This view was not unique to Hungary, but as scholars in different contexts illustrated, a wider European phenomenon. For a comparative perspective, see Florence Tamagne's *The History of Homosexuality in Europe: Berlin, London, Paris, 1919–1939* (New York: Algora Publishing, 2004), pt. 2, 149–303.

10. Scholarship on Berlin, London, and Paris is extensive. For some of the latest works, see Robert Beachy, *Gay Berlin: Birthplace of a Modern Identity* (New York: Knopf, 2015); Spector, *Violent Sensations*; Simon Avery and Katherine M. Graham, eds., *Sex, Time and Place Queer Histories of London, c. 1850 to the Present* (London: Bloomsbury Academic, 2018); Julian Jackson, *Living in Arcadia: Homosexuality, Politics, and Morality in France from the Liberation to AIDS* (Chicago: University of Chicago Press, 2009).

11. John Lukacs, *Budapest 1900: A Historical Portrait of a City and Its Culture* (New York: Weindenfeld & Nicolson, 1988), 106.

12. The modern West was by no means a homogenic entity. At the same time, Hungary, along with other (future) East-Central European states, constantly looked to the West (particularly to England, France, and Germany, which itself was not considered "Western" until after the Second World War) and defined their own progress by how quickly they could attain Western European standards. As Larry Wolf, in *Inventing Eastern Europe: The Map of Civilization on the Mind of the Enlightenment* (Stanford, CA: Stanford University, 1994), has demonstrated, the idea of the "backwardness" of the East and the "modernity" of the West was as much as an intellectual construction as it was a reality.

13. By Eastern and Western Europe, I refer to both geographic and cultural boundaries as well as intellectually invented differences. Neither Eastern nor Western Europe can be reduced to homogenous entities.

14. The connection between urban places and emerging queer and homosexual activities has been extensively documented in the Western context. The literature on the historical relationship between cities and homosexual identity and subcultures is also extensive. For an overview of the historiography of existing literature, see Robert Aldrich, "Homosexuality and the City: An Historical Overview," *Urban Studies* 41, no. 9 (2004): 1719–37.

15. This was markedly different for countries where conservative politics targeted both female and male nonnormative sexual acts and identities. See, for instance, Lorenzo Benadusi, *The Enemy of the New Man: Homosexuality in Fascist Italy*, trans. by Suzanne Dingee and Jennifer Pudney (Madison: University of Wisconsin Press, 2012); and more generally Florence Tamagne's *A History of Homosexuality in Europe*, pt. 3, 303–93.

16. Scholars in various contexts have shown how the interplay between existing regulations, the medicalization of nonnormative sexualities, and cultural norms (particularly about gender) was crucial in shaping both the treatment and experiences of queer sexualities. George Chauncey's *Gay New York: Gender, Urban Culture, and the Making of the Gay Male World, 1890–1940* (New York: Basic Books, 1994), and Matt Houlbrook's *Queer London* (Chicago: University of Chicago Press, 2005), and more recently Laurie Marhoefer's *Sex and the Weimar Republic: Homosexual Emancipation and the Rise of the Nazis* (Toronto: University of Toronto Press, 2015), and Scott Spector's *Violent Sensations* are excellent examples.

17. Works with similar conclusions include William A. Peniston, *Pederasts and*

Others: Urban Culture and Sexual Identity in Nineteenth Century Paris (New York: Harrington Park Press, 2004); James N. Green, *Beyond Carnival: Male Homosexuality in Twentieth-Century Brazil* (Chicago: University of Chicago Press, 1999); Lorenzo Benadusi, *The Enemy of the New Man*.

18. Kornél Tábori, *Bünös Nők* (Budapest: A Nap Nyomda, 1909), 65–69.

19. There were several exceptions to the official silence, notably in medical, police, and to a lesser extent, legal literature. These sources, following the example of leading European sexologists and physicians like August Forel and Richard Krafft-Ebing, dedicated considerable attention to female (homo)sexualities. Forel's *Die sexuelle Frage: Eine naturwissenschaftlische, psyhologische, hygienische und sozioloische Studie für Gebildete* (Munich: Ernst Reinhardt, 1905) and Krafft-Ebing's *Psychopathia Sexualis Psychopathia Sexualis: A visszás nemi érzések különös figyelembe vételével. Orvostörvényszéki tanulmány*, trans. by Jakab Fischer (Budapest: Singerés Wolfner Kiadása, 1894), which became standard references for medical experts.

20. Albert Shaw, "Budapest: The Rise of a New Metropolis," *Century Magazine* 44, no. 2 (1892): 163.

21. Thanks to the Hungarian invention of the "middling purifier" and gradual reduction system, which were also implemented by millers in Minnesota, Budapest and Minneapolis became the two milling centers in the world. By 1900, in terms of railway tracks and accessibility, Budapest and Hungary were on par with the railway system of Paris and France. Károly Vörös, "A Fővárostól a Székesfővárosig 1873–1896," in *Budapest története a márciusi forradalomtól az őszirózsás forradalomig*, ed. Károly Vörös (Budapest: Akadémia Kiadó, 1978), 325.

22. For political history and especially the success of "Magyarization," see Robert Nemes, *The Once and Future Budapest* (DeKalb: Northern Illinois University Press, 2005). For economic development during the period, see Iván T. Berend et al., *Evolution of the Hungarian Economy, 1848–1998*, vol. 1, *One-and-a-Half Centuries of Semi-Successful Modernization, 1848–1989* (Boulder, CO: Social Science Monographs; distributed by Columbia University Press, 2000), chap. 1. For cultural history, the seminal books remain John Lukacs, *Budapest 1900*, and Péter Hanák, *The Garden and the Workshop: Essays on the Cultural History of Vienna and Budapest* (Princeton, NJ: Princeton University Press, 1998). For social history, see Gábor Gyáni et al., eds., *Social History of Hungary from the Reform Era to the End of the Twentieth Century* (New York: distributed by Columbia University Press, 2004), pt. 1. Gábor Gyáni, *Az utca és a szalon: A társadalmi térhasználat Budapesten (1870–1940)* (Budapest: Új Mandátum Könyvkiadó, 1999).

23. During the late nineteenth century, Budapest and Berlin were the fastest growing European cities. Their population growth was only matched by cities of the New World. István Bart, *Budapest krónikája: A kezdetektol napjainkig* (Budapest: Corvina, 2007), 277–330.

24. *Budapest székesfőváros statisztikai évkönyve az 1944–1946 évekről* (Budapest: Budapest Székesfőváros Irodalmi és Művészeti Intézete, 1948), 12.

25. *Budapest székesfőváros statisztikai évkönyve az 1944–1946 évekről*.

26. *Budapest székesfőváros statisztikai évkönyve az 1944–1946 évekről*. Villagers who moved to the city of course did not become urbanites overnight. Rather, they took their village backgrounds with all their rural habits to the city.

27. Budapest's urban environment was similar to the mixing of tenants in apartment buildings in Berlin. Gábor Gyáni, *Identity and the Urban Experience: Fin-de-Siécle Budapest* (Boulder, CO: East European Monographs; distributed by Columbia University Press, 2004), 48.

28. While there were changes in the ethnic makeup of the city, its character and urban design changed little in the interwar years. For a useful history of Budapest's architectural and urban landscape from a comparative perspective, see Pál Granasztói's *Budapest arculatai* (Budapest: Szépirodalmi Könyvkiadó, 1980).

29. According to historian Balázs Mihályi, of the 39,317 buildings in Budapest, 47 percent were damaged, 23 percent seriously damaged, and 4 percent totally destroyed. "Épületkárok Budapest ostroma nyomán," http://budapest-ostroma.hu/adattar/, accessed January 9, 2019.

30. On the dramatic architectural changes and city planning post-1948, see Endre Prakfalvi, *Architecture of Dictatorship: The Architecture of Budapest between 1945 and 1959* (Budapest: Municipality of Budapest, Office of the Mayor, 1999); and Endre Prakfalvi and György Szücs, *A szocreál Magyarországon* (Budapest: Corvina, 2010).

31. Lukacs's *Budapest 1900* is an illustrative example.

32. During the pre-1989 Communist period, Hungarian historians viewed the Hungarian Soviet Republic and the Károlyi regime in a much more favorable light. And even when they presented more complex accounts of the period, they were much more critical of Károlyi and remained generally positive about the achievements of the "Dictatorship of the Proletariat." This took a distinct turn following the end of Communist one-party system in 1989. After this moment the scholarship treated Károlyi more favorably and was much more critical of the Kun regime.

33. Since 1989, historians have been very critical of and by and large focus on the negative effects of the Kun regime. See, for instance, Ignác Romsics' *Hungary in the Twentieth Century* (Budapest: Corvin; Osiris, 1999); János Gyurgyák's *Ezzé lett magyar hazátok: A magyar nemzeteszme és nacionalizmus története* (Budapest: Osiris, 2007).

34. Throughout the interwar years, these two forces, which were both overlapping and at times bitterly antagonistic, contributed to a constant shifting in Hungarian politics between antidemocratic parliamentarism and fascism. For a concise political history of interwar history in English, see István Deák, *Hungary from 1918 to 1945* (New York: Columbia University, 1989).

35. Ignác Romsics, "Nyíltan vagy titkosan? A Horthy-rendszer választójoga," *Rubicon* 1, no. 2 (1990): 4–5.

36. Current historical scholarship on the period emphasizes that following the Treaty of Trianon in "Csonka (Mutilated) Hungary," Budapest assumed an even greater significance, even though the city itself lost its intellectual and creative vanguardism. Miklós Lackó, "Budapest during the Interwar Years," in *Budapest: A History from Its Beginnings to 1998*, ed. Andras Gerő and János Poór, trans. Judit Zinner, Cecil B. Elby, and Nóra Arató (New York: Columbia University Press, 1997), 166; Tibor Frank, "Berlin Junction: Patterns of Hungarian Intellectual Migrations, 1919–1933," *Storicamente* 2 (2006), http://www.storicamente.org/05_studi_ricerche/02frank.htm, accessed December 11, 2017. In addition, historians underscore the transition from a multiethnic and liberal political state to an ethnically homogenous, authoritarian political system that ended

up fighting on the side of Germany in the World War II. For Hungarian works, see Gábor Gyáni and György Kövér, *Magyarország társadalomtörténete a reformkortól a második világháborúig* (Budapest: Osiris, 2006); and Ignác Romsics, *Magyarország története a XX. Században* (Budapest: Osiris, 2010). For English, see Mária Kovács, *Liberal Professions and Illiberal: Politics Hungary from the Habsburgs to the Holocaust* (New York: Oxford University Press, 1994); Paul Hanebrink, *In Defense of Christian Hungary: Religion, Nationalism, and Antisemitism, 1890–1944* (Ithaca, NY: Cornell University Press, 2006); Iván Z. Dénes, *Conservative Ideology in the Making*, trans. Judit Pokoly (Budapest: CEU Press, 2009).

37. The so-called numerus clausus that required the number of Jewish students in higher education to be proportionate to Hungary's Jewish population (6 percent) was introduced in 1920.

38. Herzog, *Sexuality in Europe: A Twentieth-Century History* (New York: Cambridge University Press, 2011), 1.

39. More recently there have been a number of publications in East-Central European languages that focused on the history of homosexuality. See, for instance, Jan Seidl, Jan Wintr, and Lukáš Nozar, *Od žaláře k oltáři: Emancipace homosexuality v českých zemích od roku 1867 do současnosti* [From prison to the altar: Emancipation of homosexuality in the Czech lands from 1867 to the present] (Brno: Host, 2012); Krzysztof Tomasik, *Gejerel: Mniejszości seksualne w PRL-u* [Gejerel: Sexual minorities in the People's Republic of Poland] (Warsaw: Wydawn "Krytyki Politycznej," 2012).

40. With the exception of the Háttér Archivum, http://hatter.hu/tevekenysegunk/archivum-es-konyvtar, accessed February 10, 2018.

41. Gayle Rubin's "Thinking Sex: Notes for a Radical Theory of the Politics of Sexuality," in *Pleasure and Danger: Exploring Female Sexuality*, ed. Carole S. Vance (London: Pandora, 1992), 267–293, was one of the first scholarly inquires that recognized that nonnormative sexualities are often outside of institutional memory. Rubin highlights how historians of queer sexualities have to build upon archives often not assembled for queer purposes.

42. Dagmar Herzog, "Sexuality in the Postwar West," *Journal of Modern History* 78 (2006): 144–71, and "Syncopated Sex: Transforming European Sexual Cultures," *American Historical Review* 24, no. 5 (2009): 1287; Margot Canaday, "AHR Forum: Transnational Sexualities—Thinking Sex in the Transnational Turn; An Introduction," *American Historical Review* 24, no. 5 (2009): 1250.

43. The only country from the former Eastern Bloc where sexuality has received considerable attention in English is East Germany. There are few books, however, which explicitly address same-sex sexuality in East-Central European contexts. These include Dan Healey's *Homosexual Desire in Revolutionary Russia: The Regulation of Sexual and Gender Dissent* (Chicago: University of Chicago Press, 2004); Tracie Matysik's *Reforming the Moral Subject! Ethics and Sexuality in Central Europe, 1890–1930* (Ithaca, NY: Cornell University Press, 2008); and *The Devil's Wall: The Nationalist Youth Mission of Heinz Rutha* (Cambridge, MA: Harvard University Press, 2012) by Mark Cornwall.

44. Important works on the history of rural sexualities include John Howard's *Men Like That: Southern Queer History* (Chicago: University of Chicago Press, 2001); Jen Rydström's *Sinners and Citizens: Bestiality and Homosexuality in Sweden, 1880–*

1950 (Chicago: University of Chicago Press, 2003); and Rydström and Kati Mustola, eds., *Criminally Queer: Homosexuality and Criminal Law in Scandinavia, 1842–1999* (Amsterdam: Aksant, 2007).

45. The Budapesti Fővárosi Levéltár (BFL) Budapest City Archives.

46. The names of the archives in the order mentioned are the following: Országos Széchényi Könyvtár; Országgyűlési Könyvtár; Semmelweis Orvostörténeti Múzeuml és Levéltár.

47. For an overview of approaches to studying the history of sexuality, see Victoria Harris, "Sex on the Margins: New Directions in the Historiography of Sexuality and Gender," *Historical Journal* 53, no. 4 (2010): 1085–104. For male homosexuality more particularly, see David M. Halperin's *How to Do the History of Homosexuality* (Chicago: University of Chicago Press, 2002). On women, see, for instance, Sharon Marcus's *Between Women: Friendship, Desire, and Marriage in Victorian England* (Princeton, NJ: Princeton University Press, 2007). In addition, for thinking about different methods and approaches, see the conversation between Anjali Arondekar, Ann Cvetkovich, Christina B. Hanhardt, Regina Kunzel, Tavia Nyong'o, Juana Mara Rodriguez, Susan Stryker, Daniel Marshall, Kevin P Murphy, and Zeb Tortorici in "Queering Archives," *Radical History Review Radical History Review* 2015, no. 122 (2015): 211–31.

48. The historiography of the political, social, and cultural history of Budapest and Hungary is extensive. I relied both on Hungarian and English scholarship. See note 22 above. In addition, I am indebted to Gábor Gyáni's work on the urban and social history of Budapest. On prostitution I relied on the works by Tünde Császtvay, Judit Forrai, Gábor Kiss, Pál Léderer, János Miklóssy, and Mihály Szécsényi.

49. For the history of Hungarian feminists, I relied on the works of Andrea Pető, Judit Szapor, Judit Acsády, and Ágnes Horváth. In English, see Agatha Schwartz, *Shifting Voices: Feminist Thought and Women's Writing in Fin-de-Siècle Austria and Hungary* (Montreal: McGill-Queen's University Press, 2008).

50. It is only within the past two decades that gender has been incorporated into historical analyses within Hungarian and Eastern European histories, thus, secondary literature is still sparse in comparison to Western Europe. Maria Bucur, "An Archipelago of Stories: Gender History in Eastern Europe," *American Historical Review* 113, no. 5 (2008): 1375–89.

51. While there is limited scholarly work on Hungary, the literature on masculinity and gender of the period is substantial. On Hungary, Miklós Hadas has been the sole authority; see, for instance, *A férfiasság kódjai* (Budapest: Balassi Kiadó, 2010). For ideas on Word War I's effect on gender roles particularly during the war, I found Belinda J. Davis's *Home Fires Burning: Food, Politics, and Everyday Life in World War I Berlin* (Chapel Hill: University of North Carolina Press, 2000) a useful model. For a comparative history of gender perspective, see Susan R. Grayzel, *Women's Identities at War: Gender, Motherhood, and Politics in Britain and France during the First World War* (Chapel Hill: University of North Carolina Press, 1999). On masculinity, see the review essay by Robert A. Nye, "Western Masculinities in War and Peace," *American Historical Review* 112, no. 2 (2007): 417–38. For Eastern Europe specifically, the edited collection by Nancy M. Wingfield and Maria Bucur, *Gender and War in Twentieth-Century Eastern Europe* (Bloomington: Indiana University Press, 2006), is useful.

52. In addition to the extensive historiography on Western Europe, for the East-Central European context, I drew on the works of Maria Bucur, Mark Cornwall, Melissa Feinberg, Dan Healey, Kateřina Lišková, Tracie Matsyk, Keely Stauter-Halsted, Alfred Thomas, Nancy M. Wingfield, and Susan Zimmermann.

53. The historiography on the formation of homosexual identity is substantial. Following Michele Foucault's *The History of Sexuality* (1st American ed., New York: Pantheon books, 1978), where he argued that creating the category of "homosexual" and the consequent criminalization and pathologizing of homosexual acts was essential to homosexual identity formations, there has been an ongoing debate among scholars about the causes and processes of identity formation. For an overview see, Halperin, *How to Do the History of Homosexuality*.

54. Each of these terms has its own historiography and has been subject to fierce scholarly debates. For the genealogy of the understanding and use of homosexuality, see David Halperin, "How to Do the History of Male Homosexuality," *GLQ: A Journal of Lesbian and Gay Studies* 6, no. 1 (2000): 87–123. For the genealogy of the understanding and use of queer, see Sharon Marcus, "Queer Theory for Everyone: A Review Essay," *Signs* 31, no. 1 (2005): 191–218. For a more recent review, see Victoria Harris's "Histories of 'Sex,' Histories of 'Sexuality,'" *Contemporary European History* 22, no. 2 (2013): 295–301.

55. Following Foucault's now classic *The History of Sexuality*, the history of sexual subjecthood has been the subject of a by now extensive historiography.

56. For the conceptual history or genealogy of the term "homosexuality," see David M. Halperin's *How to Do the History of Homosexuality*, 109–34.

57. For a seminal work on the relationship between the state and sexuality, see R W. Connell, "The State, Gender, and Sexual Politics," *Theory and Society* 19, no. 5 (1990): 507–44. While initial works centered on Western states, recent scholarship has increasingly focused on authoritarian states outside of Europe. See, for instance, Lynette J. Chua, *Mobilizing Gay Singapore: Rights and Resistance in an Authoritarian State* (Philadelphia: Temple University Press, 2015), or Valeria Manzano's "Sex, Gender and the Making of the 'Enemy Within' in Cold War Argentina," *Journal of Latin American Studies* 47, no. 1 (2015): 1–29.

58. See Arch Paddington's report on "Illiberal Democracies," in *Breaking Down Democracy: Goals, Strategies, and Methods of Modern Authoritarians*, https://freedomhouse.org/report/special-reports/breaking-down-democracy-goals-strategies-and-methods-modern-authoritarians (Freedom House, June 2017), 35–41, for a detailed explanation of the term "illiberal democracy" in the case of Hungary, which emerged in 2014.

59. For up-to-date discussion of LGBT issues in East and East-Central Europe, see ILGA Europe, https://www.ilga-europe.org/.

CHAPTER ONE

1. "Szerelmes Budapest," *Magyar Hirlap*, September 24, 1905, 9.

2. István Bart, *Budapest krónikája: A kezdetektol napjainkig* (Budapest: Corvina, 2007), 277–429.

3. There is a growing and already extensive historical scholarship on prostitution in Hungary. Works appearing after 1989 include János Miklóssy, *A budapesti prostitúció*

története (Budapest: Népszava Kiadó Vállalat, 1989); Mihály Szécsényi, "A bordélyrendszer Budapesten," *Rubicon*, no. 8 (1993): 58–63; Judit Forrai, "Kávéházak és kéjnők," *Budapesti Negyed* 4, no. 2 (1996): 110–20; Pál Léderer, *A nyilvánvaló nők: Prostitúció, társadalom, társadalomtörténet* (Budapest: Új Mandátum Könyvkiadó, 1999); Császtvay, *Éjjeli lepkevadászat: Bordélyvilág a történeti Magyarországon* (Budapest: Osiris, 2009).

4. The matrimonial law introduced in 1895 made divorce legal for Hungarian citizens regardless of their religious denominations. Sándor Nagy, "One Empire, Two States, Many Laws: Matrimonial Law and Divorce in the Austro-Hungarian Monarchy," *Hungarian Historical Review: New Series of Acta Historica Academiae Scientiarum Hungaricae* 3, no. 1 (2014): 194–95.

5. Lukacs, *Budapest 1900*, 11.

6. Seminal works that established the relationship between cities and (homo)sexuality include John D'Emilio's "Capitalism and Gay Identity," in *Powers of Desire: The Politics of Sexuality*, ed. Ann Snitow (New York: Monthly Review Press, 1983); Martin Duberman, *Hidden from History: Reclaiming the Gay and Lesbian Past* (New York: New American Library, 1989). More recently, see Robert Aldrich, "Homosexuality and the City: An Historical Overview," *Urban Studies* 41, no. 9 (2004): 1719–37.

7. Zoltán Nemes Nagy, *Katasztrófák a szerelmi életben: Sexualpathologiai tanulmány* (Budapest: Aesculap, 1933), 73.

8. For a comprehensive history of the evolution of Hungarian legal system, see Andor Csizmadia's *Magyar állam- és jogtörténet: Egyetemi tankönyv* (Budapest: Nemzeti Tankönyvkiadó, 1998).

9. The king of Hungary and emperor of the monarchy Franz Joseph I sanctioned it as the first Hungarian criminal code on May 27, 1878. It was declared in the National Statute Book as Article V of 1878: "Hungarian Criminal Code of Crimes and Infringements." In addition, Csemegi also drafted Article XL of 1879, "Hungarian Criminal Code of Petty Offences," and the Hungarian criminal codes went into effect on September 1, 1880.

10. On the history of the German penal code, which did not get unified until 1896, see Michael John, *Politics and the Law in Late Nineteenth-Century Germany: The Origins of the Civil Code* (Oxford: Clarendon Press, 1989).

11. In terms of the criminal codes prior to the nineteenth century, same-sex acts, if mentioned, were criminalized under the Latin term *Sodomiticum* (sodomy), which in theory encompassed both male and female same-sex activity. For a discussion of the history of legal treatments of "unnatural" sexual acts in the Hungarian context until 1878, see Pál Angyal, *A szemérem elleni büntettek és vétségek (A magyar büntetőjog kézikönyve 14.)* (Budapest: Attila-Nyomda, 1937), especially 71–76.

12. For a discussion of the different legal regulations of homosexuality within European states, see Herzog, *Sexuality in Europe*, 36–38.

13. In addition to Cisleithanian Austria, Finland also criminalized both female and male sodomy. On the history of the regulation of female homosexuality in Austria, see Claudia Schoppmann, *Verbotene Verhältnisse: Frauenliebe 1938–1945* (Berlin: Querverlag, 1999); Tracie Matysik, *Reforming the Moral Subject: Ethics and Sexuality in Central Europe, 1890–1930* (Ithaca, NY: Cornell University Press, 2008), 153–55. For Finland, see Kati Mustola and Jens Rydström, "Women and the Laws on Same-Sex Sexuality," in *Criminally Queer*, 41–61.

14. Balázs Kenyeres, *Törvényszéki orvostan* (Budapest: Magyar Orvosi Könyvkiadó Társulat, 1909), 355.

15. János Belky, *Törvényszéki orvostan* (Budapest: Magyar Orvosi Könyvkiadó Társulat, 1895), 96.

16. The Hungarian prison system consisted of three tiers, *fogház*, *börtön*, and *fegyház*, the most severe and strict form of incarceration. The debates and discussions of the German term *widernatürliche unzucht* and Paragraph 175 have an extensive historiography. The seminal work is James Steakley's *The Homosexual Emancipation Movement in Germany* (New York: Arno Press, 1975).

17. For a discussion on different interpretations prior to 1937, see Angyal, *A szemérem elleni büntettek és vétségek*, 80–83. In case of the German interpretation, the lower courts settled on convicting men only if a para-coital (*beischlafsähnlich* or intercourse-like) act could be proven. This was reaffirmed by the Imperial Court of Justice, which ruled that Paragraph 75 required "an analogue of natural [heterosexual] intercourse." Geoffrey Giles, "Legislating Homophobia in the Third Reich: The Radicalization of Prosecution against Homosexuality by the Legal Profession," *German History* 23, no. 3 (2005): 1.

18. Ernő Emil Moravcsik and Andor Sólyom, *Az orvos működési köre az igazságügyi közszolgálatban* (Budapest: Magyar Orvosi Könyvkiadó Társulat, 1901), 459.

19. Moravcsik and Sólyom.

20. Paul Lendvai, *The Hungarians: A Thousand Years of Victory in Defeat* (Princeton, NJ: Princeton University Press, 2003), 284–88.

21. On April 11, 1881, the Hungarian parliament ratified Article XXI, which established the nationalized Hungarian kingdom's Budapest Metropolitan Police, which was no longer responsible to the Budapest City Council but directly to the Ministry of Interior. Nóra Kollár, ed., *A fővárosi rendőrség története (1914-ig)* (Budapest: BRFK, 1995), 205.

22. Kollár.

23. Thaisz initially served as the chief captain of the police of Pest (1861–73).

24. Zoltán Borbély and Rezső Kapy, eds., *A 60 éves magyar rendőrség 1881–1941* (Budapest: Halász Irodalmi és Könyvkiadó Vállalat, 1942), 196. On the reign of Thaisz, see Kollár, *A fővárosi rendőrség története*, 190–239.

25. Kollár, *A fővárosi rendőrség története*, 260.

26. Borbély and Kapy, *A 60 éves magyar rendőrség 1881–1941*, 232; Baksa, *Rendőrségi almanach* (Budapest: Stephaneum Nyomda és Könyvkiadó R.T., 1923), 59–84.

27. The Berlin police introduced a system of criminal registry in 1876. Baksa, *Rendőrségi almanach*, 43.

28. The Galton-Henry method was introduced in Budapest in 1902 and in the subsequent years throughout Hungary.

29. Baksa, *Rendőrségi almanach*, 42.

30. Tolnai Nagylexikon, http://www.netlexikon.hu/yrk/Gbyanv/8097, accessed May 14, 2016.

31. Borbély and Kapy, *A 60 éves magyar rendőrség 1881–1941*, 157.

32. For the police's detailed documentation of men who engaged in sexual activities with other men in Paris, see William A. Peniston, *Pederasts and Others: Urban Culture and Sexual Identity in Nineteenth Century Paris* (New York: Harrington Park

Press, 2004). For Berlin, see Edward Dickinson, "Policing Sex in Germany, 1882–1982: A Preliminary Statistical Analysis," *Journal of the History of Sexuality* 16, no. 2 (2007): 204–50.

33. Baksa, *Rendőrségi almanach*, 106.
34. Kollár, *A fővárosi rendőrség története*, 301.
35. Nemes Nagy, *Katasztrófák a szerelmi életben*, 74.
36. Nemes Nagy, 73.
37. Nemes Nagy.
38. On the features of the Austrian registry, see Nancy Wingfield's *The World of Prostitution in Late Imperial Austria* (New York: Oxford University Press, 2017), 20–21.
39. On the history of criminology and the different approaches in different countries, see Peter Becker and Richard F. Wetzell, eds., *Criminals and Their Scientists: The History of Criminology in International Perspective* (New York: Cambridge University Press, 2006). On the effects and influence of each of these schools on the Hungarian legal system, see Andor Csizmadia, ed., *Magyar állam- és jogtörténet: Egyetemi tankönyv* (Budapest: Nemzeti Tankönyvkiadó, 1998), 448–50.
40. Csizmadia, *Magyar állam- és jogtörténet*, 449.
41. Tibor Király, Gábor Máthé, and Barna Mezey, "A Polgári Büntetőjog Története," in *Magyar Jogtörténet*, ed. Barna Mezey (Budapest: Osiris, 2003), 303–5.
42. Liszt (1851–1919) was one of the most influential criminologists and legal scholars of his era. He was widely read in Europe, and two of the most influential Hungarian legal scholars, Pál Angyal and Ferenc Finkey, were followers. On the history of Liszt and his approach, see chap. 1 of Richard F. Wetzell's *Inventing the Criminal: A History of German Criminology, 1880–1945* (Chapel Hill: University of North Carolina Press, 2000).
43. Melinda Bogdán, "A Rabosító Fénykép: A Rendőrségi Fényképezés Kialakulása," *Budapesti Negyed* 13, nos. 1–2 (2005): 143–65.
44. The phrase "notorious homosexuals" comes from the 1930s.
45. Upon arriving in Budapest, new residents had to register at the local office of registry.
46. The Hungarian Statistical Office was officially established in 1871. However, it was only in 1881 that it set up to collect nationwide statistical data. It took considerably longer before the office provided regular statistical analysis of criminals. For the history of the beginning of criminological statistical analysis, see József Balázs, *A magyar bűnügyi statisztika kialakulása és fejlődése: Különös tekintettel annak módszertani kérdéseire* (Szeged: Szegedi Nyomda, 1969).
47. For the trajectory of the medicalization of sexuality, see the seminal works of Jeffrey Weeks, *Sex, Politics, and Society: The Regulation of Sexuality since 1800* (London: Longman, 1981); and Vern Bullough, *Science in the Bedroom: A History of Sex Research* (New York: Basic Books, 1994).
48. Moravcsik and Sólyom, *Az orvos működési köre az igazságügyi közszolgálatban*, 454.
49. Zoltán Szász, "A mai magyar irodalom sorvadásának okairól," *Huszadik Század* 18 (July–December 1908): 596–97.
50. For Ulrich's theory, see Hubert Kennedy, "Karl Heinrich Ulrichs," in *Science and Homosexualities*, ed. Vernon A. Rosario (New York: Routledge, 1997), 26–46. For the use

of *urning* within the Hungarian context, see Moravcsik and Sólyom, *Az orvos működési köre az igazságügyi közszolgálatban*, 451–68.

51. Beachy, *Gay Berlin*, 18.

52. Cited by Judit Takács in "The Double Life of Kertbeny," in *Past and Present of Radical Sexual Politics*, ed. Gert Hekma (Amsterdam: Mosse Foundation, 2004), 39.

53. Kertbeny campaigned for the decriminalization of homosexuality in Germany, on the grounds that the state had no right to regulate people's sexual life in private.

54. On Krafft-Ebing, see Harry Oosterhuis, *Stepchildren of Nature: Krafft-Ebing, Psychiatry, and the Making of Sexual Identity* (Chicago: University of Chicago Press, 2000). The first Hungarian edition was published in 1894.

55. In addition to Krafft-Ebing's *Psychopathia Sexualis*, Vay was also featured in Havelock Ellis's *Studies in the Psychology of Sex*, vol. 1, *Sexual Inversion* (London: University Press, 1900).

56. Harry Oosterhuis, "Sexual Modernity in the Works of Richard von Krafft-Ebing and Albert Moll," *Medical History* 56, no. 2 (2012): 133–55.

57. The term of "pseudo homosexuality" comes from German sexologists Ivan Bloch.

58. Moravcsik and Sólyom, *Az orvos működési köre az igazságügyi közszolgálatban*, 460.

59. Kenyeres, *Törvényszéki orvostan*, 255.

60. The Hungarian Ministry of Interior began to publish an official police journal in 1869. It had various names. From 1894 to 1907, it was called *Rendőri Lapok*. From 1907 onward, it was named *Közbiztonság*, but *Rendőri Lapok* remained a subtitle.

61. T. S. E., "Az önfertőzès ès kóros nemi èletről," *Rendőri Lapok*, September 23, 1900, 7:39; Bèla Újhegyi, "A nemi ösztön kóros tèvelygèsei," *Rendőri Lapok*, October 28, 1900, 7:44. In 1903 the journal once more ran an informative and educational series on the "legal implications of sexual perversions," "Bevezetès a büntető ismeretekbe: Szemèrem elleni erőszak," *Rendőri Lapok*, January 1, January 11, 1903; "On Pornography," December 18, 1904; "A Harmadik Nem," January 27, February 3, February 10, March 10, 1907; "A Harmadik Nem: Homosexualitás," September 27, October 4, October 11, 1908.

62. On homosexuals in Paris, May 6, May 13, May 20, and May 27, 1906; on Berlin, "A kóros szerelem," November 3, 1907; on Vienna, "Pederasták Bécsben," October 18, 1908.

63. "Harmadik Nem" 3. Rész, March 10, 1907.

64. For an explanation, see David Halperin's "How to Do the History of Male Homosexuality," *GLQ: A Journal of Lesbian & Gay Studies* 6, no. 1 (2000): 87–123, especially 95–96.

65. Italics are mine. "Harmadik Nem: Homosexualitás" II. A férfi prostituált," *Rendőri Lapok*, October 4, 1908.

66. As we learn from Jenő Szántó, initially the police marked/tagged men who sold sex with "monetary interest," before establishing a separate registry for male homosexual prostitutes in the 1920s. "A homosexualis férfiprostitutio kérdése," *Népegészségügy*, no. 20 (1934): 774–79; no. 21 (1934): 826–34.

67. "A homosexualitásról, különös tekintettel a budapesti viszonyokra," *Bőrgyógyászati, Urológiai és Venereologiai Szemle*, no. 1 (1933): 21.

68. Szántó was practicing as a chief medical doctor during the 1920s and 1930s. The circumstances and actual details of Szántó's connection to police in Budapest remain unknown.

69. For a statistical analysis of the criminal registry prior to World War I, see Roland Perényi, "A 'figyelő, megelőző és felfedező' rendőrség: Egy bűnözői névjegyzék tanulságai," *Budapesti Negyed* 13, nos. 47–48 (2005): 63–92.

70. Matt Houlbrook believes that the reason young Jewish men were underrepresented had to with their particularly strong investment in family, heterosociability, and work. *Queer London*, 187–88.

71. According to John Lukacs, because the rapid industrialization of Budapest attracted so many young men (and women), "the average age of the population remained fairly young, younger than the generally urban aging population of other European cities." In *Budapest 1900*, 75.

72. Perényi, "A 'figyelő, megelőző és felfedező' rendőrség," 89–91.

73. In addition to the statistics Szántó presents, this is implicit in articles in *Rendőri Lapok*; for instance, in the article "Homosexualitás a bűnözők között," July 21, 1912.

74. József Vogl in Gyula Turcsányi, ed., *A modern bűnözés II* (Budapest: Rozsnyai Károly kiadása, 1929), 142. See, for instance, Matt Cook's discussion about the Metropolitan Police in London. *London and the Culture of Homosexuality, 1885–1914* (New York: Cambridge University Press, 2003), 46–48.

75. Géza Buzinkay, "A bűnügyi hír, a riporter és a rendőr," *Budapesti Negyed* 47–48, nos. 1–2 (2005): 7–30; Buzinkay, *Mokány Berczi és Spitzig Itzig, Göre Gábor mög a többiek . . . : A magyar társadalom figurái az élclapokban 1860 és 1918 között* (Budapest: Magvető, 1988), 742–44.

76. *Borsszem Jankó* (1868–1936) was the first truly urban comic journal, claiming the highest circulation, around fifteen thousand to twenty thousand per issue.

77. Between 1882 and 1902, András Mihaszna was a regular in *Borsszem Jankó*. Even after his departure, he continued to serve as a reference point. Géza Buzinkay, "The Budapest Joke and Comic Weeklies as Mirrors of Cultural Assimilation," in *Budapest and New York: Studies in Metropolitan Transformation, 1870–1930*, ed. Thomas Bender (New York: Russell Sage Foundation, 1994), 224–48.

78. The silent film Keystone Cops, 1912–17, are a US equivalent that portrayed incompetent policemen.

79. Buzinkay, "The Budapest Joke and Comic Weeklies as Mirrors of Cultural Assimilation," 229.

80. Cited in Kollár, *A fővárosi rendőrség története*, 243.

81. On the relationship between the police and the Budapest City Council, see Károly Vörös, "Budapest Politikai Élete," in *Budapest története a márciusi forradalomtól az őszirózsás forradalomig*, 459–73.

82. The two articles that explicitly acknowledge the failure of the police in respect to the registry are Miklós Rédey, "Az Országos Bűnügyi Nyilvantartás," *Rendőri Lapok*, March 5, 1899, 6:10, and Gyula Fekete, "A Berlini bűnügyi rendőrsèg," *Rendőri Lapok*, April 23, 1899, 6:17. The National Criminal Registry was finally established in 1908.

83. "Statistics on Criminality in Budapest 1901," *Rendőri Lapok*, August 3, 1902.

84. Borbély and Kapy, *A 60 éves magyar rendőrség*, 196. Italics are mine.
85. "Az önfertőzés és a kóros szexuális élet," *Rendőri Lapok*, September 23, 1900.
86. "Bevezetés a Büntető törvénykönyvbe," *Rendőri Lapok*, January 11, 1903.
87. Székesfővárosi Közgyűlès jegyzőkönyve, February 20, 1901–March 20, 1901, cited in Kollár, *A fővárosi rendőrség története*, 258.
88. T. S. E., "Az önfertőzés és kóros nemi életről," *Rendőri Lapok*, September 23, 1900; Béla Újhegyi, "A nemi ösztön kóros tévelygései," *Rendőri Lapok*, October 28, 1900.
89. For instance, in 1901, 36 percent of the population of Budapest lived in what was considered at the time "worrisome bad conditions" (six or more persons per room), and 30 percent of the population shared the same room with three or four persons. Judit Frigyesi, *Béla Bartók and Turn-of-the Century Budapest* (Berkeley: University of California Press, 1998), 45.
90. Imre Nyigri, *Budapest bűnélete 1881-től 1940-ig: A budapesti rendőrség hatvan éve a bűnügyi statisztika tükrében* (Budapest: Halász Irodalmi és Könyvkiadó Vállalat, 1942), 527–29. *Rendőri Lapok*'s annual crime statistics of Budapest were published by the journal every year in August and September with a short analysis. For instance, in August 3, 1902, in their analysis the editors basically acknowledge that amidst the continuing rise of population, the police simply cannot keep up, crime rates are rising, and there are not enough personnel to even assure public safety.
91. According to the Law of 1879, XL, Sections 62–73, begging and vagrancy became illegal. The punishment varied from simple warning to arrest and detention. In addition, the so-called *toloncszabályzat* of 1885 entrusted the police with the power to forcefully return vagabonds, beggars, and prostitutes to the town or village of origin. See Susan Zimmermann's "Making a Living from Disgrace: The Politics of Prostitution, Female Poverty and Urban Gender Codes in Budapest and Vienna, 1860–1920," in *The City in Central Europe: Culture and Society from 1800 to the Present*, ed. Malcolm Gee (Aldershot: Ashgate, 1999), 175.
92. Kollár, *A fővárosi rendőrség története*, 316; József Parádi, "A polgári magyar állam rendősége, 1867–1918," *Rubicon* 20, no. 3 (2010): 4–13.
93. Lajos Molnár, *Az erkölcsök, a közegészség, a prostitúció* (Budapest: Neumayer Ede Könyvnyomda, 1899); Mór Linka, "A prostitúció rendezése Budapesten," *Huszadik Század* 15 (1907): 245–54. Dr. Emil Schreiber, *A prostitúció* (Budapest: Pátria Irodalmi Vállalat es Nyomdai Részvénytársaság, 1917).
94. Baksa, *Rendőrségi almanach*, 120.
95. On Captain Thaisz's regime and his involvement in prostitution, see Baksa, *Rendőrségi almanach*, 260–63. On the period from 1873 to 1918 more generally, see Miklóssy, *A budapesti prostitúció története*, 30–67.
96. On Vienna, see Wingfield, *The World of Prostitution in Late Imperial Austria*, 6–10. For a similar discussion of the German case, see Edward Dickinson, "Policing Sex in Germany, 1882–1982," 213–14.
97. Főkapitányi Jelentés 1894, 187–88, cited in Kollár, *A fővárosi rendőrség története*, 301.
98. *Rendőri Lapok*, November 29, 1908.
99. Gábor Kiss, "Nemi betegsègek az osztrák—magyar haderőben az első világháború

idejèn," *Orvosi Hetilap* 147, no. 46 (2006): 2237–38; Judit Forrai, "Szép lányok csúnya betegsége, avagy szemelvények a bűnös szex és a szifilisz történetéből," *Orvosi Hetilap* 149, no. 40 (2008): 1895–901.

100. For changes in terms of the police, see Baksa, *Rendőrségi almanach*, 104.

101. Law no. L/1912. Following this new legislation, a new department was established, with the sole responsibility of suppressing trafficking in women and the distribution of pornographic (perverse) publications. The office began its work in April 1913.

102. Baksa, *Rendőrségi almanach*, 120.

103. Tamagne, *A History of Homosexuality in Europe*, 135.

104. While in 1912 the number of criminal prosecutions significantly increased, the following year saw an unprecedented 60 percent increase, making 1913 the year with the highest number of criminal prosecutions since statistics were in place. Baksa, *Rendőrségi almanach*, 125.

105. Baksa, 129–81.

106. Herzog, *Sexuality in Europe*, 1–16. For Hungary, see Andrea Pető, *Társadalmi nemek képe és emlékezete Magyarországon a 19-20. században* (Budapest: A nők a valódi esélyegyenlőségért alapítvány, 2004).

107. For an overview of the cultural significance of the Hungarian gentry, see the essay by Eszter Tarjányi, "A dzsentri exhumálása," *Valóság* 46, no. 5 (2003): 38–64. For the Habsburg monarchy more generally, see Alexander Maxwell, "Nationalizing Sexuality: Sexual Stereotypes in the Habsburg Empire," *Journal of the History of Sexuality* 14, no. 3 (2005): 266–90, and also "National Endogamy and Double Standards: Sexuality and Nationalism in East-Central Europe during the 19th Century," *Journal of Social History* 41, no. 2 (2008): 413–33.

108. This was as much a cultural construct as a reality. Gyáni and Kövér, *Magyarország társadalomtörténete a reformkortól a második világháborúig*, 164–69.

109. Lukacs, *Budapest 1900*, 105.

110. Despite growing critiques, the acceptance of sexual virility for men was characteristic not only of Hungarian cities but also in the countryside. Molnár, *Az erkölcsök, a közegészség, a prostitúció*; Judit Forrai, "Kávéházak és kéjnők," 110–20; and Császtvay, *Éjjeli lepkevadászat*.

111. The seminal work on the relationship between male sexual morality and respectability is George Mosse's *Nationalism and Sexuality: Respectability and Abnormal Sexuality in Modern Europe*, 1st ed. (New York: H. Fertig, 1985). In the Hungarian context, see Frigyesi, *Béla Bartók and Turn-of-the Century Budapest*, 44–49, Lukacs, *Budapest 1900*, 105–7; Alexander Maxwell, "The Nation as a 'Gentleman's Agreement,'" *Men and Masculinities* 18, no. 5 (2015): 536–58.

112. *Rendőri Lapok*, November 29, 1908.

113. Zimmermann, "Making a Living from Disgrace," 187.

114. "Harmadik Nem," *Rendőri Lapok*, March 10, 1907.

115. "Harmadik Nem."

116. Founded in 1904, the members of the Hungarian Feminist Association were openly challenging existing sexual norms. For a short history of the association, see Judit Acsády, "A feminista gondolat megjelenése Magyarországon," *Nőszemély* 4 (1994): 10–12; and Andre Pető, "The History of the Hungarian Women's Movement," in *Thinking Differ-*

ently: A Reader in European Women's Studies, ed. Gabriele Griffin and Rosi Braidotti (London: Zed Books, 2002), 361–71.

117. Roland Perényi, "A bőnügyi statisztika Magyarországon a 'hosszú' XIX. században," *Statisztikai Szemle* 85 (2007): 537.

118. Before 1900 *Rendőri Lapok* published only one article related to same-sex sexuality, a piece about the Oscar Wilde trial (July 7, 1895).

119. On the policing of different neighborhoods and districts of Budapest, see Roland Perényi, "Városi tér és hatalom: Utcapolitika századfordulós Budapesten," *Századvég* 11 (2006): 29.

120. This was an amendment to the penal code supplementing the Code on Criminal Procedure. Csizmadia, *Magyar állam- és jogtörténet: Egyetemi tankönyv*, 449–50.

121. The number of policemen per inhabitant also increased. Whereas in 1884 there were 673 inhabitants to one policeman, by 1939 the rate was 220 inhabitants to one. Borbély and Kapy, *A 60 éves magyar rendőrség*, 541. For a comparative European history of the Metropolitan Police, see Hsi-huey Liang's *The Rise of Modern Police and the European State System from Metternich to the Second World War* (New York: Cambridge University Press, 1992).

122. "Perverzek," *Rendőri Lapok*, October 6, 1912.

123. On the WhK, see Elena Mancini, *Magnus Hirschfeld and the Quest for Sexual Freedom: A History of the First International Sexual Freedom Movement* (New York: Palgrave Macmillan, 2010).

124. Physician and soon to be a superstar of psychoanalysis Sándor Ferenczi was an early supporter of the efforts of the WhK.

125. "A homoszexualitás kérdéséhez," *Huszadik Század*, no. 1 (1910): 157–60, 160.

126. For an explanation of Hirschfeld's role in conceptualization of homosexuality and gender, see J. Edgar Bauer's entry "Magnus Hirschfeld," in the GLBTQ Archive, http://www.glbtqarchive.com/ssh/hirschfeld_m_S.pdf, accessed February 2, 2017.

127. As was the case with beggars and vagabonds, surviving records indicate that homosexuals who were repeatedly caught having sex in public were sent back to their hometowns. Budapesti Forradalmi Törvényszék Kisérleti Kriminológiai Osztály és az Országos Kriminológiai Intézet iratainak gyűjteménye 1919, 2818/1919, 2236/1919, 623–25, Budapest City Archives (BFL).

128. Articles in *Rendőri Lapok* that explicitly acknowledge this connection include "Budapest 1903-as Kriminál Statisztikája," July 24, 1904; articles on homosexuals in Paris, May 6 and 13, 1907; "Harmadik Nem: Homosexualitás," September 27, 1908 and October 4, 1908; "A tiltott szerelem áldozata," June 7, 1909.

129. Nemes Nagy, *Katasztrófák a szerelmi életben*, 73.

130. Most notably George Chauncey in *Gay New York* observes that it was well into the twentieth century before "active" men who had sex with men became a concern for the authorities.

131. Scholars in other European contexts have demonstrated that prior to the interwar period, and perhaps even later, such a phenomenon was present in large urban areas. See, for instance, Dan Healey, "Masculine Purity and 'Gentlemen's Mischief': Sexual Exchange and Prostitution between Russian Men, 1861–1941," *Slavic Review* 60, no. 2 (2001): 233.

CHAPTER TWO

1. "A Harmadik Nem," *Rendőri Lapok*, September 27, 1908.

2. Herzog, "Sexuality in Twentieth Century Austria," in *Sexuality in Austria*, ed. Bischof et al. (Piscataway, NJ: Transaction Publishers, 2007), 11.

3. While scholars highlight the cultural and economic dynamism of the period, more recent accounts of Budapest also portray a society filled with fears about the decline and composition of modern Hungarians. See, for instance, Paul Hanebrink, *In Defense of Christian Hungary*, 10–46; Marius Turda, "The First Debates on Eugenics in Hungary, 1910–1918," in *"Blood and Homeland": Eugenics and Racial Nationalism in Central and Southeast Europe, 1900–1940* (Budapest: Central European University Press, 2007), 185–223. For a work in Hungarian that highlights this issue, see János Gyurgyák's *Ezzé lett magyar hazátok*, 90–135.

4. For the history of emerging political voices and groups at the turn of the century, see Monika Kozári, *A dualista rendszer, 1867–1918* (Budapest: Pannonica, 2005), 143–48.

5. Gyáni, *Identity and the Urban Experience*, 90–92; Frigyesi, *Béla Bartók and Turn-of-the Century Budapest*, 10; Lukacs, *Budapest 1900*, 24–29.

6. In addition to the published materials that are housed in the National Hungarian Library, I rely on Kornél Tábori's personal diaries and collection of papers, which are held in Országos Széchényi Könyvtár Kézirattár (Manuscript Collection of the National Széchény Library; hereafter OSZKK).

7. Seth Koven's approach to his subjects in *Slumming: Sexual and Social Politics in Victorian London* (Princeton, NJ: Princeton University Press, 2004) has been formative for my own approach.

8. Carl Schorske's *Fin-de-Siècle Vienna: Politics and Culture* (New York: Knopf; distributed by Random House, 1979) and Peter Gay's *The Bourgeois Experience: Victoria to Freud* (New York: Oxford University Press, 1984) are the seminal works that examine the intimate connection between city and Eros in a Central European context. For more recent approaches, see Scott Spector, *Violent Sensations*.

9. On psychoanalysis's role, see Eli Zaretsky, *Secrets of the Soul: A Social and Cultural History of Psychoanalysis* (New York: Alfred A. Knopf, 2004).

10. On the expansion, see Géza Buzinkay and György Kókay, *A magyar sajtó története*, 151–62.

11. Péter Szigeti, "A szexualitás nyilvánossága a századfordulő Budapestjén," *Médiakutató* 6 (Spring, 2002): 85–101; János Miklóssy, *A budapesti prostitúció története*, 106–8. On the relationship between the commercialization of sex and changing ideas around sexuality, see Lawrence Birken, *Consuming Desire: Sexual Science and the Emergence of a Culture of Abundance, 1871–1914* (Ithaca, NY: Cornell University Press, 1988).

12. According to the publisher, the books were available in "every bookstore across Hungary." Tábori Kornél Hagyaték 160/88:1–13.

13. There is conflicting information about the exact date of the beginning of Székely's employment. Although the public relations office of the police was established in 1880, it only became operational in the late 1890s. *A Budapesti Napilapok Rendőri Rovatvezetőinek Szindikátusa 50 éves jubileumi* (Budapest: B. N. R. SZ. 1930), 4–7.

14. Székely was the author of the following books: *Házi rendőr: Közhasznú rendőri*

tanácsadó (Budapest: Omnia, 1929); *Árny és derü: Egy rendőrtiszt naplójából* (Budapest: Centrál Nyomda, 1930).

15. For a more comprehensive account of Tábori's life, see Péter Buza's introduction, in *Tábori bűnös Budapestje*, ed. Péter Buza (Budapest: Budapesti Városvédő Egyesület: Országos Széchenyi Könyvtár, 2013).

16. Daily papers included but were not limited to *Pesti Hirlap* and *Budapesti Hirlap*, and the weekly paper was *Vasárnapi Újság*.

17. Conan Doyle, *Sherlock Holmes feltámadása és egyéb bűnügyi elbeszélések* (Budapest: Csendőrségi Könyvtár, 1904); *A feltámadt detektiv. Sherlock Holmes legújabb bűnesetei* (Budapest: Csendőrségi Könyvtár, 1907).

18. *A borzalom országa* (1907). He was a war correspondent during World War I.

19. Béla Albertini, "Az első magyar szociofotó album," *Budapesti Negyed* 13 (2005): 119–42.

20. Although the Central Statistical Office was established in 1867, its reports became influential only by the 1880s. The Social Science Society was established in 1901 as a hub for progressive ideas.

21. The historiography of the relationship between "sinfulness" and the birth of the modern metropolis is extensive. For London, see Judith Walkowitz's *City of Dreadful Delight: Narratives of Sexual Danger in Late-Victorian London* (Chicago: University of Chicago Press, 1992); Seth Koven's *Slumming*; for Paris, Judith Surkis's *Sexing the Citizen: Morality and Masculinity in France, 1870–1920* (Ithaca, NY: Cornell University Press, 2006); and for Berlin, Dorothy Rowe's *Representing Berlin: Sexuality and the City in Imperial and Weimar Germany* (Aldershot: Ashgate Publishing, Ltd., 2003).

22. *Pesti Hirlap*, December 28, 1907; Tábori Kornél Hagyaték 160/88:17.

23. For a detailed account of the scandal, see Isabel V. Hull, *The Entourage of Kaiser Wilhelm II, 1888–1918* (Cambridge: Cambridge University Press, 2004), 45–146. See also Norman Domeier, *The Eulenburg Affair: A Cultural History of Politics in the German Empire*, trans. Deborah Lucas Schneider (Rochester, NY: Camden House, 2015).

24. James D. Steakly, "Iconography of a Scandal: Political Cartoons and the Eulenburg Affair in Wilhelmin Germany," in *Hidden from History: Reclaiming the Gay and Lesbian Past*, ed. Martin Duberman et al. (New York: Plume, 1990), 233–64.

25. In addition to *Budapesti Hirlap*, other daily papers such as *Pesti Napló*, as well as the weekly *Borsszem Jankó*, also published multiple reports.

26. Scott Spector, "The Wrath of the 'Countess Merviola': Tabloid Exposé and the Emergence of Homosexual Subjects in Vienna in 1907," in *Sexuality in Austria*, 35.

27. Spector.

28. Spector.

29. Papers that reviewed *Sinful Budapest* and *Sick Love* include *Aradi Közlöny*, *Budapesti Hírlap*, *A Hír*, *A Friss Újság*, *A Hadi Közlöny*, *Magyar Nemzet*, *Népszava*, *Pesti Hirlap*, *Pesti Napló*, *Tonal Világlapja*, and *Független Magyarország*. OSZKK, Tábori Kornél Hagyaték 160/88:13–71.

30. *Független Magyarország*, December 28, 1907, OSZKK, Tábori Kornél Hagyaték 160/88:13. The word "apache"—the Hungarian (as well as the English) language adopted it from early twentieth-century French—originally used in Paris, referred to "violent street ruffian."

31. *Magyar Nemzet*, February 8, 1908. Tábori Kornél Hagyaték 160/88:14.

32. "A beteg szerelem lovagjai," *A bűnös Budapest* (Budapest: ANAP Ujságvállalat nyomdája, 1908).

33. On the many competing scientific interpretations about the nature of homosexuality in fin de siècle Europe, see Vernon A. Rosario, ed., *Science and Homosexualities* (New York: Routledge, 1997), 26–155; and also Rosario, *Homosexuality and Science: A Guide to the Debates* (Santa Barbara, CA: ABC-CLIO, 2002), chaps. 1 and 2.

34. Tábori and Székely, *A bűnös Budapest*, 47.

35. Carolyn J. Dean, "The 'Open Secret,' Affect, and the History of Sexuality," in *Sexuality at the Fin de Siècle: The Makings of a "Central Problem,"* ed. Peter Cryle and Christopher E. Forth (Newark: University of Delaware Press, 2008), 156.

36. For some representative works that address the conflicting coexisting interpretations of same-sex sexuality, see Robert Beachy, "The German Invention of Homosexuality," *Journal of Modern History* 82, no. 4 (2010): 801–38.; Edward Ross Dickinson, "'A Dark, Impenetrable Wall of Complete Incomprehension': The Impossibility of Heterosexual Love in Imperial Germany," *Central European History* 40, no. 3 (2007): 467–97.

37. *A bűnös Budapest*, 47. Italics are mine. In this instance, the phrase "devotees of pederasty" refers to men who desire young men or even boys.

38. Italics are mine.

39. See, for instance, William Peniston's discussion of the term in the French context. *Pederasts and Others: Urban Culture and Sexual Identity in Nineteenth Century Paris* (New York: Harrington Park Press, 2004). For Austria, see Scott Spector, "The Wrath of the 'Countess Merviola.'"

40. For the discussion of the meaning of "pederasty," see Michael L. Wilson, "The Despair of Unhappy Love: Pederasty and Popular Fiction in the Belle Époque," in *Sexuality at the Fin de Siècle: The Makings of a "Central Problem,"* 109–42.

41. *A bűnös Budapest*, 48–49. Prior to 1914 the Austro-Hungarian monarchy's currency, Corona, or *korona* in Hungarian, was among the strongest in Europe. Consequently, 1,000 *korona* was more money than an average factory worker earned in a year.

42. Tábori Kornél, "A ponyvairodalom társadalmi hatása," presented at the meeting of Magyar Társadalomtudományi Egyesület, December 3, 1908. Tábori Kornél Hagyaték 160/88.

43. Beachy, *Gay Berlin*, 58.

44. Tábori traveled extensively and published a number of informative articles on homosexuals and queer subcultures in *Rendőri Lapok*. Some of the articles include "A kóros szerelem," November 3, 1906; "A Harmadik Nem: A perverzek társas élete," February 10, March 10, 1907.

45. *Beteg szerelem* (Budapest: Nap Kiadó, n.d.). Its exact publication date is unknown, but it was most certainly sometime after 1909 and before 1914. The Hungarian National Library estimates that it was published in 1910.

46. In Tábori Kornél Hagyaték 160/88.

47. Tábori Kornél, "Hírhedt uri gyilkosok es rejtve maradt emberírtók," *Tolnai Világnapja*, November 26, 1924, 11.

48. *Beteg szerelem*, 1–2.

49. *Beteg szerelem*, 2.

50. *Beteg szerelem*, 1.
51. *Beteg szerelem*, 2–3.
52. *Beteg szerelem*, 3.
53. According to the news reports from 1903, many of which were written by Tábori himself, members of the "club" included business apprentices, musicians, and hairdressers' assistants as well as lawyers, directors, and even a retired councilor. "Niobe és Társai," *Pesti Napló* April 21, 1903, 6.
54. According to Pesti Napló, Székely was one of the policemen who interrogated the suspects.
55. *Beteg szerelem*, 3–4.
56. *Beteg szerelem*, 4.
57. *Beteg szerelem*.
58. For an explanation of the age-differential model that was characteristics of ancient Greek and Roman societies, see David Halperin's *One Hundred Years of Homosexuality: And Other Essays on Greek Love* (New York: Routledge, 1990); and also John Boswell's *Same-Sex Unions in Premodern Europe* (New York: Villard Books, 1994).
59. For New York, see Timothy J. Gilfoyle, *City of Eros: New York City, Prostitution, and the Commercialization of Sex, 1790–1920* (New York: W. W. Norton, 1992). For London, see Judith Walkowitz, *Prostitution and Victorian Society: Women, Class, and the State* (New York: Cambridge University Press, 1980); and Seth Koven's *Slumming*.
60. For the relationship between degeneration and homosexuality, see Lucy Bland and Laura Doan, *Sexology Uncensored: The Documents of Sexual Science* (Chicago: University of Chicago Press, 1999), 39–73.
61. *Beteg szerelem*, 2.
62. *Beteg szerelem*, 12.
63. *Beteg szerelem*. Italics are mine.
64. See, for instance, the article written by Gyula Kramolin in *Huszadik Század*.
65. I am using the phrase "relative freedom" with full awareness that queers could be and were harassed and lacked protection.
66. For a theoretical description of "respectable" and respectability in terms of sexuality, see George Mosse's *Nationalism and Sexuality: Respectability and Abnormal Sexuality in Modern Europe* (New York: H. Fertig, 1985). In the Central European context, see Tracie Matysik's *Reforming the Moral Subject*.
67. Moravcsik and Sólyom, *Az orvos működési köre az igazságügyi közszolgálatban*, 456.
68. *Beteg szerelem*, 6.
69. *Beteg szerelem*, 4.
70. It is difficult to verify the claims of Tábori and Székely about homosexual establishments outside of Budapest. There is one article in *Arad és Vidéke* (January 1, 1908), which in reviewing Tábori and Székely's book supports the existence of homosexual clubs in other cities/towns by explicitly naming a club in Arad (today in Romania). OSZKK, Tábori Kornél Hagyaték 160/88:50–55.
71. According to a 1903 *Pesti Napló* article, "Niobe és Társai," Modell Café subscribed to *Der Eigene*, April 21, 1903, 6. On the history and content of "Der Eigene," see Harry Oosterhuis, *Homosexuality and Male Bonding in Pre-Nazi Germany: The*

Youth Movement, the Gay Movement, and Male Bonding before Hitler's Rise: Original Transcripts from Der Eigene, the First Gay Journal in the World (New York: Haworth Press, 1991).

72. For a description of these catalogs, see Császtvay, *Éjjeli lepkevadászat*, which showcases a remarkable set of contemporary erotic images that were in circulation in Budapest.

73. The word *buzeráns*, adopted from Germany during the last two decades of the nineteenth century, became the most common derogatory word to refer to homosexuals. It was first written in Hungarian in 1896. *Buzeráns* was increasingly shortened to *buzi* after 1900. The word *buzi* was used until the 1990s when the word *meleg* became the politically correct expression for homosexuality. Ádám Nádasdy, "Az örömtelen eretnekek," *Magyar Narancs*, February 15, 2001, 40.

74. Beachy, *Gay Berlin*, 58.

75. *Beteg szerelem*, 13–15.

76. *A bűnös Budapest*, 47; *Beteg szerelem*, 14.

77. *Beteg szerelem*, 14.

78. Cited in *Beteg szerelem*, 13.

79. Jeffrey Weeks, "Inverts, Perverts, and Marry-Annes: Male Prostitution and the Regulation of Homosexuality in England in the 19th and Early 20th Centuries," in *Hidden from History*, 211.

80. Mack Friedman, "Male Sex Work from Ancient Times to the Near Present," in *Male Sex Work and Society*, ed. Victor Minichiello and John Scott (New York: Harrington Park Press, 2014), 25. Trevon D. Logan, *Economics, Sexuality, and Male Sex Work* (Cambridge: Cambridge University Press, 2017), 24.

81. *Beteg szerelem*, 12.

82. *Beteg szerelem*.

83. Jeffrey Weeks has made this point in the case of Britain. See "Inverts, Perverts, and Marry-Annes," 202.

84. Matt Houlbrook, "Soldier Heroes and Rent Boys: Homosex, Masculinities, and Britishness in the Brigade of Guards, circa 1900–1960," *Journal of British Studies* 42, no. 3 (2003): 351–88.

85. Moravcsik, Sólyom, *Az orvos működési köre az igazságügyi közszolgálatban*, 457.

86. Moravcsik.

87. *Beteg szerelem*, 16.

88. Existing social histories on the Hungarian Army, while mostly concerned with the officers and military schools, include Béla Király and Walter Scott Dillard, eds., *East Central European Officer Corps, 1740–1920s: Social Origins, Selection, Education, and Training* (Boulder, CO: Social Science Monographs; distributed by Columbia University Press, 1988); and first and foremost, István Deák, *Beyond Nationalism: A Social and Political History of the Habsburg Officer Corps, 1848–1918* (New York: Oxford University Press, 1990).

89. Kámán Kéri, "A soldier does not engage in politics; his entire conduct is determined by the rules of the service and the official obligations of his calling," in *The East Central European Officer Corps, 1740–1920s*, 151.

90. *Beyond Nationalism*, 145. Deák used the court-martial proceedings of the Military War Archive in Vienna for his study. Although Deák refers to the multiethnic Habsburg army, his observation would have been very likely true for the Hungarian home army Honvédség.

91. Describing Hungarian soldiers, another historian remarks, "It is commonly held that Hungarians have always been a nation of proud warriors, born to ride and fight on horseback and little inclined to settle down and work hard." Tibor Hajdú, "Social Origins, Selection, and Training of the Officer Corps in Hungary after the Ausgleich, 1867–82," in *The East Central European Officer Corps, 1740–1920s*, 167. Similarly, John Lukacs in *Budapest 1900* without any probing also underscores and takes for granted that masculinity and virility were simply unquestioned in fin de siècle Hungarian society, 105.

92. *A bűnös Budapest*, 47; *Beteg szerelem*, 9; in addition, *Bűnös nők*, 97.

93. *A bűnös Budapest*, 47.

94. Contemporary works on erotic relationships between women attest to this view. See, for instance, the series by Irma Nagy (pseudonym), which was immensely popular. *Bűnös szerelmek: Egy úrileány vallomásai* (Budapest: Magyar Könyvkiadó, 1908); *Sötét bűnök: Egy úrileány vallomásai* (Budapest: Kereskedelmi Reklámvállalat, 1908); *Nagy Irma utolsó könyve: A szerelem színháza Párisban* (Budapest: Szerző, 1909).

95. *Beteg szerelem*, 9.

96. *Beteg szerelem*.

97. Faderman, *Odd Girls and Twilight Lovers: A History of Lesbian Life in Twentieth-Century America* (New York: Columbia University Press, 1991), 4.

98. *Beteg szerelem*, 10.

99. Irma Nagy, *Sötét bűnök: Egy úrileány vallomásai* (Budapest: Kereskedelmi Reklámvállalat, 1908).

100. Sharon Marcus, *Between Women*, introduction.

101. *Beteg szerelem*, 10.

102. *Beteg szerelem*.

103. For a discussion on the process and timing of the stigmatization of romantic female friendship, see Martha Vicinus's *Intimate Friends: Women Who Loved Women, 1778–1928* (Chicago: University of Chicago Press, 2004).

104. Some examples from the literary representation of homosexuals include Gyula Krúdy, *A szobrok megmozdulnak: Írások az irodalomról* (Budapest: Gondolat, 1974); Gyula Krúdy, *Hét bagoly: regény* (Budapest: Szépirodalmi Könyvkiadó, 1974); Ernő Szép, *Natália* (Budapest: Noran, 2008), György Pál, *A homoszexuális probléma modem megvilágításban* (Budapest: Mai Henrik Kiadó, 1926); Zoltán Nemes Nagy, *Katasztrófák a szerelemi életben*. For an analysis of queer themes in poetry, see Zoltán Csehy, *Szodoma és környéke: Homoszocialitás, barátságretorika és queer irányulások a magyar költészetben* (Pozsony: Kalligram, 2014).

105. Female homosexuality had been criminalized in Austria since 1532, and the new penal code in 1909 simply continued an existing practice; it did not generate a legal or public debate. Matysik, *Reforming the Moral Subject*, 153.

106. The revised government proposal under Paragraph 250 would have criminalized female homosexuality and also made the punishment for homosexuality more

severe. There was an ongoing debate around the proposal, which was only brought to an unexpected end by the outbreak of World War I in 1914. For an analysis of the debate, see Matysik's *Reforming the Moral Subject*, 153–72.

107. The lectures were published in the journal of Hungarian legal association, *Magyar jogászegyleti értekezések*, in 1909.

108. Ignácz Fischer, "A homosexualitás és annak forensikus méltatása," *Magyar jogászegyleti értekezések* 38, no. 295 (1909).

109. Italics are mine. Fischer, 34.

110. For a concise summary of the politics of homosexuality in the Weimar Republic, see the introduction to Laurie Marhoefer's *Sex and the Weimar Republic*.

111. Zoltán Halász, "A szemérem elleni bűncselekményekről, különös tekintettel az erőszakos nemi közösülésre és a természet elleni fajtalanságra," *Magyar jogászegyleti értekezések* 38, no. 296 (1909).

112. Halász, 6.

113. Halász, 20. Italics are mine. In accordance with contemporary European practice of sexologists, medical and forensic doctors, and lawyers, Halász used Latin to describe "offensive" and "compromising" terms such erection or sexual impotence.

114. Same-sex relationships were also gendered; masculine, rough men paired with soft, feminine men. In "The Drive for Sexual Equality," *Sexualities* 11, nos. 1–2 (2008): 46–50.

115. Apart from underage males, according to the Hungarian criminal code, it was only women who could be victims of sexual and domestic violence.

116. Marius Turda, "'The Magyars: A Ruling Race': The Idea of National Superiority in Fin-de-Siècle Hungary," *European Review of History* 10, no. 1 (2003): 5–33. See also *The Idea of National Superiority in Central Europe, 1880–1918* (Lewiston: Edwin Mellen Press, 2004).

117. For England, see Seth Koven, *Slumming*, 25–88; for France, Peniston, *Pederasts and Others*, 149–77.

118. The creation of the category of homosexuals cut across the different legal and political constellations around homosexuality. Tamagne, *A History of Homosexuality*, 11–13.

CHAPTER THREE

1. See note 33 in the introduction.

2. The Budapesti Forradalmi Törvényszék Kisérleti Kriminológiai Osztály és az Országos Kriminológiai Intézet iratainak gyűjteménye (hereafter BFTKKO—OKI) is housed at BFL. The journal *Proletárjog: A Szocialista Jogászszövetség hivatalos lapja* is located at the Hungarian National Library. An important secondary source is a full issue of *Levéltári közlemények* (Archival Releases) that provides a comprehensive analysis of the surviving historical documents as well as of the legality and the actual functioning of the department. Issue no. 29 (1959).

3. The seminal work that established that relationship is Carl E. Schorske's *Fin-de-Siècle Vienna*. More recent works include Eli Zaretsky, *Secrets of the Soul: A Social and Cultural History of Psychoanalysis* (New York: Alfred A. Knopf, 2004); and George

Makari, *Revolution in Mind: The Creation of Psychoanalysis* (New York: Harper Collins, 2008).

4. BFTKKO—OKI, XVI.2, BFL.

5. Prior to 1914, women were completely excluded from voting, and less than 6 percent of the male population were eligible to vote.

6. Baron Móric Kornfeld, *Reflections on Twentieth Century Hungary: A Hungarian Magnate's View*, trans. Thomas J. DeKornfeld and Helen D. Kornfeld (Boulder, CO: Social Science Monographs; distributed by Columbia University Press, 2007), 219. For the different social, political, and economic issues that European capitals faced during World War I, see Jay M. Winter and Jean-Louis Robert, eds., *Capital Cities at War: Paris, London, Berlin, 1914–1919* (New York: Cambridge University Press, 1999). For how food shortage became politicized in Berlin, Belinda Davis's study, *Home Fires Burning: Food, Politics, and Everyday Life in World War I Berlin* (Chapel Hill: University of North Carolina Press, 2000), is most instructive. For the situation of Vienna during the war, see Maureen Healy, *Vienna and the Fall of the Habsburg Empire: Total War and Everyday Life in World War I* (New York: Cambridge University Press, 2004).

7. For the different political and social programs of the social democratic, liberal, and Communist opposition parties, see András Siklós, *A Habsburg-birodalom felbomlása, 1918: A magyarországi forradalom* (Budapest: Kossuth, 1987), 145–272.

8. For the comprehensive program of Károlyi and the Hungarian Democratic Republic, see Pál Schönwald, *A nagyarországi 1918–1919-es polgári demokratikus forradalom állam- és jogtörténeti kérdései* (Budapest: Akadémia Kiadó, 1969).

9. For the "Red Book" of Hungarian Communists, see Miklós Gerencsér, *Vörös könyv, 1919* (Lakitelep: Antológia Kiadó, 1993).

10. Universal suffrage meant voting rights were extended to all Hungarians over eighteen years old with the exception of political enemies and members of the clergy.

11. For a comprehensive list of policies, see Rudolfné Dósa, Ervinné Liptai, and Mihály Ruff, *A Magyar Tanácsköztársaság egészségügyi politikája* (Budapest: Medicina, 1959).

12. Order no. 1 of the People's Commissar of Justice suspended the previous court and prosecution system on March 22, 1919. Order no. 4 established the Revolutionary Tribunals. The most comprehensive book on the system of Revolutionary Tribunals remains Béla Sarlós's *A Tanácsköztársaság forradalmi törvényszékei* (Budapest: Közgazdasági és Jogi Kiadó, 1961).

13. Sarlós, *A Tanácsköztársaság forradalmi törvényszékei*, 58.

14. György Bónis, "Adatok a Budapesti Forradalmi Törvényszék történetéhez," *Levéltári Közlemények*, no. 29 (1959): 307–8.

15. 2818/1919, 2236/1919, BFL, BFTKKO—OKI 1919, 684–85.

16. Sándor Ferenczi, "Pszichoanalízis és társadalompolitika," *Nyugat* 15, no. 1 (1922): 554–55.

17. Ernő Jendrassik on March 25, 1919, at a Hungarian Medical Board Meeting, quoted in Pál Harmat, *Freud, Ferenczi és a magyarországi pszichoanalizis: A budapesti mélylélektani iskola története, 1908–1983* (Bern: Európai Protestáns Magyar Szabadegyetem, 1986), 71.

18. On May 12, 1919, Sándor Ferenczi, became a lecturer and full-time professor at the medical university in Budapest. Under the new leadership, psychoanalysis was insti-

tutionalized as part of the medical university, and Ferenczi was made the head of the new department. By being appointed a lecturer, Ferenczi became not only the first psychoanalyst in the world who was appointed as a psychoanalysis professor at a university, but also the head of the first psychoanalytical department at a medical university in the world. Ferenc Erős, "Ferenczi Sándor professzori kinevezése: Háttér és kronológia," *Thalassa* 20, no. 4 (2009): 3–28.

19. On the history of psychoanalysis in Vienna and Berlin, see Elizabeth Ann Danto, *Freud's Free Clinics: Psychoanalysis and Social Justice, 1918–1938* (New York: Columbia University Press, 2005). For London, see Sally Alexander, "Psychoanalysis in Britain in the Early Twentieth Century: An Introductory Note," *History Workshop Journal*, no. 45 (1998): 135–43.

20. The associating of psychoanalysis as a bourgeois science is long-standing. Stalinism and orthodox Marxism believed that psychoanalysis was not a "science" but rather an ideology, which served to mold the individual to fit in a bourgeois world. Accordingly, psychoanalytic practice would be incapable to truly transform individuals. In addition, they also considered psychoanalysis a pseudoscience based on its "unscientific" methodologies. Stanley Aronowitz, *Science as Power: Discourse and Ideology in Modern Society* (Minneapolis: University of Minnesota Press, 1988), 111. Two of the most influential historical works that highlight the bourgeois (and Jewish) connection are Carl Schorske's *Fin-de-siècle Vienna* and Peter Gay's *The Bourgeois Experience: Victoria to Freud* (New York: Oxford University Press, 1984).

21. On the resistance to psychoanalysis, see Harmat, *Freud, Ferenczi és a magyarországi pszichoanalizis*, 42–46.

22. The study of psychology was, similar to psychoanalysis, a relatively new science, which had been professionalizing—but had only achieved partial success, due to the stern resistance of established medical professions and hierarchical institutional structures of organized sciences. Sociology was associated with *Huszadik Század* and the *Társadalomtudományi Társaság*, and under the Károlyi government there were initiatives to strengthen sociology, but it was only with the Communists coming to power that the Faculty of Social Sciences was established in 1919.

23. The height of psychoanalysis in Russia was between 1921 and 1923. Martin A. Miller, *Freud and the Bolsheviks: Psychoanalysis in Imperial Russia and the Soviet Union* (New Haven, CT: Yale University Press, 1998), 53.

24. 2818/1919, 2236/1919, BFL, BFTKKO—OKI 1919, 684–85.

25. Ferenc Erős, "Ferenczi Sándor professzori kinevezése: Háttér és kronológia," 6–7.

26. Some recently surfaced documents make it apparent that many of the reforms within higher education and to some extent even in medicine that the Communists instituted had actually been initiated during the preceding democratic Károlyi regime.

27. The new evidence about the link between the reform aims of the democratic and Communist governments also explains the speed of which the Communists were able to carry out and institute some of the reforms. And this piece of information is important to keep in mind when considering the swift rise of psychoanalysis and psychology and their incorporation into the Communist medical and justice systems. Of course, not all reform aims were shared, nor were all Communist reforms swiftly instituted.

28. Emphasis in the original document.

29. 2818/1919, 2236/1919, BFL, BFTKKO—OKI 1919, 684–85.

30. 2818/1919, 2236/1919, BFL, BFTKKO—OKI 1919, 684–85.

31. XVI.2, BFL; Imre Kádár, "Aktuális kriminálpolitikai reformok," *Proletárjog* 1, no. 11 (1919): 76–78.; Bónis, "Levéltári Közlemények," 307.

32. It is difficult to know the political or ideological inclinations of the experts and workers of the department. For one there is no comprehensive list of the employees, nor is there in the existing records ever a mention of the political views of the staff.

33. For a comprehensive analysis of the department's approach in an international context, see Viola Lászlófi, Zsófia Nagy, and Trádler Henrietta, "'Fajtalanság,' pszichoanalízis és kriminológia a Magyar Tanácsköztársaságban. F. Gy. esete a Kísérleti Kriminológiai Osztály anyagában," *Sic Itur ad Astra* 66 (2017): 45–76.

34. The first surviving case is numbered file 3/1919, dated from May 8, 1919, while the last case in the file is numbered 2929/1919 and was dated July 3, 1919. 2818/1919, 2236/1919, 615–32, BFL.

35. Antal Neumann, "Az orvospszichologus szerepe az igazságszolgáltatásban," *Proletárjog* 1, no. 13–14 (1919): 92.

36. Neumann, 93.

37. 382/1919, BFL; Imre Kádár, "Aktuális kriminálpolitikai reformok," 76–78.

38. 2818/1919, 2236/1919, BFL.

39. Emphasis in the original document.

40. The rest of the questionnaire is missing—but it is unlikely that there were additional fixed questions. Rather, it was an "open" discussion with the experts and the description of the criminal act that completed the questionnaire.

41. Florence Tamagne, *A History of Homosexuality in Europe*, introduction.

42. Some of the latest works that show links include Marius Turda, ed. *The History of East-Central European Eugenics, 1900–1945: Sources and Commentaries* (London: Bloomsbury Academic, 2015); Marius Turda and Paul Weindling, eds., *"Blood and Homeland": Eugenics and Racial Nationalism in Central and Southeast Europe, 1900–1940* (Budapest: Central European University Press, 2007); Maria Bucur, *Eugenics and Modernization in Interwar Romania* (Pittsburgh: University of Pittsburgh Press, 2002).

43. N.A., "Az elmebetegügy ideiglenes rendezése," *Proletárjog* 1, no. 8 (1919): 61.

44. Andor Östreicher, "A bűnözés es bűntetés fogalmához," *Proletárjog* 1, nos. 9–10 (1919): 73.

45. Östreicher.

46. One of the most crucial aspects of Freud's theories is that he assigned meaning to behavior.

47. Psychoanalytic theories and the writings of Ferenczi assigned a crucial importance to early child-parent relationship in shaping human character. On Ferenczi especially, see Harmat, *Freud, Ferenczi és a magyarországi pszichoanalizis*, 87–92.

48. Based on people's political, religious, and class affiliation, the tribunals, which sprung up across Hungary, sentenced thousands of people and ordered hundreds of executions under the charge of "enemies of the revolution." The Revolutionary Tribunals avoided sending political cases to the Criminology Department. "It is obvious that in political charges, there was no need for criminal examination." Ference Rákos, quoted in Bónis, "Adatok a Budapesti Forradalmi Törvényszék történetéhez," 309.

49. In Communist ideology, the seeds and the origin of crime (of the lower classes) laid with bourgeois (capitalist) exploitation. Ferenc Rákos, *Állam és alkotmány a Magyar Tanácsköztársaságban* (Budapest: Jogi Kiadó, 1953), 76–103.

50. Imre Kádár, "Kriminológiai alapkérdések," *Proletárjog* 1, no. 12 (1919): 84.

51. 2818/1919, 2236/1919, 616, BFL.

52. 2818/1919, 2236/1919, 617, BFL.

53. 2818/1919, 2236/1919, 618, BFL.

54. 2818/1919, 2236/1919, 618, BFL.

55. 2818/1919, 2236/1919, 623–25, BFL.

56. The use of Latin was commonplace until the end of World War II in both medical and legal documents.

57. 2818/1919, 2236/1919, 629, BFL.

58. The question about childhood fantasizing reflects psychoanalytic and more specifically Freud's interest in the interpretation of dreams and an assumed connection between dreams and people's subconscious.

59. Födesi Kálmán, "A proletárállam büntetőjoga: Különös rész," *Proletárjog* 1, no. 2 (1919): 13.

60. 2818/1919, 2236/1919, 629, BFL.

61. Both Freud and Ferenczi thought that there were homosexuals, who could not be "converted." While eventually they both came to believe that most homosexuals could not be transformed to heterosexuals, they also believed that in many cases there were developmental and environmental factors that "caused" homosexuality. In these cases, there was potential to steer people back to heterosexual life. On Freud's ideas of sexuality, see Paul Robinson's "Freud and Homosexuality," in *Homosexuality and Psychoanalysis*, ed. Tim Dean and Christopher Lane (Chicago: University of Chicago Press, 2001), 91–98. On Ferenczi's views, see Miklós Eszenyi and László Zahuczky, "Ferenczi és kortársai a homoszexualitásról," *Thalassa* 21, no. 4 (2008): 87–100.

62. Béla Sarlós, for instance, talks about how when it was believed that a person under investigation was not a "recidivist offender," the Experimental Criminology Department in collaboration with the Budapest Revolutionary Tribunal arranged a job (often in a factory), as they believed that providing economic livelihood and social structure was the most beneficial "punishment" for both the accused as well as for the Communist society as a whole. In *A Tanácsköztársaság forradalmi törvényszéke*, 110–12.

63. Depending on their "condition," reforming people would take place at different reformatory camps, where they would be required to work. Kádár, "Aktuális kriminálpolitikai reformok," 78.

64. "A kommunista állam családjoga," *Proletárjog* 1, no. 1 (1919): 5.

65. On the Bolshevik vision and the Soviet Family Law, see Wendy Z. Goldman, *Women, the State and Revolution: Soviet Family Policy and Social Life, 1917–1936* (Cambridge: Cambridge University Press, 1993), 1–58.

66. Appeared in *Vörös Újság*, May 20, 1919. Cited in Tibor Pap, "A házasság felbontásának problematikája a Magyar Tanácsköztársaságban," *Jogtudományi Közlöny* 15, nos. 2–3 (1959): 64.

67. Pap, "A házasság felbontásának problematikája a Magyar Tanácsköztársaságban."

68. Bentsur Eytan, *Láng Európa szívében: Kun Béla hatalmának 133 napja*, trans. Tamás Berczi (Budapest: K.U.K. Könyv-És Lapkiadó, 2010), 137–38.

69. Foucault, *The History of Sexuality*, 1:17–35.

70. For a discussion of venereal diseases, see Gábor Szegedi, "Good Health Is the Best Dowry: Marriage Counseling, Premarital Examinations, Sex Education in Hungary, 1920–1952" (PhD diss., Central European University, 2014), 34–44.

71. For comprehensive analyses of the Communist Party's approach to sex in Russia, see Eric Naiman's *Sex in Public: The Incarnation of Early Soviet Ideology* (Princeton, NJ: Princeton University Press, 1997) and also Gregory Carleton's *Sexual Revolution in Bolshevik Russia* (Pittsburgh: University of Pittsburgh Press, 2005).

72. Britta McEwen, *Sexual Knowledge: Feeling, Fact, and Social Reform in Vienna, 1900–1934* (New York: Berghahn Books, 2012), 54.

73. I have not been able to locate primary documents on what exactly Lukács proposed as sex education in schools, but there are secondary sources, which describe how during his time as deputy people's commissar of education he ordered mandatory sex education in schools. For instance, in László Szabó, *A bolsevizmus Magyarországon: A proletárdiktatúra okirataiból* (Budapest: Athenaeum, 1919), 73; Miklós Gerencsér, *Vörös könyv, 1919*, 397.

74. Eytan, *Láng Európa szívében*, 137.

75. "A venereas betegségek és a háború—beszélgetés Nékám tanárral," *Egészségügyi Lapok* 9, no. 1 (1916): 1–3; Dezső Hahn, "A fertőző nemi betegségek és a háború," *Huszadik Század* 17, no. 2 (1916): 1–19.

76. Eric Naiman, *Sex in Public*, 4.

77. There is no comprehensive study on sex education in fin de siècle Hungary. For Vienna, see McEwen, *Sexual Knowledge*, 54–63.

78. For a discussion on the Bolshevik ideas of sexuality, see Dan Healey's *Bolshevik Sexual Forensics: Diagnosing Disorder in the Clinic and Courtroom, 1917–1939* (DeKalb: Northern Illinois University Press, 2009), 3–12.

79. Frances Bernstein, *The Dictatorship of Sex: Lifestyle Advice for the Soviet Masses* (DeKalb: Northern Illinois University Press, 2007), 8; Dan Healy, *Bolshevik Sexual Forensics*, 164–65.

80. "A kommunista állam családjoga," 6.

81. On a brief history of understanding of *faj*, see János Gyurgyák, *Magyar fajvédők: Eszmetörténeti tanulmány* (Budapest: Osiris, 2012), introduction.

82. "A kommunista állam családjoga," 6.

83. On the relationship between prostitution and Communist ideology, see the speech by Alexandra Kollontai, "Prostitution and Ways of Fighting It," in Alexandra Kollontai, *Selected Writings* (New York: W. W. Norton & Company, 1980), 261–75.

84. "Razzia a fővárosi prostitúció mocsarában," *Népszava*, July 5, 1919, 6.

85. "Razzia a fővárosi prostitúció mocsarában."

86. Kálmán Födesi, "A proletárállam büntetőjoga: Különös rész," *Proletárjog* 1, no. 2 (1919): 13.

87. Same-sex relations between consenting adults were decriminalized in the Soviet Union in 1922. Following the solidification of Stalin's power, homosexuality was recrimi-

nalized in 1934. For the history of legal debates in the Soviet context, see Dan Healy's *Homosexual Desire in Revolutionary Russia*.

88. Födesi, "A proletárállam büntetőjoga: Különös rész," 13.

89. The Hungarian Communists were likely preceded by some of their Russian counterparts. Peter Holquist argues the ethos of self-mobilization and building revolutionary subjects in Russia began with the total mobilization during World War I; *Making War, Forging Revolution: Russia's Continuum of Crisis, 1914–1921* (Cambridge, MA: Harvard University Press, 2002), introduction.

90. Sarlós, *A Tanácsköztársaság forradalmi törvényszékei*, 106.

CHAPTER FOUR

1. Rudolf Paksa, *A magyar szélsőjobboldal története* (Budapest: Jaffa Kiadó, 2012), 44–61.

2. On the circumstances of the coming to power of the counterrevolutionaries, see Romsics, *Magyarország története a XX. században*, chap. 5.

3. There were competing accounts of the White Terror from the onset. While Communist émigrés accounted for huge numbers, the sympathizers of Horthy denied the Terror and put the blame on the Soviet Republic. During the Communist era, between 1948 and 1989, the numbers of White Terror victims were highly exaggerated. Since the 1990s, there have been different interpretations. The best summary of different numbers and accounts of the events is Gergely Bödők, "Vörös és fehér: Terror, retorzió és számonkérés Magyarországon 1919–1921," *Kommentár*, no. 3 (2011), http://kommentar.info.hu/iras/2011_3/voros_es_feher, accessed July 10, 2012.

4. Bödők.

5. Horthy was named regent of Hungary on March 1, 1920.

6. Romsics, *Magyarország története a XX. században*, 147.

7. Romsics, 188.

8. On the nature of Christian nationalism, see Paul Hanebrink's *In Defense of Christian Hungary*, 77–108.

9. Deák, *Hungary from 1918 to 1945*, 20.

10. On the initial years of Horthy rule, see Krisztián Ungváry, *A Horthy-rendszer mérlege: Diszkrimináció, szociálpolitika és antiszemitizmus Magyarországon* (Budapest: Jelenkor Kiadó, 2013), especially 86–107.

11. More recent Hungarian scholarship stresses that the extent to which the nature and degree of conservatism varied throughout the 1920s. See, for instance, Gyurgyák, *Ezzé lett magyar hazátok*, 289–315.

12. Cécile Tormay, *Bujdosó könyv. Feljegyzések 1918–1919-ből* (Budapest: Pallas, 1921).

13. Since 1989, historians have revealed that Tormay could not have been present at many of the events she recounts as an "eyewitness."

14. János Hankiss, *Tormay Cécile* (Budapest: Singer & Wolfner, 1939), pt. 6.

15. Cécile Tormay, *An Outlaw's Diary*, vol. 1 (London: P. Allan & Company, 1923), 141.

16. János Hankiss's biography of Tormay (1939) remains one of the most compre-

hensive books on the details of Tormay's life albeit omitting any information that might negatively portray her.

17. For additional details of Pallavicini's life, see the Hungarian Catholic Lexicon, http://lexikon.katolikus.hu/P/Pallavicini.html, accessed March 19, 2017.

18. On the most accomplished members of the Zichy family, see the entries in the Hungarian Biographical Lexicon, http://mek.oszk.hu/00300/00355/html/, accessed March 19, 2017.

19. On the details of the scandal, see John Sadler and Silvie Fisch, *Spy of the Century: Alfred Redl and the Betrayal of Austria-Hungary* (Barnsley: Pen and Sword, 2016), 103–41.

20. *Pesti Hírlap* was an exception along with the satirical weekly *Borszem Jankó*, with both alluding to Redl's homosexuality.

21. Under the Bethlen government (1921–31), a so-called press conference committee was established to censor publications. Ignác Romsics, "A Horthy-rendszer jellegéről: Elitizmus, tekintélyelv, konzervativizmus," *Rubicon: Történelmi Magazin* 1 (1997), http://www.rubicon.hu/magyar/oldalak/a_horthy_rendszer_jellegerol_elitizmus_tekintelyelv_konzervativizmus/, accessed March 16, 2017.

22. VII.2.c. Királyi Büntetö Törvényszék 45162/1923, BFL (hereafter Divorce Suit).

23. Divorce Suit, 2.

24. "Gróf Zichy válópörének epilógusa," *Az Est*, November 19, 1925, 4.

25. "Gróf Zichy Rafaelné a katolikus vallás törvényeire való hivatkozással az itélet ellenére sem hajlandó elválni férjétől," *Esti Kurir*, November 28, 1925, 5. In addition, some of the papers that provided extensive coverage included *Pesti Hírlap*, *Magyar Hírlap*, *Esti Kurir*, *Népszava*, *Pesti Napló*, and *8 Órai Újság*.

26. "Gróf Zichy Rafalèk házasságának históriája," *8 Órai Újság*, November 28, 1925, 5.

27. On the press and sexual customs of the time, see Géza Buzinkay, in *A Magyar Sajtó Története I*, 161–63.

28. "Gróf Zichy Rafeal másfèlèvi börtönre itélte a biróság," *Pesti Hirlap*, November 27, 1925, 4.

29. "Gróf Zichy Rafaelné a katolikus vallás törvényeire való hivatkozással az itélet ellenére sem hajnadó elválni férjétől," *Esti Kurir*, November 28, 1925, 5.

30. On the interrelationship between the emergence of the New Woman and the discursive appearance of female homosexuality, see Judith Halberstam's *Female Masculinity* (Durham, NC: Duke University Press, 1998). More recently, Marti Lybeck's *Desiring Emancipation: New Women and Homosexuality in Germany, 1890–1933* (Albany: State University of New York Press, 2014) provides an especially instructive explanation about the complex relationship between the ideas of New Woman and homosexuality.

31. Mihály Szécsényi, "Kalauznők konfliktusai a villamoson: Társadalmi nem és térhasználat Budapesten," *Sic Itur Ad Astra* 20 (2009): 149–79.

32. Gyáni and Kövér, *Magyarország társadalomtörténete a reformkortól a második világháborúig*, 265.

33. On the history of Hungarian women's movement and efforts to greater equality, see Rita Antoni, "A Magyarországi Feminista Megmozdulások Története," in *Nőképek kisebbségben: Tanulmányok a kisebbségben (is) élő nőkről*, ed. Lilla Bolemant (Pozsony: Phoenix PT, 2014), 18–29.

34. For the origin of the term "conservative modernity," see Alison Light, *Forever England: Femininity, Literature, and Conservatism between the Wars* (New York: Routledge, 1991), and for its definition; Laura Doan and Jane Garrity, *Sapphic Modernities: Sexuality, Women, and National Culture* (New York: Palgrave Macmillan, 2006), introduction.

35. Tormay, *An Outlaw's Diary*, 1:182–83.

36. Paola Bacchetta and Margaret Power, eds., *Right-wing Women: from Conservatives to Extremists around the World* (New York: Routledge, 2002); Kevin Passmore, ed., *Women, Gender, and Fascism in Europe, 1919–45* (New Brunswick, NJ: Rutgers University Press, 2003).

37. For the history of feminism and women's movements in Hungary, see Andrea Pető, "Minden tekintetben derék nők: A nők politikai szerepei és a nőegyesületek a két világháború közötti Magyarországon," in *Szerep és alkotás: Női szerepek a társadalomban és az alkotóművészetben* (Debrecen: Csokonai Kiadó, 1997), 268–79; and Maria M. Kovacs, "Hungary," in *Women, Gender, and Fascism in Europe, 1919–45*, 79–91. By the 1930s the rhetoric of women staying at home became impossible to support, as it was no longer a viable option for most. Nevertheless, the rhetoric of separate spheres remained a stable feature of MANSz.

38. Divorce Suit, 2.

39. Italics are mine to indicate that the two words were written in Latin rather than in Hungarian.

40. Following Count Zichy's appeal after the decision of the Royal Criminal Court, the Royal Tribunal (Appeals Court) as well the Royal Curia (Hungary's Highest Court of Justice) sided with the Royal Criminal Court: both denied Count Zichy's petition and did not grant the divorce.

41. VII.5.c. Királyi Büntető Törvényszék Budapest 4516/1924, BFL (hereafter Criminal Suit).

42. The Royal Curia found Count Zichy and the servants guilty on November 18, 1927.

43. For an attempt to reconstruct the legal cases, see Attila Döme, *Egy "nyomdafestéket el nem bíró" ügy: A Tormay Cécile per* (Keszthely: Balaton Akadémiai Kiadó, 2013).

44. Scholars have repeatedly shown the frankness with which domestic servants could speak about intimate bodily matters. For a classic example, see Lawrence Stone's *Road to Divorce: England, 1530–1987* (Oxford: Oxford University Press, 1990).

45. Morris B. Kaplan, *Sodom on the Thames* (Ithaca, NY: Cornell University Press, 2005), 224–51.

46. The testimonials of servants were recorded by public notaries between December 1922 and October 1923.

47. Walter József nyilatkozata in Jeszenszky 1141/1923, 10, BFL.

48. Walter József nyilatkozata in Jeszenszky 1141/1923, 10–11, BFL.

49. Walter József nyilatkozata in Jeszenszky 1141/1923, 11, BFL.

50. The idea of the "Third Sex" comes from Magnus Hirschfeld. See note 130 in chap. 1.

51. Esther Newton, "The Mythic Mannish Lesbian: Radclyffe Hall and the New Woman," *Signs* 9, no. 4 (1984): 557.

52. Zeisler Mária nyilatkozata in Jeszenszky 1398/1921, 10, BFL.

53. Jeszenszky 105/1922, 2, BFL.
54. Jeszenszky 105/1922, 2, BFL.
55. D'Artagnan was one of Vay's pen names, but Gyula Krúdy, the famous Hungarian novelist, also often referred to Vay as D'Artagnan. See *Szobrok megmozdulnak: Írások az irodalomról* (Budapest: Gondolat, 1974).
56. On the life of Vay, see Anna Borgos's "Vay Sándor/Sarolta: Egy konvencionális nemiszerep-áthágó a múlt századfordulón," *Holmi*, no. 2 (2007): 185–94.
57. The trial of Vay, which received international attention, took place in 1899 when Vay was sued by her father-in-law for marrying under false pretense and intentionally deceiving her wife and in-laws about her biological sex. Based on the opinion of medical experts who determined that Vay had a congenital and, therefore, unstoppable sexual passion for her own sex, she was acquitted and continued to live as a man. For an analysis of the greater implications of the trial in English, see Geertje Mak, "Sandor Sarolta Vay: From Passing Woman to Sexual Invert," *Journal of Women's History* 16, no. 1 (March 8, 2004): 54–77.
58. Richard von Krafft-Ebing, *Psychopathia sexualis. Mit besonderen Berücksichtigung der konträren Sexualempfindung. Eine klinisch-forensische Studie*, 6th ed. (Stuttgart: Ferdinand Enke, 1892), 311–28; Havelock Ellis, *Studies in the Psychology of Sex*, vol. 1, *Sexual Inversion* (London: University Press, 1900), 94.
59. Borgos, "Vay Sándor/Sarolta," 190.
60. Quoted in Zsuzsa Török, "A férfiruhás írónő: Vay Sarolta/Sándor és az átöltözés társadalomtörténete," *Irodalomtörténet* 95, no. 4 (2014): 467.
61. Some of Krúdy's pieces as well as Vay's own appeared in daily newspapers and were widely circulated. For a list of articles, see Borgos, "Vay Sándor/Sarolta," 193–94.
62. On the circulation of narratives of nonnormative (female) gender and sexualities in the Hungarian context, see Judit Takács and Gábor Csiszár, "Nemváltások és nemiszerep-áthágások reprezentációi az Estben 1910 és 1939 között," *REPLIKA* 85–86, no. 1 (2014): 209–25.
63. Poszlik Ferencné szolgáló nyilatkozata in Jeszenszky 1260/1923, 4–5, BFL.
64. *Csira*, in *Magyar etymologiai szótár I. könyv*, ed. Zoltán Gombocz and János Melich (Budapest: Magyar Tudományos Akadémia, 1914), 30.
65. For instance, Kenyeres, *Törvényszéki orvostan*, 232.
66. Esther Newton, "The Mythic Mannish Lesbian," 557.
67. Walter József nyilatkozata, 8.
68. Walter József nyilatkozata, 9.
69. On the unintelligibility of contemporary legal and medical discourse on female homosexuality, see George Chauncey's article "From Sexual Inversion to Homosexuality: Medicine and Changing Concept of Female Deviance," *Salmagundi*, nos. 58–59 (Fall 1982/Winter 1983): 114–46, and more recently, Laura Doan and Jane Garrity in their introduction in *Sapphic Modernities*.
70. Deák István nyilatkozata in Jeszensky 1277/1923, 5, BFL.
71. Divorce Trial note. By the time of the Criminal Court's decision on the libel case, the papers were allowed to address the specific charges, which included the explicit details of the case.
72. VII.5.c. 4516/1924, 125, BFL.

73. VII.5.c. 4516/1924, 125, BFL.
74. VII.5.c. 4516/1924, 125, BFL.
75. The courts, in rejecting granting the divorce on moral grounds (based on §80), cited that hiring someone with whom he had a sexual relationship (one of the female servants) to spy on his wife, along with the fact that he moved out not for the reason of the countess's tribadism but rather his own affair with another woman, made the count's appeal for divorce on moral grounds objectionable. Divorce Suit, 19–20.
76. This was part of an older legal code that was invoked only rarely by the 1920s.
77. Divorce Suit Decision of Royal Tribunal, 27.
78. Divorce Suit Decision of Royal Tribunal.
79. Divorce Suit, Curia's verdict, 2. Italics are mine.
80. This seemed to be a transnational phenomenon. See, for instance, George Chauncey's reconstruction of the trial of Reverend Samuel Kent in 1920, "Christian Brotherhood or Sexual Perversion? Homosexual Identities and the Construction of Sexual Boundaries in the World War One Era," *Journal of Social History* 19, no. 2 (Winter, 1985): 189–211.
81. For the particular circumstances of servants in the 1920s Hungary, see Gyáni and Kövér, *Magyarország társadalomtörténete a reformkortól a második világháborúig*, 205–11.
82. Tormay, *An Outlaw's Diary*, 2:43.
83. Dezső Kosztolányi, *Édes Anna* (Budapest: Genius, 1926).
84. The recent arrival of universal suffrage in 1918 had yet to translate into equal treatment in the courts. Moreover, universal suffrage was seriously compromised by the Minister Decree of 1922 and Voting Law of 1925, both of which raised the prerequisites of voting in terms of education, thereby successfully shutting out most of working-class, peasant, and servant votes.
85. The sentences for the three servants sued were lowered from a year to ten months, from seven months to six months, and from six months to four months in prison, respectively.
86. Criminal Suit, Verdict of Court of Appeal, 136, Verdict of Royal Curia, 167.
87. Criminal Suit, Royal Criminal Court of Budapest, 86.
88. Criminal Suit, Royal Criminal Court of Budapest, 76.
89. For a discussion on the timing of the stigmatization of romantic female friendship, see Vicinus's *Intimate Friends: Women Who Loved Women, 1778–1928*.
90. Divorce Suit, Criminal Court, 3.
91. Divorce Suit, Criminal Court, 3.
92. P.VII.2.c. 45162/1923, 19, BFL.
93. P.III. 4997/1924/5 Divorce Suit, 33, BFL.
94. Divorce Suit, 18–19, Orvosi Vélemény, Függelék, 12.
95. Divorce Suit, Royal Tribunal, 4.
96. Doan, *Fashioning Sapphism* (New York: Columbia University Press, 2001), 32.
97. The historical elite, while having no tolerance for Communists, had also cracked down on radical right groups and openly revisionist voices, since during the 1920s, they still believed—incorrectly—that they could convince the Allies and the international community to "correct the fatal mistakes of Trianon" without military intervention. Romsics, *Magyarország története a XX. században*, 146–56.

98. István Deák, *Hungary from 1918 to 1945*, 3. With approximately 5 percent of the population, Hungary had an exceedingly high proportion of nobility, comparable in Europe only to Poland and Spain. For the historical origins of Hungary's social makeup, see Paul Lendvai, *The Hungarians*, 319–23.

99. See, for instance, Nemzetgyűlés, parliamentary session no. 475, 1925.

100. Most notably the social democrat Imre Györki.

101. Páter Zadravecz, *Páter Zadravecz titkos naplója* (Budapest: Kossuth Könyvkiadó, 1967).

102. Zadravecz, 216–17.

103. Zadravecz. For the first balanced assessment of Horthy's life in Hungarian, see Dávid Turbucz, *Horthy Miklós* (Budapest: Napvilág, 2011).

104. Thomas Sakmyster, *Hungary's Admiral on Horseback: Miklós Horthy, 1918–1944* (Boulder, CO: East European Monographs; distributed by Columbia University Press, 1994).

105. Judit Kádár, "Az antiszemitizmus jutalma: Tormay Cécile és a Horthy korszak," *Kritika*, no. 3 (2003): 9–12. For an analysis of Tormay's literary scholarship, see Krisztina Kollarits's *Egy bujdosó írónő—Tormay Cécile* (Vasszilvágy: Magyar Nyugat, 2010).

106. P.III. 4997/1924, 2. Divorce Suit, 30, BFL.

107. On the rise of Fidesz and Jobbik, see András Bozóki, "Consolidation or Second Revolution? The Emergence of the New Right in Hungary," *Journal of Communist Studies and Transition Politics* 24, no. 2 (June 1, 2008): 191–231. On their historical revisionism, see Krisztián Ungváry, *Tettesek vagy áldozatok? Feltáratlan fejezetek a XX. század történelméből* (Budapest: Jaffa Kiadó, 2014).

108. For a detailed analysis of Tormay's reappearance, see Anita Kurimay, "Interrogating the Historical Revisionism of the Hungarian Right: The Queer Case of Cécile Tormay," *East European Politics & Societies* 30, no. 1 (February 1, 2016): 10–33.

109. On using female figures as representations of the nation, the seminal works include Nira Yuval-Davis, *Gender and Nation* (London: Sage Publications, 1997), and Mrinalini Sinha, *Gender and Nation* (Washington, DC: American Historical Association, 2006).

CHAPTER FIVE

1. For the explanation of the case, see Roland Perényi, "Találkahelyek, bűnügyi helyszínek és 'dzsungel-erkölcsök': Homoszexuális szubkultúra, városi tér és bűnözés Budapesten a 20. század elején," *Sic Itur ad Astra* 66 (2017): 109–12.

2. "Szerelmi ügynökök, homoszexuális apacsok garázdálkodnak a főváros szívében," *Város*, January 23, 1932, 1–2.

3. Nazi Germany led the large-scale persecution of homosexuals, but, as scholars have pointed out, homosexuals were also prosecuted in fascist Italy and increasingly policed even in France. There is substantive scholarship on Germany; the classic work is Richard Plant's *The Pink Triangle: The Nazi War against Homosexuals*, 1st ed. (New York: H. Holt, 1986). On Italy, see Benadusi, *The Enemy of the New Man*. On France, see Tamagne, *A History of Homosexuality in Europe*, 336–53.

4. On Horthy's aversion to Budapest, see Sakmyster, *Hungary's Admiral on Horse-*

back, 1–24. The word *bűnös*, which Horthy used in his speech in English, can actually mean both "guilty" and "sinful."

5. Lajos Fülep, *A magyarság pusztulása* (Budapest: Magvető, 1984).

6. On the role of "Christian values" and, more generally, the role of Hungarian churches in working with the ruling elite to shape interwar society and national culture, see Paul Hanebrink's *In Defense of Christian Hungary*, 108–36. On the history of the Catholic Church and its influence during the same period, see Jenő Gergely, *A katolikus egyház története Magyarországon 1919–1945* (Budapest: Pannonica Kiadó, 1997).

7. Ungváry, *A Horthy-rendszer mérlege*, 111–57.

8. Károly Pósch, *Utam a gólyafészek körül: Tanulmány a nemi felvilágosítás problémájáról szülők és nevelők részére* (Budapest: Szerző, 1923), 55.

9. David L. Hoffmann, in "Mothers in the Motherland: Stalinist Pronatalism and Its Pan-European Context," *Journal of Social History* 34, no. 1 (2000): 35–54.

10. Public discourse moreover also acknowledged that many respectable women had to work outside of the home. For a detailed analysis of how expectations for women within the private sphere changed during the interwar years, see Krisztina Sedlmayr, "A modern háztartás születése az 1930-as években Magyarországon" (PhD diss., Eötvös Loránd Tudományegyetem, 2007), especially 16–48.

11. This was a general European-wide phenomenon. Robert A. Nye, "Western Masculinities in War and Peace," 417–38.

12. Mandatory conscription was introduced only in 1939. Ágnes Nagy-Juhász Vargáné, "Az önkéntes haderő tartalék biztosításának szervezési—vezetési kérdései" (PhD diss., Zrinyi Miklos Nemzetvedelmi Egyetem, Hadtudományi Kar, 2010), 20–23.

13. The law "Lex Karafiáth," as the so-called physical education law, which was adopted in 1921 and implemented by the Order V.KM 9000/1924, codified Levente or "paladin." The law stated that ensuring the physical education of the Hungarian people was the responsibility of the state even if they were not in school. Henriette Pusztafalvi, "Az egészségnevelés intézményesülésének folymata hazánkban a dualizmus korától a második világháború végéig" (PhD diss., A Pécsi Tudományegyetem Bölcsészettudományi Kar Oktatás és Társadalom Neveléstudományi Doktori Iskola, 2011), 18–21.

14. Count Kuno von Klebelsberg, who was the minister of religion and public education between 1922 and 1931, was the central figure coordinating the new national discourse on public morality. The importance of physical education in strengthening the morality and ethics of Hungarian youth was recognized by the 1920s and increasingly built into the education system, which expanded substantially under Klebelsberg. Pusztafalvi, "Az Egészségnevelés Intézményesülésének Folymata Hazánkban," 87–94. On the Hungarian education policy between the two world wars, see Miklós Mann's *Oktatáspolitikusok és koncepciók a két világháború között* (Budapest: Országos Pedagógiai Könyvtár és Múzeum, 1997).

15. For an overview of Hungarian sex education, see Gábor Szegedi, "Good Health Is the Best Dowry," introduction.

16. Kókay and Buzinkay, *A magyar sajtó története*, 190–206.

17. György Lukács, *Népegészségügy Magyarországon* (Budapest: Magyar Tudományos Társaság Nyomdája, 1924), 16–18.

18. "A m. kir. belügyminiszternek 151.000/1927 B.M. számú körrendelete: a közerkölcsiség védelme," *Belügyi Közlöny* 32 (1927): 327–28.

19. "A m. kir. belügyminiszternek 151.000/1927 B.M. számú körrendelete: a közerkölcsiség védelme."

20. István Szikinger, "A magyar rendvédelmi jog 1919–1944," *Rendvédelem-Történeti Füzetek* 23, no. 27–30 (2013): 191.

21. 151.000/1927 §1.

22. 151.000/1927 §3.1–4.

23. 160.100/1926, BM.

24. 160.100/1926, BM, §28.

25. Nemes Nagy, *Katasztrófák a szerelemi életben*, 87–99.

26. Nemes Nagy never named his patient. K was born in 1893.

27. Nemes Nagy was a sexual pathologist and a medical doctor. He published a number of books on sexual pathologies, as well as on sexuality, from the 1920s to the late 1940s. Other than his publications, there is very little known about his life and practice.

28. For a comprehensive account of the effects of the war on Budapest, see Vörös Károly, "Budapest a Világháborúban," in *Budapest története a márciusi forradalomtól az őszirózsás forradalomig*, 725–44.

29. Nemes Nagy, *Katasztrófák a szerelemi életben*, 92.

30. Nemes Nagy.

31. Tamagne, *A History of Homosexuality in Europe*, 28–33.

32. Turcsányi, *A modern bűnözés I*, 13, 133.

33. Turcsányi, 133.

34. Turcsányi, 13–30, 131; Szántó, "A homosexualitásról, különös tekintettel a budapesti viszonyokra," 43.

35. Estimates ranged from ten thousand to fifteen thousand homosexuals in greater Budapest (population 1.44 million). See Turcsányi, *A modern bűnözés I*, 133; Szántó "A homosexualitásról, különös tekintettel a budapesti viszonyokra," 40.

36. Borbély and Kapy, *A 60 éves magyar rendőrség, 1881–1941*, 579.

37. About 10–15 percent of ethnic Hungarians (especially professionals and bureaucrats) who, following the Treaty of Trianon, were outside the newly drawn boundaries of Hungary decided to relocate to Budapest or one of the other (remaining) larger cities. *Budapest Székesfőváros Statisztikai Évkönyve az 1944–1946 Évekről* (Budapest, Központi Statisztikai Hivatal, 1948), 14.

38. Nemes Nagy, *Katasztrófák a szerelemi életben*, 94.

39. Chauncy, *Gay New York*, 6.

40. Nemes Nagy, *Katasztrófák a szerelemi életben*, 94.

41. "Küzdelem a világvárois Bűnök ellen," *Detektív*, August 1921, 1–2, cited in Perényi, "Találkahelyek, bűnügyi helyszínek és 'dzsungel-erkölcsök,'" 100.

42. Cited in Perény, "Találkahelyek, bűnügyi helyszínek és 'dzsungel-erkölcsök,'" 95.

43. Nemes Nagy, *Katasztrófák a szerelemi életben*, 94–96.

44. Turcsányi, *A modern bűnözés I*, 13–30, 120–21; Jenő Szántó, "A homosexualis férfiprostitució kérdése," 826–34, "A homosexualitásról, különös tekintettel a budapesti viszonyokra, 40–44.

45. Nemes Nagy, *Katasztrófák a szerelemi életben*, 96.

46. Gyáni and Kövér, *Magyarország társadalomtörténete a reformkortól a második világháborúig*, 189–362.

47. Chauncey, *Gay New York*, 152–53.

48. In 1925, for example, about half of Budapest's population lived in a one-bedroom flat, and almost one-third of these people shared their living space with more than five other people. Béla Biró, *A prostitúció* (Budapest: Magyar Királyi Rendőrség, 1933), 78. Borbély and Kapy, *A 60 éves magyar rendőrség, 1881–1941*, introduction.

49. Borbély and Kapy, *A 60 éves magyar rendőrség, 1881–1941*, 10–35; Nyigri, *Budapest bűnélete*, 520–25.

50. Nemes Nagy, *Katasztrófák a szerelemi életben*, 98.

51. According Nemes Nagy, the number by the 1930s reached five thousand; *Katasztrófák a szerelemi életben*, 74. In Jenő Szántó's account, until 1929 the homosexual registry contained about two thousand men, and by 1933 it had 3,500. This is a significant increase, which he attributed to both the rise of homosexuals and greater police attention. "A homoszexualitásról különös tekintettel a Budapesti viszonyokra," 43.

52. Nemes Nagy, *Katasztrófák a szerelemi életben*, 74; Turcsányi, *A modern bűnözés I*, 135.

53. László Tóth, ed., *A homoszexualitásról* (Pompeji: T-Twins Kiadó, 1994).

54. László Tóth, "A modern kori homoszexualitás néhány kérdése," in *A homoszexualitásról*, 76.

55. Tóth.

56. The only other place where the police indicated the existence of a homosexual subculture was Debrecen, a city of 120,000 inhabitants (after Budapest and Szeged, the largest city) in northeast Hungary.

57. My data comes from the documents of the Budapest City Archives (BFL). Specifically, I am relying on the indexes as well as the actual documentation of court cases within the Budapest Criminal Court system. VII.13.b. indicates cases of Royal Budapest Criminal District Courts of Justice to Budapest. VII.5.c. stands for the cases tried at the Budapest Royal Criminal Court.

58. On the Criminal Court system of Budapest, see György Bónis, *Fővárosi Levéltár (volt Budapesti 1. Sz. Állami Levéltár) 4: A jogszolgáltatás budapesti területi szervei* (Budapest: Művelődésügyi Minisztérium Levéltári Osztálya, 1961).

59. I arrived at this data by going through the annual index of the Criminal Courts and cataloging the number of cases with the charge of crime against nature.

60. The numbers reflect the cases tried according to the annual index of the Budapest Criminal Court and Criminal District Courts, BFL.

61. József Vogl, "Homoszexualitas," in Turcsányi, *A modern bűnözés I*, 142. The numbers Vogl cites come from police statistics between 1926 and 1929. During this time, according to Vogl, there were 345 people from the homosexual registry who had been already prosecuted and an approximately similar number who were being prosecuted at the time of him writing the report.

62. Vogl.

63. Sex with a minor: All following cases in VII.5.c. 5083/22/1923, 13295/4/1924 (one month), 15222/7/1926, B.III., 13331/2/1928, 1779/6/1928, 7093/3/1928, 12237/7/1929, BFL.

Penalties ranged from one month (in the case of having consensual sex with a seventeen-year-old) to a year and a half (for having sexual acts with boys under fourteen). In terms of nonconsensual sex between adult men Paragraph 242): All following cases in VII.5.c. 11928/20/1922, 13295/4/1924, 7310/18/1925. Depending on the severity of harm and level of force applied, the sentences ranged from six months in prison to two and a half years.

64. *Ügyészség* in Hungarian.

65. A detailed description of what some of the major contemporary differences were both in other countries as well as in Hungary is provided by Pál Angyal in *A szemérem elleni büntettek és vétségek*, 80–83.

66. It is likely that while following the arrest and registering of men who were allegedly homosexuals, unless their acts could be definitely labeled as "unnatural fornication," the police let the men free without any charges. VII.5.c. 9302/9/1925, VII.5.c. 15222/7/1926.

67. Out of the approximately fifty-five cases between 1910 and 1930 and forty cases between 1930 and 1940, there were only seven cases where people with social and economic means were involved.

68. Ten out of fifty-five men were married between 1918 and 1930, and eight out of forty cases between 1930 and 1940. The percentage of men who were married among the accused was much lower than average marriage rate in Budapest during this period. The marriage rate for men between twenty and sixty in Budapest during the 1920s and 1930s was about 55 percent. Gábor Doros and József Melly, *A nemi betegségek kérdése Budapesten II* (Budapest: Székesfővárosi házinyomda, 1930), 123.

69. About two hundred thousand Jews lived in Budapest during the interwar period, constituting over 20 percent of the population. In contrast to the criminal cases, in the homosexual registry Jewish men were actually underrepresented. The study of the reasons for higher representation of Jewish men in the criminal system would be an important inquiry. In this respect the situation of Budapest would make an interesting comparison to London, where according to Matt Houlbrook in *Queer London*, Jewish men were systematically underrepresented.

70. If the accused were under eighteen years old, the court would direct their cases to the Juvenile Criminal Court.

71. England seemed to be an exception where the courts tended to sentence older men (between thirty and sixty years old). For a comparative European account, see Tamagne's *A History of Homosexuality in Europe*, 137, 164.

72. The actual sentence depended on the specific circumstances as well as the defendant's mental and physical well-being. For this reason, the courts could require a forensic medical opinion.

73. The cases in which the punishment was suspended include VII.13.b. 12970/1919, VII.13.b. 22050/1921, VII.5.c. 7550/1922; or when the fine was suspended: All cases in VII.5.c. 12600/6/1921, 4051/7/1926, 13298/3/1927, 8614/15/1930.

74. Eight cases (in VII.13.b.: 17438/1919, 21944/1920, 19630/1921; in VII 5.c.: 16136/9/1921, 8785/5/1922, 78/1926, 5552/7/1927, 3259/5/1930) out of fifty-five were dismissed for the lack of adequate proof during the 1920s, and five (B.I. 31406/2/1931, B.X. 31917/14/1934, Bf.I. 6045/17/1939, Bf.II. 3546/6/1939, Bf.I. 18270/7/1942) of forty during the 1930s.

75. That was at times true even when the witness was a policeman.

76. In addition, quite often when the suspect was given an actual prison sentence for consensual homosexuality, the courts would rule to have a prison sentence include the length of time the accused had already been in custody, in which case the person was set free soon after the trial ended. See, for instance, VII.13.b. 26199/1920, VII.5.c. 13589/17/1927, VII.5.c. 8990/8/1927.

77. In 1931 I found only seven cases in the criminal courts of Budapest, while in 1932–36 the numbers ranged from twenty-five to thirty-six.

78. It is impossible to provide the exact statistical breakdown of the percentage of "unnatural fornication" cases in which minors were involved. Nevertheless, out of the surviving cases, there were seven cases: All following cases in VII.5.c.: 8614/15/1930, B.VII. 1920/7/1930, B.IX. 36393/7/1931, B.II. 16116/25/1931, B.II. 21.366/49/1932, B.II. 40130/13/1937, B.II. 34158/5/1940.

79. Cases of Paragraph 242 include B.VII. 5315/8/1934, B.XI. 7687/5/1937, B.VIII. 2825/3/1938, B.VIII. 9551/6/1940, B.VIII. 7157/10/1940, B.VIII. 360/4/1941.

80. Theft and stealing: All following cases in VII.5.c.: 11539/3/1929, B.XIX. 119/2/1936, B.XXVIII. 8522/3/1936, B.XXX. 12060/13/1936, B.VIII. 13359/10/1936, B.XXX. 741/4/1938, B.XXVIII. 11.012/3/1938, B.XXIX. 10566/5/1941. Bribery: VII.5.c. 11985/10/1920, B.V. 11082/6/1939.

81. Punishment ranged from a month to years in prison.

82. Péter Héczey in *A modern bűnözés I*, 13–30, 120–21. For a European perspective, see Herzog, *Sexuality in Europe*, 45–95.

83. Szántó, "A homosexualis férfiprostitutio kérdése," *Népegészségügy*, nos. 20–21 (1934): 774–79, 826–34, 829.

84. Szántó, 827.

85. Szántó, 828.

86. Szántó.

87. Szántó, 829.

88. For a concise summary of regulations of female prostitution, see Anka László's "A budapesti prostitúció és szexpiac története a boldog békeidőkben," *Valóság* 47, no. 2 (2004): 82–105.

89. Ordinance 151.000/1927 §4.

90. For a comprehensive list of regulations of female prostitutes and women accused of prostitution, see Biró, *A prostitúció*, 206–20.

91. Herzog, *Sexuality in Europe*, 45–83.

92. Szántó, "A homosexualis férfiprostitutio kérdése," 829.

93. Hungary's confinement of prostitution into fixed state-controlled brothels was similar to fascist Italy's treatment of prostitution. On the Italy, see Victoria De Grazia, *How Fascism Ruled Women: Italy, 1922–1945* (Berkeley: University of California Press, 1992), 44.

94. Matt Houlbrook's "Soldier Heroes and Rent Boys: Homosex, Masculinities, and Britishness in the Brigade of Guards, circa 1900–1960," *Journal of British Studies* 42, no. 3 (2003): 351; Jeffrey Weeks's "Inverts, Perverts, and Mary-Annes," 130–32.

95. Szántó, "A homosexualis férfiprostitutio kérdése," 829.

96. 1913. évi XXI. Törvénycikk: A közveszélyes munkakerülőkről.

97. Unlike in the case of women, it did not require any deeds or actions on behalf of the men who were registered. According to Szántó the 1,695 registered male prostitutes faced no (forced) medical exam and did not have to file paperwork for permits or go through regular check-ins with the police.

98. Szántó, "A homosexualis férfiprostitutio kérdése," 831.

99. Szántó advocated for Paragraph 66 of the municipal order 881-1008/1907 of 1907 (that grants license to restaurants and cafés to have prostitution) to be implemented for male prostitution as well. Thus, those establishments (cafés and restaurants) would be granted permission to host and facilitate homosexual prostitution.

100. Hospitals were set up in the Austro-Hungarian monarchy from 1916. On the relationship between soldiers' trauma on the front and interwar medical practices and gender politics in the German context, see Paul F. Lerner's *Hysterical Men: War, Psychiatry, and the Politics of Trauma in Germany, 1890–1930* (Ithaca, NY: Cornell University Press, 2003).

101. Nancy Wingfield and Maria Bucur, eds., *Gender and War in Twentieth-Century Eastern Europe* (Bloomington: Indiana University Press, 2006), introduction, and especially Maureen Healy's "Civilizing the Soldier in Postwar Austria," which is a more specific case study and analysis of Central Europe post–World War I. Robert A. Nye, "Western Masculinities in War and Peace," 417–38.

102. László Foscher, "A nemi élet zavarai," in *A család egészsége: Népszerű orvosi tájékoztató és tanácsadó*, 2nd ed., ed. Béla Somogyi (Budapest: Dante Könyvkiadó, 1928), 588–90.

103. Szántó, "A homosexualis férfiprostitutio kérdése," 831.

104. Szántó.

105. György Lukács, in his report on Hungary's public health points out how 50 percent of infertility is caused by sexually transmitted diseases in *Népegészségügy Magyarországon*, 16.

106. Szántó, "A homosexualis férfiprostitutio kérdése," 830. The statement could also be interpreted as a manifestation of a greater cultural change, where, at least in some people's view, the satisfaction of individual desire became a basic principle of life. On the relationship between sexology and cultural shift to a consumerist culture and society, see Matt Cook's *London and the Culture of Homosexuality, 1885–1914*, 82; and Harry Oosterhuis, in *Stepchildren of Nature*, 80. For an even more positive approach to homosexuality, see György Pál, *A homoszexuális probléma modem megvilágításban*.

107. For an example, see Doros and Melly, *A nemi betegségek kérdése Budapesten II*, 547–60.

108. Szántó, "A homosexualis férfiprostitutio kérdése," 830.

109. See György Pál, in *A homoszexuális probléma modem megvilágításban*.

110. The distinction between pseudo- and constitutional homosexuality was widely shared in Central Europe and beyond. See, for instance, in Sweden, Jen Rydström's *Sinners and Citizens*, 178.

111. József Vogl, "Homosexualitas," in Turcsányi, *A modern bűnözés I*, 115.

112. Mark Cronwall, *The Devil's Wall: The Nationalist Youth Mission of Heinz Rutha* (Cambridge, MA: Harvard University Press, 2012).

113. Sándor Márai, *Zendülők* (Budapest: Pantehon, 1930); Antal Szerb, *Utas és holdvilág* (Budapest: John Rodker, 1937).

114. For a detailed analysis of sexuality in *Utas és holdvilág*, see József Havasréti, "'Egyesek és mások' Szerb Antal: Utas és holdvilág," *Jelenkor: Irodalmi és művészeti folyóirat* 54, no. 4 (2011) 427–50.

115. György Sárközi, "A Zendülők," *Nyugat*, no 14. (1930), http://epa.oszk.hu/00000/00022/00494/15359.htm, accessed April 24, 2019.

116. Sárközi.

117. This approach stood in sharp contrast to the approach of Nazi Germany, where authorities used the idea of "fluid sexuality" for punitive effects. See chaps. 1, 2, and 3 in Dagmar Herzog's *Sex after Fascism: Memory and Morality in Twentieth-Century Germany* (Princeton, NJ: Princeton University Press, 2007).

118. Hungary had sixty-eight people with sexually transmitted diseases per ten thousand inhabitants; while Germany had fifty-eight; Sweden, twenty-three; and Norway, thirty. However, considering that about 70 percent of sexually transmitted illnesses were concentrated in urban areas and that Budapest was an urban monopoly in Hungary, the rates of sexually transmitted diseases in Budapest were seriously alarming. Doros and Melly, *A nemi betegségek kérdése Budapesten I–II*, introduction. While in 1932 there were nine facilities, by 1940 there were thirty-two facilities that specialized in treating venereal disease.

119. The organized fight against venereal disease and sexually transmitted diseases in more general started before and intensified during World War I under the aegis of Professor Lajos Nékám. From the late 1920s, the Anti-Venereal Association received wide attention in official publications as well as in the mass media. The issue of venereal disease and syphilis was also regularly discussed in the parliament throughout the 1930s.

120. On Catholic ideas on homosexuality, see Gábor Szegedi, "Stand by Your Man: Honor and Race Defilement in Hungary, 1941–44," *Hungarian Historical Review* 4, no. 3 (2015): 580–81.

121. Illés II. 296, cited in Angyal, *A szemérem elleni büntettek és vétségek*, 86.

122. On the evolution of eugenics in the Hungarian context pre-1918, see Turda, "The First Debates on Eugenics in Hungary, 1910–1918." While a comprehensive history of eugenics of the interwar era is yet to be written, János Gyurgyák's *Magyar fajvédők: Eszmetörténeti tanulmány* provides a useful overview of the relationship between different political actors and eugenics. Attila Kund and Marius Turda both contextualize Hungarian eugenic ideas in relation to Western ones. See Turda's "In Pursuit of Greater Hungary: Eugenic Ideas of Social and Biological Improvement, 1940–1941," *Journal of Modern History* 85, no. 3 (2013): 558–91; Kund, in "'Duties for Her Race and Nation': Scientific Racist Views on Sexuality and Reproduction in 1920s Hungary," *Sexualities* 19, nos. 1–2 (February 1, 2016): 190–210.

123. This was true not only for Hungary but all nations fighting in World War I. Marius Turda, *Modernism and Eugenics* (New York: Palgrave Macmillan, 2010), 40–63.

124. Kund, "'Duties for Her Race and Nation,'" 204.

125. The most well-known race biologist was Lajos Méhely, who was the editor of *Cél* (Goal), the publication of the radical right, which served as the primary public face

of the Hungarian race protectors. On Méhely's work, see Attila Kund, "Méhely Lajos és a magyar fajbiológiai kísérlete (1920–1931)," *Múltunk* 57, no. 4 (2012): 239–89.

126. On the power of eugenic ideas in shaping attitudes toward homosexuality in the broader European context during the interwar years, see Herzog's analysis in chap. 2 of *Sexuality in Europe*.

127. During these discussions, female homosexuality was never raised as an issue requiring medical intervention.

128. In 1930 Pope Pius XI condemned sterilization explicitly, and more generally, the Catholic Church was against negative eugenic measures. The Hungarian Catholic Church followed the *Casti connubii* encyclical. For a contemporary view of the Hungarian church and its rejection of negative eugenics, see Tihamér Tóth, "Eugenika és katolicizmus," in *Az 1934. évi előadások: Eugenika-élettan-származástan-örökléstan-embertan-pedagógia* (Budapest: Korda R. T. kiadása, 1935), 1–41. In addition to the Christian churches' resistance to negative eugenics, the fact that the Hungarian state was financially unsound also played a role in why eugenics, particularly negative eugenic policies, did not become institutionalized.

129. Judit Takács and Gábor Csiszár, "Nemváltások és Nemiszerep-áthágások Reprezentációi Az Estben 1910 és 1939 Között," 209–25.

130. Major radical right daily publications of the 1930s and 1940s include *Egyedül Vagyunk*, *Függetlenség*, *Nemzet Szava*, *Magyarság*, and *Magyar Futár*, as well as the periodical publications *Nép* and *Nyilas évkönyv*.

131. See, for instance, Gyula Dessewffy "Népközösség, új szociálpolitika, néphadsereg," *Egyedül Vagyunk*, October 6, 1938, 1.

132. There is an extensive scholarship on the role of the radical right parties and their effects on government policies directed at Hungary's Jewish population. The seminal work in English is Randolph L. Braham's *The Politics of Genocide: The Holocaust in Hungary* (New York: Columbia University Press, 1981). More recent works by Hungarian historians include Vera Ranki's *The Politics of Inclusion and Exclusion: Jews and Nationalism in Hungary* (New York: Holmes & Meier, 1999) and János Gyurgyák's *A zsidókérdés Magyarországon: Politikai eszmetörténet* (Budapest: Osiris, 2001).

133. The few exceptions include racial scientists such as János Gáspár, "A Fajok Összehasonlító Pathologiája," cited in Kund, "'Duties for Her Race and Nation,'" 202.

134. On homosexuality in the SA, see Andrew Wackerfuss, *Stormtrooper Families: Homosexuality and Community in the Early Nazi Movement* (New York: Harrington Park Press, 2015).

135. The pro-German National Socialist paper *Függetlenség* published some of the earliest articles on the Nazi eugenic laws and advocated sterilization. See, for instance, "Finom Kis Család: Terméktelenítsük-e az elmebetegeket?," April 19, 1936, 19. One of the first articles to address Nazi eugenic policy in the Arrow Cross Party's paper, *Nemzet Szava*, is "Fajegészségtan a nemzeti szocializmus szolgálatában: Vitéz Csík László dr. előadása a szegedi nyilasoknál," April 4, 1937, 5. Following these reports articles about eugenics become frequent in both papers.

136. Newspapers across the political spectrum reported on Röhm's homosexuality. See, for instance, *Népszava*, April 7, 1933; April 4, 1934; *Pesti Napló*, July 1, July 3, 1934.

137. Angyal, *A szemérem elleni büntettek és vétségek*, 77–83.

138. See, for instance, Angyal, 8–20, 71–87; Albert Irk, "A sterilizáció és kasztráció kriminálpolitikai szempontból," in *Büntetőjogi dolgozatok: Finkey Ferenc irodalmi munkássága négy évtizedes évfordulójának emlékére*, ed. Albert Irk (Pécs: Dunántúl Pécsi Egyetemi Könyvkiadó és Nyomda, 1936), 133.

139. On the Nazi's prosecution of homosexuals, see Günter Grau et al., eds., *Hidden Holocaust? Gay and Lesbian Persecution in Germany, 1933–45* (Chicago: Fitzroy Dearborn, 1995). More recent works include William Spurlin, *Lost Intimacies: Rethinking Homosexuality under National Socialism* (New York: Peter Lang, 2009); Edward Dickinson, "Policing Sex in Germany, 1882–1982." As most of this recent scholarship points out, the treatment of homosexuals, unlike of the Jewish people, was by no means uniform and varied considerably in the Third Reich.

140. Angyal, *A negatív eugenikai irány büntetőjogi vonatkozásai*, 133.

141. Angyal, *Fajvédelem és büntetőjog* (Budapest: Attila-Nyomda Részvénytársaság Kiadása, 1938), 13–14.

142. At the same time, Angyal and his legal contemporaries were in favor of institutionalizing positive eugenic measures that were already in place in Nazi Germany. Angyal, *Fajvédelem és büntetőjog*, 14. On positive eugenics in Nazi German, see Aly Götz, *Hitler's Beneficiaries: Plunder, Racial War, and the Nazi Welfare State* (New York: Metropolitan, 2007).

143. The Nazis passed an amendment to §175 of the German penal code that made all same-sex sexual contacts illegal and prohibited any behavior that was deemed to have a sexual intent, including kissing, fondling, or even simply looking. On the history of the legal amendment to §175, see Geoffrey Giles, "Legislating Homophobia in the Third Reich: The Radicalization of Prosecution against Homosexuality by the Legal Profession," *German History* 23, no. 3 (2005): 339–54.

144. On the intellectual debates between so-called *urbanus* (urban) and *népi* (folk) groups, see Gyurgyák, *Ezzé lett magyar hazátok*, 150–300.

145. Herzog, *Sexuality in Europe*, 55.

146. As Laurie Marhoefer in *Sex and the Weimar Republic* (Toronto: University of Toronto Press, 2015) shows, the greater toleration of certain nonnormative sexuality could be predicated on the more intense policing and controlling of other sexuality in general.

CHAPTER SIX

1. Until 1938 fascist Italy was a much closer ally to Hungary. From 1938 on, however, ties with Nazi Germany became more extensive, including economic, cultural, and eventually military relations. For a comprehensive account of Hungary's political and military history during World War II, see Ignác Romsics, ed., *Magyarország a második világháborúban* (Budapest: Kossuth Könyvkiadó, 2011). In English see Deborah S. Cornelius, *Hungary in World War II: Caught in the Cauldron*, 3rd ed. (New York: Fordham University Press, 2011).

2. Between 1937 and 1939, there were a number of restrictions placed on leaders of the Hungarian radical right movements. Despite conservatives' attempts to curtail Ferenc

Szálasi's Nyilaskeresztes párt–Hungarista mozgalom (Arrow Cross Party–Hungarista movement), the party gained new members at an unprecedented pace.

3. At the onset of the war in September 1939, the government essentially suspended parliamentary rule of law and granted extensive power to the military and political leadership. Using the 1912 LXIII law, the government introduced the practice of *kivételes hatalom* (exceptional power).

4. On Hungary's internal politics during the war, see Pál Pritz, "Hátország: Kormánypolitika és a Társadalom," in Romsics, *Magyarország a második világháborúban*, 65–73.

5. As the result of the German and Italian arbitration in October 1938, territories in southern Slovakia and southern Carpathian Ruthenia, the areas known as the "Upper Land" in Hungarian, were returned to Hungary.

6. The fraught relationship between pro-Nazi politicians and more Anglophone members of the government took a drastic turn after the suicide of Pál Teleki, the Hungarian prime minister, on April 3, 1941.

7. An illustrative example is the article "Regényes Házasság a XIX században: Egy Európára szóló botrány, amely először buktatta meg a polgári házassági törvényjavaslatot," *Egyedül Vagyunk*, September 7, 1943, 4.

8. See, for instance "Embervásár," in *Nemzet Szava*, May 2, 1937, 2, and "Ismét letartóztattak két zsidónőt," in *Magyarság*, September 17, 1938, 4.

9. "Tömegesen züllenek el a falusi lányok Budapest zugelhelyező irodáiban," *Nép*, May 4, 1939, 7.

10. The most extreme representation of Jewish sexuality as the seed of all evil and something that needed to be eradicated comes from the pages of *Harc* (Fight), the official paper of the Hungarian Research Institute for the Jewish Question (established in 1944).

11. By allowing the German Army to travel through Hungary and, crucially, by accepting the promise of the return of its former territories, and by occupying *Vajdaság* (parts of Vojvodina), Hungary essentially entered the war in April 1941.

12. Article XV of Law of 1938, which became known as the *első zsidó törvény* (first [anti-]Jewish law), limited the percentage of Jews in white-collar professions. In determining Jewishness, the law defined Jewishness based on people's religious affiliation prior to 1920. Thus, by denying the legal recognition of converts post-1920, the law introduced the seeds of the Nuremberg Laws. The second Jewish law, Article IV of Law of 1939, in addition to further limiting public participation of Jews, defined people as part of the Jewish race by relying on their birth religion as well as of the religion of their parents and grandparents. The third Jewish Law (Article XV of Law 1941) fully adopted the terminology of the Nuremberg Laws and defined Jewishness as having two Jewish grandparents. The contributions of a recent publication by Judit Molnár, ed., *Számokba zárt sorsok: A numerus clausus 90 év távlatából* (Budapest: Holokauszt Emlékközpont, 2012), provides a succinct overview of the evolution of anti-Jewish laws during the interwar period.

13. 1941. Évi XV. Tc. A házassági jogról szóló 1894:XXXI. Törvénycikk kiegészítéséről és módosításáról, valamint az ezzel kapcsolatban szükséges fajvédelmi rendelkezésekről [Article XV of Law of 1941: The amendment of 1894 Marriage Law and Provisions of Related Required Race Protections]. The first paragraph of the law also mandated premarital medical examinations of both partners. The full text of the law is available in Hungarian at http://www.1000ev.hu/index.php?a=3&param=8168.

14. §15 of XV Article 1941. On the legal opinion of the interpretation of miscegenation law and on the contemporary concerns over its implementation into prosecutorial and legal practice, see the Decree no. 70651/1941 of B.M. [the Ministry of Interior].

15. According to Sándor Nagy, who studied the surviving court records of miscegenation cases, there were a couple of thousand cases (the great majority in Budapest) prosecuted under miscegenation charges, and ultimately the number of cases tried was at least a few hundred. Nagy, "A fajvédelem útvesztőjében: Bírói gyakorlat 'fajgyalázási' perekben," *Fons* 22, no. 4 (2015): 491. András Lugosi, "Sztalin főhercege: Kohn báró vacsorái a Falk Miksa utcában a fajgyalázási törvény idején," *Fons* 17, no. 4 (2010): 555–56; Gábor Szegedi, "Tisztaság, tisztesség, fajgyalázás: Szexuális és faji normalizáció a Horthy-korban," *Socio.hu* 5, no. 1 (2015): 70–73.

16. For an overview of the health screening, see Gábor Szegedi's "Good Health Is the Best Dowry," 164–92.

17. Szegedi.

18. According to the Budapest Criminal Court index, in 1935 there were thirty-two cases; in 1936, thirty-five cases; twenty-four in 1937; thirty-two in 1938; thirty-plus (one index book is missing) in 1939; and forty cases in 1940.

19. As an entry from the *Arrow Cross Yearbook* demands, the perfecting of the Hungarian race (to become a master military race) required "the legislation of eugenic laws that mandate public health interventions to prohibit the reproduction of unhealthy and those people who are unable to produce healthy offspring." Pál Vágó, "Vér és faj törvénye," *Nyilas évkönyv*, 1941, 20. For the demands about the expulsion of Jews, see Nagy József, "Kereszténység és nemzetiszocializmus két édestestvér!," *Nyilas évkönyv*, 1941, 48–53. On the quarantining of the Roma, see "Az bizonyos cigánykérdés: Tiltakozzunk a vérkeveredés ellen," *Magyarság*, August 19, 1940, 12.

20. This was especially the case in terms of the two Arrow Cross papers, *Nemzet Szava* and *Magyarság*. A revealing example is Dr. Negyessy, Zoltán, "A magyar jövő álma," *Nemzet Szava*, August 18, 1940, 3.

21. The exclusion of Roma people (also known as Gypsies) was much less systematic than the Jewish people. For instance, until 1944 Romas could fight in the Hungarian Army. At the same time, during the war, there were increased numbers of atrocities against their communities, especially in the recently annexed territories. In 1944, however, the situation of Romas rapidly deteriorated; they were conscripted into forced labor and also sent to concentration camps. For the history of the Roma during World War II, see László Karsai, *A cigánykérdés Magyarországon, 1919–1945: Út a cigány Holocausthoz* (Budapest: Cserépfalvi, 1992).

22. A thorough examination of the archives holding material formerly belonging to the national army and national guard requires further study.

23. For the years of 1943 and 1944, the annual indexes of the Budapest Criminal Courts are missing. Thus, it is impossible to determine whether the charges continued to rise.

24. According to the National Security Law of 1939 II, during wartime and a time of alert, all people between seventeen and sixty could be called on to work to defend the nation.

25. Homoszexuális egyének bevonultatása munkaszolgálatra (benne névjegyzék a

fővárosi lakosokról.), 1942 HM 68763/Eln.1b. 1-1942, Hadtörténelmi Levéltár [Military History Archive]. German homosexuals along with asocial and political prisoners were used as forced laborers from the outbreak of the war. On forced labor and German homosexuals, see Plant, *Pink Triangle*, 152–82, and Grau et al., *Hidden Holocaust?*, 264–81.

26. I would like to thank Dr. Judit Takács for bringing the source to my attention.

27. 1942 HM 68763/Eln.1b. 1-1942.

28. 1942 HM 68763/Eln.1b. 1-1942, 2. The so-called *megbízhatatlan katonakötelesek* (unreliable military aged) was a category created as early as 1920. But it was a new law passed by Ministry of Defense in 1939—according to which those "unreliable" in military age could be required to perform forced labor service—that set up an extensive, and in many respects unique, forced labor system that operated throughout the war years. The most detailed account in English is Randolph L. Braham's *The Hungarian Labor Service System, 1939–1945* (Boulder, CO: East European Quarterly; distributed by Columbia University Press, 1977).

29. 1942 HM 68763/Eln.1b. 1-1942, 2.

30. 1942 HM 68763/Eln.1b. 1-1942, 3.

31. 1942 HM 68763/Eln.1b. 1-1942.

32. 1942 HM 68763/Eln.1b. 1-1942.

33. 1942 HM 68763/Eln.1b. 1-1942.

34. Dessewffy, "Népközösség, új szociálpolitika, néphadsereg."

35. Cecil D. Eby, *Hungary at War: Civilians and Soldiers in World War II* (University Park: Pennsylvania State University Press, 1998), 17–18.

36. Eby, 17.

37. Eby.

38. On the Hungarian Army in World War II in English, see Thomas Nigel and László P. Szabó, *The Royal Hungarian Army in World War II* (New York: Osprey Publications, 2008).

39. 1942 HM 68763/Eln.1b. 4.

40. 1942 HM 68763/Eln.1b. 3.

41. 1942 HM 68763/Eln.1b. 3. Italics are mine. Vilmos Nagy de Nagybaczoni, the former commanding officer of Hungarian First Army, was the minister of defense between September 24, 1942, and June 12, 1943.

42. The situation of Nagy de Nagybaczoni illustrates the pressure that old conservatives felt to comply with the rapidly radicalizing rightist demands. He categorically rejected the attempts of radical right politicians to apply Nazi measures on the treatment of Jews and more generally "enemies" of the state. In turn, Nagy de Nagybaczoni was constantly attacked for being a "Jewish hireling" and anti-Axis. In this respect the request and consequent denial of the conscription of homosexuals by Nagy in December 1942 can be seen as a victory, albeit brief, for the old conservatives. Feeling he lost the support of Horthy, he stepped down on June 12, 1943. Following the official takeover of the Arrow Cross, Nagy was arrested.

43. For an overview of the Kállay government and its foreign and domestic policies, see Braham's *The Politics of Genocide*, vol. 1, chap. 7.

44. Rudolf Paksa, *Szálasi Ferenc és a hungarizmus* (Budapest: Jaffa Kiadó, 2013), 155–56.

45. On the situation of Jewish people from March 1944 until the end of the war, the most comprehensive work remains Braham's *The Politics of Genocide*, 181–98. On the prosecution of Roma during the same time, see Karsai's *A cigánykérdés Magyarországon, 1919–1945*, 85–136.

46. On the leader of the Arrow Cross Party and his vision, see Paksa, *Szálasi Ferenc és a hungarizmus*. The legal proposal and a comprehensive explanation of the Family Law are found in the collection of political and military documents (K814) at the Hungarian National Archives (MNL).

47. There is yet to be a comprehensive analysis of the historical origins and content of the Family Law. Krisztián Ungváry has addressed it in an interview, "Milyen volt a Hungarista családmodell?," in *Népszabadság Online*, June 8, 2002, http://nol.hu/archivum/archiv-65754-49654, accessed February 16, 2016. In addition, see László Karsai, *Szálasi Ferenc: Politkai életrajz* (Budapest: Balassi Kiadó, 2016), 291–95.

48. §9 of the Family Law made premarital medical examination mandatory and prohibited marriage not only between Hungarians and Jews but also between Roma and Jews and between people of mixed Jewish and mixed Roma heritage.

49. Szeredi testvér, "Általános indoklás a család tervezetehez," MNL/K814/ X7076 -16722/1057.

50. Szeredi testvér, "Általános indoklás a család tervezetehez."

51. §32 of the Family Law, MNL/K814/ X7076-16.729/50–51.

52. §32 of the Family Law, MNL/K814/ X7076-16.729/50–51.

53. On the issue of castration and homosexuals in the Germany, see Geoffrey J. Giles, "The Most Unkindest Cut of All: Castration, Homosexuality, and Nazi Justice," *Journal of Contemporary History* 27, no. 1 (1992): 41–61. The castration of homosexuals had become part of a broader trend of the treatment of homosexuality. Castration of homosexuals, for instance, had been performed in the US since the 1880s. See Jennifer Terry, *An American Obsession: Science, Medicine, and Homosexuality in Modern Society* (Chicago: University of Chicago Press, 2010), 81.

54. The most explicit evidence comes from a postwar interview with Szálasi, who stated that homosexuality was natural for some people. In Rezső Szirmai, *Fasiszta lelkek: Pszichoanalitikus beszélgetések a háborús főbűnösökkel a börtönben* (Budapest: Pelikán, 1993). This was not unlike in the case of Nazi Germany where in terms of their personal opinions many of the high-ranking Nazi officials also cared little about homosexuality in private or believed in the monogamous sanctity of marriage. On the personal views of Nazi officials, see Anna Maria Sigmund's *"Das Geschlechtsleben bestimmen wir": Sexualität im Dritten Reich* (Munich: Heyne, 2008). Also, Andrew Wackerfuss's *Stormtrooper Families*.

55. Although Hungary signed a peace agreement with the Allies in January 20, 1945, the actual fighting between the retreating German and Hungarian fascist armies and the Soviet forces continued until April 1945.

56. By the end of the war, the vast majority of police records including registries were either destroyed or taken outside of the country. As to what happened during the last few months of the war, for instance, in terms of the Arrow Cross's access to the homosexual registry, there is no existing evidence.

57. For Hungary's case vis-à-vis other countries within the Soviet sphere, see Robert

Gellately, *Stalin's Curse: Battling for Communism in War and Cold War* (New York: Vintage, 2013), 225–61.

58. On the internal deportations of Hungarians deemed "enemies of the state," see Kinga Szechenyi's *Stigmatized: A History of Hungary's Internal Deportations during the Communist Dictatorship* (Budapest: Central European University Press, 2016).

59. Krisztian Ungváry, *Battle for Budapest: 100 Days in World War II*, trans. Ladislaus Lob (London: I. B. Tauris, 2011).

60. The Yalta Conference in February 1945 confirmed the Moscow agreement. Peter Kenez, *Hungary from the Nazis to the Soviets: The Establishment of the Communist Regime in Hungary, 1944–1948* (New York: Cambridge University Press, 2006), 61–66.

61. Ungváry, *The Battle for Budapest*, introduction.

62. On the platform of each of these parties, see György Litván, "Koalíciós közjáték, 1945–1948," *Rubicon* 7, nos. 1–2 (1996), http://www.rubicon.hu/magyar/oldalak/koalicios_kozjatak_1945_1948/, accessed July 17, 2017.

63. Kenez, *Hungary from the Nazis to the Soviets*, 107–8.

64. Kenez, 119–40.

65. For an overview, see Kateřina Lišková, *Sexual Liberation, Socialist Style: Communist Czechoslovakia and the Science of Desire, 1945–1989* (New York: Cambridge University Press, 2018), chap. 1.

66. On the effects of that change, see Lynne Haney, *Inventing the Needy Gender and the Politics of Welfare in Hungary* (Berkeley: University of California Press, 2002), 91–131.

67. Sándor Horváth, *Stalinism Reloaded: Everyday Life in Stalin-City, Hungary*, trans. Thomas Cooper (Bloomington: Indiana University Press, 2017), 146–48.

68. On leftist ideologies on homosexuality, see Gert Hekma et al., eds., *Gay Men and the Sexual History of the Political Left* (New York: Harrington Park Press, 1995).

69. Hekma et al., "Leftist Sexual Politics and Homosexuality: A Historical Overview," in *Gay Men and the Sexual History of the Political Left*, 8.

70. On Communists' interpretations of fascisms, see Kata Bohus, "Not a Jewish Question? The Holocaust in Hungary in the Press and Propaganda of the Kádár Regime during the Trial of Adolf Eichmann," *Hungarian Historical Review* 4, no. 3 (2015): 737–72.

71. István Ötvös, "Koncepciós perek," *Rubicon* 26, no. 10 (2015): 54–58.

72. The (re)discovery of Hannah Arendt's *The Origins of Totalitarianism* (New York: Schocken Books, 1951) among Hungarian historians especially on the right is significant. By labeling both the Arrow Cross and post–World War II Communist regime as "totalitarian," conservative historians work to exonerate the Horthy regime. At the same time, historians associated with the left and liberals in and outside of Hungary emphasize the continuities within these regimes. For an overview of the historians' debate, see Máté Rigó, "A Hungarian Version of the Historikerstreit? A Summary of the Romsics-Gerő Debate among Hungarian Historians" (2012), in Forum Geschichtskulturen, Hungary, http://www.imre-kertesz-kolleg.uni-jena.de/index.php?id=415&l=0, accessed February 7, 2018.

73. László Borhi, "Stalinist Terror in Hungary, 1945–1956," in *Stalinist Terror in*

Eastern Europe: Elite Purges and Mass Repression, ed. Kevin McDermott and Matthew Stibbe (New York: Manchester University Press, 2010), 119–40.

74. MDP Budapesti Pártbizottságának ülései (XXXV.95.a.), November 17, 1953.

75. MDP Budapesti Pártbizottságának ülései (XXXV.95.a.), June 29, 1952.

76. Paul Betts, *Within Walls: Private Life in German Democratic Republic* (Oxford: Oxford University Press, 2010), 33.

77. On the framing of homosexuals as Communist in the US, see David K. Johnson, *The Lavender Scare: The Cold War Persecution of Gays and Lesbians in the Federal Government* (Chicago: University of Chicago Press, 2006), introduction.

78. Borhi, "Stalinist Terror in Hungary, 1945–1956," 123.

79. On Western Europe, see Herzog, *Sexuality in Europe*, 117–19; on the US, see Chauncey, *Gay New York*, 360; on East Germany, see Jennifer V. Evans, "Decriminalization, Seduction, and 'Unnatural Desire' in East Germany," *Feminist Studies* 36, no. 3 (2010): 553–77.

80. While until 1953 the treatment of homosexuals was relatively lenient in East Germany, following 1953 homosexuals became seen as the enemy of the socialism. Evans, "Decriminalization, Seduction, and 'Unnatural Desire,'" 557.

81. XXV.4.a. 198/1955/11, BFL.

82. Evans, "Decriminalization, Seduction, and 'Unnatural Desire' in East Germany," 558.

83. XXV.4.a. cases involving charges of Paragraph 337 "unnatural fornication," BFL.

84. On the history of judiciary under Communists, see Ervin Belovics, *Büntetőjog I.; Általános rész*, 2nd ed. (Budapest: HVG—ORAC Lap és Könyvkiadó Kft., 2018), 35–42.

85. XXV.4.a. 3663/1954, BFL.

86. XXV.4 a. 1649/1955, BFL.

87. XXV.4.a. 633/1953, BFL.

88. XXV.4a. 7355/1952, BFL.

89. XXV.4.a. 7355/1952, BFL.

90. XXV.4a. 7355/1952, BFL. For a discussion of bourgeois morality in the East German context, see Günter Grau, "Return of the Past: The Policy of the SED and the Laws against Homosexuality in Eastern Germany between 1946 and 1968," *Journal of Homosexuality* 37, no. 4 (1999): 1–21.

91. There were some rare exceptions, when citing the court would order a retrial based on improper police procedures. See, for instance, XXV.4.a. 6843/1955, BFL.

92. For an illustrative example, see XXV.4.a. 3018/1954, BFL.

93. See, for instance, all following cases in XXV4.a: 7355/1952; 5621/1952; 2118/1952; 1255/1955, BFL.

94. On the initial reforms of Hungarian institutions, see György Gyarmati, *A Rákosi-korszak: Rendszerváltó fordulatok évtizede Magyarországon, 1945–1956* (Budapest: Rubicon-Ház B.T., 2013), 130–48.

95. On the transformation of cultural institutions during the early 1950s, see György Gyarmati, *Demokráciából a diktatúrába 1945–1956* (Budapest: Kossuth Kiadó, 2010), 73–81.

96. XXV4.a. 1199/1953, BFL.

97. XXV4.a. 1199/1953, BFL.

98. XXV4.a. 3077/1954, BFL.

99. Judit Takács and Tamás P. Tóth, "Az 'Idegbizottság' szerepe a homoszexualitás magyarországi dekriminalizációjában," *Socio.hu: Társadalmi Tudományi Szemle*, no. 2 (2016): 226–42.

100. XXVIII. 4908/1959, BFL.

101. XXVIII. 4908/1959, BFL.

102. The first Polish penal code of 1932 no longer criminalized consensual male homosexual acts with the exception of solicitation, which remained criminalized for both sexes. East Germany decriminalized consensual homosexual acts in 1968, West Germany in 1969, the United Kingdom in 1967. In the US, Illinois was the first state to remove sodomy laws from its criminal code in 1962, with most northern and midwestern states following in the 1970s and 1980s. However, it was not until 2003 that sodomy was constitutionally outlawed, invalidating the still existing criminalization of same-sex sexual acts in fourteen (mostly southern) states.

103. Takács and P. Tóth, "Az 'Idegbizottság,'" 235.

104. Takács and P. Tóth, 233.

105. On the relationship between Hungarian medical communities and their Western counterparts, see Dora Vargha's *Polio across the Iron Curtain: Hungary's Cold War with an Epidemic* (Cambridge: Cambridge University Press, 2018).

106. MNL OL 1958a:6. Cited in Takács and P. Tóth, "Az 'Idegbizottság,'" 236.

107. On the succinct summary of medical understanding of homosexuality during this time, see Béla Buda, "Adalékok a férfi homoszexualitás etiológiájához és pszichodinamikájához," *Magyar Pszichológiai Szemle* 35, no. 4 (1978): 322–40.

108. On the Communists' views on sex and everyday practices of sex and contraception, see Eszter Zsófia Tóth and András Murai, *Szex és szocializmus* (Budapest: Libri Könyvkiadó, 2014), 13–27.

109. Dagmar Herzog, *Sexuality in Europe*, 124–25.

110. Herzog, 125. Italics in the original.

111. Takács and P. Tóth, "Az 'Idegbizottság,'" 238.

112. Cited in Takács and P. Tóth, "Az 'Idegbizottság,'" 236.

113. Cited by Adorján Linczényi, "A homoszexualitasról," in *A szexuális élet zavarai*, ed. Erzsébet Krúdy (Budapest: Medicina Könyvkiadó, 1977), 134.

114. Vera Sokolova, "State Approaches to Homosexuality and Non-Heterosexual Lives in Czechoslovakia during State-Socialism," in *Expropriated Voice: Transformations of Gender Culture in State-Socialist Czechoslovakia*, ed. Hana Havelkova and Libora Oates-Indruchova (New York: Routledge, 2014), 83.

115. Linczényi, "A homoszexualitasról," in *A szexuális élet zavarai*, 134.

116. The age of consent for homosexual sex was made higher in most countries that decriminalized it.

117. 1960. V. §279.

118. In 1978, in the new penal code, the age of consent for homosexuality was reduced to eighteen years.

119. Cited in Takács and P. Tóth, "Az 'Idegbizottság,'" 238.

120. On the political police, see Gábor Tabajdi and Krisztián Ungváry, *Elhallgatott múlt: A pártállam és a belügy: A politikai rendőrség működése Magyarországon 1956–1990* (Budapest: 1956-os Intézet; Corvina, 2008).

121. Bűnügyi nyilvántartási utasítás jelzet, 4.2. 50-6/5/1958, 6–7, ÁBTL.
122. Bűnügyi nyilvántartási utasítás jelzet, 4.2. 50-6/5/1958, 6–7, ÁBTL, 40.
123. For example, in the trial records of a murder case from 1966, the registry is cited as an instrument that "helped to track down the suspect and solve the case." BFL XXV.44.b—1966-30948.
124. This is evident from interviews conducted by László Cseh-Szombathy. Cseh-Szombathy László irathagyatéka XIV.77.4.d., BFL. See also Judit Takács and Tamás P. Tóth, "Megbélyegzett kapcsolatok az államszocialista Magyarországon," Socio.hu 7, no. 3 (2017): 63–85.
125. XIV. 77. 4.d, 14, BFL.
126. Cseh-Szombathy László irathagyatéka, 15.
127. Tóth and Murai, Szex és szocializmus, 41.
128. Anna Borgos, "Secret Years: Hungarian Lesbian Herstory, 1950s–2000s," Aspasia 9 (2015): 87–112; Judit Takács, "Homofóbia Magyarországon és Európában," in Homofóbia Magyarországon, ed. Judit Takács (Budapest: L'Harmattan, 2011), 15–34.
129. Prior to 1956, when the fear of internal enemies reached paranoid heights, State Security functioned essentially as the "fist" of the Communist Party. After 1957, while its power was no longer unrestrained, State Security remained the most important instrument in the hands of Communist leadership in controlling the population.
130. József Muzslai, Az ügynökség beszervezése (1957) 4.1. A—3081, 6.1., ÁBTL.
131. Muzslai, 71.
132. Personal conversation with archivist, ÁBTL, July 2015.
133. On the history of Communist policies against different religions, see contributions of Margit Balogh and Sándor Ladányí in the subchapter, "Egyházak a szovjet rendszerben (1945–1989)," in Magyarország a XX. században II: Természeti környezet, népesség és társadalom, egyházak és felekezetek, gazdaság, ed. István Kollega Tarsoly (Szekszárd: Babits Kiadó, 1997), 386–440.
134. On the details of the Mindszenty trial, see Margit Balogh, "A Mindszenty-per," Korunk 23, no. 7 (2012): 3–17. More generally, see Attila Viktor Soós, "Harc a 'klerikális reakció' ellen: Egyházüldözés Magyarországon 1945–1956 között," Rubicon 26, no. 10 (2015): 34–43.
135. Balogh, Magyarország a XX. században II, 398.
136. MSZMP Központi Bizottsága Agitációs és Propaganda Osztályának (APO) iratai 1–5. ő. e. May 5, 1960, 185.
137. 3.1.5. O-11802/18; 3.1.5. O-13838/1, ÁBTL.

EPILOGUE

1. Recently there have been a number of important publications in Hungarian that aim to recover Hungarian queer histories. For instance, Judit Takács's Meleg század: Adalékok a homoszexualitás 20. századi magyarországi társadalomtörténetéhez (Kalrigram: Budapest, 2018) as well as the publications of Roland Perényi and Borgos Anna.
2. The silence around queer sexualities prior to 1989 (and 1991) in the former countries of the Eastern Bloc is a general phenomenon. See, for instance, Vera Sokolova, "'Don't Get Pricked!': Representation and the Politics of Sexuality in the Czech Repub-

lic," in *Over the Wall/After the Fall: Post-Communist Cultures through an East-West Gaze*, ed. Sibelan Forrester et al. (Bloomington: Indiana University Press, 2004), 251–67. The exception is GDR, where from the 1970s, there is a more open discussion of homosexuality. Josie McLellan, "Glad to Be Gay behind the Wall: Gay and Lesbian Activism in 1970s East Germany" *History Workshop Journal* 74, no. 1 (2012): 105–30.

3. Gábor Tabajdi and Krisztián Ungváry, *Elhallgatott múlt*, 14.

4. More recently, there have been some important exceptions and people who are willing to share their experiences. See, for instance, interviews in Borgos, *Eltitkolt évek*, or the men in Mária Takács's documentary *Hot Men Cold Dictatorship* (2015).

5. Jobbik Magyarországért Mozgalom (The Movement for a Better Hungary) was founded in 2002. The party can be described as a ring-wing populist party based on ethnonationalism, antisemitism, anti-immigration, homophobia, and opposition to EU and globalization more generally. Amidst the global financial downturn and growing social tensions within Hungary, since 2008 Jobbik has seen a spectacular rise in popularity. In 2014 election it received over 20 percent of the popular vote.

6. The request of the amendment was filed by Ádám Mirkóczki, April 12, 2012. For the full text in Hungarian, see http://www.parlament.hu/irom39/06721/06721.pdf, accessed March 20, 2019.

7. "Büntetné a homoszexualitás népszerűsítését a Jobbik," MTI, April 11, 2012.

8. "Jobbik Considers the Propagation of Homosexuality on the Streets Socially Harmful," https://jobbik.hu/hireink/jobbik-tarsadalmilag-karosnak-tartja-homoszexualitas-propagalasat-budapest-utcain, accessed February 13, 2016.

9. Fidesz—Hungarian Civic Union (Magyar Polgári Szövetség). In the 2010 election, Fidesz, with the Christian Democratic People's Party (KDNP—an even more conservative party), won over two-thirds of the parliamentary seats. Since being in power, Fidesz has been systematically centralizing power in the hands of the government and weakening the institutions of checks and balances. In the 2014 election, Fidesz-KDNP won 45 percent of the popular vote and continues to be largest parliamentary party holding 117 of 199 seats.

10. For contemporary situation of LGBT issues for countries in East and East-Central Europe, see Chuck Stewart, *The Greenwood Encyclopedia of LGBT Issues Worldwide* (Santa Barbara: ABC-CLIO, 2010).

11. I use the word "queer" to denote the different identity groups based on sexual orientation. The main Hungarian LGBTQ organizations include Háttér Társaság, Labrisz Leszbikus Egyesület, and the more recent Inter Alia Alapítvány.

12. This is also implicit in more recent works that focus on queer sexualities in post-1989 East-East-Central European context. See Robert Kulpa and Joanna Mizielinska, eds., *De-Centring Western Sexualities: Central and Eastern European Perspectives* (London: Ashgate Publishing Limited, 2011), introduction, 11–26.

BIBLIOGRAPHY

ARCHIVES

Állambiztonsági Szolgálatok Történeti Levéltára (Historical Archives of the Hungarian State Security)
Budapesti Fővárosi Levéltár (Budapest City Archive)
Hadtörténelmi Levéltár (Military History Archive)
Magyar Nemzeti Levéltár (Hungarian National Archive)
Országgyűlési Könyvtár (Library of the Hungarian Parliament)
Országos Széchényi Könyvtár (National Széchényi Library)
Országos Széchényi Könyvtár Kézirattár (Manuscript Collection of the National Széchény Library)
Semmelweis Orvostörténeti Múzeuml és Levéltár (Semmelweis Medical History Museum and Archive)

PRIMARY SOURCES

Áldor, Viktor. *A prostitúció*. Vita Sexualis 4. Budapest: Viktória Nyomda, 1929.
Angyal, Pál. *Fajvédelem és büntetőjog*. Budapest: Attila-Nyomda Részvénytársaság Kiadása, 1938.
———. *A negatív eugenikai irány büntetőjogi vonatkozásai*. Budapest: Kisfaludi Nyomda, 1936.
———. *A psychoanalysis és a büntetőjog*. Budapest: Jogállam, 1937.
———. *A szemérem elleni büntettek és vétségek*. (A magyar büntetőjog kézikönyve 14.) Budapest: Attila-Nyomda Részvénytársaság Kiadása, 1937.
Baksa, János. *Rendőrségi almanach*. Budapest: Stephaneum Nyomda és Könyvkiadó R.T., 1923.
Balányi, Lajos. *Szabadítsuk meg a büntetettség keresztjétől a jó útra tért büntetett előéletőeket!* Budapest: Budai Nyomda, 1936.
Barcza, Ferenc. *Nemzeti szocializmus: Fasizmus magyar vonatkozásban*. Kalocsa: Szerző, 1932.

Belky, János. *Törvényszéki orvostan*. Budapest: Magyar Orvosi Könyvkiadó Társulat, 1895.

———. *A Törvényszéki orvostan alapvonalai, különös tekintettel az új magyar büntető törvénykönyvre*. Budapest: Eggenberger, 1880.

Biró, Béla. *A prostitúció*. Budapest: Magyar Királyi Rendőrség, 1933.

Borbély, Zoltán, and Rezső Dr. Kapy, eds. *A 60 éves magyar rendőrség 1881–1941*. Budapest: Halász Irodalmi és Könyvkiadó Vállalat, 1942.

Bovill, W. B. Forster. *Hungary and the Hungarians*. London: Methuen & Co, 1908.

Brichta, Kálmán. *Budapestnek vesznie kell! Röpirat*. Budapest: Heisler nyomda, 1891.

Buda, Béla. "Adalékok a férfi homoszexualitás etiológiájához és pszichodinamikájához." *Magyar Pszichológiai Szemle* 35, no. 4 (1978): 322–40.

Budapest székesfőváros statisztikai évkönyve az 1944–1946 évekről. Budapest: Központi Statisztikai Hivatal, 1948.

Doros, Gábor. *A nemi egészségügy problémái*. Budapest, 1928.

———. *A Prostitúció kérdése*. Budapest: Arany János Nyomda, 1935.

Doros, Gábor, and József Melly. *A nemi betegségek kérdése Budapesten I–II*. Budapest: Székesfővárosi házinyomda, 1930.

Ferenczi, Sándor. *A homosexualitas szerepe a paranoia pathogenesisében*. Budapest: Franklin Kiadó, 1911.

———. "Pszichoanalízis és kriminológia." *Új Forradalom* 1 (1919): 5–6.

———. "Pszichoanalízis és társadalompolitika." *Nyugat* 15 (1922): 554–55.

———. *A pszichoanalízis felé: Fiatalkori írások 1897–1908*. Edited by Judit Mészáros. Budapest: Osiris Kiadó, 1999.

Finkey, Ferenc. *A magyar büntetőjog tankönyve*. Budapest: Grill, 1914.

Fischer, Ignácz. "A homosexualitás és annak forensikus méltatása." *Magyar Jogászegyleti Értekezések* 295, no. 38: 4 (1909): 347–79.

Forel, August. *Die sexuelle Frage: Eine naturwissenschaftliche, psyhologische, hygienische und sozioloische Studie für Gebildete*. Munich: Ernst Reinhardt, 1905.

Foscher, László. "A nemi élet zavarai." In Béla Somogyi, *A család egészsége: Népszerű orvosi tájékoztató és tanácsad*, 388–90. 2nd ed. Budapest: Dante Könyvkiadó, 1928.

Fülep, Lajos. *A magyarság pusztulása*. Budapest: Magvető, 1984.

Gerencsér, Miklós. *Vörös könyv, 1919*. Lakitelep: Antológia Kiadó, 1993.

Guthi, Soma. *Homosexuális szerelem (Tuzár detektív naplója): Bűnügyi Regény*. Budapest: Kunossy, Szilágyi és társa Könyvkiadóvállalat, 1908.

Halász, Zoltán. "A szemérem elleni bűncselekményekről, különös tekintettel az erőszakos nemi közösülésre és a természet elleni fajtalanságra." *Magyar Jogászegyleti Értekezések* 296, no. 38 (1909): 5.

Hankiss, János. *Tormay Cécile*. Budapest: Singer & Wolfner, 1939.

Hetényi, Gyula. *A nőkérdés*. Budapest: Szociális Missziótársaság, 1920.

Imrédy, Béla. *Egyedül vagyunk!* Budapest: Stádium Nyomda, 1941.

Irk, Albert. *Büntetőjogi dolgozatok: Finkey Ferenc irodalmi munkássága négy évtizedes évfordulójának emlékére*. Pécs: Dunántúl Pécsi Egyetemi Könyvkiadó és Nyomda, 1936.

Kádár, Imre. "Aktuális kriminálpolitikai reformok." *Proletárjog: A Szocialista Jogászszövetség hivatalos lapja*, no. 11 (1919): 76–78.

Kenyeres, Balázs. *Törvényszéki orvostan*. Budapest: Magyar Orvosi Könyvkiadó Társulat, 1909.

Kollontai, Alexandra. *Selected Writings*. New York: W. W. Norton & Company, 1980.

Kornfeld, Móric. *Reflections on Twentieth Century Hungary: A Hungarian Magnate's View*. Translated by Thomas J. DeKornfeld and Helen D. Kornfeld. Boulder, CO: Social Science Monographs; distributed by Columbia University Press, 2007.

Kostyál, Jenő. *A budapesti leányvásár titkai*. Budapest: Fritz Ármin könyvnyomdája, 1902.

Kosztolányi, Dezső. *Édes Anna*. Budapest: Genius, 1926.

Krafft-Ebing, Richard. *Psychopathia Sexualis: A visszás nemi érzések különös figyelembe Vételével. Orvos-törvényszéki tanulmány*. Translated by Jakab Fischer. Budapest: Singerés Wolfner Kiadása, 1894.

Krúdy, Erzsébet, ed. *A szexuális élet zavarai*. Budapest: Medicina Könyvkiadó, 1977.

Krúdy, Gyula. *Hét bagoly: regény*. Budapest: Szépirodalmi Könyvkiadó, 1974.

———. *A szobrok megmozdulnak: Írások az irodalomról*. Budapest: Gondolat, 1974.

Lukács, György. *Népegészségügy Magyarországon*. Budapest: Magyar Tudományos Társaság Nyomdája, 1924.

Márai, Sándor. *Zendülők*. Budapest: Pantehon, 1930.

Molnár, Lajos. *Az erkölcsök, a közegészség, a prostitúció*. Budapest: Neumayer Ede Könyvnyomda, 1899.

Moravcsik, Ernő Emil, and Andor Sólyom. *Az orvos működési köre az igazságügyi közszolgálatban*. Budapest: Magyar Orvosi Könyvkiadó Társulat, 1901.

Nagy, Dénes. *Beszédek a szerelemről: tanulmányok a logoi erótikoi-hoz*. Budapest: Hornyánszky Nyomda, 1907.

Nagy, Irma. *Bőnös szerelmek: Egy úrileány vallomásai*. Budapest: Magyar Könyvkiadó, 1908.

———. *Nagy Irma utolsó könyve: A szerelem színháza Párisban*. Budapest: Szerző, 1909.

———. *Sötét bűnök: Egy úrileány vallomásai*. Budapest: Kereskedelmi Reklámvállalat, 1908.

Nemes Nagy, Zoltán. *Katasztrófák a szerelmi életben: Sexualpathologiai tanulmány*. Budapest: Aesculap, 1933.

———. *Sexuálpedagógia és -ethika: Nemi felvilágosítás irányelvei és módjai: Sexuálpedagógiai tanulmány*. Budapest: Aesculap, 1944.

Nemes, Sándor. *Gyakorlati nyomozás*. Budapest: Griff, 1943.

Nyigri, Imre. *Budapest bűnélete 1881-től 1940-ig: A budapesti rendőrség hatvan éve a bűnügyi statisztika tükrében*. Budapest: Halász Irodalmi és Könyvkiadó Vállalat, 1942.

Pál, György. *A homoszexuális probléma modem megvilágításban*. Budapest: Mai Henrik Kiadó, 1926.

Pósch, Károly. *Utam a gólyafészek körül: Tanulmány a nemi felvilágosítás problémájáról szülők és nevelők részére*. Budapest: Szerző, 1923.

Schreiber, Emil. *A prostitúció*. Budapest: Pátria Irodalmi Vállalat és Nyomdai Részvénytársaság, 1917.

Shaw, Albert. "Budapest: The Rise of a New Metropolis." *Century Magazine* 44, no. 2 (1892): 163.

Somogyi, Béla, ed. *A család egészsége: Népszerű orvosi tájékoztató és tanácsadó.* 2nd ed. Budapest: Dante Könyvkiadó, 1928.

Szabó, László. *A bolsevizmus Magyarországon: A proletárdiktatúra okirataiból.* Budapest: Athenaeum, 1919.

Szántó, Jenő. "A homosexualis férfiprostitutio kérdése." *Népegészségügy,* no. 20 (1934): 774–79; no. 21 (1934): 826–34.

———. "A homosexualitásról, különös tekintettel a budapesti viszonyokra." *Bőrgyógyászati, Urológiai és Venereologiai Szemle,* no. 1 (1933): 21–27; no. 2 (1933): 40–44.

Szatmáry, Sándor. *Nagyvárosi erkölcsök: Budapest sexuális élete.* Budapest: Országos Laptudósító, 1908.

Székely, Vladimir. *Árny és derü: Egy rendőrtiszt naplójából.* Budapest: Centrál Nyomda, 1930.

———. *Házi rendőr: Közhasznú rendőri tanácsadó.* Budapest: Omnia, 1929.

Szép, Ernő. *Natália.* Budapest: Noran, 2008.

Szerb, Antal. *Utas és holdvilág.* Budapest: John Rodker, 1937.

Tábori, Kornél, and Vladimir Székely. *A bűnös Budapest.* Budapest: A Nap Újságvállalat nyomdája, 1908.

———. *Beteg szerelem: Kragujevics bajtársai.* Budapest: A Nap Újságvállalat nyomdája, n.d.

———. *Bűn és szerelem: Budapesti erkölcsrajz.* Budapest: Haladás Nyomda, 1910.

———. *Bünös nők.* Budapest: A Nap Újságvállalat nyomdája,1909.

———. *Az erkölcstelen Budapest.* Budapest: A Nap Újságvállalat nyomdája, 1908.

———. *Humor a bűnben: Megtörtént viccek, Pesti anekdóták.* Budapest: Budapesti Hírlap Nyomdája, 1909.

———. *Nyomorultak, gazemberek.* Budapest: A Nap Újságvállalat nyomdája, 1908.

Tóth, Tihamér. "Eugenika és katolicizmus." In *Az 1934. évi előadások: Eugenika-élettan-származástan-örökléstan-embertan-pedagógia.* Budapest: Korda R. T. kiadása, 1935.

Tormay, Cécile. *Bujdosó könyv. Feljegyzések 1918–1919-ből.* I. kötet. Budapest: Pallas irodalmi és nyomda kiadása, 1921.

———. *An Outlaw's Diary.* London: P. Allan & Company, 1923.

Turcsányi, Gyula, ed. *A modern bűnözés I–II.* Budapest: Rozsnyai Károly kiadása, 1929.

Weiss, Emil. *Védekezés a ragályos nemi betegségek ellen: Közérdekű felvilágosítás.* Budapest: Szerző, 1907.

Weisse, S., Viktor Áldor, and Kurt Moreck. *A titkos prostitúció és a félvilág.* Vita Sexualis 5. Budapest: Sándor József és társa Kiadó, 1920.

Zadravecz, István. *Páter Zadravecz titkos naplója.* Szerkesztette és a bevezetőt írta: Borsányi György. Budapest: Kossuth Könyvkiadó, 1967.

NEWSPAPERS AND PERIODICALS

Budapesti Hírlap
Egyedül Vagyunk
A Friss Újság
Független Magyarország

Függetlenség
A Hír
Huszadik Század
Magyar Futár
Magyar Nemzet
Magyarság
Nemzet Szava
Nép
Népegészségügy
Népszava
Nyilas évkönyv
Pesti Hirlap
Pesti Napló
Proletárjog: A Szocialista Jogászszövetség hivatalos lapja
Rendőri Lapok
Város: Várospolitikai és közigazgatási hetilap
Vörös Újság

SECONDARY SOURCES

Abelove, Henry, Michele Aina Barale, and David M. Halperin, eds. *The Lesbian and Gay Studies Reader.* 1st ed. New York: Routledge, 1993.

Ablovatski, Eliza. "The 1919 Central European Revolutions and the Judeo-Bolshevik Myth." *European Review of History: Revue Europeenne d'histoire* 17, no. 3 (June 2010): 473–89.

Abraham, Julie. *Metropolitan Lovers: The Homosexuality of Cities.* Minneapolis: University of Minnesota Press, 2009.

Albertini, Béla. "Az első magyar szociofotó 'album.'" *Budapesti Negyed: Lap a Városról* 13, nos. 1–2 (2005): 119–42.

Aldrich, Robert. "Homosexuality and the City: An Historical Overview." *Urban Studies* 41, no. 9 (2004): 1719–37.

Alexander, Sally. "Psychoanalysis in Britain in the Early Twentieth Century: An Introductory Note." *History Workshop Journal*, no. 45 (1998): 135–43.

Aly, Götz. *Hitler's Beneficiaries: Plunder, Racial War, and the Nazi Welfare State.* New York: Metropolitan, 2007.

Anka, László. "A budapesti prostitúció és szexpiac története a boldog békeidőkben." *Valóság* 47, no. 2 (2004): 82–105.

Antoni, Rita. "A magyarországi feminista megmozdulások története." In *Nőképek kisebbségben: Tanulmányok a kisebbségben (is) élő nőkről,* edited by Lilla Bolemant, 18–29. Pozsony: Phoenix PT, 2014.

Arendt, Hannah. *The Origins of Totalitarianism.* New York: Schocken Books, 1951.

Arondekar, Anjali, Ann Cvetkovich, Christina B. Hanhardt, Regina Kunzel, Tavia Nyong'o, Juana María Rodríguez, Susan Stryker, Daniel Marshall, Kevin P. Murphy, and Zeb Tortorici. "Queering Archives." *Radical History Review*, no. 122 (2015): 211–31.

Avery, Simon, and Graham M. Katherine, eds. *Sex, Time and Place Queer Histories of London, c. 1850 to the Present*. London: Bloomsbury Academic, 2018.
Bacchetta, Paola, and Margaret Power, eds. *Right-Wing Women: From Conservatives to Extremists around the World*. New York: Routledge, 2002.
Bácskai, Vera. *Budapest története: A kezdetektől 1945-ig*. Budapest: Budapesti Fővárosi Levéltára, 2000.
Balázs, József. *A magyar bűnügyi statisztika kialakulása és fejlődése: Különös tekintettel annak módszertani kérdéseire*. Szeged: Szegedi Nyomda, 1969.
Balogh, Margit. "A Mindszenty-per." *Korunk* 23, no. 7 (2012): 3–17.
Baran, Brigitta. "Károly Schaffer and His School: The Birth of Biological Psychiatry in Hungary, 1890–1940." *European Psychiatry: The Journal of the Association of European Psychiatrists* 23, no. 6 (2008): 449.
Bart, István. *Budapest krónikája: A kezdetektol napjainkig*. Budapest: Corvina, 2007.
Bauer, Heike. "Theorizing Female Inversion: Sexology, Discipline, and Gender at the Fin de Siècle." *Journal of the History of Sexuality* 18 (2009): 84–102.
Beachy, Robert. *Gay Berlin: Birthplace of a Modern Identity*. New York: Knopf, 2015.
———. "The German Invention of Homosexuality." *Journal of Modern History* 82, no. 4 (2010): 801–38.
Beccalossi, Chiara. *Female Sexual Inversion: Same-Sex Desires in Italian and British Sexology, c. 1870–1920*. New York: Palgrave Macmillan, 2011.
Becker, Peter, and Richard F. Wetzell, eds. *Criminals and Their Scientists: The History of Criminology in International Perspective*. New York: Cambridge University Press, 2006.
Beller, Steven, ed. *Rethinking Vienna 1900*. New York: Berghahn Books, 2001.
Belovics, Ervin. *Büntetőjog I.; Általános rész*. 2nd ed. Budapest: HVG—ORAC Lap és Könyvkiadó Kft., 2018.
Benadusi, Lorenzo. *The Enemy of the New Man: Homosexuality in Fascist Italy*. Translated by Suzanne Dingee and Jennifer Pudney. Madison: University of Wisconsin Press, 2012.
Bender, Thomas, and Carl Schorske. *Budapest and New York: Studies in Metropolitan Transformation, 1870–1930*. New York: Russell Sage Foundation, 1994.
Bennett, Judith. "'Lesbian-Like' and the Social History of Lesbianisms." *Journal of the History of Sexuality* 9, no. 2 (2000): 1–24.
Berend, Ivan T. *History Derailed: Central and Eastern Europe in the Long Nineteenth Century*. Berkeley: University of California Press, 2005.
Berend, Iván T., Tamás Csató, János Kornai, György Csáki, and Gábor Karsai. *Evolution of the Hungarian Economy, 1848–1998*. New York: Distributed by Columbia University Press, 2000.
Bernstein, Frances. *The Dictatorship of Sex: Lifestyle Advice for the Soviet Masses*. DeKalb: Northern Illinois University Press, 2007.
Bernstein, Mary. "Identities and Politics: Toward a Historical Understanding of the Lesbian and Gay Movement." *Social Science History* 26, no. 3 (2002): 531–81.
Betts, Paul. *Within Walls: Private Life in the German Democratic Republic*. Oxford: Oxford University Press, 2010.

Birken, Lawrence. *Consuming Desire: Sexual Science and the Emergence of a Culture of Abundance, 1871–1914*. Ithaca, NY: Cornell University Press, 1988.
Bischof, Gunter, Anton Pelinka, and Dagmar Herzog, eds. *Sexuality in Austria (Contemporary Austrian Studies 15)*. Piscataway, NJ: Transaction Publishers, 2007.
Bland, Lucy, and Laura L. Doan, eds. *Sexology in Culture: Labelling Bodies and Desires*. Chicago: University of Chicago Press, 1998.
Bödők, Gergely. "Vörös és fehér: Terror, retorzió és számonkérés Magyarországon 1919–1921." *Kommentár*, no. 3 (2011): 15–31.
Bogdán, Melinda. "A Rabosító fénykép: A rend őrségi fényképezés kialakulása." *Budapesti Negyed: Lap a Városról* 13, nos. 1–2 (2005): 143–65.
Bohus, Kata. "Not a Jewish Question? The Holocaust in Hungary in the Press and Propaganda of the Kádár Regime during the Trial of Adolf Eichmann." *Hungarian Historical Review* 4, no. 3 (2015): 737–72.
Bónis, György. "Adatok a Budapesti Forradalmi Törvényszék történetéhez." *Levéltári Közlemények* 29 (1959): 293–312.
———. *Fővárosi Levéltár (volt Budapesti 1. Sz. Állami Levéltár) 4: A jogszolgáltatás budapesti területi szervei*. Budapest: Művelődésügyi Minisztérium Levéltári Osztálya, 1961.
Borgos, Anna. *Eltitkolt évek: Tizenhat leszbikus életút*. Budapest: Labrisz Leszbikus Egyesület, 2011.
———. "Secret Years: Hungarian Lesbian Herstory, 1950s–2000s." *Aspasia* 9 (2015): 87–112.
———. "Vay Sándor/Sarolta: Egy konvencionális nemiszerep-áthágó a múlt századfordulón." *Holmi*, no. 2 (2007): 185–94.
Borhi, László. "Stalinist Terror in Hungary, 1945–1956." In *Stalinist Terror in Eastern Europe: Elite Purges and Mass Repression*, edited by Kevin McDermott and Matthew Stibbe, 119–40. New York: Manchester University Press, 2010.
Borus, Judit. "A Hivatásosak: Fejezetek a Prostitúció Történetéből." *Rubicon* 22, no. 1 (2011): 58–62.
Boswell, John. *Same-Sex Unions in Premodern Europe*. New York: Villard Books, 1994.
Bozóki, András. "Consolidation or Second Revolution? The Emergence of the New Right in Hungary." *Journal of Communist Studies and Transition Politics* 24, no. 2 (2008): 191–231.
Braham, Randolph L. *The Hungarian Labor Service System, 1939–1945*. Boulder, CO: East European Quarterly; distributed by Columbia University Press, 1977.
———. *The Politics of Genocide: The Holocaust in Hungary*. New York: Columbia University Press, 1981.
Brooks, Ross. "Transforming Sexuality: The Medical Sources of Karl Heinrich Ulrichs (1825–95) and the Origins of the Theory of Bisexuality." *Journal of the History of Medicine and Allied Sciences* 67, no. 2 (2012): 177–216.
Brühöfener, Friederike. "Sex and the Soldier: The Discourse about the Moral Conduct of Bundeswehr Soldiers and Officers during the Adenauer Era." *Central European History* 48, no. 4 (2015): 523–40.
Brunner, José. "Psychiatry, Psychoanalysis, and Politics during the First World War." *Journal of the History of the Behavioral Sciences* 27, no. 4 (1991): 352–65.

Bruns, Claudia. "The Politics of Masculinity in the (Homo-)Sexual Discourse (1880 to 1920)." *German History* 23, no. 3 (2005): 306–20.
Bucur, Maria. *Eugenics and Modernization in Interwar Romania*. Pittsburgh: University of Pittsburgh Press, 2002.
Bullough, Vern. *Science in the Bedroom: A History of Sex Research*. New York: Basic Books, 1994.
Buza, Péter, and Tamás Gusztáv Filep, eds. *Tábori bűnös Budapestje*. Budapest: Budapesti Városvédő Egyesület; Országos Széchenyi Könyvtár, 2013.
Buzinkay, Géza. *Borsszem Jankó és társai: Magyar élclapok és karikatúráik a XIX. század második felében*. Budapest: Corvina, 1983.
———. "A bűnügyi hír, a riporter és a rendőr." *Budapesti Negyed* 47–48, nos. 1–2 (2005): 7–30.
———. *Mokány Berczi és Spitzig Itzig, Göre Gábor mög a többiek . . . : A magyar társadalom figurái az élclapokban 1860 és 1918 között*. Budapest: Magvető, 1988.
Buzinkay, Géza, and György Kókay. *A magyar sajtó története I.: A kezdetektől a fordulat évéig*. Budapest: Ráció, 2005.
Canaday, Margot. "AHR Forum: Transnational Sexualities—Thinking Sex in the Transnational Turn; An Introduction." *American Historical Review*. 24, no. 5 (2009): 1250–57.
Carleton, Gregory. *Sexual Revolution in Bolshevik Russia*. Pittsburgh: University of Pittsburgh Press, 2005.
Chauncey, George. "From Sexual Inversion to Homosexuality: Medicine and Changing Concept of Female Deviance." *Salmagundi*, nos. 58–59 (Fall 1982/Winter 1983): 114–46.
———. *Gay New York: Gender, Urban Culture, and the Making of the Gay Male World, 1890–1940*. New York: Basic Books, 1994.
Chemouni, Jacquy, and David Alcorn. "Lenin, Sexuality and Psychoanalysis." *Psychoanalysis & History* 6, no. 2 (2004): 135–59.
Chua, Lynette J. *Mobilizing Gay Singapore: Rights and Resistance in an Authoritarian State*. Philadelphia: Temple University Press, 2015.
Clark, Anna, Karen Hagemann, and Stefan Dudink, eds. *Representing Masculinity: Male Citizenship in Modern Western Culture*. 1st ed. New York: Palgrave Macmillan, 2007.
Clement, Elizabeth A. *Love for Sale: Courting, Treating, and Prostitution in New York City, 1900–1945*. Chapel Hill: University of North Carolina Press, 2006.
Cleminson, Richard, and Francisco Vázquez García. *"Los Invisibles": A History of Male Homosexuality in Spain, 1850–1939*. Cardiff: University of Wales Press, 2007.
Cline, Sally. *Radclyffe Hall: A Woman Called John*. 1st ed. Woodstock, NY: Overlook Press, 1998.
Cocks, Harry. "Modernity and the Self in the History of Sexuality." *Historical Journal* 49, no. 4 (2006): 1211–27.
———. *Nameless Offences: Homosexual Desire in the Nineteenth Century*. New York: I. B. Tauris, 2003.
Congdon, Lee. *Exile and Social Thought: Hungarian Intellectuals in Germany and Austria, 1919–1933*. Princeton, NJ: Princeton University Press, 1991.

Connell, R. W. "The State, Gender, and Sexual Politics." *Theory and Society* 19, no. 5 (1990): 507–44.
Cook, Matt. *London and the Culture of Homosexuality, 1885–1914*. New York: Cambridge University Press, 2003.
Cornelius, Deborah S. *Hungary in World War II: Caught in the Cauldron*. 3rd ed. New York: Fordham University Press, 2011.
Cornwall, Mark. *The Devil's Wall: The Nationalist Youth Mission of Heinz Rutha*. Cambridge, MA: Harvard University Press, 2012.
———. "Heinrich Rutha and the Unraveling of a Homosexual Scandal in 1930s Czechoslovakia." *GLQ: A Journal of Lesbian and Gay Studies* 8, no. 3 (2002): 319–47.
Crouthamel, Jason. *Intimate History of the Front: Masculinity, Sexuality, and German Soldiers in the First World War*. New York: Palgrave Macmillan, 2016.
Cryle, Peter, and Christopher E. Forth. *Sexuality at the Fin de Siécle: The Makings of a "Central Problem."* Newark: University of Delaware Press, 2008.
Császtvay, Tünde. "Bordélyvilág a békebeli Budapesten: A prostitúció társadalomtörténete a 19. századvégen, a 20. századelőn." *Rubicon* 22, no. 1 (2011): 42–55.
———. *Éjjeli lepkevadászat: Bordélyvilág a történeti Magyarországon*. Budapest: Osiris, 2009.
Csehy, Zoltán. *Szodoma és környéke: Homoszocialitás, barátságretorika és queer irányulások a magyar költészetben*. Pozsony: Kalligram, 2014.
Csizmadia, Andor, ed. *Magyar állam- és jogtörténet: Egyetemi tankönyv*. Budapest: Nemzeti Tankönyvkiadó, 1998.
Danto, Elizabeth Ann. *Freud's Free Clinic: Psychoanalysis & Social Justice, 1918–1938*. New York: Columbia University Press, 2005.
Davidson, Roger, and Lesley A. Hall, eds. *Sex, Sin, and Suffering: Venereal Disease and European Society since 1870*. New York: Routledge, 2001.
Davis, Belinda J. *Home Fires Burning: Food, Politics, and Everyday Life in World War I Berlin*. Chapel Hill: University of North Carolina Press, 2000.
Deák, István. *Beyond Nationalism: A Social and Political History of the Habsburg Officer Corps, 1848–1918*. New York: Oxford University Press, 1990.
———. *Hungary from 1918 to 1945*. New York: Columbia University, 1989.
De Grazia, Victoria. *How Fascism Ruled Women: Italy, 1922–1945*. Berkeley: University of California Press, 1992.
D'Emilio, John. "Capitalism and Gay Identity." In *Powers of Desire: The Politics of Sexuality*, edited by Ann Snitow, Sharon Thompson, and Christine Stansell, 100–113. New York: Monthly Review Press, 1983.
D'Emilio, John, and Estelle B. Freedman. *Intimate Matters: A History of Sexuality in America*. 3rd ed. Chicago: University of Chicago Press, 2012.
Dénes, Iván Z. *Conservative Ideology in the Making*. Translated by Judit Pokoly. Budapest: CEU Press, 2009.
Dickinson, Edward Ross. "Biopolitics, Fascism, Democracy: Some Reflections on Our Discourse about 'Modernity.'" *Central European History* 37, no. 1 (2004): 1–48.
———. "'A Dark, Impenetrable Wall of Complete Incomprehension': The Impossibility of Heterosexual Love in Imperial Germany." *Central European History* 40, no. 3 (2007): 467–97.

———. "Policing Sex in Germany, 1882–1982: A Preliminary Statistical Analysis." *Journal of the History of Sexuality* 16, no. 2 (2007): 204–50.

———. *Sex, Freedom, and Power in Imperial Germany, 1880–1914*. Cambridge: Cambridge University Press, 2015.

Doan, Laura L. *Disturbing Practices: History, Sexuality, and Women's Experience of Modern War*. Chicago: University of Chicago Press, 2013.

———. *Fashioning Sapphism*. New York: Columbia University Press, 2001.

Doan, Laura, and Jane Garrity. *Sapphic Modernities: Sexuality, Women, and National Culture*. New York: Palgrave Macmillan, 2006.

Döme, Attila. *Egy "nyomdafestéket el nem Bíró" ügy: A Tormay Cécile per*. Keszthely: Balaton Akadémiai Kiadó, 2013.

Domeier, Norman. *The Eulenburg Affair: A Cultural History of Politics in the German Empire*. Translated by Deborah Lucas Schneider. Rochester, NY: Camden House, 2015.

———. *Der Eulenburg-Skandal: Eine politische Kulturgeschichte des Kaiserreichs*. New York: Campus-Verlag, 2010.

Dósa, Rudolfné, Ervinné Liptai, and Mihály Ruff. *A Magyar Tanácsköztársaság egészségügyi politikája*. Budapest: Medicina, 1959.

Duberman, Martin Bauml, Martha Vicinus, and George Chauncey, eds. *Hidden from History: Reclaiming the Gay and Lesbian Past*. New York: Plume, 1990.

Dudink, Stefan, Karen Hagemann, and John Tosh, eds. *Masculinities in Politics and War: Gendering Modern History*. New York: Manchester University Press; distributed by Palgrave, 2004.

Duggan, Lisa. "The Trials of Alice Mitchell: Sensationalism, Sexology and the Lesbian Subject in Turn of the Century America." *Signs* 18, no. 4 (1993): 791–814.

Eby, Cecil D. *Hungary at War: Civilians and Soldiers in World War II*. University Park: Pennsylvania State University Press, 1998.

Ellis, Havelock, and John Addington Symonds. *Sexual Inversion: A Critical Edition*. Edited by Ivan Crozier. New York Palgrave Macmillan, 2008.

Erős, Ferenc. "Ferenczi Sándor professzori kinevezése: Háttér és kronológia." *Thalassa* 20, no. 4 (2009): 3–28.

———. *Pszichoanalízis és forradalom: Ferenczi Sándor és a budapesti egyetem 1918/19-ben*. Budapest: Jószöveg Műhely, 2011.

Erős, Ferenc, István Kapás, and György Kiss. "Pszichoanalizis a hadseregben 1914–1918." *Hadtörténelmi Közlemények*, no. 1 (1988): 141–48.

Erőss, László. *Furcsa párok: A homoszexuálisok titkai nyomában*. Budapest: Editorg, 1984.

Eszenyi, Miklós. *"Férfi a férfival, nő a nővel": Homoszexualitás a történelemben*. Budapest: Corvina Kiadó, 2006.

Eszenyi, Miklós, and László Zahuczky. "Ferenczi és kortársai a homoszexualitásról." *Thalassa* 21, no. 4 (2008): 87–100.

Etkind, Alexander. *Eros of the Impossible: The History of Psychoanalysis in Russia*. Boulder, CO: Westview Press, 1997.

Evans, Jennifer V. "Decriminalization, Seduction, and 'Unnatural Desire' in East Germany." *Feminist Studies* 36, no. 3 (2010): 553–77.

Evans, Richard. *The German Underworld: Deviants and Outcasts in German History.* New York: Routledge, 1988.
Eytan, Bentsur. *Láng Európa szívében: Kun Béla hatalmának 133 napja.* Translated by Tamás Berczi. Budapest: K.U.K. Könyv-És Lapkiadó, 2010.
Faderman, Lillian. *Odd Girls and Twilight Lovers: A History of Lesbian Life in Twentieth-Century America.* Reprint ed. New York: Columbia University Press, 2012.
Farkas, Tamás. "Eugenics: The Building of Society and the Nation in Fin de Siècle and Interwar Hungary." Master's thesis, Central European University, 2012.
Forrai, Judit. "Beautiful Girls' Ugly Malady—Selected Passages from the History of Guilty Sex and Syphilis." *Orvosi Hetilap* 149, no. 40 (2008): 1895–901.
———. "Kávéházak és kéjnők." *Budapesti Negyed* 12–13, nos. 2–3 (1996): 110–20.
———. "Militarizált szex: Katonák, prostitúció, nemi betegségek a Nagy Háborúban." *Per Aspera Ad Astra* 5, no. 2 (2018): 93–114.
———. "Szép lányok csúnya betegsége, avagy szemelvények a bűnös szex és a szifilisz történetéből." *Orvosi hetilap* 149, no. 40 (2008): 1895–901.
Foucault, Michel. *The History of Sexuality.* 1st American ed. New York: Pantheon Books, 1978.
Frank, Tibor. *Double Exile: Migrations of Jewish-Hungarian Professionals through Germany to the United States, 1919–1945.* New York: Peter Lang, 2009.
Frigyesi, Judit. *Béla Bartók and Turn-of-the Century Budapest.* Berkeley: University of California Press, 1998.
Gay, Peter. *The Bourgeois Experience: Victoria to Freud.* New York: Oxford University Press, 1984.
———. *Freud: A Life for Our Time.* 1st ed. New York: W. W. Norton & Company, 1998.
———. *A Godless Jew: Freud, Atheism, and the Making of Psychoanalysis.* New Haven, CT: Yale University Press, 1987.
Gee, Malcolm, ed. *The City in Central Europe: Culture and Society from 1800 to the Present.* Aldershot: Ashgate, 1999.
Gellately, Robert. *Stalin's Curse: Battling for Communism in War and Cold War.* New York: Vintage, 2013.
Gergely, Jenő. *A Katolikus egyház történéte Magyarországon 1919–1945.* Budapest: Pannonica Kiadó, 1997.
Gerő, András, and János Poór. *Budapest: History from Its Beginnings to 1998.* New York: Columbia University Press, 1997.
Giles, Geoffrey. "Legislating Homophobia in the Third Reich: The Radicalization of Prosecution against Homosexuality by the Legal Profession." *German History* 23, no. 3 (2005): 339–54.
Gilfoyle, Timothy J. *City of Eros: New York City, Prostitution, and the Commercialization of Sex, 1790–1920.* New York and London: W. W. Norton & Company, 1992.
Goldman, Wendy Z. *Women, the State and Revolution: Soviet Family Policy and Social Life, 1917–1936.* Cambridge: Cambridge University Press, 1993.
Granasztói, Pál. *Budapest arculatai.* Budapest: Szépirodalmi Könyvkiadó, 1980.
Grau, Günter. "Return of the Past: The Policy of the SED and the Laws against Homo-

sexuality in Eastern Germany between 1946 and 1968." *Journal of Homosexuality* 37 no. 4 (1999): 1–21.

Grau, Günter, Claudia Schoppmann, and Patrick Camiller. *Hidden Holocaust? Gay and Lesbian Persecution in Germany, 1933–45*. Chicago: Fitzroy Dearborn, 1995.

Green, James N. *Beyond Carnival: Male Homosexuality in Twentieth-Century Brazil*. Chicago: University of Chicago Press, 2001.

Gyáni, Gábor. *Identity and the Urban Experience: Fin-de-Siécle Budapest*. New York: Distributed by Columbia University Press, 2004.

———. *Magánélet Horthy Miklós korában*. Budapest: Corvina, 2011.

———. *Parlor and Kitchen Housing and Domestic Culture in Budapest, 1870–1940*. Budapest: Central European University Press, 2002.

———, ed. "Tömegkultúra a Századfordulós Budapesten." *Budapesti Negyed* 16–17, nos. 2–3 (1997).

———. *Az utca és a szalon: A társadalmi térhasználat Budapesten (1870–1940)*. Budapest: Új Mandátum Könyvkiadó, 1999.

Gyáni, Gábor, and György Kövér. *Magyarország társadalomtörténete a reformkortól a második világháborúig*. Budapest: Osiris, 2006.

Gyáni, Gábor, György Kövér, and Tibor Valuch. *Social History of Hungary from the Reform Era to the End of the Twentieth Century*. New York: Distributed by Columbia University Press, 2004.

Gyarmati, György. *Demokráciából a diktatúrába 1945–1956*. Budapest: Kossuth Kiadó, 2010.

———. *A Rákosi-korszak: Rendszerváltó fordulatok évtizede Magyarországon, 1945–1956*. Budapest: Rubicon-Ház B.T., 2013.

Gyurgyák, János. *Ezzé lett magyar hazátok: A magyar nemzeteszme és nacionalizmus története*. Budapest: Osiris, 2007.

———. *Magyar fajvédők: Eszmetörténeti tanulmány*. Budapest: Osiris, 2012.

———. *A zsidókérdés Magyarországon: Politikai eszmetörténet*. Budapest: Osiris, 2001.

Hadas, Miklós. *A férfiasság kódjai*. Budapest: Balassi Kiadó, 2010.

———. *Férfiuralom: Írások nőkről, férfiakról, feminizmusról*. Budapest: Replika Kör, 1994.

Halberstam, Judith. *Female Masculinity*. Durham, NC: Duke University Press, 1998.

Halperin, David M. *How to Do the History of Homosexuality*. Chicago: University of Chicago Press, 2002.

———. "How to Do the History of Male Homosexuality." *GLQ: A Journal of Lesbian and Gay Studies* 6, no. 1 (2000): 87–123.

Hanák, Péter. *The Garden and the Workshop: Essays on the Cultural History of Vienna and Budapest*. Princeton, NJ: Princeton University Press, 1998.

Hanebrink, Paul. *In Defense of Christian Hungary: Religion, Nationalism, and Antisemitism, 1890–1944*. Ithaca, NY: Cornell University Press, 2006.

Haney, Lynne. *Inventing the Needy Gender and the Politics of Welfare in Hungary*. Berkeley: University of California Press, 2002.

Harmat, Pál. *Freud, Ferenczi és a magyarországi pszichoanalizis: A budapesti mélylélektani iskola története, 1908–1983*. Bern: Európai Protestáns Magyar Szabadegyetem, 1986.

Harris, Victoria. "Histories of 'Sex,' Histories of 'Sexuality.'" *Contemporary European History* 22, no. 2 (2013): 295–301.

Havasréti, József. "'Egyesek és mások' Szerb Antal: Utas és holdvilág." *Jelenkor: Irodalmi és művészeti folyóirat* 54, no. 4 (2011) 427–50.

Havelková, Hana, and Libora Oates-Indruchová, eds. *The Politics of Gender Culture under State Socialism: An Expropriated Voice*. London: Routledge, 2014.

Healey, Dan. *Bolshevik Sexual Forensics: Diagnosing Disorder in the Clinic and Courtroom, 1917–1939*. DeKalb: Northern Illinois University Press, 2009.

———. "Comrades, Queers, and 'Oddballs': Sodomy, Masculinity, and Gendered Violence in Leningrad Province of the 1950s." *Journal of the History of Sexuality* 21, no. 3 (2012): 496–522.

———. *Homosexual Desire in Revolutionary Russia: The Regulation of Sexual and Gender Dissent*. Chicago: University of Chicago Press, 2004.

———. "Masculine Purity and 'Gentlemen's Mischief': Sexual Exchange and Prostitution between Russian Men, 1861–1941." *Slavic Review* 60, no. 2 (2001): 233–65.

Healy, Maureen. *Vienna and the Fall of the Habsburg Empire: Total War and Everyday Life in World War I*. New York: Cambridge University Press, 2004.

Hekma, Gert. "The Drive for Sexual Equality." *Sexualities* 11, nos. 1–2 (February 1, 2008): 46–50.

Hekma, Gert, Harry Oosterhuis, and James D. Steakley. *Gay Men and the Sexual History of the Political Left*. New York: Harrington Park Press, 1995.

Hellbeck, Jochen. *Revolution on My Mind: Writing a Diary under Stalin*. Cambridge, MA: Harvard University Press, 2006.

Herzog, Dagmar. *Sex after Fascism: Memory and Morality in Twentieth-Century Germany*. Princeton, NJ: Princeton University Press, 2007.

———. *Sexuality in Europe: A Twentieth-Century History*. New York: Cambridge University Press, 2011.

———. "Syncopated Sex: Transforming European Sexual Cultures." *American Historical Review* 24, no. 5 (2009): 1287–308.

Hoffmann, David L. "Mothers in the Motherland: Stalinist Pronatalism and Its Pan-European Context." *Journal of Social History* 34, no. 1 (2000): 35–54.

Holquist, Peter. *Making War, Forging Revolution: Russia's Continuum of Crisis, 1914–1921*. Cambridge, MA: Harvard University Press, 2002.

Horváth, Miklós, ed. *Budapest története a forradalmak korától a felszabadulásig*. Budapest: Akadémia Kiadó, 1980.

Horváth, Sándor. *Stalinism Reloaded: Everyday Life in Stalin-City, Hungary*. Translated by Thomas Cooper. Bloomington: Indiana University Press, 2017.

Houlbrook, Matt. *Queer London: Peril and Pleasures in the Sexual Metropolis, 1918–1957*. Chicago: University of Chicago Press, 2005.

———. "Soldier Heroes and Rent Boys: Homosex, Masculinities, and Britishness in the Brigade of Guards, circa 1900–1960." *Journal of British Studies* 42, no. 3 (2003): 351–88.

Howard, John. *Men Like That: Southern Queer History*. Chicago: University of Chicago Press, 2001.

Hull, Isabel V. *The Entourage of Kaiser Wilhelm II, 1888–1918*. Cambridge: Cambridge University Press, 2004.

Jackson, Julian. *Living in Arcadia: Homosexuality, Politics, and Morality in France from the Liberation to AIDS*. Chicago: University of Chicago Press, 2009.

Johnson, David K. *The Lavender Scare: The Cold War Persecution of Gays and Lesbians in the Federal Government*. Chicago: University of Chicago Press, 2006.

Kádár, Judit. Az antiszemitizmus jutalma: Tormay Cécile és a Horthy korszak." *Kritika*, no. 3 (2003): 9–12.

Kaplan, Morris B. *Sodom on the Thames*. Ithaca, NY: Cornell University Press, 2005.

Karsai, László. *A cigánykérdés Magyarországon, 1919–1945: Út a cigány Holocausthoz*. Budapest: Cserépfalvi, 1992.

———. *Szálasi Ferenc: Politkai életrajz*. Budapest: Balassi Kiadó, 2016.

Kenez, Peter. *Hungary from the Nazis to the Soviets: The Establishment of the Communist Regime in Hungary, 1944–1948*. New York: Cambridge University Press, 2006.

Király, Béla, and Walter Scott Dillard, eds. *The East Central European Officer Corps, 1740–1920s: Social Origins, Selection, Education, and Training*. New York: Distributed by Columbia University Press, 1988.

Kiss, Gábor. "Nemi betegségek az osztrák-magyar haderőben az első világháború idején." *Orvosi Hetilap* 147, no. 46 (2006): 2237–38.

Kollár, Nóra, ed. *A fővárosi rendőrség története (1914-ig)*. Budapest: Budapesti Rendőrfőkapitányság, 1995.

Kollarits, Krisztina. *Egy bujdosó írónő—Tormay Cécile*. Szombathely: Magyar Nyugat Könykiadó, 2010.

Kollega Tarsoly, István, ed. *Magyarország a XX. században II: Természeti környezet, népesség és társadalom, egyházak és felekezetek, gazdaság*. Szekszárd: Babits Kiadó, 1997.

Kovács, M. Mária. *Liberal Professions and Illiberal Politics: Hungary from the Habsburgs to the Holocaust*. New York: Oxford University Press, 1994.

———. *Törvénytol sújtva: A numerus clausus Magyarországon, 1920–1945*. Budapest: Napvilág Kiadó, 2012.

Koven, Seth. *Slumming: Sexual and Social Politics in Victorian London*. Princeton, NJ: Princeton University Press, 2004.

Kozári, Monika. *A dualista rendszer, 1867–1918*. Budapest: Pannonica, 2005.

Kulpa, Robert, and Joanna Mizielinska, eds. *De-Centering Western Sexualities: Central and Eastern European Perspectives*. London: Ashgate Publishing Limited, 2011.

Kund, Attila. "'Duties for Her Race and Nation': Scientistic Racist Views on Sexuality and Reproduction in 1920s Hungary." *Sexualities* 19, nos. 1–2 (2016): 190–210.

———. "Méhely Lajos és a magyar fajbiológiai kísérlete (1920–1931)." *Múltunk* 57, no. 4. (2012): 239–89.

Kurimay, Anita. "Interrogating the Historical Revisionism of the Hungarian Right: The Queer Case of Cécile Tormay." *East European Politics & Societies* 30, no. 1 (2016): 10–33.

Kurimay, Anita, and Judit Takács. "Emergence of the Hungarian Homosexual Movement in Late Refrigerator Socialism." *Sexualities* 20, nos. 5–6 (2017): 585–603.

Lászlófi, Viola, Zsófia Nagy, Trádler Henrietta. "'Fajtalanság,' pszichoanalízis és kriminológia a Magyar Tanácsköztársaságban. F. Gy. esete a Kísérleti Kriminológiai Osztály anyagában." *Sic Itur ad Astra* 66 (2017): 45–76.

Léderer, Pál. *A nyilvánvaló nők: Prostitúció, társadalom, társadalomtörténet.* Budapest: Új Mandátum Könyvkiadó, 1999.

Lee, Julian C. H. *Policing Sexuality: Sex, Society, and the State.* London and New York: Zed Books, 2011.

Lendvai, Paul. *The Hungarians: A Thousand Years of Victory in Defeat.* Princeton, NJ: Princeton University Press, 2003.

Lerner, Paul F. *Hysterical Men: War, Psychiatry, and the Politics of Trauma in Germany, 1890–1930.* Ithaca, NY: Cornell University Press, 2003.

Liang, Hsi-huey. *The Rise of Modern Police and the European State System from Metternich to the Second World War.* New York: Cambridge University Press, 1992.

Light, Alison. *Forever England: Femininity, Literature, and Conservatism between the Wars.* New York: Routledge, 1991.

Lipták, Dorottya. "A családi lapoktól a társasági lapokig: Újságok és újságolvasók a századvégen." *Budapesti Negyed: Lap a Városról* 5, nos. 2–3 (1997): 45–70.

Lišková, Kateřina. *Sexual Liberation, Socialist Style: Communist Czechoslovakia and the Science of Desire, 1945–1989.* Cambridge University Press, 2018.

Lukacs, John. *Budapest 1900: A Historical Portrait of a City and Its Culture.* New York: Weindenfeld & Nicolson, 1988.

Lybeck, Marti M. *Desiring Emancipation.* Albany: State University of New York Press, 2014.

Mak, Geertje. "Sandor Sarolta Vay: From Passing Woman to Sexual Invert." *Journal of Women's History* 16, no. 1 (2004): 54–77.

Mancini, Elena. *Magnus Hirschfeld and the Quest for Sexual Freedom: A History of the First International Sexual Freedom Movement.* New York: Palgrave Macmillan, 2010.

Mann, Miklós. *Oktatáspolitikusok és koncepciók a két világháború között.* Budapest: Országos Pedagógiai Könyvtár és Múzeum, 1997.

Manzano, Valeria. "Sex, Gender and the Making of the 'Enemy Within' in Cold War Argentina." *Journal of Latin American Studies* 47, no. 1 (2015): 1–29.

Marcus, Sharon. *Between Women: Friendship, Desire, and Marriage in Victorian England.* Princeton, NJ: Princeton University Press, 2007.

———. "Queer Theory for Everyone: A Review Essay." *Signs* 31, no. 1 (2005): 191–218.

Marhoefer, Laurie. *Sex and the Weimar Republic: German Homosexual Emancipation and the Rise of the Nazis.* Toronto: University of Toronto Press, 2015.

Matysik, Tracie. *Reforming the Moral Subject: Ethics and Sexuality in Central Europe, 1890–1930.* Ithaca, NY: Cornell University Press, 2008.

Maxwell, Alexander. "National Endogamy and Double Standards: Sexuality and Nationalism in East-Central Europe during the 19th Century." *Journal of Social History* 41, no. 2 (2007): 413–33.

———. "Nationalizing Sexuality: Sexual Stereotypes in the Habsburg Empire." *Journal of the History of Sexuality* 14, no. 3 (2005): 266–90.

McEwen, Britta. *Sexual Knowledge: Feeling, Fact, and Social Reform in Vienna, 1900–1934.* New York: Berghahn Books, 2012.

McLellan, Josie. "Glad to Be Gay behind the Wall: Gay and Lesbian Activism in 1970s East Germany." *History Workshop Journal* 74, no. 1 (2012): 105–30.

———. *Love in the Time of Communism: Intimacy and Sexuality in the GDR*. New York: Cambridge University Press, 2011.
Miklóssy, János. *A budapesti prostitúció története*. Budapest: Népszava Kiadó Vállalat, 1989.
Miller, Martin A. *Freud and the Bolsheviks: Psychoanalysis in Imperial Russia and the Soviet Union*. New Haven, CT: Yale University Press, 1998.
Molnár, Judit, ed. *Számokba zárt sorsok: A numerus clausus 90 év távlatából*. Budapest: Holokauszt Emlékközpont, 2012.
Mosse, George L. *The Image of Man: The Creation of Modern Masculinity*. New York: Oxford University Press, 1996.
———. "Nationalism and Respectability: Normal and Abnormal Sexuality in the Nineteenth Century." *Journal of Contemporary History* 17, no. 2 (1982): 221–46.
———. *Nationalism and Sexuality: Respectability and Abnormal Sexuality in Modern Europe*. 1st ed. New York: H. Fertig, 1985.
Nagy, Ágnes. *Harc a lakáshivatalban: Politikai átalakulás és mindennapi érdekérvényesítés a fővárosban, 1945–1953*. Budapest: Korall, 2013.
Nagy-Juhász Vargáné, Ágnes. "Az önkéntes haderő tartalék biztosításának szervezési—vezetési kérdései." PhD diss., Zrinyi Miklos Nemzetvedelmi Egyetem, Hadtudományi Kar, 2010.
Nagy, Sándor. "A fajvédelem útvesztőjében: Bírói gyakorlat 'fajgyalázási' perekben (1942–1944)." *Fons* 22, no. 4 (2015): 487–532.
———. "One Empire, Two States, Many Laws: Matrimonial Law and Divorce in the Austro-Hungarian Monarchy." *Hungarian Historical Review* 3, no. 1 (2014): 190–221.
Naiman, Eric. *Sex in Public: The Incarnation of Early Soviet Ideology*. Princeton, NJ: Princeton University Press, 1997.
Nemes, Robert. *The Once and Future Budapest*. DeKalb: Northern Illinois University Press, 2005.
Newton, Esther. "The Mythic Mannish Lesbian: Radclyffe Hall and the New Woman." *Signs* 9, no. 4 (1984): 557.
Nye, Robert A. "Western Masculinities in War and Peace." *American Historical Review* 112, no. 2 (2007): 417–38.
Oosterhuis, Harry. *Homosexuality and Male Bonding in Pre-Nazi Germany: The Youth Movement, the Gay Movement, and Male Bonding before Hitler's Rise*. New York: Haworth Press, 1991.
———. "Sexual Modernity in the Works of Richard von Krafft-Ebing and Albert Moll." *Medical History* 56, no. 2 (2012): 133–55.
———. *Stepchildren of Nature: Krafft-Ebing, Psychiatry, and the Making of Sexual Identity*. Chicago: University of Chicago Press, 2000.
Ötvös, István. "Koncepciós Perek." *Rubicon* 26, no. 10 (2015): 54–58.
Paksa, Rudolf. *A magyar szélsőjobboldal története*. Budapest: Jaffa Kiadó, 2012.
———. *Szálasi Ferenc és a hungarizmus*. Budapest: Jaffa Kiadó, 2013.
Pap, Tibor. "A házasság felbontásának problematikája a Magyar Tanácsköztársaságban." *Jogtudományi Közlöny* 15, nos. 2–3 (1959): 61–68.

Parádi, József. "A polgári magyar állam rendőrsége, 1867–1918." *Rubicon* 20, no. 3 (2010): 4–13.
Passmore, Kevin. ed. *Women, Gender, and Fascism in Europe, 1919–45*. New Brunswick, NJ: Rutgers University Press, 2003.
Peniston, William A. *Pederasts and Others: Urban Culture and Sexual Identity in Nineteenth Century Paris*. New York: Harrington Park Press, 2004.
Perényi, Roland. "A bűn és a nyomor tanyái: A szegénység és bűnözés tere Budapesten a 19–20. század fordulóján." *Urbs: Magyar Várostörténeti Évkönyv* 4 (2009): 205–26.
———. "A bűnügyi statisztika Magyarországon a 'hosszú' XIX. században." *Statisztikai Szemle* 85 (2007): 524–41.
———. "A 'figyelő, megelőző és felfedező' rendőrség: Egy bűnözői névjegyzék tanulságai." *Budapesti Negyed: Lap a Városról* 13, nos. 1–2 (2005): 63–92.
———. "A jogtörténettől az 'új kultúrtörténetig': A bűnözés társadalomtörténete." *Sic Itur Ad Astra* 18, no 1–2 (2006): 85–108.
———. "Találkahelyek, bűnügyi helyszínek és 'dzsungel-erkölcsök': Homoszexuális szubkultúra, városi tér és bűnözés Budapesten a 20. század elején." *Sic Itur ad Astra* 66 (2017): 109–12.
———. "Városi tér és hatalom: 'Utcapolitika' századfordulós Budapesten." *Századvég* 11, no. 39 (2006): 29–55.
Pető, Andrea. "The History of the Hungarian Women's Movement." In *Thinking Differently: A Reader in European Women's Studies*, edited by Gabriele Griffin and Rosi Braidotti, 361–71. London: Zed Books, 2002.
———. "Minden tekintetben derék nők: A nők politikai szerepei és a nőegyesületek a két világháború közötti Magyarországon." In *Szerep és alkotás: Női szerepek a társadalomban és az alkotóművészetben*, 268–79. Debrecen: Csokonai Kiadó, 1997.
———. *Társadalmi nemek képe és emlékezete Magyarországon a 19–20. században*. Budapest: A nők a valódi esélyegyenlőségért alapítvány, 2004.
Plant, Richard. *The Pink Triangle: The Nazi War against Homosexuals*. 1st ed. New York: H. Holt, 1986.
Prakfalvi, Endre. *Architecture of Dictatorship: The Architecture of Budapest between 1945 and 1959*. Budapest: Municipality of Budapest, Office of the Mayor, 1999.
Prakfalvi, Endre, and György Szücs. *A szocreál Magyarországon*. Budapest: Corvina, 2010.
Pusztafalvi, Henriette. "Az egészségnevelés intézményesülésének folymata hazánkban a dualizmus korától a második világháború végéig." PhD diss., A Pécsi Tudományegyetem Bölcsészettudományi Kar "Oktatás és Társadalom" Neveléstudományi Doktori Iskola, 2011.
Püski, Levente. *A Horthy-korszak 1920–1941*. Budapest: Kossuth Könyvkiadó, 2013.
Ranki, Vera. *The Politics of Inclusion and Exclusion: Jews and Nationalism in Hungary*. New York: Holmes & Meier, 1999.
Rákos, Ferenc. *Állam és alkotmány a Magyar Tanácsköztársaságban*. Budapest: Jogi Kiadó, 1953.
Robinson, Paul. "Freud and Homosexuality." In *Homosexuality and Psychoanalysis*, edited by Time Dean and Christopher Lane. Chicago: University of Chicago Press, 2001, 91–98.

Romesburg, Don. "'Wouldn't a Boy Do?': Placing Early-Twentieth-Century Male Youth Sex Work into Histories of Sexuality." *Journal of the History of Sexuality* 18, no. 3 (2009): 367–92.

Romsics, Ignác. "A Horthy-rendszer jellegéről: Elitizmus, tekintélyelv, konzervativizmus." *Rubicon: Történelmi Magazin* 1 (1997). Online.

———. "A Horthy-rendszer szociálpolitikája." *Rubicon* 1, no. 6 (1990): 24–25.

———. *Hungary in the Twentieth Century*. Translated by Timothy Wilkinson. Budapest: Corvina; Osiris, 1999.

———, ed. *A magyar jobboldali hagyomány, 1900–1948*. Budapest: Osiris, 2009.

———, ed. *Magyarország a második világháborúban*. Budapest: Kossuth Könyvkiadó, 2011.

———. *Magyarország története a XX. században*. Budapest: Osiris, 2005.

———. "Nyíltan vagy titkosan?: A Horthy-rendszer választójoga." *Rubicon* 1, no. 2 (1990): 4–5.

Rosario, Vernon A. *Homosexuality and Science: A Guide to the Debates*. Santa Barbara, CA: ABC-CLIO, 2002.

———, ed. *Science and Homosexualities*. New York: Routledge, 1997.

Rowe, Dorothy. *Representing Berlin: Sexuality and the City in Imperial and Weimar Germany*. Aldershot: Ashgate Publishing, Ltd., 2003.

Rydström, Jens. *Sinners and Citizens: Bestiality and Homosexuality in Sweden, 1880–1950*. Chicago: University of Chicago Press, 2003.

Rydström, Jens, and Kati Mustola, eds. *Criminally Queer: Homosexuality and Criminal Law in Scandinavia, 1842–1999*. Amsterdam: Aksant, 2007.

Sadler, John, and Silvie Fisch. *Spy of the Century: Alfred Redl and the Betrayal of Austria-Hungary*. Barnsley: Pen and Sword, 2016.

Sakmyster, Thomas. *Hungary's Admiral on Horseback: Miklós Horthy, 1918–1944*. Boulder, CO: East European Monographs; distributed by Columbia University Press, 1994.

Sarlós, Béla. *A Tanácsköztársaság forradalmi törvényszékei*. Budapest: Közgazdasági és Jogi Kiadó, 1961.

Schoppmann, Claudia. *Verbotene Verhältnisse: Frauenliebe 1938–1945*. Berlin: Querverlag, 1999.

Schorske, Carl. *Fin-de-Siècle Vienna: Politics and Culture*. 1st ed. New York: Knopf; distributed by Random House, 1979.

Schönwald, Pál. *A nagyarországi 1918–1919-es polgári demokratikus forradalom állam- és jogtörténeti kérdései*. Budapest: Akadémia Kiadó, 1969.

Schwartz, Agatha. *Shifting Voices: Feminist Thought and Women's Writing in Fin-de-Siècle Austria and Hungary*. Montreal: McGill-Queen's University Press, 2008.

Sedlmayr, Krisztina. "A modern háztartás születése az 1930-as években Magyarországon." PhD diss., Eötvös Loránd Tudományegyetem, 2007.

Seidl, Jan, Jan Wintr, and Lukáš Nozar. *Od žaláře k oltáři: Emancipace homosexuality v českých zemích od roku 1867 do současnosti* [From prison to the altar: Emancipation of homosexuality in the Czech lands from 1867 to the present]. Brno: Host, 2012.

Sigmund, Anna Maria. *"Das Geschlechtsleben bestimmen wir": Sexualität im Dritten Reich*. Munich: Heyne, 2008.

Siklós, András. *A Habsburg-birodalom felbomlása, 1918: A Magyarországi forradalom*. Budapest: Kossuth, 1987.

Sinha, Mrinalini. *Gender and Nation*. Washington, DC: American Historical Association, 2006.

Sipos, Balázs. *Sajtó és hatalom a Horthy-korszakban: Politika- és társadalomtörténeti vázlat*. Budapest: Argumentum, 2011.

Snitow, Ann, Sharon Thompson, and Christine Stansell, eds. *Powers of Desire: The Politics of Sexuality*. New York: Monthly Review Press, 1983.

Sokolova, Vera. "'Don't Get Pricked!': Representation and the Politics of Sexuality in the Czech Republic." In *Over the Wall/After the Fall: Post-Communist Cultures through an East-West Gaze*, 251–67. Bloomington: Indiana University Press, 2004.

———. "State Approaches to Homosexuality and Non-Heterosexual Lives in Czechoslovakia during State-Socialism." In *Expropriated Voice: Transformations of Gender Culture in State-Socialist Czechoslovakia*, ed. Hana Havelkova and Libora Oates-Indruchova, 82–109. New York: Routledge, 2014.

Soós Viktor, Attila. "Harc a 'klerikális reakció' ellen: Egyházüldözés Magyarországon 1945–1956 között." *Rubicon* 26, no. 10 (2015): 34–43.

Spector, Scott. *Violent Sensations: Sex, Crime, and Utopia in Vienna and Berlin, 1860–1914*. Chicago: University of Chicago Press, 2016.

Spector, Scott, Helmut Puff, and Dagmar Herzog. *After the History of Sexuality: German Genealogies with and beyond Foucault*. New York: Berghahn Books, 2012.

Spira, György, and Vörös, Károly. *Budapest története a márciusi forradalomtól Az őszirózsás forradalomig*. Budapest: Akadémia Kiadó, 1978.

Spurlin, William. *Lost Intimacies: Rethinking Homosexuality under National Socialism*. New York: Peter Lang, 2009.

Stauter-Halsted, Keely, and Nancy M. Wingfield. "Introduction: The Construction of Sexual Deviance in Late Imperial Eastern Europe." *Journal of the History of Sexuality* 20, no. 2 (2011): 215–24.

Steakley, James. *The Homosexual Emancipation Movement in Germany*. New York: Arno Press, 1975.

———. "Iconography of a Scandal: Political Cartoons and the Eulenburg Affair in Wilhelmine Germany." In *Hidden from History: Reclaiming the Gay and Lesbian Past*, edited by Martin B. Duberman, Martha Vicinus, and George Chauncey, 233–63. London: Penguin, 1991.

Stipta, István. *A magyar bírósági rendszer története*. Budapest: Multiplex Media, 1998.

Stone, Lawrence. *Road to Divorce: England, 1530–1987*. Oxford: Oxford University Press, 1990.

Surkis, Judith. *Sexing the Citizen: Morality and Masculinity in France, 1870–1920*. Ithaca, NY: Cornell University Press, 2006.

Szechenyi, Kinga. *Stigmatized: A History of Hungary's Internal Deportations during the Communist Dictatorship*. Budapest: Central European University Press, 2016.

Szécsényi, Mihály. "A bordélyrendszer Budapesten." *Rubicon* 4, nos. 8–9 (1993): 58–63.

———. "Kalauznők konfliktusai a villamoson: Társadalmi nem és érhasználat Budapesten, 1915–1920." *Sic Itur Ad Astra* 20 (2009): 149–79.

Szegedi, Gábor. "Good Health Is the Best Dowry: Marriage Counseling, Premarital Examinations, Sex Education in Hungary, 1920–1952." PhD diss., Central European University, 2014.

———. "Stand by Your Man: Honor and Race Defilement in Hungary, 1941–44." *Hungarian Historical Review* 4, no. 3 (2015): 577–605.

———. "Tisztaság, tisztesség, fajgyalázás: Szexuális és faji normalizáció a Horthy-korban." *Socio.hu* 5, no. 1 (2015): 57–76.

Szigeti, Péter. "A szexualitás nyilvánossága a századfordulo Budapestjén." *Médiakutató*, no. 6 (Spring, 2002): 85–101.

Szikinger, István. "A magyar rendvédelmi jog 1919–1944." *Rendvédelem-Történeti Füzetek* 23, nos. 27–30 (2013): 187–97.

Szirmai, Rezső. *Fasiszta lelkek: Pszichoanalitikus beszélgetések a háborús főbűnösökkel a börtönben*. Budapest: Pelikán, 1993.

Tabajdi, Gábor, and Krisztián Ungváry. *Elhallgatott múlt: A pártállam és a belügy: A politikai rendőrség működése Magyarországon 1956–1990*. Budapest: 1956-os Intézet; Corvina, 2008.

Takács, Judit, ed. "The Double Life of Kertbeny." In *Past and Present of Radical Sexual Politics*, edited by Gert Hekma, 26–40. Amsterdam: Mosse Foundation, 2004.

———. *Homofóbia Magyarországon*. Budapest: L'Harmattan, 2011.

———. *Meleg század: Adalékok a homoszexualitás 20. századi magyarországi társadalomtörténetéhez*. Budapest: Kalrigram, 2018.

Takács, Judit, and Gábor Csiszár. "Nemváltások és nemiszerep-áthágások reprezentációi az Estben 1910 és 1939 között." *Replika* 85–86, nos. 1–2 (2014): 209–25.

Takács, Judit, and Tamás P. Tóth. "Az 'Idegbizottság' szerepe a homoszexualitás magyarországi dekriminalizációjában." *Socio.hu: Társadalmi Tudományi Szemle*, no. 2 (2016): 226–42.

———. "Megbélyegzett kapcsolatok az államszocialista Magyarországon." *Socio.hu Társadalomtudományi Szemle* 7, no. 3 (2017): 63–85.

Tamagne, Florence. *The History of Homosexuality in Europe: Berlin, London, Paris, 1919–1939*. New York: Algora Publishing, 2004.

Tarjányi, Eszter. "A dzsentri exhumálása." *Valóság* 46, no. 5 (2003): 38–64.

Thomas, Nigel, and László P. Szabó. *The Royal Hungarian Army in World War II*. New York: Osprey Publications, 2008.

Tomasik, Krzysztof. *Gejerel: Mniejszości seksualne w PRL-u* [Gejerel: Sexual minorities in the People's Republic of Poland]. Warsaw: Wydawn "Krytyki Politycznej," 2012.

Tóth, Eszter Zsófia, and András Murai. *Szex és szocializmus*. Budapest: Libri Könyvkiadó, 2014.

Tóth, László, ed. *A homoszexualitásról*. Pompeji: T-Twins Kiadó, 1994.

———. "Homoszexuálisok Magyarországon—Beszélgetés Romsauer Lajossal, a Homérosz Egyesület elnökével." *Mozgó Világ* 17, no. 3(1991): 110–17.

Turbucz, Dávid. *Horthy Miklós*. Budapest: Napvilág, 2011.

Turda, Marius. "The Biology of War: Eugenics in Hungary, 1914–1918." *Austrian History Yearbook* 40, no. 1 (2009): 238–64.

———. *Eugenics and Nation in Early 20th Century Hungary*. Houndmills, Basingstoke: Palgrave Macmillan, 2014.

———. "The First Debates on Eugenics in Hungary, 1910–1918." In *"Blood and Homeland": Eugenics and Racial Nationalism in Central and Southeast Europe, 1900–1940*, edited by Mariua Turda and Paul J. Weindling, 183–223. Budapest: Central European University Press, 2007.

———, ed. *The History of East-Central European Eugenics, 1900–1945: Sources and Commentaries*. London: Bloomsbury Academic, 2015.

———. *The Idea of National Superiority in Central Europe, 1880–1918*. Lewiston: Edwin Mellen Press, 2004.

———. "In Pursuit of Greater Hungary: Eugenic Ideas of Social and Biological Improvement, 1940–1941." *Journal of Modern History* 85, no. 3 (2013): 558–91.

———."'The Magyars: A Ruling Race': The Idea of National Superiority in Fin-de-Siecle Hungary." *European Review of History* 10, no. 1 (2003): 5–33.

Turda, Marius, and Paul J. Weindling, eds. *"Blood and Homeland": Eugenics and Racial Nationalism in Central and Southeast Europe, 1900–1940*. Budapest: Central European University Press, 2007.

Ungváry, Krisztián. *Battle for Budapest: 100 Days in World War II*. Translated by Ladislaus Lob. London: I. B. Tauris, 2011.

———. *A Horthy-rendszer mérlege: Diszkrimináció, szociálpolitika és antiszemitizmus Magyarországon*. Budapest: Jelenkor Kiadó, 2013.

———. *Tettesek vagy áldozatok? Feltáratlan fejezetek a XX. század történelméből*. Budapest: Jaffa Kiadó, 2014.

Vicinus, Martha. *Intimate Friends: Women Who Loved Women, 1778–1928*. Chicago: University of Chicago Press, 2004.

Völgyesi Zoltán: *Harctértől a hátországig—Az első világháború gazdasági és társadalmi hatásai Magyarországon a levéltári források tükrében*. Budapest: L'Harmattan Kiadó, 2016.

Vörös, Károly. "A világváros útján: 1873–1918." *Budapesti Negyed: Lap a Városról* 6, nos. 2–3 (1998): 106–72.

Wackerfuss, Andrew. *Stormtrooper Families: Homosexuality and Community in the Early Nazi Movement*. New York: Harrington Park Press, 2015.

Walkowitz, Judith. *City of Dreadful Delight: Narratives of Sexual Danger in Late-Victorian London*. Chicago: University of Chicago Press, 1992.

———. *Prostitution and Victorian Society: Women, Class, and the State*. New York: Cambridge University Press, 1980.

Weeks, Jeffrey. "Pleasure and Duty." *Contemporary European History* 22, no. 2 (2013): 277–82.

———. *Sex, Politics, and Society: The Regulation of Sexuality since 1800*. London: Longman, 1981.

———. "The Sexual Citizen." *Theory, Culture & Society* 15, no. 3 (1998): 35–52.

Wetzell, Richard F. *Inventing the Criminal : A History of German Criminology, 1880–1945*. Chapel Hill: University of North Carolina Press, 2000.

Wingfield, Nancy M. *The World of Prostitution in Late Imperial Austria*. New York: Oxford University Press, 2017.

Winter, Jay M., and Jean-Louis Robert. *Capital Cities at War: Paris, London, Berlin, 1914–1919*. New York: Cambridge University Press, 1997.

Wolf, Larry. *Inventing Eastern Europe: The Map of Civilization on the Mind of the Enlightenment*. Stanford, CA: Stanford University, 1994.

Yuval-Davis, Nira. *Gender and Nation*. London; Thousand Oaks, CA: Sage Publications, 1997.

Zaretsky, Eli. *Secrets of the Soul: A Social and Cultural History of Psychoanalysis*. 1st ed. New York: Alfred A. Knopf, 2004.

Zsuzsa, Török. "A férfiruhás írónő: Vay Sarolta/Sándor és az átöltözés társadalomtörténete." *Irodalomtörténet* 95, no. 4 (2014): 466–84.

INDEX

Page numbers in italics refer to illustrations.

Angyal, Pál, 190–91, 250n42, 282n142
anti-Jewish laws: during Horthy regime, 120; during World War II, 195, 196–97, 283n12, 284n14, 286n48
Anti-Venereal Association, 280n119
Arad és Vidéke, 259n70
Arcanum, 15
Arendt, Hannah, *The Origins of Totalitarianism*, 209, 287n72
Arrow Cross Government of National Unity (1944–45), 4, 194; attempt to create *Hungarista* society guided by eugenic ideas and ultranationalism, 195, 202–3, 282n2, 286nn47–48; criminalization of male and female homosexual acts, 12, 229; prosecution of officials of in People's Republic of Hungary, 209; reign of terror and murder of Jews, 205; sterilization and castration laws against "sexual deviancy," 203–6, 229; use of term *emberek* when referring to abnormal sexual instinct, 204–5
Arrow Cross Yearbook, 284n19
Aster Revolution of 1918, 94, 122, 149
Austria, criminalization of both male and female homosexuality, 85, 261n105
Austro-Hungarian Compromise (*Kiegyezés* or *Ausgleich*), 8, 22, 24, 241n5
Austro-Hungarian monarchy (1867–1918), 4, 5, 8, 10, 24, 29, 81

Bárdossy government (April 1941–March 1942), 195
baths. *See* thermal baths

Battle of Budapest, 13–14
Beer sanatorium/Szörszanatorium, 212
Berlin: as early twentieth-century homosexual "Mecca," 78, 163; high-profile sexual scandals, 61–62; introduction of criminal registry in 1876, 249n27; psychoanalysis in early twentieth century, 92; use of city spaces across class lines, 9
Berlin Square (Budapest), 163
Bernstein, Frances, 111
Bertillon, Alphonse, anthropometric system, 25
Bethlen government (1921–31), 269n21
Binet, Alfred, 219
Bloch, Ivan, 251n57
Bokányi, Dezső, 122
Bolshevik Code on Marriage, the Family, and Guardianship of 1918, 109
Borsszem Jankó, 38–39, 252nn76–77, 269n20
Buda, 8, 9, 24, 164
Budapest, interwar, World War II, and postwar periods: designated as "Sinful Budapest," 156, 191, 241n6; economic hardships, 161–62, 164; homosexual meeting places, 162–65, 212; increase in male homosexual prostitution, 178–82; increase in visibility of male homosexuality, 161–62, 164, 191; reestablishment of traditional gender norms under Horthy regime, 156–58; siege of during WWII, 10, 205, 206. *See also* Budapest Criminal Courts; Budapest Metropolitan Police; same-sex sexualities, interwar period

Budapest, late nineteenth/early twentieth century: birth of city as unified metropolis in 1873, 5, 8; and "butterflies of the night," 19, 181; cafés, promenades, and thermal baths, 9, 67, 78–79; concentration of population and cramped living conditions, 9, 20, 40–41, 244n27, 253n89, 276n48; emergence of homosexual subculture, 21, 54, 68, 231, 232; expansion of print media and penny press, 56–57, 60, 241n5; and fall of Habsburg monarchy in 1918, 10; and fears about decline of modern Hungary, 256n3; geographies of queer subculture, 67, 78–79; Golden Age of, 9–10, 19; increasing divorce rates, 20; liberal politics and economic and cultural growth, 19–20, 54–55, 156; map of, 1899, 10; as milling center, 243n21; and modern scientific management of city, 60; population growth, 9, 243n23; public sexual culture, 2–3, 4, 20, 51, 60, 89, 106; transformation following Austro-Hungarian Compromise, 8; and Western theories on sexuality, criminology, and penal reform, 6. *See also* Budapest Metropolitan Police; same-sex sexualities, early twentieth century

Budapest City Archives (BFL), 14

Budapest Criminal Courts: ambiguities in definitions of "unnatural fornication," 175; cases of theft or blackmail against homosexuals, 173–74, 177; change in number of charges for homosexuality from 1935–41 and post-1941 period, 197, 198; characteristics of men involved in homosexuality cases, 175, 277n69; courts as extension of police and State Security, 214; criminal prosecution of homosexuals during 1950s, 211–15; destruction of records during Battle of Budapest, 13–14; and homosexuality, 14, 172–78, 174; leniency of interwar courts, 177–78, 193, 278n76; penalties for consensual public homosexual acts during 1920s, 175–76; "unnatural fornication" charges pressed in cases of sex with minors and nonconsensual sex, 173, 177, 276n63. *See also* Hungarian State Security Service (ÁBTL)

Budapesti Hírlap, 62, 257n16

"Budapest in Love," (Tábori), 19–20

Budapest Metropolitan Police: criminal registry based on fingerprinting, 25; difficulties in implementing criminal registry, 39–40; establishment in 1881, 24–25, 39–40, 249n21; inadequate personnel to deal with rising population and crime, 41, 253n90; policing of urban poor and socialist and workers' union, 41; portrayal of in newspapers in first decade of twentieth century, 38–39; public relations department, 57–58, 60; relationship with civic leadership, 39. *See also Rendőri Lapok* (Police Pages)

Budapest Metropolitan Police, sexual crimes and non-normative sexuality: approaches to male homosexuals, 21, 47–51, 165–72, 182, 191, 192; attribution of non-normative male sexual practices to experience of WWI, 162, 183; differential treatment of homosexual men based on gender representation, sexual performativity, and social class, 33, 50–52; distinction between innate and acquired homosexuality, 31–33, 185, 192; double standard of policing male versus female behavior in public, 45–46; focus on theft, blackmailing, and nonconsensual sex, 47, 50, 182, 186, 192; and golden age of prostitution, 40; "homosexual squad," 34, 38, 182; and male prostitutes, 33–34, 182, 183–85; regulation of female prostitution in early twentieth century, 26, 33–34, 45, 81; regulation of female prostitution in interwar period, 6, 12, 154, 158, 159–60, 180–81, 278n93; Vice Squad Department, 41–42, 180; views of sex, 40–43. *See also* Budapest Criminal Courts; homosexual registry, Budapest Metropolitan Police; *Rendőri Lapok* (Police Pages)

Bulletin of the Chief of the Police, 42

buzeráns (homosexual), 78, 138, 260n73

buzeráns tanyát (homosexual bar), 71

Buzinkay, Géza, 38–39

Castle Gardens, 78

castration, and homosexuals: in Germany, 286n53; and laws against "sexual deviancy" under Arrow Cross Government, 203–6, 229; in the United States, 286n53

Catholic Church: Communist efforts to damage reputation of Church leadership using homosexuals as informants, 227–29, 233; efforts toward conservative gender and sexual norms in interwar era, 20, 157–58, 274n6; resistance to negative eugenics, 204, 281n128

Catholic Women's Journal, 124
Cél (Goal), 280n125
Charcot, Jean-Martin, 145
Chauncey, George, 163, 271n69
China, and building of socialist society, 116
Churchill, Winston, 207
City Park/Városliget, Budapest, 67, 78, 106, 163, 231
Cleveland Street affair, 130
Cocteau, Jean, 77–78
Cold War, 91
Communism: and building of socialist society, 116; fall of, 91; "goulash communism," 217; on origin of crime in bourgeois exploitation, 266n49; and psychoanalysis, 92–93, 95–96; war on religion, 226–29. See also People's Republic of Hungary (1948–89)
Compromise of 1867. See Austro-Hungarian Compromise (*Kiegyezés* or *Ausgleich*)
Cornwall, Mark, 185
criminal anthropology, 28
criminal sociology, 28
Császár Bath, Budapest, 67
Csemegi, Károly, 22
csira (sprout), used to indicate "hermaphrodite," 136–38
Czechoslovakia, decriminalization of homosexuality, 219, 221

Dandár bath, Budapest, 1643
Danube promenade/Dunakorzó, Budapest, 67, 78, 163, 170, 231
Deák, István, 81, 261n90, 273n98
Deák Square, Budapest, 212
Debrecen, 276n56
decriminalization of male homosexuality, 5, 13, 113, 195, 217–23, 230, 289n102
Der Eigene (The Unique), 77
Detektív (police journal), 163
divorce: among highest rates in Europe in late nineteenth/early twentieth-century Hungary, 20; female homosexuality as grounds for under Hungarian civil code, 126; and People's Republic of Hungary, 208–9; and Zichy divorce scandal, 7, 14, 17, 131–32
Doyle, Sir Arthur Conan, 58
Duna Strandfürdő, men at (1929), 166, 168

East-Central European capitals: appearance of sexuality in public sphere in early 1900s, 56; decriminalization of homosexual acts in 1968, 289n102; historical silencing of issues of same-sex sexuality, 4, 232; lack of archives on queer sexualities, 13–17; post-1989 attitudes toward LGBTQ communities, 18; view of homosexuals as enemies of state after 1953, 288n80; and Western European standards, 242n12
Eastern Bloc: and religious organizations, 227; and same-sex sexualities, 208, 211, 213–14, 235, 290n2
East Germany, 213
Eby, Cecile, 200
economic crisis of 1929, 164, 171, 176, 179, 188
8 Órai Újság (8 O'clock News), 126
Elisabeth Square/Erzsébet tér, Budapest, 67, 78, 163
Ellis, Havelock, study of Vay's sexuality, 135, 251n55
Emberek a kövek közt (People between the stones) (Tormay), 122
Emke Kávézó, Budapest, 163, 165
Esti Kurir (Evening Courier), 127
eugenics: and Arrow Cross Government, 195, 202–3, 282n2, 286nn47–48; and Hungarian Soviet Republic (1919), 102, 111–12; resistance of Catholic Church to, 204, 281n128; and World War I, 187–88; and World War II, 187–92, 196–97, 284nn14–15, 286n48
Eulenburg scandal. See Harden-Eulenburg sex scandal
Evans, Jennifer V., 212
Experimental Criminology Department, Budapest Revolutionary Tribunal, 266n62; archival collections of, 92, 93; case of Gyula Fekete, 98–100, 102, 104–9, 116; establishment of, 95–98; focus on identifying roots of abnormal practices, 103–4; and importance of sexual history and socio-economic background as determinants of behavior, 92, 104–5, 108; integration of theories of sociology, psychology, and psychoanalysis in case studies, 91–92, 99–100, 103, 107–8, 115, 116–17; link between criminal behavior and biological abnormalities, 102; prescribed therapy to "heal" and reintegrate homosexuals to heterosexuality, 108–9, 266nn62–63; questionnaire used to assess people referred from the courts, 100–102; statutes of, 95; tolerance of sexual crimes viewed as no threat to "Dictatorship of the Proletariat,"

Experimental Criminology Department, Budapest Revolutionary Tribunal (cont.) 116; view of homosexuality as result of environmental and psychological factors, 108, 115, 116–17; work rules, 97–98

Faculty of Hungarian Medicine, 96
Faderman, Lillian, *Odd Girls and Twilight Lovers*, 83, 84
fajvédők ("race protectors"), 188, 280n125
fascist Italy: and Hungary, until 1938, 282n1; persecution of homosexuals, 273n3
Fekete, Gyula, case study of, 98–100, 102, 104; background and sexual history, 105–6; medical opinion on, 106–9, 116
Felvidék (Upper lands), 194, 283n5
female homosexuality: as grounds for divorce under Hungarian civil code, 126; interwar discourses on, 7, 154; lack of primary sources on, 14; in medical, police, and legal literature, 243n19; not considered as threat to public morals, 23, 81; police focus on "inauthentic" women who blackmailed and preyed upon other women, 83–84; portrayal as unnaturally close bond between women, 82–83; proposed criminalization of in pre-WWI Germany, 85, 261n106; among prostitutes, 81–82; silence about in public records and discourse, 7; unimaginable prior to interwar era, 16. *See also* Zichy-Tormay sex scandal
female prostitution: and female homosexuality, 81–82; Golden Age of, 40; and Hungarian Soviet Republic (1919), 112–13, 114; increased regulation of during interwar years, 6, 12, 154, 158, 159–60, 180–81, 188, 192, 278n93; officially legalized in 1869, 6; public view of, 80–81; regulation of in early twentieth century, 26, 33–34, 45–46, 78, 81
feminism, police attitudes toward in early twentieth century, 46–47
Ferenczi, Sándor, 93, 98, 265n47; Budapest Psychoanalytical School, 103; on factors causing homosexuality, 266n61; first professor and head of psychoanalytical department at a medical university, 263n18; "Psychoanalysis and Social Policy," 96; and *Wissenschaftlich-humanitäres Komitee* (WhK) (Scientific-Humanitarian Committee), 255n124
Fidesz Party: anti-West platform, 151; attempts to rehabilitate Tormay, 151, 152; promotion of homophobia and anti-LGBTQ attitudes, 18, 234–35; results in 2010 and 2014 elections, 291n9
fingerprinting, 25, 249n28
Finkey, Ferenc, 250n42
Fischer, Ignácz: "Homosexuality and Its Forensic Contemplation," 85–86, 88–89; testimony on tribadism in Zichy-Tormay trial, 145
Forel, August, 243n19
forensic scientists, beliefs about same-sex sexuality, 30–31
Foucault, Michel, 110; *The History of Sexuality*, 247n53
Franz Joseph I, 125, 248n9
Freud, Sigmund, 6, 92–93, 96, 103, 145, 266n58, 266n61
fridzsider szocializmus (refrigerator socialism), 217

Galton-Henry classification method of fingerprinting, 25, 249n28
Gay, Peter, *The Bourgeois Experience*, 256n8, 264n20
Gellért Bath, Budapest, 163
gender ideologies and roles: differential approach of police to homosexual men based on gender roles and performativity, 33, 51; gender-based understanding of female homosexuality, 130–36; ideas of masculinity, 15, 44; male *dzsentri* (gentry), 44; moral double standards for men and women, 43–46; reestablishment of traditional gender norms under Horthy regime, 156–58; and same-sex sexualities, early twentieth-century, 7, 33, 51, 262n114; uncontested masculinity of soldiers, 79–80, 81, 261n91
German SA (Sturmabteilung), 189
Germany: discourses on non-normative sexuality, 89; homosexuality in Weimar era, 86; legal debates around reformation of penal codes, 85; move toward World War II, 194. *See also* Nazi Germany
Gide, Andre, 77
"goulash communism," 217
Great Depression, 164, 171, 176, 179, 188
Guthi, Soma, *Homosexual Love*, 1–2, 3
Gyáni, Gábor, 246n48
gyógyintézet, "healing institution" for criminals, 109
Gyurgyák, János, 187

INDEX 319

Habsburg monarchy. *See* Austro-Hungarian monarchy (1867–1918)
Halász, Zoltán, 87–89
Harc (Fight), 283n10
Harden, Maximilian, 61–62
Harden-Eulenburg sex scandal, 15, 61–62, 120, 125
Háttér Társaság, 291n11
Healey, Dan, 111
Hekma, Gert, 88
Herzog, Dagmar, 13, 54, 220, 281n126
Heves County, 136
Hirschfeld, Magnus, 6, 67, 86, 219; theory of *sexuelle Zwischenstufen* (sexual intermediary stages), 49; and *Wissenschaftlich-humanitäres Komitee* (WhK) (Scientific-Humanitarian Committee), 49
Hitler, Adolf, 189, 194
Holquist, Peter, 268n89
"homosexuality," term coined by Karl-Maria Kertbeny, 30
homosexual registry, Budapest Metropolitan Police: additional information gathered in interwar period, 165–66; age distribution of registrants, 36, 36–37; and association of effeminacy with homosexuality, 46; continuation of in post-WWII era, 13; criminal history of registrants, 37, 37–38; descriptions of physical attributes and social history of registrants, 26–28; differentiation of registrants based on gender representation and sexual performativity, 33, 51; disappearance of, 201, 233, 286n56; distinction between innate and acquired homosexuality, 29, 31–33; distinction between men who engaged in consensual sex and male prostitutes, 33–34; effects of forensic medicine on, 28–34; *érdek* label to designate male prostitutes, 179; establishment of, 5, 25–26; as form of protection from blackmailers and criminals, 50, 66; information on female names of homosexuals, 29, 33; *közvetítő iskola* (go-between school) approach to causes of crime, 28; and management of sexual economy of city, 52; marital status of registrants, 36; number and percentage of registrants convicted of blackmailing, 38; number of people prosecuted for misdemeanors and crimes between 1926 and 1929, 173; occupational statistics of registrants, 35; police belief that registration reduced crimes associated with homosexuality, 47; in practice, 38–40; quantifying data from, 34–38, 35; religious affiliation of registrants, 36; role in official and public silence around homosexuality, 5, 232; and state ability to control lives of citizens, 21–22, 52; use of by Hungarian State Security during Communist years, 223–26
homosexual registry, national: use of after 1961, 224; use of by Hungarian State Security Service to blackmail and turn homosexuals into informants, 223–26
Honfoglalás, 25
Horthy, Miklós, regime of, 17, 123; attempts to rehabilitate, 151, 287n72; and regulations to establish sexual and moral order, 156–60, 172, 183, 197; and "Sinful Budapest," 156, 273n4; and tolerance of particular queer sexualities, 121; and Treaty of Trianon (*See* Treaty of Trianon); and White Terror, 119, 268n3; work for separate peace with Allies, 201–2; and Zichy-Tormay scandal, 125, 148–49, 152, 154. *See also* interwar regime, Hungary (1920–44)
Horváth, Sándor, 208
Hot Men Cold Dictatorship (2015), 235
Houlbrook, Matt, 80, 252n70
Hungária Bath, 67, 212
Hungarian Association of Legal Scholars, lectures on homosexuality, 85–89
Hungarian Boy Scouts Association, 158, 185
Hungarian Communist dictatorship (1948–89). *See* People's Republic of Hungary (1948–89)
Hungarian Democratic Republic (1918–1919), 4, 10, 94
Hungarian *faj*, 111, 113, 188, 195, 197
Hungarian Feminist Association, 15, 254n116
Hungarian legal system: establishment of criminal vice court in 1911, 28; and *közvetítő iskola* (go-between school), 28
Hungarian Medical Archives, 15
Hungarian medical discourse, influence of German-speaking world on, 29–30
Hungarian National Archives (OSZK), 14–15
Hungarian Penal code of 1878 (*Büntető törvénykönv*), 22; and criminalization of consensual sex between adult men, 6, 14, 22–23, 154; criminalization of *természet elleni fajtalanság* (unnatural fornication), 23–24, 98, 154–55; view of sex between women as unworthy of criminalization, 23

Hungarian Research Institute for the Jewish Question, 283n10
Hungarian Revolution of 1956, 217
Hungarian Socialist Workers' Party: action plan, "Exploiting the Homosexual Affairs of Catholic Priests," 228; forced merger of social democrats into, 208; purging of homosexuals and suspected homosexuals from ranks of, 210
Hungarian Soviet Republic (1919): approaches to sex and non-normative sexuality, 4, 5, 10–11, 17, 92–93, 106–17, 209; belief in potential of people to change and society to be transformed, 92–93, 95–96, 108–9, 112, 115–16, 155, 204; embrace of Social Darwinism and eugenics, 102, 111–12; *gyógyintézet*, "healing institution" for criminals, 109; intent to decriminalize consensual male homosexuality, 113; intent to secularize marriage and liberalize divorce laws, 109–10; interest in cutting-edge scientific work, 97–98; lack of discussion about female homosexuality, 113–14; promotion of *szexuális felvilágosítás* (sexual enlightenment), 110–11; Revolutionary Tribunals, 91–92, 95, 104, 173, 263n12, 265n48; transformation of social, medical, and public health care systems, 94–95; and universal suffrage, 94, 263n10; view of female prostitution, 112–13, 114; view of in pre-1989 Communist period, 244n32; White Terror, 119, 268n3. *See also* Experimental Criminology Department, Budapest Revolutionary Tribunal
Hungarian State Security Service (ÁBTL): Historical Archives of, 15, 223; homosexuality as tool for purposes of blackmail and recruitment of state informants, 12–13, 195, 223–26, 228–29; instrument of Communist leadership for controlling population, 211, 290n129; Operation Black Raven and Operation Apostles, 228; training manual for recruitment of informants, 225–26
Hungarian youth movements, 185, 189
Hungária Restaurant and Café, Budapest, 106
Hungary, late nineteenth/early twentieth century: Austro-Hungarian Compromise (*Kiegyezés* or *Ausgleich*), 8, 22, 24, 241n5; Austro-Hungarian monarchy (1867–1918), 4, 5, 8, 10, 24, 29, 81; criminal codes of 1880, 248n9; defining of progress according to Western standards, 242n12; first era of mass politics during first decade of twentieth century, 54–55; loss of territory and population, 1918–19, 10–11; Office of National Criminal Registry, 25; prison system, 249n16; Revolution of 1848–49, 10–11; unification of, 24. *See also* Budapest, late nineteenth/early twentieth century; same-sex sexualities, early twentieth century

Huszadik Század (Twentieth Century), 49, 58, 264n22

inclination, and police distinction between innate and acquired homosexuality, 31–32
Inter Alia Alapítvány, 291n11
interwar regime, Hungary (1920–44): censorship in media, art, and politics, 120; characterized by Christian nationalism, anti-Semitism, and antiliberalism, 11–12, 120, 191; efforts to protect public morality, 120, 158–59; eugenics and influence of Nazi Germany, 187–91; introduction of first anti-Jewish laws in post-WWI period, 120; Levente Associations, 158; media conformism, 158; pronatalism in wake of territorial and population losses, 156–57; prosecution of abortion providers, 158, 188; Protection of Public Morality Ordinance, 1927, 180. *See also* Horthy, Miklós, regime of; Treaty of Trianon
interwar regime, Hungary (1920–44), sex and same-sex sexualities: attribution of non-normative male sexual practices to experience of WWI, 162, 183, 186, 191; belief in rehabilitation of non-normative sexuality, 186, 192; Budapest Criminal Courts and homosexuality, 14, 172–78, 174, 205–6; Budapest Metropolitan Police and homosexuality, 165–72, 183; campaign against venereal disease, 184, 186–87, 280nn118–19; continuities in treatment of male homosexuality from pre-WWI period, 5, 17, 118, 155, 177, 205–6, 282n146; discussions of homosexuality only around murders and scandals, 153–54; distinction between innate and acquired homosexuality, 184, 185, 186; fear of contagiousness of homosexuality and fragility of heterosexual masculinity, 185–86, 189, 232; and

female homosexuality, 154, 192; ideas on centrality of sex and sexuality to individual and societal health, 183–84, 191, 205; idea that homosexuality could be acquired through exposure to ideas and discourses, 4, 187, 188–89, 192–93, 205, 232; increased regulation of female prostitution, 6, 12, 154, 158, 159–60, 180–81, 188, 192, 278n93; and male homosexual prostitution, 154, 178–82. *See also* eugenics

Jászi, Oscar, 122
Jewish people: anti-Jewish laws against in Hungary during WWII, 120, 196–97; and numerus clausus requirement for number of Jewish students in higher education, 245n37; reign of terror against, under Arrow Cross Government of National Unity, 205; underrepresentation of men in queer urban life, 36, 252n70. *See also* World War II, Hungary
Jobbik Party: anti-West platform, 18; attempts to rehabilitate Tormay, 151, 152; promotion of homophobia and anti-LGBTQ attitudes, 234; rise in popularity since 2008, 291n5
Juhász, Pál, 223

Kádár, János, era of, 217–18, 225
Kállay, Miklós, 201-2
Kálvin Square, Budapest, 163
Károlyi, Mihály, regime of, 10, 94, 96, 122, 244n32, 264n22, 264n26
Keleti Train Station, Budapest, 212
Kertbeny, Karl-Maria, 30, 251n53
Kinsey, Alfred, 219
Király Bath, Budapest, 212
Klebelsberg, Kuno von, 274n14
Kościańska, Agnieszka, 208
Kosztolányi, Dezső, *Édes Anna*, 142
közvetítő iskola (go-between school), or neoclassical school, 28
Krafft Ebing, Richard von, 1, 6, 29, 243n19; ideas of homosexuality as medical rather than criminal matter, 30, 99; later understanding of homosexuality as a variant of sexual inclination, 31; *Psychopathia Sexualis*, 30, 251n55; study of Vay's sexuality, 135
Kragujevics, Spázó, 68–70; in *Tolnai Világlapja*, 69

Kramolin, Gyula, "To the Issue of Homosexuality," 49
Krúdy, Gyula, 85; *Hét bagoly*, 135; writings on Sándor Vay, 135, 271n55
Kun, Béla, regime of, 10, 94, 96, 110, 244nn32-33
Kund, Attila, 187

Labrisz Leszbikus Egyesület, 291n11
Lakatos de Csíkszentsimon, Géza, 202
Lebzelter, Ferdinand, 62
Levente movement, 158, 185, 274nn13-14
LGBTQ community, contemporary: assumed connection between democracy and sexual freedom among, 234–35; organizations, 291n11; and Tormay, 152
Liberal Party, 54
Lišková, Kateřina, 208, 221
Lorenz, Konrad, 219
Lovászi, Márton, 122
Löwenfeld, Leopold, 86
Lukács, György, 110, 279n105; and sex education in schools, 267n73
Lukacs, John: *Budapest 1900*, 44, 252n71; on homosexuality and Hungarian culture, 4, 261n91; on sexually charged atmosphere of Budapest, 20
Lukács Bath, Budapest, 67, 212

Magyar Nemzet, 63
Magyarság, 284n20
male homosexual prostitution: better prospects for men in later life than for female prostitutes, 181; in Budapest during interwar years, 154, 178–82; and Budapest Metropolitan Police in early twentieth century, 33–34; gathering places in Budapest, 78–79; low number of juveniles registered by police, 180; and military men, 79–81; registered male prostitutes, 1932, by socioeconomic background, occupation, and age, 179–80, 179. *See also* Szántó, Jenő, "The Issue of Male Homosexual Prostitution"
Márai, Sándor, *Zendülők* (The rebels), 185, 186
Marcus, Sharon, 83
Marhoefer, Laurie, *Sex and the Weimar Republic*, 282n146
Marriage Law of 1941, 112, 129, 141
McLellan, Josie, 208
Méhely, Lajos, 280n125

Merzbach, Georg, 86
Metropolitan Mores, on same-sex love, 3–4
Mihaszna, András (Useless Andrew), 38–39, 251n57, 252n77
Mikszáth, Kálmán: *Gavallérok*, 44; *A Noszty Fiú Esete Tóth Marival: Regény*, 44
military men, as homosexual prostitutes, 79–81
Mindszenty, Cardinal József, 227
Minta Café, Budapest, 67
mitmachers, 80
Moll, Albert, 67
Moltke, Kuno von, 61, 125
Morality of Budapest, The, 2–3, 4
Moravcsik, Ernő, 29, 31, 80
My Way around the Stork's Nest, 157

Näcke, Paul, 86
Nagy, Irma (pseud.), *Sötét bűnök* (Dark sins), 83, 261n94
Nagy, Sándor, 284n15
Nagy de Nagybaczoni, Vilmos, 285nn41–42
Napkelet (Eastern Sunrise), 124
National Association of Hungarian Women (MANSz), 128, 232, 270n37
National Criminology Institute, Budapest City Archives, 92
National Peasant party, 207–8
Nazi Germany: eugenic measures, 189–90; and homosexuals, 229, 273n3, 282n139, 282n143, 284n25, 286n54
Nemes Nagy, Zoltán, 275n27; *Catastrophies of Love Life*, 26–27, 33, 34, 50, 161–72, 173, 178, 182
Németh, Ödön, 145
Nemzet Szava, 284n20
Népegészségügy (Public Health), 178
Newman, Antal, "The Role of Medical Psychologists in the Justice System," 99–100
New Woman, 269n30
numerus clausus, 245n37
Nuremberg Laws, 112, 196, 283n12
Nyirő, Gyula, 220
Nyugat (West), 124
Nyugati (Marx) Square, Budapest, 212
Nyugati Train Station, Budapest, 212

Óbuda, 8, 24
Office of National Criminal Registry, 25
Orbán, Viktor, 18
Österreichische Kriminal-Zeitung (Austrian Criminal Newspaper), ÖKZ, 60–61, 62

paederastia, 65
Pallavicini, Eduardina, 7, 121–22; as conservative Catholic national patriot, 149; conservative gender views, 128–29; founder with Tormay of National Association of Hungarian Women (MANSz), 128; involvement in charitable associations, literary world, and political circle of Horthy regime, 124; medical and psychological arguments about in trial, 145–47
Parliamentary Archives, 15
"Pearl of the Danube," 19
penny press, and discussion of sex and sexuality beginning in 1890s, 56–57, 60, 125
People's Park/Népliget, Budapest, 67
People's Republic of Hungary (1948–89): Constitution of 1949, 208, 213; continuing social stigma against homosexuality into 1980s, 224–26, 230–33; courts as transformers of sexual orientation, 215–17, 230; early gender equality, liberation of divorce, and legalization of abortion, 208–9; exploitation of homosexuals for purposes of blackmail and as state informants, 12–13, 18, 221, 223–26, 228–29, 230, 233; Family Law of 1952, 208; "goulash communism," or *fridzsider szocializmus* (refrigerator socialism), 217; Kádár era, 217–18, 225; late 1950s acceptance of contraception and nonprocreative sex, 220; medical pathologizing of homosexuality, 219–21; post-1956 decriminalization of homosexuality, 217–23, 230; post-1956 prosecution of perversion "conducted in a scandalous manner," 222–23; post-1956 setting of age of consent for men and women in homosexual and heterosexual relationships, 222; prosecution of homosexual men and women between 1948 and 1956, 12–13, 17, 118, 206, 210–15, 229–30; prosecution of officials in Horthy and Arrow Cross regimes, 209; Rákosi era, 206, 210, 230; return to conservative sexuality in 1950s, 208–11, 230. *See also* Hungarian State Security Service (ÁBTL)
personal ads, 79
Pest, 8, 9, 24, 51; homosexual gathering places, 77
Pesti Hírlap (Gazette of Pest), 61, 127, 257n16, 269n20
Petőfi Square, Budapest, 212
Philip, prince of Eulenburg, 61–62, 120

INDEX   323

Pius XI, Pope, condemnation of sterilization, 281n128
Poland, and legal status of homosexuality, 219, 289n102
post-1989 democratic era, assumed connection between democracy and sexual freedom among public and LGBTQ community, 234–35
Poszlik, Ferencné, 130
Pride Parade, 234
Proletárjog (Proletarian Law) (journal), 92, 99, 113
pronatalism, 156–57
prostitution. *See* female prostitution; male homosexual prostitution
Proust, Marcel, 77
pseudo homosexuality, 251n57
psychoanalysis: and dreams, 266n58; and early twentieth-century Communism, 92–93, 95–96, 264n20, 264n27; effect on discourse on sexuality, 56; and importance of child-parent relationships, 265n47; role of sexual history in character development, 104; in Vienna and Berlin in first two decades of twentieth century, 92
psychology, resistance of medical professions to, 264n22

Radclyffe Hall, Marguerite, *The Well of Loneliness*, 120, 144, 149
Rákosi, Mátyás, 206
Redl, Colonel Alfred, 125, 269n20
Régi ház (Old house) (Tormay), 122
Reich Central Office for Combatting Homosexuality and Abortion, 190
religion, under People's Republic of Hungary: nationalization of all church holdings, 227; State Office of Religion, 227; use of homosexuals as informants against Catholic priests and church officials, 228–29
Rendőri Lapok (Police Pages), 60, 251n60, 252n73; annual crime statistics of Budapest, 253n90; article on Oscar Wilde trial, 255n118; articles on sexual abnormalities and approaches of European cities to homosexuality, 31, 48–49; discussion of innate and acquired homosexuality, 32; illustrative of transnational influence of sexological theories, 31–32; "The Male Prostitute," 33–34; "The National Registry System," 39; "Prostitution and the Vice Police," 45

respectable homosexuals: blackmailing of, 28; distinguished from immoral, "inauthentic" homosexuals, 6–7, 55–56, 74–75, 86, 89–90
Röhm, Ernst, 190, 281n136
Röhm Putsch (Night of the Long Knives), 190
Római Part, two men at, in 1929, *169*
Romas, in Hungary during WWII: call for expulsion of, 198; conscription of into forced labor and concentration camps, 284n21; deaths of, 207
Rónái, Zoltán, 109
Rudas Bath, 67
Rudnay, Béla, 25
Russo-Japanese War, 58

same-sex sexualities, early twentieth century: active culture of, in turn-of-century Budapest and other Hungarian cities, 6, 9, 54, 67, 76–77, 89; both biological and psychological explanations for, 70, 72–74, 87, 88–89, 144–47, 262n118; and concept of respectability, 6–7, 55–56, 74–75, 86, 89–90; continuities in regulation of, across political and ideological divides, 4, 5, 7, 13, 17, 155, 177; discourse on, in first decade, 3, 41–43, 53–54; and gender ideologies, 7, 33, 51, 262n114; and homosexual "Meccas" of Berlin and Paris, 78, 163; lack of archives on, in East-Central Europe, 13–17; little mention of, in official documents and popular press between 1873 and 1960s, 4–5; medicalization of, by early twentieth century, 29, 106, 145; and modern penal code, 22–24; primary sources and secondary sources for study of, 14–15; and queer publications, 77–78; regional and dialectical variation in expressions associated with, 137; role of regulation of, in establishment of modern Hungarian capital, 5, 93; silencing of, in historical record, 4, 18, 232. *See also* Budapest Metropolitan Police, sexual crimes and non-normative sexuality; female homosexuality; homosexual registry, Budapest Metropolitan Police; Tábori, Kornél, and Székely, Vladimir
same-sex sexualities, interwar period: additional personal information on homosexual registry, 165–67; and Budapest Criminal Courts, 172–78; and Budapest Metropolitan Police, 165–72; Duna Strandfürdő, men at, in 1929, *166*, *168*; homosexual meeting places, 162–65; implications of conserva-

same-sex sexualities, interwar period (cont.) tive sexual order, 182–87; increase in visibility of male homosexuality, 161–62, 164; interviews about era with homosexuals in 1980s and 1990s, 167, 169; Római Part, two men at, in 1929, 169; two men embracing in 1943, 167; "unnatural fornication" charges pressed in cases of sex with minors and nonconsensual sex, 173; view of homosexuality as abnormal, 170; vulnerability of homosexual men to blackmailing and social stigma, 170

same-sex sexualities, post-1944. See LGBTQ community, contemporary; People's Republic of Hungary (1948–89); World War II, Hungary

Sarlós, Béla, 266n62

Schorske, Carl, *Fin-de-Siécle Vienna*, 256n8, 264n20

schwester (sister), 30, 78

Second Republic of Hungary, 207–8

sexual scandals: Colonel Alfred Redl scandal, 125; Harden-Eulenburg sex scandal, 15, 61–62, 120, 125; Oscar Wilde trial, 15, 62, 74, 75, 120, 125, 130, 149; Radclyffe Hall and *The Well of Loneliness*, 120, 144, 149. See also Zichy-Tormay sex scandal

Shaw, Albert, "Budapest," 8–9, 52

Sherlock Holmes detective novels, 58

Smallholders' Party, 207

Social Darwinism, 102, 188

Socialist Governing Council, Hungarian Soviet Republic, 94

sociology, 71, 264n22

Sokolova, Vera, 221

Soviet Union: attempts to secularize sexuality, 111; decriminalization and recriminalization of same-sex relations between consenting adults, 267n87; intent of building socialism and creating Communist subjects, 116

Spector, Scott, 62

Stalin, Josef, 207

Szálasi, Ferenc, 12, 202, 204, 282n2, 286n54

Szántó, Jenő, 252n68; "A homosexualitásról, különös tekintettel a budapesti viszonyokra," 34–38, 276n51; "The Issue of Male Homosexual Prostitution," 178–82, 183–85, 251n66

Széchenyi Bath, Budapest, 163, 171, 212

Székely, Vladimir: contributor and editor of *Rendőri Lapok* (Police Pages), 58; editor of "Criminal Chronicle section of *Huszadik Század* (Twentieth Century), 58; head of public relations for Budapest Metropolitan Police, 57–58, 256n13; photograph of, 59. See also Tábori, Kornél, and Székely, Vladimir

Szép, Ernő, 85

Szerb, Antal, *Utas és holdvilág* (Journey by moonlight), 185–86

Szövetség Street, bar on, Budapest, 67

Sztójay, Döme, 202

Tábori, Kornél: contributor and editor of newspapers and book series and author/coauthor, 58–59; deportation from Hungary and death at Auschwitz, 59; father of Hungarian investigative journalism and photography, 57, 58–59, 258n44; photograph of, 60. See also Tábori, Kornél, and Székely, Vladimir

Tábori, Kornél, and Székely, Vladimir: "A beteg szerelem lovagjai" ("The knights of sick love"), 63–66; account of Hungarian homosexual association, 76–77, 259n53; ambiguous depiction of homosexuality, 55, 89; contributors to *Rendőri Lapok* (Police Pages), 60; distinction between respectable authentic and immoral inauthentic homosexuals, 55–56, 74–75, 86, 89–90; gendered understanding of non-normative sexuality, 80–81; on geographies of queer subculture, 67; *Immoral Budapest*, 62; investigative journalism linked to sensationalist style, 57, 60–61, 71; lasting impact of publications, 84–89; on "lesbos love," 81–84; *Les Miserables and Villains*, 62; on male homosexual prostitutes (*pervezek parazitái* [parasites of perverts]), 78–81, 178; motives of, 57–62; *Railway Thieves*, 62; *The Secrets of Thieves*, 62; *Sick Love*, 68–75, 76, 77, 78, 84, 89; *Sinful Budapest*, 61, 62, 63–68, 76, 84, 86, 89; *Sinful Love*, 62, 86; *Sinful Women*, 62; view of homosexuality as age-differential model, 65, 73; view of homosexuality as both biological and medical problem and as moral issue, 70; view of homosexuality as effect of urban degeneration, 74; view of homosexuality as public health epidemic, 70, 72–74, 87; widely read sources on homosexuals of Budapest in first decade of twentieth century, 17, 53, 57, 63, 84–85, 89

Tanácsköztársaság (Communist-run Soviet Republic). *See* Hungarian Soviet Republic (1919)
Teleki, Pál, 283n6
természet elleni fajtalanság (unnatural fornication): criminalization under Hungarian Penal code of 1878 (*Büntető törvénykőny*), 23–24, 98, 154–55; criminalization under provisional Socialist Criminal Law, 212
Thaisz, Elek, Budapest Metropolitan police, 24, 25, 45, 249n23
thermal baths, 9, 67, 79, 106, 163–64, 212, 216, 231
Third Reich. *See* Nazi Germany
Tormay, Cécile, 268n13; anti-Semitic, antiliberal, and anti-Communist views, 123; co-founder of National Association of Hungarian Women (MANSz), 128, 149; conservative Catholic national patriot, 149; conservative gender views, 128–29; embraced by far right as ideal patriotic woman of past century, 151–52; first female editor in chief of *Napkelet*, 123–24, 149; one of most influential women of conservative social order, 122–24, 127; *An Outlaw's Diary*, 122–23, 128, 142–43, 149; photograph of, *123*; relationship with Horthy, 148–49; servants' portrayal of in trials, 131–36; statue of, *150*, 151; undamaged respectability following Zichy case, 149; and Zichy divorce scandal, 7, 14, 17, 131–32
Treaty of Peace, 1947, 207
Treaty of Trianon, 91, 157, 172, 187, 191; attempts to revise, 194, 272n97; and Budapest, 244n36, 275n37; loss of Hungarian territory and population, 91, 119–20
tribadia (tribadism), 29, 30, 140, 145, 147
Turda, Marius, 187

Ulrichs, Karl Heinrich, 1, 29, 30
universal suffrage, 272n84; under Hungarian Soviet Republic, 94, 263n10; under post-WWII republic, 207
uranism, 29
urning, 1, 30, 78
urning partik (male homosexual parties), 77

Város (City) (journal), 153–54
Vasárnapi Újság, 257n16
Vay, Sarolta/Sándor, 30, 133–39; drawing of, *134*; pen name D'Artagnan, 134, 271n55;
references to in Zichy-Tormay scandal, 133–35; self-identification as man, 135; trial of, 135, 271n57
venereal disease: campaign against in interwar Hungary, 184, 186–87, 280nn118–19; rate of in armed forces, 42–43; and regulation of female prostitutes, 45
Vienna: discourses on homosexuality, 78; high-profile sexual scandals, 61–62; public image of sexual cultures in, 241n3
Vogl, József, 37, 173, 276n61
von Liszt, Franz Eduard Ritter, 28

Walter, József, 130, 131–32
warme bruder or *warme schwester*, 30, 78
Weeks, Jeffrey, 79
Weimar Germany, and homosexuality, 86
Western sexuality morality, conceptual shift in, 220
Westphal, Carl von, 29
White Terror, 119, 268n3
Wilde, Oscar, trial of, 15, 62, 74, 75, 120, 125, 130, 149, 255n118
William II, Kaiser, 61–62, 125
Wolfenden Report of 1957, 220
Women and Girls, 124
women's rights: policies directed against in interwar years, 6. *See also* National Association of Hungarian Women (MANSz)
World War I, Hungary: demands for social and political reforms, 93–94; diverse sexual experiences of men in trenches and prison camps, 161–62, 172; focus on strength of Hungarian men, 158; and gender politics, 156; physical and psychological damage to soldiers, 182–83; and postwar eugenic ideas, 187–88
World War II, Hungary: alignment with Nazi Germany, 194; Allied support for democratic government, 207; anti-Jewish laws, 195, 196–97, 283n12, 284nn14–15, 286n48; Bárdossy government (April 1941–March 1942), 195; call for expulsion of Jews and Roma and hereditarily ill, 198; conscription of Roma and Jewish men into forced labor service, 199, 284n21, 285n28; deaths of Hungarian Jews and Roma and Hungarian soldiers, 207; demonization of Jewish sexuality, 196, 283n10; Döme Sztójay (March 1944–August 1944), 202; entry into war, 194, 195, 283n11; and establishment of People's Republic of Hungary, 208; and

World War II, Hungary (cont.)
eugenic ideas and measures, 187–92, 195, 202 (see also World War II, Hungary: anti-Jewish laws); German occupation of, 201; ill-preparedness of Hungarian Army, 200; and *kivételes hatalom* (exceptional power), 283n3; National Security Law of 1939, 284n24; and Nazi racial policies, 194–95; peace agreement with Allies, 286n55; political division over alignment with Nazi Germany, 201–2; postwar political parties, 207; refusal of Ministry of Defense to conscript registered homosexuals into forced labor service, 198–201, 285n42; Second Republic of Hungary, 207–8; structural devastation, 207; treatment of homosexuality, 197–201; Treaty of Peace, 1947, 207

Yalta Conference, 287n60

Zadravecz, Páter, *Secret Diary of Father Zadravecz*, 148–49
Zeisler, Mária, 130
Zichy-Tormay sex scandal: accusation of *tribádia* (tribadism) found unsubstantiated by courts, 140; class bias in the courts, 142–47, 148; difficulty of understanding female homosexuality among servants and contemporary press, 138–39; disappearance of materials relating to homosexuality charges from court records, 149, 232; divorce petition of Count Rafael Zichy, 126, 127, 129–31, 139; failure to increase public understanding of homosexuality, 149–50; influence of political figures on case, 148–49, 154; legal battles over defining of female homosexuality, 139–42; legal suits, 129–30, 270n42; outcomes of legal suits, 127, 130, 270n40, 270n42, 272n75, 272n85; participants and outbreak of, 121–26; public and press reaction to, 126–30; redemption of Countess Zichy and Tormay by courts, 143–44; selective use of medical and psychological discourses by courts, 144–47; servants' description of female homosexuality, 136–38; servants' gender-based understanding of women's relationship, 130–36; servants' reference to Sándor Vay in testimony, 133–35; and "sitting at the same table" legal principle, 140
Zimmerman, Susan, 45–46
zsidótörvények (Jewish laws), 195, 196–97, 283n12, 284nn14–15, 286n48

www.ingramcontent.com/pod-product-compliance
Lightning Source LLC
Chambersburg PA
CBHW051349290426
44108CB00015B/1944